Justice and Tort Law

Justice and Tort Law

Alan Calnan

CAROLINA ACADEMIC PRESS

Durham, North Carolina

Calnan, Alan, 1959–
    Justice and tort law / Alan Calnan.
        p.   cm.
    Includes bibliographical references and index.
    ISBN 0-89089-701-8 (hardcover)
    1. Torts. 2. Liability (Law) 3. Justice I. Title.
K923.C35   1996
346.0--dc20   96-20114
[342.63]   CIP

Carolina Academic Press
700 Kent Street
Durham, North Carolina 27701
Telephone (919) 489-7486
Fax (919) 493-5668

Printed in the United States of America

To my parents,
Thomas J. Calnan, Jr. and Ann Calnan,
who taught me more about ethics
than any book ever could.

Contents

Acknowledgments

In the *Introduction* which follows, I describe the musings in this book as a kind of intellectual voyage in search of certain truths about law and ethics. This journey did not begin with the writing of this book, but commenced long before and was assisted by a great number of individuals. Although it is not possible to thank them all, I wish to acknowledge a few of the people whose contributions made the dream of this sojourn a reality.

The faculty of the History Department at Kutztown University were some of the earliest and most important underwriters of my passage into the academy. Provocative and challenging, these mentors individually and collectively inspired my quest and started it on the right course.

Navigation and provisions for this voyage were later supplied by the faculty at Syracuse University School of Law. By sharpening my analytical skills, they provided me with the equipment necessary to captain my own ship and to steer it in the right direction. Peter Bell, in particular, stimulated my interest in tort law and caused it to blossom into a life-long passion.

The late Honorable Donald E. Wieand of the Superior Court of Pennsylvania permitted me to explore this passion under his wise and magnanimous tutelage. A meticulous author and fair-minded decision-maker, he taught me how to consider all contingencies before setting sail into unknown waters. His inspiration will be with me always.

Jules Coleman, Stephen Perry and Ernest Weinrib, though more remote contributors, have nevertheless had a profound influence on the ultimate destination of this journey. Through their prolific writings and thoughtful ruminations on the morality of tort law, these scholars not only have awakened my moral sensibilities, and enhanced my understanding of ethical issues, they ultimately have motivated the writing of this book.

The crew for this expedition have given generously of their time and talents and have ensured that the juggernaut remained on track. Jay Chavkin, Annette Gerber, Shanna Davis, Julie Ocheltree, Michael Moore, Lisa Machii, Lani Miller, Michelle Chambers, Misty Murray and Neil Stoliar all provided valuable research assistance along the way. Special mention must go to Michelle, whose critical eye, sharp investigative instincts, acute editorial skills and tireless dedication helped to make this mammoth task a lot less onerous, and a lot more enjoyable than I ever believed it could be.

Even with such a stalwart crew, my pilgrimage would not have reached fruition without some capable overseers. Jim Fischer, Robert Lind and Marin Scordato filled this bill by reading previous drafts of the book and providing thoughtful comments and suggestions. In addition, the editors at Carolina Academic Press, especially Mayapriya Long, Tim Colton and Greta Strittmatter, supplied the patience and technical expertise necessary to keep the ship sailing smoothly.

Of course, no journey as lengthy and trying as this would be possible without the unselfish dedication of a loyal first mate. My special thanks to my partner in life, Sandy Glanzrock, who not only listened to my rantings, and offered many commonsense insights, but who gave up untold weekends and substantial portions of our home so that I might complete this project. Now that my work here is done, she finally gets her dining room back...at least until the next book.

Table of Authorities

STATE CASES

ARTICLES

BOOKS

RESTATEMENTS & U.C.C.

Justice and Tort Law

Introduction

The Transformation of Tort Law

The American law of torts has reached a critical crossroads. In the last few decades, tort law as we have known it has undergone enormous change. Not the kind of glacial transformation characteristic of the common law generally, but something far more significant. It is a movement that, if left unabated, could render the law of torts obsolete or extinct. For the changes made do more than simply alter its direction, they explode the very cornerstones upon which it is built.

English Antecedents

Tort law started out as a publicly implemented means of private dispute resolution and social control. Spawned during the chaotic period following the Norman Invasion of England, it was used by foreign sovereigns to secure and maintain power over a captive populace.[1] In this unstable milieu, any hostile encounter was seen as a serious threat to the crown. From blood feuds to fistfights, such raucous behavior displayed an insolent indifference towards, if not an utter contempt for, the monarch and the authority of his laws.

To quell this recalcitrance, the king's courts developed the writ of trespass. This writ empowered any royal court to haul a suspected transgressor into custody and force him to justify his apparent misdeed.[2] Initially, trespass would lie only against those who acted with force and arms. As time passed, however, the culprit could be held responsible simply for performing an affirmative act which directly caused harm to another.[3] Where force was used, the wrongdoer often was imprisoned and required to pay a fine to buy his release.[4] Yet in any type of case, the wrongdoer also could be made to pay compensation to the victim or his relatives.[5] While this nascent legal system made no distinction between criminal and civil law, one already can see in the latter sanction the seeds of modern tort liability.

As harsh as early Anglo-Norman jurisprudence seemed to be, it never completely endorsed the concept of absolute liability.[6] Although the reason for this restraint is not entirely clear, it certainly was not occasioned by any lack of political power or justification. Indeed, because of the king's "divine right" and his place atop the hierarchical pyramid of England's feudal system, the royal courts certainly possessed the authority to limit the autonomy of the vassals and manorial lords who came before them. Nevertheless, even in the earliest trespass actions, royal courts were unwilling to prosecute a defendant who could prove that the plaintiff's injury was the result of an inevitable accident or had been caused by some third party.[7] Of the many possible reasons for this reluctance, the most plausible explanation is also the simplest: the courts seem to have been driven by an instinctive concern for justice. Indeed, even by medieval standards, it must have appeared immoral if not illogical to hold an innocent protagonist responsible for an injurious occurrence which was completely beyond his power of control.

Once the Normans became firmly entrenched in English society, the crown no longer needed to employ the civil law as an instrument of subjugation. As a result, the royal courts gradually relaxed the standard of liability by openly embracing the moral principle of fault. In cases of trespass, for example, the defendant could now escape liability by showing that his actions were "utterly without fault."[8] For other encounters which did not fall neatly within the parameters of a trespass action, a new fault-based theory of recovery—called trespass on the case—was created. Under this new form of action, a party who either failed to act, or acted in a way that had only an indirect effect upon the plaintiff's interests, could not be held liable unless the plaintiff established that the offending conduct was in some way wrongful.[9]

American Reception

This mixed scheme of justice was brought to America by English settlers fleeing from political and religious persecution. Though undergoing gradual adaptation, it remained in much the same form throughout the colonial period.[10] Following the American Revolution, however, the civil law of the newly liberated states began to take on a distinctive character of its own. It slowly shed the constraining precepts of absolute rule and began to display the ideals of freedom and autonomy that had fueled the move toward independence. Under this new conception of liability, trespass would not lie merely because someone's act or omission caused another harm. Such a broad liability rule, it was feared, would be inimical to the spirit of individual initiative which already had begun to permeate the common law. Before such an action could prevail, therefore, it became necessary for the injured party to demonstrate that the defendant's conduct violated some external standard of behavior.[11] With this additional burden in place, there remained little difference between the traditional tort forms of action; under either trespass or case, the liberty-restricting sanction of liability could not be invoked unless the defendant was in some way at fault. This innovation in legal analysis, while inspired by principles long recognized in the early English common law, was as original as it was momentous. It meant that negligence had finally overtaken and replaced causal responsibility as the most powerful determinative concept in the law of civil reparations.[12]

Paradigm Found; Paradigm Lost?

By most accounts, this transition from strict liability to negligence was well under way by the middle of the nineteenth century.[13] From this time on, American tort law generally has possessed three defining characteristics. First, it has been promulgated and administered primarily by judges rather than legislators. Second, it routinely has required proof of wrongful misconduct, and has continued to demand evidence of causation and harm. Third, it has aspired merely to undo the personal wrong flowing from private interactions, both by compensating the victim and by punishing or deterring the wrongdoer.[14]

In recent years, however, this paradigm has begun to crumble piece by piece, and is now in jeopardy of becoming outdated. In fact, today each of these hallmarks of tort law is undergoing substantial modification or vitiation.

Not surprisingly, the first characteristic to bend with the winds of change was the law's modest policy objective of resolving private disputes. In this regard, it has long been thought that, by the late nineteenth century, judges were not so much concerned with facilitating the litigation of individual cases as they were with setting social policy. Indeed, many believe that such industrial-age courts consciously adopted and applied a large assortment of duty-limiting doctrines to protect growing business concerns which promised to strengthen the economy of the nation.[15] Whether or not this was true, it is clear that policy-making increasingly was becoming an accepted function of tort law. In fact, by the early twentieth century, the social objectives of the law often seemed to dwarf the personal interests and private justice concerns of the litigants. Nowadays, social engineering remains a constant feature in almost every type of tort case. From loss spreading to risk avoidance, courts currently employ tort law to accomplish a wide variety of goals extraneous to the nullification of wrongful encounters.

What precipitated this purposive movement toward judicial activism? At least part of the answer may be found in the changes which American society itself has undergone during the last century and a half. Gone are the days when handcrafted products or personalized service could be obtained from a neighbor with a handshake and a smile. With the industrial revolution has come the age of national, and even international, commerce. Goods and services seldom are offered in sporadic, personal exchanges; instead, they are mass-produced and distributed to thousands if not millions all at the same time. As these networks of distribution have grown, so too have the entities providing them. Mighty corporations with thousands of employees, and millions of dollars in capital, have sprawled their long tentacles across the country. Now, people in New York may purchase the same product from the same manufacturer as people in California. And those in Texas are just as likely to endure the effects of the same railroad system as those in Oregon. In each case, the risks posed by these enterprises are not private, but public. Indeed, if the product is made with a dangerous design, or the railroad cars continuously discharge sparks from their wheels, the injurious consequences of these hazards often will be felt not only by a single individual or community, but by innumerable others throughout the country.

It is not surprising, then, that courts now employ tort law to address the long-term social ramifications that a finding of liability will engender. For instance, most judges recognize that product liability judgments do not merely censure a single, random act of carelessness, but amount to a condemnation of an entire product line or way of doing business. In cases like this, therefore, courts applying tort principles routinely consider the interests of individuals other than those involved in the dispute. On the one hand, they might use the law as a shield to protect not only the private litigant who already has been harmed, but all others who are subject to the same hazard. On the other hand, they may wield the law as a sword to discourage both the wrongdoer and other enterprises from creating and disseminating similar risks in the future. Perhaps most importantly, they often employ it to diffuse the private impact of injurious transactions by distributing their costs to other members of society.

Because of the quasi-public character of modern tort cases, changes also have been made in the way the law is promulgated. Judges and juries today are far less influential in determining the direction of tort law than their nineteenth century counterparts. The reason is that state and federal governments increasingly are legislating tort law by enacting safety laws and regulations. Where conflicts arise, these enactments often replace competing common law tort principles. This is most apparent in the area of federal preemption. The Cigarette Labeling Act,[16] The Federal Insecticide, Fungicide and Rodenticide Act[17] and The Medical Device Amendments to the Federal Food, Drug and Cosmetic Act,[18] among others, all provide dispositive standards which exempt complying actors from the threat of tort liability.[19] On the state level, many jurisdictions have passed legislation designed to supplant old tort doctrines with more contemporary liability rules, particularly in the areas of products liability[20] and medical malpractice.[21] Other statutes curtail traditional tort remedies in these and other types of litigation.[22]

Even in those enclaves of the tort realm where common law principles still reign supreme, the law's doctrinal underpinnings are quickly crumbling. In many states, the notion of compensable harm has been substantially redefined.[23] Frequently, plaintiffs may recover for "fear" of contracting a disease,[24] for medical monitoring,[25] for being exposed to increased risks of harm[26] and for lost chances of surviving certain maladies, even if they have suffered no physical harm.[27] Causation requirements also have been relaxed, in some cases almost to the point of being meaningless. Plaintiffs who cannot identify their wrongdoers may avoid summary dismissal by asserting such theories as market share liability,[28] enterprise liability[29] or alternative liability.[30] In other scenarios, the plaintiff need not establish that her injuries were the probable consequence of her adversary's actions; rather, she need only demonstrate the mere possibility of that nexus.[31]

Foundational Crisis

These developments have cast the law of torts into a foundational crisis. From this precarious station, the law will either collapse from its own intrinsic weakness,[32] or emerge stronger and more resplendent than before. Its fate depends upon its pathology. If the decline of the tort system is premised upon its moral deficiency, then it is probably better left for dead, for it could never satisfy our unending hunger for justice. But if its moral constitution is sound, then perhaps it suffers only from the cyclical infirmity of political fashion. In such a case, there would be reason enough to forestall its demise.

To make the appropriate diagnosis, a growing segment of the tort intelligencia has sought to discover the law's true moral basis. For many of these scholars, the search has led to the Aristotelian concept of corrective justice.[33] Not since the advent of the law and economics movement has a single idea attracted such interest.[34] Nor has any concept had such an impact on legal philosophy. Indeed, as the novelty of efficiency analysis fades, more and more tort theorists are looking to corrective justice to provide a complete or at least partial justification for tort law.[35]

This excursion into the critical morality of tort law has proven to be a mixed blessing. On the one hand, it has fixed the attention of the legal community where it should be—on the intrinsic morality or justness of the law. Indeed, it is only through such an inquiry that we can determine whether the tort system in its present form is fundamentally desirable or at least tolerable, and if not, how it might be modified, supplemented or replaced.

On the other hand, it is not clear whether this analysis has advanced our understanding of this subject, or merely served to obfuscate it. For one thing, there presently is no consensus as to what role corrective justice is to play in the adjudication of tort disputes. In fact, no one really knows for sure what corrective justice requires. For example, Ernest Weinrib contends that corrective justice provides an *exclusive formal* structure for the resolution of all tort disputes, but contains *no substantive* standard for deciding them.[36] This, he argues, is supplied by the Kantian theory of agency and the Hegelian idea of abstract right.[37] Jules Coleman, by contrast, sees corrective justice as the predominant, though not the only, principle underlying modern tort law.[38] And, unlike Weinrib, Coleman asserts that its substantive basis is as much a matter of legal and political practices as it is of deontological first principles.[39] Finally, Stephen Perry has proposed a moral theory of tort law that views corrective justice as a localized scheme of distributive justice.[40] Under his theory, corrective justice applies only to those actors whose faulty or "fault-like" behavior produces harm to others.[41]

Beyond this problem of indeterminacy, much of recent tort scholarship has suffered from a sort of analytic tunnel vision. Indeed, the interest in corrective justice seems to have become a preoccupation.[42] As a result, it has stifled further reflection on other aspects of morality which may have explanatory value for tort law.[43] This would not be so bad if corrective justice provided a comprehensive model for our tort system. But as many in the tort field finally have come to realize, it does not.[44] Thus, to truly understand tort law, and to assess its viability in our system of justice, we must both intensify and broaden our investigation into its underlying moral foundation.

Searching for Tort Law's Moral Basis: An Overview

In the chapters which follow, I will undertake this rather daunting task. The inquiry will unfold in five parts. The first two parts examine the concept of justice generally. The remaining three parts explore the justice of tort law in particular.

The Nature of Justice

Part I, entitled *The Nature of Justice*, begins by emphasizing a point which, in the jurisprudence of tort law, often has gone overlooked. It is that, in societies with centralized governments, justice has two levels, not just one. The first level is that of private justice. It requires that each participant in a private transaction treat the other fairly. Most corrective justice theorists focus exclusively upon this aspect of justice in evaluating the morality of tort law. For these theorists, the critical question is whether losses wrongfully imposed upon the victim are adequately redressed by the wrongdoer. No doubt, this is an important factor in the determination of justice. But it is not the only one. In fact, it is more a check on the tort *system* generally than it is a requirement of tort *law*.

There is another, more efficacious, barometer for evaluating the justice of the law. It is the requirement of political justice. As a social institution, the law establishes a relationship between the lawgiver and those subject to it. Like any relationship, the political compact requires that its constituents treat each other fairly. Citizens pledge their obedience to the law. In return, the lawgiver must enact fair rules of behavior and distribute them in an even-handed manner. The propriety of these rules, and the way in which they are allocated to the public, is not a matter of corrective justice. Rather, it concerns the justice of distributions, a predominantly political notion. All publicly imposed rules of behavior, including tort law, are subject to this constraint.

But how do we know when the law is politically unjust, or is likely to engender private injustice? The remaining chapters in Part I are devoted to this question. The answer depends upon a premise which also is all too often ignored. It is that our notion of justice is not determined only by our sense of morality, but also by our political ideology. In our culture, autonomy is the base value which permeates both our moral and political sensibilities. Thus, to be just, the law must give appropriate deference to the autonomy interests of those whose conduct it regulates. This is accomplished through the creation and distribution of rights. Rights, I argue, are prima facie markers of the autonomy interests which others must respect. Political injustice occurs when the lawgiver fails to create rights to protect our most important attributes of autonomy, or allocates recognized rights unfairly among people similarly situated. Private injustice, by contrast, results when an individual exceeds her prima facie right of autonomous action and violates a superior, actual right of another. Tort law, which establishes public rules for resolving private disputes, is concerned with each type of injustice.

The remainder of Part I examines in detail the underlying attributes which together determine our sense of injustice. One attribute of injustice is the notion of harm. Harm is simply the impairment of an interest. When the invaded interest enjoys legal protection, thus attaining the status of a right, the resulting violation amounts to a denial of something "owed to" or "due" the victim. Yet the mere infliction of harm by another is not enough to satisfy our sense of injustice. It must also appear that the harm was caused by some specific actor's conduct. Causal responsibility, a second attribute of injustice, identifies the party against whom remedial action can be taken. Only she has created the injustice, and only she can undo it. Still, the harm-inflicting actor has no legal obligation to repair the loss unless her conduct was wrongful. Contrary to prevailing dogma, the concept of wrongfulness, which completes our sense of injustice, is not necessarily synonymous with moral depravity. Rather, I shall argue that it is also a political notion characterized by one's usurpation of a disproportionate share of autonomy.

The Forms of Justice

In Part II, the focus shifts to *The Forms of Justice*. The taxonomy used in this part is borrowed substantially from Aristotle's *Nichomachean Ethics*. It begins by distinguishing two different connotations of this moral concept. Under the "broad" interpretation of justice, conduct is wrongful when it is wicked, or deliberately designed to cause harm to another. The "particular" form of justice, on the other hand, concerns only unfair behavior. As Aristotle explains, both distributive and corrective justice are aspects of this particular form of justice. These concepts are analyzed next, and are discussed in turn.

Distributive justice, we shall see, concerns the fairness of distributions. In a political context, it provides a means for evaluating the propriety of the government's distribution of common resources. One of these resources, I contend, is autonomy, which is given up by the masses in exchange for protection and is distributed back to them in return for their obedience. As indicated above, autonomy interests are guarded by rights which are distributed in the form of laws. To be fair, these legal distributions must satisfy some socially recognized criteria of fairness. In our society, "merit," "need" and "risk" are the primary factors which influence our sense of distributive justice. As one's vulnerability increases, the law must afford her greater autonomy; but as her conduct becomes more risky, the law may subject it to greater restriction. Laws which do not follow this pattern invariably offend our sense of justice.

Corrective justice is not addressed to distributions, but to transactions. As a result, it is not so much a political concept as it is theory of private intercourse. Its purpose is to right private wrongs. Where one individual wrongfully harms another, it requires that the gain of the wrongdoer and the loss of the victim both be nullified, and that the parties be restored to the status quo. In this way, corrective justice prescribes a formula for calculating damages and meting out punishment. It does not, however, determine *when* these measures should be imposed. This is because it provides no means for assessing which transactions are wrongful, and thus subject to sanction by the state. It is my contention that this void is filled by the notion of distributive justice, which delineates the freedom we may and may not exercise in our social interactions with others.

Part II concludes with a discussion of justice in exchange and retribution, two other moral considerations which complete our portrait of justice. Justice in exchange, or reciprocity as it is sometimes known, helps us evaluate the fairness of consensual transactions. It ensures that goods or interests exchanged are commensurable and roughly equivalent in value. Retributive justice, on the other hand, may apply to any type of transaction, although in different ways depending upon the moral culpability of the party in question. It defines our instinct to punish wicked behavior by exacting some comeuppance from the wrongdoer. Like distributive justice, these concepts receive scant attention in the moral dialogue of tort law. Yet, as I indicate in Part V, they both play a significant role in the resolution of many tort disputes.

Justice in the Structure of Tort Law

After establishing the groundwork for understanding the nature of justice and its many facets, Part III begins the search for justice in tort law. Denominated *Justice in the Structure of Tort Law*, this part examines the fundamental attributes of all torts, including the existence of a legal duty of care, the beneficiary status of the claimant as one to whom the duty is owed, and the invasion of a significant autonomy interest of the claimant. An exegesis of these elements reveals their indispensability to the attainment of justice. They are, in combination, a working analogue of a right. The breach of a duty owed to another is but a description of "wrongdoing;" while "harm" consists of any encroachment upon another's significant autonomy interest.

The analogue is not complete, however, without the concept of causal responsibility. It is this notion which activates the corrective right of the injured party to take action against another to redress her harm. Yet, as was recounted at the outset of this discussion, the element of causal responsibility is rapidly disappearing from many tort theories. Can this concept be eliminated without undermining or redefining our sense of justice? The rest of Part III takes up this question.

One of the problems in addressing this inquiry is the uncertain nature of causation itself. Although much ink has been spilled by legal scholars and philosophers in an attempt to define this concept, there still is no clear consensus as to its meaning. After reviewing the legal notion of factual cause, I offer yet another perspective on this definitional dilemma. In my view, the "factual cause" requirement of tort law comports with neither colloquial nor philosophic conceptions of causation. Rather, it helps to select among all possible causes the individuals or natural conditions most directly responsible for producing harm. This is a function of the power or influence these "causes" actually had, or could have had, over the injurious outcome. This nexus, I contend, is better understood as "factual responsibility."

Although factual responsibility may not be essential to the idea of justice generally, it is vital to the justice of the tort system. In compensation systems, which are founded solely upon the notion of distributive justice, the state may take from wrongdoers and distribute their ill-gotten gains to those who have been victimized by their conduct. Even though no causal relation necessarily exists between any specific wrongdoer and victim, such distributions are just so long as both the taking and giving adhere to some social norm of fairness. In the corrective framework of tort law, however, it is a private party, not the state, who seeks to invade the coffers of the wrongdoer. What gives her the power to effect this invasion? It is the factual responsibility of the wrongdoer which marks her alone as the violator of the victim's rights. Were this remedy to be leveled against any other individual, the interest invasion it entails, being neither excused nor justified, would itself be wrongful.

Justice in the Content of Tort Law

While all torts share the structural elements of wrongdoing, causal responsibility and harm, these concepts are not defined or interpreted the same in every theory of recovery. Part IV, entitled *Justice in the Content of Tort Law*, explores the different constructions given to these components under tort law's three substantive bases of liability: intent, negligence and strict liability. Although the entire elemental structure of all three theories will be considered, the primary focus here is on their alternative conceptions of wrongdoing.

For a political society to survive, its members must be willing to respect the rights of others. To inculcate this respect, a state must distribute to its citizens a duty to refrain from intentionally harming their neighbors. Every member of society enjoys the protective benefit and suffers the restrictive burden of this duty. When this mandate is violated, the transgressor.is guilty of a type of wrongdoing which is punishable as either a crime or a tort. In each case, such conduct, being deliberate or knowing, is unjust in the broad sense of being wicked. It arouses our most primitive retributive instincts. To discourage this behavior, tort law requires the wrongdoer to pay compensation or an exemplary fine to the victim. This is so even if the causal nexus between the parties is attenuated or the victim has sustained no actual damage. Whatever its corporeal effects, such conduct represents a threat to the concept of freedom and thus is injurious at least in a political sense. Under traditional tort theory, this is reason enough for subjecting the wrongdoer to these sanctions.

Unlike intentional conduct, negligent behavior is not completely other-directed. Rather, it is primarily self-regarding activity which poses some coincident risk for others. Thus, it is not wrongful in the broad sense of being wicked. The actor is permitted some autonomy to pursue her self-interest. This freedom, however, is tempered by a correlative responsibility to refrain from exposing others to undue risks. This duty is not owed to all, however, but only to those threatened by the ancillary risks it creates. While the duty to abstain from intentionally harmful conduct is largely absolute, the duty in negligence is far more flexible, adapting to the circumstances of each interaction. Where one engages in high risk activities, she is distributed greater responsibility than those conducting less dangerous endeavors. Conversely, where the actor's basic rights are in jeopardy, her responsibility is diminished, and her freedom of action is proportionally enhanced. Still, if one exceeds her distributive right of action, and so violates her distributive duty to contain the risks it engenders, she acts wrongfully and thus tortiously. Though not wicked, such negligent conduct is unjust in the particular sense of being unfair. By exercising more than her allotted share of autonomy, the wrongdoer cheats others who have relinquished the opportunity to act in a similar fashion.

Part IV closes by analyzing and comparing strict products liability and strict liability for abnormally dangerous activities. Particular attention will be given to the rarely acknowledged affinity these theories share with the theory of negligence. Like negligent conduct, strict liability activities (including manufacturing defective products) generally are not intended to harm others; rather, they advance some personal end of the actor and create attendant risks along the way. Thus, they are not subject to the clear prohibitive rules characteristic of intentional torts. Instead, just as for negligence, they must satisfy a more abstract community standard which balances the actor's autonomy interest against the risk of harm she imposes upon others. If the activity fails this community standard, the actor is liable to all those it endangers. Just as in negligence, the activity here is wrongful in the sense of being unfair since it affords the actor an advantage—that of creating abnormal risks—forsaken by others in the community. There is one area, however, where this symmetry breaks down: in cases of product category liability. Here, the determination of liability is not so much concerned with private justice and community notions of fairness as it is with spreading losses and deterring public risks.

Justice in Three Paradigms of
Tortious Interaction

The fifth and final Part of this book, which I have called *Justice in Three Paradigms of Tortious Interaction*, examines the justice of tort law in its theoretical application to different factual settings. In my view, the encounters which give rise to tort disputes can be grouped into three paradigms: calculated transactions, random transactions and relations. Because the concerns of justice vary depending upon the type of interaction involved, these paradigms serve as useful tools in analyzing the moral rectitude of the law. These paradigms are discussed in seriatim.

Calculated Transactions

Calculated transactions consist of intentional acts committed against others without their consent. These transactions come in four varieties, each distinguished by the unique motivation of the protagonist. One subcategory of this paradigm includes adversarial transactions. Such transactions may be either proactive or reactive. Proactive adversarial transactions involve the type of deliberative conduct associated with intentional torts. Cases involving such conduct are the easiest to analyze. The actor is bound by clear prohibitive rules; if she intentionally violates the rules and produces a particular consequence, often requiring no actual damage, she is liable. Retributive justice permeates the law in this scenario.

Reactive adversarial transactions, on the other hand, are quite different. Here, the actor does not initiate the interaction, but reacts to an apparent hazard. Cases of self-defense and necessity are of this sort. Because the actor's interests are in jeopardy, she is not precluded from acting, but may use reasonable force to protect her interests. In such a scenario, the necessity entitles the actor to a greater distributive share of autonomy. Her actions are wrongful only if she abuses her enhanced freedom by using more force than is needed to eliminate the danger. Even so, such conduct is not ordinarily wicked, but unfair. Thus, it is less a matter of retributive justice and more the concern of distributive and corrective justice.

The second subcategory in this paradigm includes transactions that are initiated under a mistake of fact. In this scenario, the actor's conduct again is proactive and not justified by some situational need. Thus, like proactive adversarial acts, intentional though mistaken behavior is subject to a general distributive prohibition. Violation of this preclusive rule is wrongful and thus actionable under the law. Such conduct, however, generally lacks the moral culpability found in most adversarial acts. In some cases, the actor is not even aware of the victim's presence; in others, she operates under a mistaken impression as to the victim's identity. Although the harm caused by these acts demands correction, there is little need, absent a malicious motive, to impose a retributive punishment against those that carry them out.

Calculated transactions may not only lack a malicious motive, they may even be altruistic. In these cases, a good samaritan undertakes to aid another in distress but winds up hurting rather than helping the victim.[45] The need for action entitles the good samaritan to a more generous share of autonomy. Nevertheless, if she exceeds this right and causes injury to the victim, she acts unjustly. While she is liable for her wrongdoing, her good faith quells any need for retribution.

Unlike the preceding encounters, calculated transactions of the last sort are not initiated by an unknown protagonist, but by the injured party herself. In these "self-endangering" transactions, the "victim" voluntarily exposes herself to a known dangerous condition created by somebody else. Upon making this choice, the risk-taker relieves the risk-creator of any duty of protection. Thus, while she may be harmed in the transaction, she is never wronged, for she is afforded the benefit of autonomous choice. Even if this were not so, the risk-taker alone would be causally responsible for the injurious outcome. Here, the encounter is not thrust upon her; rather, it takes place only if and when she elects to instigate it.

Random Transactions

The second paradigm of tortious intercourse consists of random transactions in which at least one party is an unexpected or unwilling participant. In contrast to the foregoing paradigm, the actions here are not designed primarily to interfere with the interests of others. Instead, they are intended to promote the actor's own interests, but fortuitously create some risk towards others. This has two significant effects upon the analysis of these cases. First, it ensures that the determination of wrongdoing will rest not on the application of rigid prohibitive rules, but on the interpretation of flexible standards of conduct. Here, the actor is granted at least some autonomy to pursue her life plan. To properly assess her conduct, one must balance this interest against the interests of others to be free from the risks she creates. Second, the randomness of the encounter reduces the moral outrage of the conduct which precipitated it. For the most part, this will obviate the desire for retributive justice.

Cases within this paradigm can be subdivided into two groups: those in which one party unilaterally causes harm to another, and those in which the harm results from a bilateral transaction. Transactions in the first group bear the characteristics described above. Those in the second group, however, possess an additional analytical nuance. In these bilateral encounters, both the alleged wrongdoer and the aggrieved party act in a way which contributes to the result. They may act simultaneously or sequentially, although neither operates at the request of nor in reliance on the other. Given the participation of both parties in the injury-producing event, the analysis here is not limited to the issue of wrongdoing, but may include difficult questions of causal responsibility.

Relations

The last paradigm consists of harms which arise out of relationships. This is the most frequently occurring scenario and the hardest one to analyze. Like the random bilateral transactions mentioned above, the parties in many relational interactions jointly contribute to the resulting harm. This often presents sticky problems of causal responsibility. However, unlike random encounters, the parties in relationships interact directly. Thus, the words and conduct of one party may influence the conduct of her relational partner.

This fact often has a profound effect upon the determination of wrongdoing. The most obvious consequence of such interaction is that the parties routinely will begin to rely upon each other in various ways, frequently to their detriment. For example, sometimes an injured party induces the reliance of her relational counterpart by manifesting her consent to accept the risks of the association. In such cases, the reliant party proceeds to act only because the consenter appears to assume full responsibility for any harm that may follow. On other occasions, the injured party herself may give up opportunities for protection. This is particularly likely where the parties to the relationship possess unequal abilities to control the risks of their relationship and the conditions under which they interact. Here, the party lacking such power typically expects the other to provide a reasonably safe environment for their association. In fact, it is not uncommon for the controlling party to accept this responsibility voluntarily, although perhaps not expressly. In other cases, the state, by operation of law, creates in the dominant party a heightened responsibility to safeguard her relational partner from preventable danger. This responsibility requires not only that that party refrain from unreasonable conduct, but also that she take action to alleviate unreasonable dangers. Such a duty to act is unique to the relational paradigm.

Besides cultivating mutual reliance interests, the bilateral association of the parties permits them to define the nature and scope of their relationship and to allocate between them the risks that flow from it. By express or implied agreement, the parties can dispense with the distributive freedoms and responsibilities ordinarily imposed upon them by the state. To effect this waiver, however, the volition of both parties must be true, and their choices informed. Whether these conditions uphold depends on many factors, including the circumstances in which the choice is made, the level of risk information available to the parties, the nature of the risks to be expected, and the type of relationship in question. While social and commercial relations present the most favorable context for consent, fiduciary and consumer relations offer the worst. Still, the nature of the relation is not necessarily determinative of the parties' ability to freely allocate risks. A further yardstick of the parties' subjective desires is the equivalency of the rights they have given up and secured. This is where the concept of justice in exchange plays an important role. If the risks are distributed unevenly, true consent is suspect and the exchange may fail the strict demands of justice.

An End and a Beginning

With this, our long excursion through the murky waters of tort law reaches its final stage. In the *Epilogue*, I attempt both to distinguish my theory of tort law from a number of its more prominent predecessors, and to use the insights gained from this new vision to assess the recent avalanche of change which threatens to make classic tort law an anachronism. Although I find some of these developments to be necessary and desirable, I conclude, in the end, that much of traditional tort law is better adapted to satisfying our need for justice than perhaps many will acknowledge. Accordingly, it is my opinion that we proceed cautiously before altering the law's delicate fabric. No doubt, those who are fanning the flames of change will instinctively recoil at even the suggestion of such reasoned restraint. Yet perhaps after making this trek with me, they will see more clearly all that they are about to throw away, and how hard it may be to replace. If so, then this book will have served its purpose. For, as most intellectual explorers will readily attest, the destination of one's pilgrimage is usually less memorable, and far less enlightening, than the journey itself. And even if it offers no other benefit, at least it may help to chart the course for future pioneers.

Part I

The Nature of Justice

Chapter 1

Private and Political Justice

When most people think of justice, they probably think of the legal system. It is that elusive commodity dispensed by judges in our courts of law. And when they think about legal justice, inevitably they think about results. Did the court (or jury) render a verdict that settles the matter at hand fairly?

But justice involves more than just the results in legal proceedings. Justice is multidimensional. It is the process of applying law and the substance of law itself. It is the test for determining whether the law suits our needs. And it does not just concern law, and our relationship with our lawgiver. It also permeates our interpersonal relationships. It is a way of evaluating our conduct towards others, and thus is part of our sense of morality. Because the notion of justice is so complex, and its influence so pervasive, we must begin by taking a closer look at this incomparably dynamic concept.

The Definition of Justice

The confusion surrounding the notion of justice begins with its definition. Distilled to its essence, justice is the requirement that one receive her "due" from another. As a moral principle, justice must of necessity be broadly conceived. The generality of its mandate, however, creates ambiguity in its application, particularly in two areas. The first problem, which will be addressed in this chapter, is in knowing against whom the directive applies. The second difficulty, discussed in Chapter Two, is in determining what one is "due."

Justice as a Relational Virtue

Aristotle tells us that justice is a virtue.[1] It is an excellence of character marked by moderation. As Aristotle describes it, it is the mean between excess and deficiency.[2] For most virtues, this balance is abstract and internal. Courage, for example, is the mean between the character traits of cowardice and rashness.[3] Likewise, the intermediate of self-indulgence and insensibility is temperance.[4] Here, the ideal dispositional balance is suggested by the spectrum of possible human qualities.

Justice differs in an important respect. Unlike other virtues, justice is a purely relational concept. The standard for evaluation which it requires is not internal but external. It is, as Ernest Weinrib has noted, "virtue practised towards others."[5] While we may be wicked even in seclusion, we may be just or unjust only when we interact with others.

Political and Private Dimensions of Justice

In prepolitical societies, the relational aspect of justice has only one dimension. Theoretically, everyone enjoys unrestricted freedom. There is no law or lawgiver. Thus, there are no formal rules delineating proper standards of conduct. If someone takes one of my possessions, there is no one but me to determine whether I have been unjustly treated. Nobody is responsible for failing to prevent the wrongful act, nor is anyone obligated to undo the wrong once it is inflicted. If I am to rectify this injustice, I must do so myself by reclaiming the object from the taker.

The simple justice of this scenario becomes far more complicated, however, when such an act is committed within a political association. As we saw above, prepolitical societies contain only one type of social relationship—that between individuals. Thus, the only justice concern is that the parties to such private interactions each receive their due. In a political association, however, there is an additional social relationship which all citizens share. It is their relationship with the state. From this relationship emanate a multitude of additional justice concerns.

To appreciate this fact, one must understand the role played by the state in the private actions of its citizens. In our system of government, the state takes on certain obligations in protecting its members. It passes laws which prohibit or restrict harmful activities of the type mentioned above. And, if those laws are violated, it provides a formal, public mechanism for punishing the wrongdoer and/or compensating the injured victim. Each of these obligations creates an entitlement in all citizens which determines their "due" from the state. Accordingly, the performance of these duties is a concern of justice.

Sources of Political Justice

A closer look at each of these obligations reveals yet other aspects of justice not found in prepolitical communities. For example, a state's ex ante restrictions on harmful conduct often take many different forms and are created by different organs of that body. Laws are enacted by the legislature. Regulations, which help implement laws, are created by administrative agencies. Common law doctrines are fashioned by courts in resolving disputes. Despite their different sources, all of these rules may regulate private conduct in a way that satisfies the state's commitment to protect its members from harm. Thus, each must satisfy our ideal of justice.

With so many rules, it is often difficult to discern what justice requires in individual cases. Frequently more than one legal directive will apply to a given form of conduct. Just identifying all the relevant constraints on such action can be a daunting task. And even where the rules are known, they may be hard to reconcile. Indeed, because they are created by different agencies of government, they often conflict. In such situations, the quest for justice is especially problematic.

Substantive and Procedural Justice

Assuming the rules can be harmonized, other justice concerns still remain. Any rule of conduct possesses both substantive and procedural components.[6] The rule, as abstractly conceived, must aspire to do justice. That is, it must not be too lenient (deficient) nor too restrictive (excessive) in its regulation of private action. If it satisfies this requirement, it is substantively just. But even such a rule may be unjust if applied the wrong way. This is the concern of procedural justice. It ensures that the just aspiration of the rule is not subverted during its interpretation and implementation.

This requirement of procedural justice is relevant not only to the evaluation of substantive rules, but also to their ex post enforcement.[7] After a wrong has been committed, the state is duty-bound to correct it in some fashion. To meet the demands of procedural justice, the mechanism which the state constructs for this purpose must appear reasonably capable of furthering this end. In our political system, the state provides two such mechanisms—one criminal, where punishment is inflicted directly by the state; the other civil, where monetary damages are assessed against the wrongdoer and awarded to the victim.[8] Each share similar formal attributes. They consist of an accuser and an accused who present evidence to a fact-finder. They are administered by a judge who declares the substantive rule to be applied to the controversy. And they impose a battery of steps that each party must follow to prosecute her case. If any part of this ex post process for remedying wrongs is unjust, the state will have failed in its commitment to its constituents, even if the rule of conduct is substantively fair and correctly interpreted.

Justice in Fact

While these procedural protections are necessary to our sense of justice, they are not necessarily sufficient to satisfy this instinct. The state's ex post obligation to enforce the law is subject to a final moral constraint—it must prove at least reasonably successful in realizing the protections promised by the rules themselves. This means that our adjudication systems not only must operate on principles which are normatively just, they must more often than not actually achieve just results in resolving our interpersonal disputes. Indeed, the justness of substantive rules would matter little if they did not afford us some acceptable measure of justice in fact.

Summary

From this brief survey, it becomes clear that every injurious interaction between citizens in a political association involves two levels of justice. On a primary level, we seek to achieve justice between the parties by righting the wrong caused by their encounter. On a secondary level, we depend upon the state to formulate rules of conduct likely to prevent such harms in the first place, and/or to provide the means for redressing them when they occur. Though presented separately, these levels of justice are in fact intimately interconnected. For, as will be discussed at greater length later on, the state's obligation to intercede often is conditioned on the commission of a private injustice; and, once this duty is activated, the manner in which the state rectifies the wrong usually will depend upon the injustice of the action which precipitated it.

Chapter 2

Justice and Rights

Having considered the relational aspect of justice, we turn now to examine its substantive content. Here we are faced with an age-old polemic. If justice requires that we receive our "due" from others, exactly what does this entail? As would be expected, the responses given by moral philosophers have been far different than those rendered by political theorists. Even within these disparate realms, there is much division. Among the philosophers, utilitarians and deontologists share little common ground; and of the politicos, autocrats and communists hold opposing views. In American society, however, the answer is as plain as our founding instrument of government. For us, justice derives from our notion of rights.

Primary Rights

Rights are prima facie entitlements to things essential for human flourishing. They come in two forms.[1] Passive, or "primary," rights presumptively guarantee their holders certain benefits. These benefits may be either positive or negative, and may be tangible or intangible. Thus, some primary rights grant us positive, tangible benefits like food, clothing, shelter or bodily integrity. Other primary rights secure positive, intangible benefits such as the freedom of speech, the freedom of association and the freedom of movement. Primary rights with a negative dimension, on the other hand, shelter the holder's interests from wrongful interference by others. They are designed to ensure that our positive rights are not taken away without our consent.

Secondary Rights

While these passive rights signify the holder's entitlements, they do not empower her to enforce them. This is accomplished by active, or "secondary," rights. With such rights, the holder can compel another either to provide her with a tangible benefit or to refrain from interfering with her interests. In essence, they bestow upon the holder a license to limit the freedom of others.[2]

Types of Secondary Rights

Such secondary rights may be implemented in a variety of ways. The most powerful secondary right is compulsory. Compulsory rights entitle the holder to demand some affirmative action by another. These rights are enjoyed by governments and private citizens alike. The government may require that we provide military service, go to jail or pay taxes. In the private sector, parents can force their children to eat peas or clean their rooms, while contracting parties can demand specific performance from those withholding unique goods. In each case, the right holder may do more than just interfere with someone else's interests, she may actually compel the other to do her bidding.

Preemptive rights are also potent, but in a different way. These rights do not command affirmative action; rather, they permit the holder to *preclude* the action of another. One way this right may be exercised is by applying direct physical restraint against some apparent wrongdoer. For example, one who reasonably perceives an immediate threat to her interests may invoke the preemptive right of self-defense. Under this right, the potential victim becomes empowered to inhibit the conduct of the aggressor so long as her response is reasonably necessary to eliminate the danger. Another way to exercise a preemptive right is to invoke the injunctive power of the state. If, for instance, a property owner operates an incinerator which fouls the air of her neighbor, the latter might obtain an injunction directing the wrongdoer to abate the nuisance.

Regulatory secondary rights are slightly less demanding. With a regulatory right, the holder may not completely bar the conduct of another, but may only alter the manner in which she performs a particular activity. Governmental regulations provide perhaps the most prominent illustrations of regulatory rights in action. Administrative agencies frequently are authorized to control the business practices of certain industries. Airlines may fly, but only if they subject their planes to regular inspections. Banks may make loans, but they may not charge usurious interest rates. And while employers may set the work hours of their employees, they may not omit lunch hours, breaks or payment for overtime. Besides these formal types of regulation, there are an infinite variety of more subtle limitations on our autonomy. From the rules of games to articles of incorporation, we are constantly subject to someone's secondary right of regulation.

Corrective rights are the least restrictive variety of secondary rights. Unlike the other secondary rights mentioned above, corrective rights do not empower one to interfere with another's right of action *before* an act has been committed. Only when the act is performed and the right holder is injured is her corrective right invoked. At that point, the right allows the victim to take remedial action against the actor. For example, one who engages in a strict liability activity like pile driving may not be prohibited from doing so. Nor, absent some specific regulation, may she be directly forced to change the manner of her operation. Rather, she may be required only to pay for any damage that her enterprise causes to others. In such a case, each of the injured parties possesses a secondary right to "correct" the loss by extracting from the pile driver some fair measure of compensation.

The Political Nature of Rights

Regardless of their form, secondary rights do not exist in a state of nature, but are uniquely a product of political association.[3] As we have seen, individuals in prepolitical societies are free to act by force and instinct. At a moment's whim, the strongest individual or group may plunder the possessions of those less powerful, or break promises without fear of reprisal. In a world of changing coalitions, however, even the most ruthless and cunning gang would be vulnerable to coercion or deception by still larger cooperative factions. Under these unstable circumstances, neither the life nor material holdings of any individual could ever be secure. Here, there are no duties to refrain from invading the interests of others; nor are there any entitlements to preferential treatment. There is only one guiding principle: might makes right.

Political associations are formed to provide the security and predictability lacking in a state of nature. In creating a body politic, individuals give up absolute freedom. They may no longer exploit their natural endowments to subjugate others. In return for this concession, the state assumes the responsibility of ensuring that all citizens receive adequate protection. It does this by enacting laws. Laws require that all members of the group respect at least certain interests of others. The interests protected by law, in turn, constitute our rights.

Privately Created Rights

Rights are not just promulgated by the state through law; they also may be created by individuals themselves. By making certain types of promises enforceable, the state empowers citizens to enter binding contracts. When contracting parties exchange oaths, each procures from the other the right to affect her interests in some way. It may entitle the parties to the performance of a particular act, to the receipt of some good or merely to the payment of money. In any case, the beneficiaries of these promises enjoy a power over others not otherwise available under the law.

The Paradox of Rights

The advantages secured by rights—of security and commercial exchange—are not obtained without some cost. Remember that rights empower individuals to prevent others from causing them harm. For example, if someone has a right to be free from bodily harm, I must suppress my urge to punch her in the nose. Thus, besides enhancing the holder's security, this right serves to restrict my freedom of action. In fact, it would inhibit anyone from engaging in such conduct. At first glance, this seems to give the right holder a power of oppression. But because rights are agent-neutral, no one individual owns a monopoly on this protection. Everyone enjoys the benefits of this right, and all bear its restrictive burdens. So, although a specific right holder may prevent me from punching her in the nose, she too is precluded from changing my profile. This leads to a rather startling paradox: just as rights assure us our liberty, they also ensure that some of our liberty will be lost.

This paradox creates the central tension in all democratic legal systems. On the one hand, the state desires to protect the interests of its members from all unwanted invasions. On the other hand, however, it seeks to guarantee its citizens the greatest possible liberty so they might pursue their life plans. The problem is that these are contradictory goals. Where few negative rights are recognized, we receive greater freedom of action, but we remain vulnerable to the rapacious designs of others. Conversely, where negative rights are created to protect all interests from even the most trivial invasions, we gain added security, but we lose many of the positive freedoms which make life worth living. As is apparent, injustice lurks in each of these extremes. We simply cannot enjoy unbridled freedom without risking domination; neither may we ensure complete safety without risking tyranny. To do justice, we must balance these competing concerns.

The Assignment of Rights

This need for balance determines how and when rights are created. They do not protect all of our interests, only some. Indeed, as we shall see in the next chapter, the interests one may possess are multitudinous and far-reaching. They range from the sublime—like the interest in living—to the ridiculous—say, the interest in having chocolate cake for desert. The state cannot guarantee each of these interests without placing correlatively excessive restrictions on our liberty. There are simply some interests which must be sacrificed as a cost of social living. Because of this, the state must be selective in choosing the interests which it will accord the status of a right.

Naturally, the more important the interest is to human flourishing, the more worthy it is of protection and the stronger that protective shield must be. In keeping with this notion, primary rights are assigned only to significant interests. This too will be considered in further detail in the next chapter. At this point, it is sufficient to say that such interests must be at least important enough to warrant imposing upon others a duty to respect them. Why use a description which focuses on how the right will affect others? Because primary rights never exist in isolation, but are accompanied by secondary rights which empower their holders to take some coercive, preemptive or corrective action against somebody else.

Rights Clusters

The rights clusters formed by primary and secondary rights are not static and inflexible.[4] Rather, they vary in weight and complexity depending upon the underlying interest being protected and the circumstances under which it is challenged. For example, the primary right to life is one of the most fundamental rights we possess. Because of its importance, this right is usually guarded by a bevy of secondary defenders and enforcers. When threatened by another, a right holder may protect her life in many ways. She may act preemptively, by physically restraining or even killing her aggressor. She might regulate the threatening behavior, as by enjoining an industrial plant from polluting the air or water. Or, in the event of her death, her estate might take corrective action by instituting a survival action against the wrongdoer. Even where the threat is not imposed by another, but is created by nature, the party in jeopardy possesses a secondary right to save her life by appropriating the lesser interests of others.[5]

On the other hand, primary rights to lesser interests—like a piece of personal property—ordinarily are accompanied by fewer of these secondary enforcement mechanisms. Although one might take preemptive action to protect her property, the measures she may use would be greatly limited. In most cases, she would be prohibited from employing force to defend her good. And, if her property were actually seized, she would be virtually powerless to take it back. Instead, she would be relegated to invoking the corrective remedy afforded her by the legal system.

The Relativity of Rights

Whatever the intrinsic value of a primary right, this factor alone is not determinative of the number and variety of secondary rights which will cluster around it. In different contexts, these protections may either expand or diminish. The reason is that rights are not absolute, but relative.[6] They accord the holder only a prima facie or presumptive entitlement to some good or power.[7] Often, the prima facie rights of different individuals come into conflict. My right to engage in blasting may clash with your right to the peaceful enjoyment of your property. While we can roughly evaluate the worth of each right independently, we cannot determine in advance of this encounter whose right is superior. And without knowing this, it would be impossible to say whose secondary rights will be activated, and what they will empower their holder to do.

Consider this illustration. Both A and B are individuals with a right to life. In the abstract their rights are identical; the life of one has no more value than that of the other. Under an immutable hierarchy of rights, where life is the ultimate interest, both should enjoy the same unqualified protection. But now assume that A pulls a gun on B without provocation. B, who is armed herself, reacts by shooting and killing A. Until B's weapon was discharged, both parties engaged in the same type of conduct—drawing a gun—and both were in jeopardy of losing their primary rights to life. Yet it is clear that B's secondary enforcement rights were far greater than those of A. B was entitled to take the preemptive action of producing her gun in order to protect her life. Indeed, she even was justified in pulling the trigger and sending A to meet her creator. A, however, enjoyed no such privilege. That B drew her gun did not empower A to shoot, even though her own well-being was now in jeopardy. Moreover, once B shot and killed A, A's estate acquired no secondary corrective right to seek damages against B. This is because A's right to life was not absolute, but only presumptive. Under the circumstances of her confrontation with B, A's prima facie right gave way to the superior, actual right of B to defend herself.

Meshing and Clashing Rights

Viewing rights in this way—as only prima facie entitlements—is a necessary first step in evaluating the justice of human interactions. It reminds us that what we are "due" from others is not certain and unwavering, but changes dynamically from one encounter to the next. As a result, it also leaves us with a great deal of uncertainty. How do we know when a prima facie right will serve as an actual right, or will succumb to the countervailing rights of others? Moreover, what kinds of secondary rights can be used to protect the parties' interests, and when are these rights invoked? Unfortunately, there are no easy answers to these questions. There are, however, some definite principles to steer us in the right direction.

Whether we notice it or not, we all exercise our rights every moment of every day. This is as true when we are acting affirmatively, say, by driving to work or taking a walk, as it is when we sit passively reading a book or taking a nap. We are each surrounded by spheres of interest which follow us wherever we go. In most cases this is not a problem. We avoid conflict by planning our transactions with others. Thus, when I go to the super-market to acquire a bag of groceries, I know I must pay money before I will be permitted to take them home. In the exchange, I accrue a right to pos-sess the commodities in my bag, and the store is entitled to an amount of my money approximating their value. In these typical interactions, the rights of the parties mesh like interlocking sprockets, and the wheels of justice keep humming smoothly.

As was noted earlier, however, there inevitably will be occasions where the rights of individuals come into conflict, and the machinery of justice will get jammed. Indeed, given the extent of our interdependence, a certain num-ber of these unwanted transactions are simply destined to happen. Yet it is not always clear when these conflicts arise or what should be done about them. As I drive ninety miles an hour on the freeway, my need for speed expos-es others who have the misfortune of being near me to an increased risk of harm. Here, my desire to drive as I please interferes with my fellow travel-ers' interest in motoring without fear for their own safety. No one would argue, however, that those threatened by my conduct would be justified in pulling me over and detaining me, adjusting my engine to limit the horse-power of my car or asking me to pay them damages for their discomfort. But if this type of other-affecting behavior does not create a tangible rights con-flict, then what will? At what point does the potential for calamity which I cre-ate cease to be purely a trivial annoyance and begin to become a concern of justice? More specifically, when do my actions activate someone else's sec-ondary rights so that she may exercise some power to restrict my behavior?

Risk and Harm as Secondary Right Activators

There are basically three ways this might happen. Because secondary rights are by nature protective, all are initially triggered by risk. Only those individuals whose primary rights are threatened by my conduct may have the power either to stop me, interfere with my activity or recover dam-ages if I cause them injury. For some secondary rights, this is enough. Thus, in our previous hypothetical involving the showdown between A and B, B's secondary right of self-defense was activated as soon as A put her life at risk by drawing a gun. For other secondary rights, however, more than mere risk is needed. For example, in some cases a remedial secondary right arises only after a contracting party fails to satisfy some promissory con-dition. In others, it often must also be shown that the holder's primary right actually has been invaded, thus causing her harm. This is typical of corrective rights which are the primary concern of tort law. Because of the importance of harm in the scheme of tort justice, the next chapter will be devoted to this concept.

Causation as Secondary Right Director

Once secondary rights have been triggered, they must be given appropriate direction. These rights are, after all, inherently relational. They bestow upon the bearer uncommon power to intrude upon the sphere of interests enjoyed by others. To be used, there must be some identifiable person against whom this power may be unleashed. Indeed, absent any such specific target, the underlying primary right invasion may be injurious, and maybe unethical, but it is not a wrong. Even where a list of likely suspects may be compiled, secondary rights may not be wielded haphazardly; rather, they must be employed with judicious discrimination. The concept of causal responsibility serves this purpose. It singles out the moral agent who may be subject to the remedial prerogative of the victim. Because causal responsibility is a central component in the corrective matrix of tort law, it will be examined more thoroughly in Chapter Four.

Wrongdoing as Right Violator

Even where secondary rights have been activated and directed against a specific individual, they often may not be implemented unless the actual or potential transgressor has acted wrongfully. Why? Because both the actor and the victim are right-holders. The victim is entitled to protection from the unwanted intrusions of others. The actor, on the other hand, is entitled to engage in those activities which help to further her life plan. In a tortious transaction where the victim suffers an injury, her primary right appears to be violated. The mere fact of her injury, however, does not necessarily establish the violation of her right. If the actor has not exceeded her own right of action, she has not acted wrongfully and there is no moral basis for allowing the victim to interfere with her interests. Although the victim's interests have been impaired, her prima facie right to be free from harm is never realized. As we have seen, some interests simply are not entitled to protection. Loss of these interests is not wrongful, but just an unfortunate consequence of social intercourse. This notion of wrongfulness, which rounds out our analysis of justice and rights, also permeates the law of torts. Consequently, it will be explored in much greater depth in Chapter Five.

Chapter 3

Harm

Previously, we determined that rights serve to delineate the interests which are protected by law. We also saw why this is important. Only when such interests are threatened or impaired is the potential victim said to have sustained "harm;" and only if she is harmed may she take corrective action against the instigator. However, we have not yet considered what interests actually are and which ones acquire favored status under the law. Nor have we examined how such interests may be violated, and exactly how this results in harm. It is to these questions which we now turn.

Derivation and Dichotomy of Interests

Joel Feinberg has described an interest as a stake in the realization of a particular outcome or condition.[1] One has a stake in an outcome or condition when she stands to gain or lose from its realization or frustration.[2] Under what circumstances will an individual be so vulnerable to the vicissitudes of chance? When she possesses either a need or desire that the outcome or condition reach fruition.[3]

Needs and desires are understandable only if life has some purpose. They are not ends in themselves, but merely instruments for attaining some ultimate goal. According to Aristotle, the goal of life is happiness, and this entails the pursuit of virtue. People form life plans to facilitate this endeavor. A life plan is a scheme of decisions and actions which one must implement in order to be happy. Each step in one's life plan is a necessary or desirable element in reaching that end. Thus, one may have an interest in anything which allows her to fulfill her life plan.

Despite their differences, every life plan has one thing in common. It cannot be achieved unless its author is alive to pursue it. Thus, survival is necessary to the success of all life plans. It follows that people have a stake in securing those things essential to survival—things like food, clothing, shelter and health. These are our basic welfare interests.[4]

Beyond survival, every life plan requires some action toward the end good chosen by its author. However, these actions will vary from individual to individual, depending upon the virtue to be obtained. For the scholar, acquiring knowledge may require studying at the finest academic institutions and reading the classics. For the artist who pursues aesthetics, it may mean traveling in search of the world's many wondrous beauties. Although the objectives of each differ, they both desire to gain the experiences necessary to implement their particular life plans. The more successful an actor is in realizing these experiences, the closer she comes to achieving her conception of virtue. Likewise, the more of these experiences the actor is denied, the more she stands to lose. These desires, then, form ulterior interests which assist in the realization of people's life plans.[5]

Interests and Autonomy

By now, the common principle underlying these interests is probably apparent. Both welfare and ulterior interests are founded on a concern for autonomy. Welfare interests arise from our need for independence. To survive, we must have the mental faculties to make rational decisions, and the physical capabilities to carry them out. Additionally, we must be afforded the basic material goods necessary to sustain these attributes of autonomy. Our ulterior interests, on the other hand, rest on our need for options from which to choose. Every life plan requires a certain range of options. These options allow us not only to distinguish good from bad, but to alter the path to our final destination. Without such options one is not truly free, for she may be compelled to abandon her life plan or make choices inconsistent with it.

Harm as the Impairment of an Interest

We now have the basis for understanding what it means to sustain a harm. A harm is the objective blocking or invading of an interest without one's consent.[6] Because interests simply represent aspects of individual autonomy, to harm someone means to interfere with her freedom. This may consist of eliminating or restricting her options, or impeding her ability to act upon them.

Direct Harm

Autonomy may be impaired in many different ways, both direct and indirect. One of the most direct, and most serious ways of obstructing autonomy is through physical injury. The greatest source of our freedom lies in our physicality. As human beings, we have the "hardware" to think and act. It is these characteristics which allow us to chase the elusive goal of virtue. Thus, an impairment of our physicality often poses a direct threat to this life plan. Indeed, one who suffers a permanent disability may be precluded from engaging in certain activities essential to that end. This, in turn, restricts that individual's universe of choices, and so inhibits her autonomy.

The disability producing this restriction can be either psychological or physiological. Physiological disabilities provide overt evidence of autonomy restriction. For example, the employee whose hand is amputated by a piece of machinery not only loses an important appendage, she is forced to change her life significantly. Many vocational, recreational and domestic activities, not to mention ordinary tactile pleasures, are lost forever. As devastating as such physiological restrictions are, accompanying psychological disabilities may be just as profound. In fact, often the fear, anger, humiliation and anguish following a physical injury (or the imposition of some other unreasonable risk of harm) may inhibit the victim's capacity to think and act more than the external impairment itself.

Another form of direct restriction of autonomy is the destruction or appropriation of one's material possessions. For individuals to manifest other-directed virtue, it is necessary for each individual to possess a modicum of property. Only then would an individual have the choice to act benevolently or altruistically. When these material holdings are reduced or eliminated, so too are the possessor's options. Though material possessions often can be replaced, the time and effort in acquiring them (representing an investment in autonomy) cannot. And even if replaced, the loss of the article, even temporarily, inhibits the possessor's opportunities for using or transferring the item for some personally beneficial purpose. While this form of autonomy restriction is usually far less permanent, and thus less serious than invasions of bodily or psychic integrity, it is significant enough to inhibit one's life plan.

The same is true of direct obstructions of one's freedom of movement. I may be confined by physical barricade, by threat or by deception. In each case, my independence is curtailed and the range of options beyond my sphere of confinement effectively eliminated. Still, I have the capacity for full exercise of my autonomy if these constraints are ever removed. Although the effect upon my freedom is direct, it is generally of less magnitude than the invasions described above.[7]

Indirect Harm

Indirect autonomy invasions also may take any one or more of a number of forms: being induced to act where one would not ordinarily act or to forebear certain opportunities which otherwise might have been pursued, or having certain opportunities eliminated from the spectrum of choice. These restrictions are indirect because they do not physically interfere with the victim's ability to chose and act; rather, they limit the options available for her choice and action.

When one makes a promise or undertakes to aid another, she creates in the recipient an expectation of some future benefit. Because of this expectation, the intended beneficiary often forgoes other opportunities to acquire the benefit from some other source. Although this restriction of choice is voluntary and not "coerced" as by injury to body or property, it is induced by the promisor and its resulting effect is an impairment, albeit indirect, of the recipient's autonomy.

When an individual is defamed, or her business pursuits are sabotaged by another, her restriction of autonomy, though still indirect, is even more concrete. Here, the impairment of life choices is not voluntarily assumed, but is precipitated by forces external to the autonomous agent. Consider the case of defamation. By definition, a defamatory statement is one which lowers the community's estimation of the subject. As a result, it induces others to avoid interaction with that individual. This inhibition of social interaction, in turn, impairs the subject's opportunities for pursuing both self- and other-directed virtue. To an even greater extent, tortious interference with contractual relationships significantly impacts the agent's business options. It deprives the individual of economic opportunities which otherwise would have been available to her. Although these injuries are more speculative and ephemeral than those involving direct invasions, they are sufficient to hinder the exercise of autonomy intrinsic to the quest for virtue.

Nonredressable Harms

All of the "harms" described above involve some actual restriction of autonomy. But will *any* actual invasion of autonomy, no matter how slight, give grounds for redress? Indeed, is an actual harm even necessary? Might a right arise even where such an interest has not in fact been obstructed or invaded?

The answer to the first question seems obvious. Even skeptics would agree that the witness to a plane crash, or other catastrophic event, may suffer long lasting emotional and psychological scars which may have a significant impact on her autonomy.[8] And, there are some sensitive individuals whose offense to what we would characterize as common indecencies might be paralyzing.[9] In each case, the victim has sustained an actual harm. Yet in both cases the law denies the aggrieved parties a right of recovery. Why?

There are a few reasons. One is the difficulty of protecting the interest allegedly violated. In both of the above examples, the number of potential claim-holders would be enormous. Cataclysmic events are by their very nature far-reaching, and their occurrences widely publicized. Similarly, nary a day goes by that one will not hear indecencies such as epithets and off-color remarks. They are an unavoidable part of social living. To vindicate all the interests affected by such events would quickly deplete the precious, limited resources of the state. Another reason for refusing to recognize rights in these circumstances is the difficulty of proving that an underlying interest has been violated. In the case of indecencies, most people exposed to such behavior suffer no harm at all. This fact casts suspicion upon the claim of a hypersensitive individual. Because the alleged harm, if any, is psychological, it may be impossible to substantiate the claim. Finally, as the indecency example suggests, the interest itself may be too unimportant, or its violation too insignificant, to warrant recognition.[10]

Abstract or Presumed Harm

So an *actual* autonomy invasion is not always sufficient to ground a right of recovery; this leads one to wonder—is it even necessary? Again, one cannot respond affirmatively without giving qualification. There *are* a few occasions where an aggrieved party will be granted a right of recovery without such a tangible injury. For example, if I tread across your property without your permission, I am liable for trespass even though I have neither done physical damage to the land, nor interfered with your ability to use and enjoy it.[11] Likewise, if I raise my fist to strike you, and have the apparent ability to complete this act, you have a right to be free from such conduct even if you are not frightened or in any other way affected by my gesture.[12] In these cases, the right arises not simply from the badness of my act, but from my utter rejection of or disregard for the dignity of my victims, and from my threatened assault upon the idea of autonomy itself. Remember that it is freedom from such random usurpations which drives us to political association. Any attack upon this freedom is an attack upon the social arrangement which allows us to survive. Thus, where one intentionally threatens the autonomy interests of another, the transgression is serious enough to afford the victim a right of redress.

The Relativity of Harm

Though these exceptional cases seem disjointed, they are united by a common thread. All embrace the notion of relativity and balance. For instance, there are degrees of interests and interest obstruction. In determining whether a right exists, one must consider the importance of the right affected. Is it an aspect of physicality from which all other autonomy interests emanate, or is it the loss of a remote option, ancillary to one's life plan? These factors must be balanced against the extent of the interference. Where bodily integrity is concerned, was the invasion a pin prick or head injury? If an option is affected, is it completely foreclosed or only made less desirable, and are there other options which can take its place?

After weighing these considerations, the interest still must be evaluated in light of the nature of the wrongdoer's conduct and the policies of the state. Thus, even a significant interest may find no legal asylum if the injury-producing conduct is socially desirable, and the administrative costs of protecting that interest are prohibitive. On the other hand, if the offending conduct displays a volition contemptuous of dignity and freedom, it may ground a right of recovery even though no actual harm has been sustained by the claimant. In this way, wrongdoing and harm are not completely independent concepts, but are inextricably intertwined. Together, they help to shape our sense of justice.

Chapter 4

Causal Responsibility

Although harm is a necessary part of our sense of injustice, it is not the only factor. Another essential aspect of this moral instinct is the concept of causal responsibility. Causal responsibility means different things to different people depending upon the context in which it is used. For the purpose of this discussion, however, it may be defined simply as the identification of an individual or group whose conduct either threatens or actually produces injury to another. As so construed, this concept serves two important functions in the resolution of legal disputes. In transactions where the right-holder appears to consent to a particular act or consequence, thereby inducing others to appropriate her interests, the notion of causal responsibility forecloses the possibility that such encounters are unjust. In other transactions where consent is lacking, so that the invasion of the right-holder's interests clearly is initiated by someone else, causal responsibility helps to determine what action the right-holder may take to defend her interests and against whom such remedial action can be taken. Because of the importance of these functions in the realm of justice, we will examine each more closely in this chapter.

Consensual Encounters

Ordinarily, a right-holder who consents to a transaction is causally responsible for any loss she may sustain in that encounter.[1] Why? Because by agreeing to interact with another, the right-holder gives up her negative right to be left alone. In fact, a consenter does more than simply lift the barriers to social intercourse, she actually empowers her transactional partner to interfere with her interests in some specified manner. As long as the other does not exceed the scope of the right-holder's consent, the transaction is not wrongful. Indeed, the encounter may not even be harmful in any moral sense if the right-holder desires to obtain some subjective benefit from the encounter. In such a scenario, the transaction affords the right-holder advantages she would not enjoy in isolation. It thus enhances, rather than restricts, her autonomy.

For instance, one who contracts to have a tattoo applied to her arm gives up part of her bodily integrity to get what she desires: a piece of artwork to enhance her appearance. Although the procedure may be painful and unpleasant, it is not a harm to the recipient. Indeed, harm is more than just something physically hurtful, it is a failure to respect the will, and thus the personhood, of another. She who voluntarily consents to a transaction, however, is not the victim of a unilateral assault upon her rights, but the beneficiary of a mutual exchange. So it is with our tattoo recipient. Far from threatening her autonomy interests, this transaction furthers these interests by allowing her to make choices about what to do with her body and how to live her life.

Suppose, however, that our tattoo recipient did not truly desire to have a permanent mark stitched into her arm. Somewhat naive, she went to the tattoo parlor unaware of the consequences of her decision. Because of her ignorance, it would be difficult to say that her subjective will was realized in the transaction. Nevertheless, by walking into the parlor, sitting in the chair and enduring hours of constant pricking, the client did express her consent. It may not have been verbalized, but it was just as clearly communicated through the objective language of her actions. Given this apparent license, the client's resulting bodily invasion, though perhaps a harm, is not a wrong for which she could seek redress. Even though she did not want a permanent tattoo, her manifestation of willingness induced the tattooist to go through with the procedure. Without her expression of consent, neither the encounter, nor the interest invasion it engendered, would have ever occurred.

We see, then, that regardless of whether the client subjectively desired the tattoo, she alone was responsible for its placement on her arm. While the client's interest in bodily integrity was affected in the transaction, this interference simply cannot be attributed to the tattooist. The client, not the tattooist, initiated the transaction and controlled the circumstances of its formation and completion. At any time, she could have revoked her consent and terminated the transaction by merely expressing her displeasure or exiting the parlor. It follows that the tattooist did not wrongfully invade the client's interest in bodily integrity; rather, the client alienated her right freely through her own actions. If she has anyone to hold causally accountable for this intrusion, it is only herself.

Nonconsensual Encounters

The same is not true, however, where the right-holder has not waived her rights and is not otherwise responsible for their transfer. In such a case, the party who threatens or impairs her interests has no special license to do so. Thus, unlike in the above situations where the right-holder's injury is self-induced, nonconsensual transactions are more likely to be unjust. Because someone other than the right-holder has caused her harm, justice allows the victim to defend her rights. But who may she take action against? To answer this question, we again must turn to the concept of causal responsibility.

The Directive Role of Causal Responsibility

In democratic societies, we have seen, all individuals engage in two types of relationships: private relations with other people and a political relationship with their lawgiver. Parties to each type of relationship are vested with certain primary rights. As citizens in a liberal democratic state, for example, we have the right to exercise certain basic liberties. In return, our government is entitled to respect and obedience. In private transactions, we are given the right to act in furtherance of our interests; yet others are entitled to be free from the dangers which our actions create. In both types of relationships, the primary rights of the parties are accompanied by secondary rights which give the holder the power to protect her interests. Thus, when we are oppressed by our government, we may take action to eliminate the oppression. Likewise, if our lives are placed in danger by an aggressor, we are entitled to employ some reasonable measure of self-defense.

But nothing in this threat requires that our reaction be directed against any particular individual. Indeed, in some situations one might be inclined to exercise these protective rights against almost anyone. Thus, if I am denied civil rights by my government, I might opt not to overthrow the system, but to ransack or loot the property of blameless merchants. Or, if my life is in danger, I might choose to defend myself not by striking back at my pursuers, but by threatening the lives of innocent hostages. Although many observers may feel that I was entitled to take some remedial action, my guess is that most instinctively would condemn my responses as misdirected and unjust. What informs this instinct? It is the notion of causal responsibility. It serves to restrict my retaliatory efforts by identifying a specific individual or group against whom my secondary rights may be exerted.

The Political Role of Causal Responsibility

Although this concept at first may seem stultifying, in reality it has more of a moderating effect, and one which is vital to our political survival. The existence of every form of government depends upon the ability of its citizens to cooperate. To this end, individuals need to be able to plan their behavior towards others. They also must develop expectations about how others may treat them. One way of doing this, of course, is through contracts. Contracts allow parties to specify their rights and responsibilities before they interact. Unfortunately, however, people have neither the time nor the resources to arrange all of their interactions with others. Where such planned transactions are not possible, the state must provide reasonably clear rules to guide the actions of its citizens. The concept of causal responsibility helps to supply this guidance.[2] Under it, an aggrieved party may not lash out arbitrarily against anyone she desires. Rather, she generally must exercise her secondary rights against those that threaten or harm her interests. By establishing this convention, the concept of causal responsibility lends predictability to interpersonal transactions and so avoids the political instability which follows from social chaos.

Causal Responsibility and Morality

It could be argued, however, that any rule of behavior would serve this same purpose. For example, a rule that required individuals to exercise their secondary rights exclusively against some predetermined scapegoat group—say, parents, teachers or political leaders—would provide just as much predictability as a rule of causal responsibility. All we really have established so far is that some rule delimiting the use of secondary rights is better than no rule at all. We have not yet cited a reason for preferring causal responsibility over any other competing rule.

Yet such a reason does exist. By providing direction to our corrective and retributive impulses, causal responsibility ensures that secondary rights will be used to vindicate the rights of their possessors, and not to desecrate the rights of others. Remember that we are all exercising our rights all of the time. Even as I sit here writing, I not only enjoy the positive right to free expression, but also the negative right not to have my thoughts censored by anyone else. Similarly, where I am threatened by an attacker or oppressed by my government, I have a secondary right to protect myself from what I perceive to be the wrongful acts of others. But if I react to such perils by taking hostages or looting stores, I now jeopardize the rights of these innocent bystanders. Both the hostages and the merchants are entitled to at least a prima facie immunity from my injurious actions. By interfering with their interests, I am transformed from victim into wrongdoer. My conduct is no longer defensive but offensive. As such, it is not simply politically undesirable, it is potentially immoral. Unless I have some specific justification for this intrusion, my actions towards my victims are as wrongful and unjust as the provocative behavior which motivated my response.

Causation in Different Interactive Contexts

The concept of causal responsibility provides at least part of the justification for directing our protective instincts towards certain individuals or entities and not against others. It does this in different ways depending on the form of the wrongdoer's misconduct and the type of secondary right the holder wishes to exercise against her. For example, where the wrongdoer's affirmative actions place the right holder in danger, the latter may respond with some preventative measure. Here, causal responsibility strongly influences, though it does not necessarily control, the direction of the right-holder's reaction. The concept's impact is greater in situations where the wrongdoer's deeds actually culminate in harm. Under these circumstances, the victim may take corrective or remedial action, but only against the agent causally responsible for her loss. And when the wrongdoer has failed to act, thus depriving the victim of needed protection, causal responsibility takes yet another form. Founded on the potential power of one's will, rather than on any specific act of misconduct, it permits the right-holder to compel the omitter to take action or to provide compensation for failing to do so.

Preemptive Reactions to Misfeasance

Let's first consider the situation where one party is endangered by someone else's affirmative act of misfeasance. In this scenario, a unique bond is forged between the actor and her prospective victim. This fusion proceeds from each side of the transactional relationship. By creating and imposing certain risks upon another, the causative agent incurs a duty to protect the endangered party from the potentially injurious consequences of her conduct. As the recipient of such causal agency, the prospective victim in turn accrues a special secondary right to protect herself from impending harm by taking preemptive action against the actor. In such cases, there are special political and moral forces arising from this causality which connect the actor to her prospective victim and vice versa.

Establishing the Actor's Duty

Actors are tied to others by the causation-infused concept of legal duty. Duties, we shall see in the next chapter, place the shackles of responsibility upon those who create risk and give the chains controlling them to the privileged few individuals who fall within the sphere of the actors' causal influence.

While most activities are subject to some duty, purely self-regarding activities are not. For example, If I play a game of solitaire in the privacy of my own home, I pose no affirmative risk to the rights of others. Such an activity is entirely personal, not social. By engaging in it, I establish no direct or indirect relations with anyone else. Because my game playing is done in isolation, it cannot be subject to the demands of justice, which is inherently relational. My conduct threatens no one, so I owe no duty of care towards others; accordingly, nobody may claim to be due any such consideration from me. Under these circumstances, I have an absolute right to proceed with my card game. Anyone who attempts to prohibit or restrict my activity violates this right.

The situation is different, however, if my conduct exposes others to certain risks. Suppose I decide to hit golf balls out of my back yard. Undoubtedly, I have the right to use and enjoy my property. But my neighbors also have rights, including the right to be free from the harmful intrusion of an errant golf ball. Thus, unlike when I played the game of solitaire, my right to hit the golf balls is not unrestricted. Because my conduct may jeopardize others in my neighborhood, I bear a duty to act reasonably. Under this duty, I owe my neighbors a degree of consideration to protect them from the hazards of my activity. As a result, they accrue an entitlement to receive this special treatment. The obligations and entitlements flowing from this duty link me and each of my neighbors together in a morally significant relationship. This relationship, like all others, is subject to the concerns of justice.

The Effect of Duties

When the lives of individuals become intertwined in this way, justice sometimes may permit one or both of the parties to invade the interests of the other. Duties are the passports which legitimate such intrusions. A duty is, after all, but the opposite of a right. Thus, depending upon the right at issue, one burdened by a correlative duty not only may lack an entitlement to act in a particular way, she may bear an obligation to others to refrain from doing so. This duty makes the actor more vulnerable to the actions of others than when her conduct is purely self-regarding. It divests its holder of some of her negative freedom by empowering others to interfere with her autonomy. So in the golfing example above, my duty to act reasonably both denies me the right to aim my drives at the bay window of my neighbor's house and authorizes my neighbor to take some reasonable measures to prevent me from doing so. In the absence of a primary right to behave in this manner, I enjoy no negative liberty to prevent others from stopping me. Thus, unlike in the solitaire hypothetical, the efforts of my neighbors to restrict my actions are not unjust.

Duties and Autonomy

As the antithesis of rights, duties seem to pose a real threat to the concept of autonomy.[3] They limit the universe of one's actions and deputize others to enforce this limitation. Yet such consequences are not always bad. Indeed, they are tolerable, if not desirable, where the conduct being regulated is more dangerous to the concept of liberty than the restriction imposed by the duty. Harmful behavior that is both deliberate and unjustified falls into this category. It represents the subordination of one person's interests to those of another. Such conduct is completely inconsistent with the tenets of a liberal democratic society. Besides repudiating the notion of equality, it undermines the rule of law necessary to orderly political association. Thus, there is good reason to deny individuals the freedom to engage in this kind of activity. We do this by subjecting everyone to the general duty of abstaining from acts which are intentionally designed to violate someone else's rights. This duty extends to all members of society, and each is given some power to enforce it.[4]

Not all duties, however, are so broadly conceived. Nor would we want them to be. This is especially true for actions which are primarily self-regarding, but happen to produce some ancillary risk towards others. In contrast to intentionally wrongful behavior, such activities may possess great personal or social utility. If these enterprises are laden with the kind of expansive responsibilities noted above, many individuals will be discouraged from undertaking them. The result would be catastrophic. By blocking the pathways to individual virtue, the entire purpose of political association would be subverted. To prevent this from happening, the duties which curtail such self-directed activities must be narrowly drawn. While protecting others from unreasonable risks of harm, these duties must also afford their holders some fair measure of freedom to pursue their life plans.

Causation as Duty Limiter

The concept of causal responsibility helps to effect this balance. In most cases, an actor pursuing some self-serving end owes no duty to the world at large to ensure that no one is harmed by her conduct. Rather, her responsibility extends only so far as the risk she creates. Thus, when I tee up a golf ball in my back yard, my duty to use care in hitting it is owed to those of my neighbors within striking distance of my drive. It is these individuals, and no others, who I have caused to suffer the hazard of my behavior. Consequently, only people within the ambit of this causality are empowered to take some preventative action against me. For all other people in the world, my misguided driving range is of no concern. Because they are not endangered by my conduct, they are not beneficiaries of my duty to exercise care. As against them, I have an absolute right to continue with my activity.

The Morality of Causally Restricted Duties

By placing such limitations on duties, the concept of causal responsibility effectively secures a fair measure of freedom for those actively pursuing their life objectives. But it is not necessarily the only way of guaranteeing such a right. There might be some other formula equally if not better adept at serving this end. For example, one's duty might be temporally or spatially restricted rather than circumscribed by causal risk. Under such a scheme, my responsibility might not extend beyond a hundred yard radius from my point of operation. Or, if my duty were cast more expansively, it might be operative for only one hour following the completion of my activity. What makes causal responsibility more viable, and thus more attractive than these or any other alternatives?

The answer, in short, is that causal responsibility comes closest to effectuating our intuitive moral sense of accountability. To understand this, we must return to an examination of our most fundamental moral precepts. As previously discussed, the purpose of existence is the attainment of virtue. Virtue, we have seen, requires autonomy, or the choice between right and wrong and the freedom to select between these options. To be virtuous, one must exercise her freedom to do what is right and refrain from doing what is wrong. Our sense of morality, therefore, depends upon the nature of our actions.

Although behavior can be characterized generally as either good or bad, it is not possible to ascribe a definite moral value to all human endeavors. For some types of conduct, this moral assessment appears to be purely subjective. For example, to one person the refusal of a bystander to intervene in a domestic dispute may be viewed as an appropriate exercise of respect for the affairs of others, while another may see the same reluctance as evidence of the bystander's cowardice or the lack of an altruistic spirit. Other actions, however, are universally condemnable from both a political and moral standpoint. In a political system such as ours in which individual autonomy is a basic good, any conduct which deliberately and unjustifiably threatens the autonomy of others is clearly bad. Even where an activity is not designed to harm others, it may be bad if it displays a callous disregard for their rights. In either case, one cannot properly evaluate the moral quality of such actions without examining the extent to which they tend to expose others to harm.

Causal Control and the Problem
of Line-Drawing

In complicated industrial societies, few actions, good or bad, are completely self-contained. Given the intricate network of relationships pervading our culture, even the most simple act is likely to have far-reaching, long-term effects. Suppose I accidentally drop a nail on the street as I leave the hardware store. Two weeks later, a car travelling over the same street strikes my nail, which becomes embedded in one of its tires. The tire, which develops a slow leak, goes flat after one hundred miles. As a result, the driver misses an important business meeting and loses an important client. She is thereafter fired and must seek public assistance. Because of her financial difficulties, her marriage deteriorates and her husband eventually files for divorce, taking their two children with him. Here my seemingly innocuous action of dropping the nail has had a startlingly significant, albeit indirect effect upon many individuals over great time and distance. Indeed, its impact on our unfortunate driver may last her entire lifetime. But few would argue that I am morally responsible for all of these consequences. At some point during this chain of events, I can no longer be held accountable for the harm that may follow.

The difficulty is in determining where this point is and when it has been reached. Where an action is performed in complete isolation, say on a deserted island, such moral line-drawing would not be so challenging. There, the only possible causal agents would be Mother Nature or the actor herself. The question of accountability becomes more problematic, however, in an environment where there are an untold number of others, all acting simultaneously. Here, an injurious event might be attributed to the acts of many possible causal agents. For instance, in the nail-dropping hypothetical mentioned above, there are several individuals, besides me, whose conduct may have contributed to the adverse consequences suffered by the driver. The driver may have caused some of her own problems by driving the car without inspecting the tires, performing inadequately at work on previous occasions or failing to devote enough time to her family. The actions of the driver's employer and spouse, no doubt, also figured significantly in the outcome. In cases like this, where the actions of many coincide and coalesce, the moral quandary is to single out from among this group the specific individual or individuals responsible for the occurrence.

Although this can never be done with absolute precision, it is not as arduous a task as may first appear. The key is to identify the actor whose conduct so influenced or controlled the outcome that it bears the unique signature of her will. While an event often may have several causal influences, these influences usually vary in the power of their effect upon the outcome. Some may be substantial or even compelling, others may be weak and attenuated.

As a general rule, the more deliberate the intention of the actor in producing the harmful effect, the greater her causal responsibility for that condition will be. Thus, if a malevolent interloper had discovered my nail and stood it on its head in the middle of the road for the express purpose of exploding the tire of our driver, she alone would be morally responsible for the driver's injuries if the tire ruptured and the car crashed. My act, though perhaps careless, displayed little contempt for the autonomy of the driver. Nor did it predetermine such an injurious conclusion. Upon falling to the ground, the nail could have laid on its side or been shunted harmlessly along the curb. But the interloper foreclosed any of these possibilities. By her calculated act, she set out to interfere with the driver's solitude. The collision which resulted from her act thus represents a clear expression of her will. Determined to play this prank, she controlled the circumstances of its occurrence. Indeed, it is quite possible that, even without my nail, she would have discovered the means necessary to bring it about. Thus, for her, the injurious event has moral ramifications. In choosing to intrude upon the driver's autonomy, the interloper committed a bad act. For me, the event is morally indifferent. It is no more the result of my autonomous action in dropping the nail than it is the act of the municipality in constructing the road upon which the prank occurred.

Some actions, of course, cannot be attributed to any human agency, and so are not the concern of justice. To illustrate, let's return to the previous scenario in which I hit golf balls off my property. Assume that after one of these strokes a large bird catches my ball in mid flight and drops it on the head of some unsuspecting individual ten miles away. True, had I not hit the ball in the first place the bird would never have had the opportunity to undertake its long range bombing mission. Still, under these bizarre circumstances it would be difficult to say that I am causally responsible for this unfortunate occurrence. If there is a culprit here, it seems to be the dexterous aviator which absconded with my ball. Were it not for this unforeseen intervention, my shot was destined to fall nary a few hundred yards from my tee. It was the bird's action, not mine, that provided the impetus for the extraordinary flight of my ball. Because I lacked the causal power to influence or control this outcome, it cannot be attributed to my exercise of autonomy.

The Interrelationship between Duty, Risk and Causation

This congruence of control and causal responsibility explains how duties are fashioned from risk. In fact, risk and causal responsibility are kindred spirits. The finite universe of obligation delimited by risk often is identical to the sphere of influence defining the actor's causal responsibility. We saw earlier that duties generally extend only so far as the risk posed by an actor's conduct. In the preceding example in which I hit golf balls out of my back yard, we concluded that my duty to exercise care while engaged in this activity was owed only to those of my neighbors who may have been within range of my drives. This is because the scope of risk which I created by my conduct also represents the maximum extent of control which I was able to exercise over my golf balls. Any ball traveling outside this perimeter, like the one intercepted by our bird or one carried by an unprecedented wind, not only would exceed the zone of expected risk inherent in my activity, it also would transcend my normal capacity for influencing or affecting my surroundings. The errant missile is not the product of any bad act on my part, but the result of some greater natural power. This tells us that I am not causally responsible for the resulting extraordinary occurrence. But it also suggests that I bear no duty either to alter my conduct or to remedy its untoward effects.

Activating Secondary Rights

So the notion of risk not only creates relationships between actors and those around them, it also delimits the scope of the former's causal responsibility. Yet its function in the realm of rights does not end here. It plays an equally important role on the other side of the relational axis. Specifically, it activates the secondary rights of prospective victims, thus legitimating and directing their preemptive responses.

Secondary rights, we have seen, are the sentinels which stand guard over our primary interests. They protect these core rights by empowering their holders to take preventative or corrective action against others. Unlike primary rights, however, secondary rights cannot be invoked and exercised at their holders' whim. Rather, they lie dormant until activated by the moral stimulus of risk. In this way they are much like the motion sensitive lights in a home security system. Although they remain "off" much of the time, they are triggered automatically by activity which threatens the solitude of the inhabitants. And, once energized, they possess the power to repulse prospective intruders.

By operating in this fashion, active secondary rights create a relationship between the right holder and other members of society which would not otherwise exist. For example, in a risk-free environment where secondary rights remain in their inert state, the holder has no justification to interfere with the autonomy of others. If she acts, she must act in isolation or take measures to contain the hazards of her conduct. Once she is threatened by the risky activity of someone else, however, she develops a power of action which links her to others in the community. Her secondary rights now animated, she is justified in protecting her interests by engaging in some autonomy-threatening action of her own.

Directing Secondary Rights

But against whom may she take such action? As a practical matter, the answer seems simple. The best way to prevent an impending harm is to stop the one who is about to inflict it. As we learned at the beginning of this discussion, however, this is not necessarily the case. In some situations, it might be more efficacious to react against some completely innocent bystander, like the merchants or hostages referenced in my earlier illustrations. Yet, on a visceral level, such a reaction seems terribly unpalatable. Instinctively, we feel it is preferable to extinguish the risk directly by impeding the conduct of those that place us at risk. What grounds this inclination is not efficiency or expediency, but moral rectitude.

The Justice of Causation's Directive Function

The reason we require the threatened party to direct her reaction against the risk-creator is that ordinarily it would be wrong to do anything else. Remember that one engaged in risky activity usually owes a duty of care to those she imperils by her conduct. In the event she breaches that duty, not only does she possess no absolute right to behave in such a hazardous manner, she often may be stopped from doing so by her potential victims. Indeed, it is as if, by acting in this way, she suddenly has become hitched to the lives of certain individuals who are handed the reigns to manipulate her freedom. Having been exposed to this risk, these parties, in turn, become authorized to seize these reigns in order to place reasonable restraints upon the actor's conduct.[5] In this way, a unique symmetry develops between the risk creator and those she causes to be placed in danger. While the actor's autonomy is vulnerable only to these potential victims, only they possess the power to take preemptive action against her, and they may exercise this power against no one else.

This symmetry often may be disrupted, however, when the secondary right holder reacts against one who either has not violated a duty of care or was not causally responsible for exposing the other to risk. Previously, we saw that those who engage in risky activities have a duty to act reasonably. In most cases, this requires only that the actor refrain from imposing *excessive* (i.e., unreasonable) risks upon others. So long as she complies with this duty, she has a right to pursue her risky endeavor. Likewise, where one is not engaged in risky activity at all, or carries on an activity which is not dangerous towards the particular right-holder who wishes to stop her, she owes no duty to alter her behavior. As against all nonthreatened parties, this innocent individual possesses a right both to continue acting as before and to prevent others from impeding her. In either case, if some secondary right-holder nevertheless proceeds to direct a defensive, but harmful attack against such blameless parties, she herself appears to act wrongfully by violating their primary rights.

Preemptive Action without Causal Direction

I say that such a reaction *appears* wrongful because, upon closer examination, we see that this is not always the case. Under certain extraordinary circumstances, a desperate party may be justified in defending herself by reacting against almost anyone. For example, where the right holder is threatened by another's intentional overtures, she is justified in responding in kind against the aggressor, even if it turns out that the aggressor was acting within her rights. Thus, if I am approached by one with a menacing look who I mistakenly believe to be brandishing a gun, I may nevertheless take preemptive action to protect myself. The fact that the aggressor has not violated her duty of reasonable action does not weaken my right.

In other situations, such preemptive measures may be exercised against a party who has had no part in placing the prospective victim in danger. Take the case of *Cordas v. Peerless Transportation Co.*[6] There, a fleeing criminal entered a taxi cab and pointed a gun at the driver's head. While the cab was in motion, the driver jumped from the vehicle in order to save his own life. In doing so, however, he caused the abandoned cab to career onto a sidewalk where it struck and slightly injured a mother and her two infant children. In this case, the driver was threatened by the act of the criminal who pressed the barrel of the gun against his temple. Nevertheless, the cabby chose to defend himself not by disarming the criminal, but by jeopardizing the interests of those on the sidewalk. The driver was exonerated for his actions because, the court said, he acted reasonably under the circumstances.

Just what are the circumstances that would permit a party to take preventative measures against someone who either has not acted wrongfully toward her or is not responsible for putting her at risk? There seem to be several important factors common to each scenario. For instance, the interest in jeopardy must be an important welfare interest, like life or bodily integrity. We certainly would not afford the same freedom to one seeking to recover some item of personal property.[7] In addition, the threat against that interest must be substantial; that is, it must appear that the risk may consume the entire interest.[8] This certainly was true for the cab driver in *Cordas* who stood to lose his life at the hands of his kidnapper. Moreover, the probability that the risk will result in harm must be great,[9] as it was when the cabby was confronted by a seemingly rash and desperate outlaw. Finally, even where the threat is great, it must also be sprung suddenly upon the prospective victim, leaving her no time to deliberate over alternative courses of action.[10] As the *Cordas* case ably demonstrates, such is the predicament of almost anyone who is subject to the imminent destructive force of a gun.

When these exigent conditions exist, there are compelling moral justifications for dispensing with the requirement that the prospective victim assert her preemptive rights only against parties who are normatively and causally responsible for exposing her to danger. Few would dispute that survival is our most important moral and political interest. Without life, political association and the virtues it affords would be meaningless. For this reason alone, the right of self-defense assumes preeminent moral significance. Yet this right is not just a creature of political invention, it is perhaps our most basic natural instinct. Consequently, it can never be suppressed or dissipated. Indeed, those facing certain extinction are stripped of the power of rational thought, and so lose the ability to control their behavior. In such a state, it is unlikely that the threatened parties could be influenced by externally imposed ethical rules. Accordingly, little attempt is made by positive law to do so. For the most part, those whose lives are in immediate jeopardy are not inhibited in their defense by restrictive duties of care. On the contrary, because of the dire need created by such exigencies and the importance of the interests at stake, they are accorded a near absolute right to take protective measures, even if they harm others not responsible for their plight. Thus, when the cabby in *Cordas* jumped from his moving vehicle, he bore virtually no obligation to consider the interests of those who might be endangered by his conduct, and they lacked the power to keep him from abandoning his taxi. Whatever other concessions we might have expected the cab driver to make for enjoying the benefits of social living, giving up the right to ensure his own existence was not one of them.

Corrective Reactions to Misfeasance

So much for preemptive rights. While they are an indispensable weapon in an individual's arsenal of rights, they of course are not the sole means by which one may secure her interests. Just as important, and perhaps more frequently used, are corrective rights. These secondary rights are invoked in situations where the victim's interests are not simply threatened, but actually impaired. After incurring this autonomy restriction, the aggrieved right-holder seeks to correct or undo the harm by taking from someone else's cache of rights. This is accomplished either by undertaking some self-help measure like repossession, or, more commonly, by instituting a legal claim for redress in a judicial proceeding.

Corrective Rights and Causal Responsibility

Like preemptive rights, corrective rights are founded in large part on the concept of causal responsibility. One who seeks redress for a wrong foisted upon her may not randomly usurp the interests of others. Rather, she must have some good reason for taking remedial action, and for directing that action against a specific individual. The concept of causal responsibility provides such a reason, albeit only a partial one. As with preemptive rights, the causal responsibility necessary to the exercise of corrective rights depends upon the existence of risk. This catalyst, we have seen, not only creates and defines the actor's duty, it also justifies and directs the defensive response of the potential victim. This is true for corrective rights as well. Only the creator of an extrinsic risk owes a duty to prevent it from being actualized in harm to others; and only those endangered by such action are empowered to take remedial action against that actor.

By linking the parties in this way, the concept of causal responsibility forges between them a distinctive relationship with its own peculiar moral concerns. In inflicting injury upon the victim, the causal agent deprives the victim of something unique. The loss is exclusively hers; it is her autonomy that has been restricted, and her distinctive life plan which has been altered. More importantly, the loss she sustains is not limited to the impairment of interests or options, but entails both a political and moral setback as well. That is, in suffering a nonconsensual invasion of her rights, she is deprived of the equality enjoyed by all other members of society. Perhaps anyone could compensate the victim for the physical loss incurred in the transaction, but the violation of her rights can only be undone by the party who usurped them. This is accomplished only when the transgressor has been required to make some symbolic gesture of supplication to the victim, either through the award of monetary damages or imposition of injunctive relief.

The Indispensability of Cause, Harm and Wrongdoing

The relational bond which justifies such corrective measures is harder to establish and more difficult to break than the one authorizing only preemptive action. Unlike preemptive rights, corrective rights may not be employed against anyone who places the right-holder at risk. While risk is a necessary element in activating a corrective response, it alone is not sufficient. The party wishing to invoke this right must also show that she has sustained actual harm as a result of some act of wrongdoing.

Both harm and wrongdoing serve to narrow the class of causally responsible actors who may be held accountable for interfering with the autonomy of another. The harm requirement identifies the specific consequence that must result from one's action before a remedial response will be warranted. Of those agents who may have contributed to the right-holder's harm, not all will have exceeded their right of action. Proof of wrongdoing further shrinks this field of responsible actors by isolating those that have violated a duty owed to the party harmed.

Each of these prerequisites is critical to the moral legitimacy of corrective rights. Without harm, which was discussed in the last chapter, there simply is nothing to correct. Having lost no autonomy, the right-holder is in need of no repair. It would seem anomalous, then, to permit her, after merely being exposed to some risk, to take from the risk-creator some positive right. Besides inviting rampant social conflict (almost every human endeavor performed in a social context poses *some* risk towards others), such an accommodation clearly offends notions of fairness and proportionality which lie at the heart of our sense of justice.

Without wrongdoing, on the other hand, there is no moral basis for exacting such a corrective action against any particular individual. As was explained with reference to preemptive rights, and will be discussed in greater detail in the next chapter, wrongdoing consists of one's breach of a duty of care. Lacking a right to engage in the offending conduct, the actor becomes vulnerable to the secondary rights of others. Still, we saw that this vulnerability need not always exist before an endangered party can exercise her right of preemptive action. Where the prospective victim faces exigent circumstances, she may defend herself by reacting against even noncausal parties.

Such is not the case, however, with corrective rights. For these remedial weapons, the wrongdoing requirement is not so flexible. In fact, it seems to be absolutely indispensable. Unlike preemptive rights, corrective rights are not exercised amidst the frenzied environment of imminent danger. Rather, they are implemented only after the danger has culminated in harm to the right-holder. Here, the right-holder does not react reflexively. Because the circumstances are more tranquil, she has the opportunity to judiciously calculate her response. Thus, there is no moral reason for affording her the freedom of countering with a random, erratic defense which may impair the rights of innocent bystanders. If she is to take corrective action, it must be directed against the party whose moral indiscretion has caused her harm.

Causal Responsibility and Nonfeasance

From the foregoing, it becomes apparent that the notion of causal responsibility plays a prominent role in evaluating the propriety of affirmative actions and the responses they illicit. Yet it does still more than this. It also helps to determine when an endangered party has a right to expect aid from others and to identify those individuals who may be held accountable for failing to provide it.

In Chapter Five, we shall see that ordinarily one owes no legal duty to act on behalf of her neighbors. Anointed with the power of autonomy, each individual may choose for herself if and when to exercise her liberty. Any effort to force her to act challenges one of her most precious rights; specifically, her negative freedom to be left alone when so desired. But as cherished as this freedom is, it is not absolute. There are some situations where a party must forego passivity and affirmatively act to benefit others.

Risk and the Scope of Causal Responsibility for Inaction

This obligation arises when the passive party is in a "special" relationship with the prospective victim. As with affirmative conduct, such a relationship must be of the sort that creates between the parties a morally distinctive reciprocation of duty and entitlement. How is such a relationship formed? Once again, risk is the key. Risk can be created and imposed upon others either directly or indirectly. In the preceding analysis of preemptive and corrective rights, we've seen how affirmative conduct may directly endanger the lives of other people. Some acts, however, do not in themselves threaten harm to strangers; rather, they create conditions which increase the likelihood that the prospective victims will be harmed by some other causal agency.

Consider the following hypothetical. Suppose I promise a drowning man that I will throw him a line, but then fail to live up to my commitment. I have not created the danger that the man will drown. Someone or something else has placed him in that predicament. But if because of my promise the drowning man gave up the opportunity to swim to safety, or some potential rescuer discontinued his effort to help him, then through my action I have created a condition which exposes him to greater danger than if I had not acted at all. The same would be true if I encouraged the man to enter my supermarket and, because of my inaction, he slipped on a slick of rain water tracked into the store by some other customer. Or, if I permitted the man to lease space in my high-security apartment building, and he nevertheless is attacked by a robber in my lobby. In each of these scenarios, I have not just failed to assist the man in danger, I have helped to control the environment of risk in which he is now trapped. By inducing the drowning victim and his potential rescuers to forego other safety measures, my failed promise to save him ensures that he will languish in a sea of danger. Similarly, when I invite a patron into my supermarket or apartment building—spheres of influence over which I have substantial control—I determine the risks to which he will be exposed. Thus, it is my exercise of autonomy, perhaps in combination with others who act more directly upon the victim, which have dictated the outcomes in these cases. My causally fecund undertaking thus has a special moral significance which vests in me a responsibility not shared by others who, without any control over the victim's condition, simply failed to intervene on his behalf.

Reprise: The Causal Power of Consent

Just because I have enveloped the right-holder in a milieu pregnant with risk, however, does not necessarily mean that I am causally responsible for the harm she may eventually sustain. Indeed, as we saw at the outset of this discussion, one who consents to encounter a danger may herself bear full causal responsibility for the harmful consequences of her actions. Thus, if a risk-taker makes an informed decision to encounter a dangerous condition which I have failed to remediate, she may be prevented from asserting against me her corrective right of redress. In such a case, it is not my exercise of autonomy (by refusing to act) which has caused her harm; instead, she is the victim of her own choice.

To illustrate, suppose that I fail to shovel my sidewalk after a heavy snow. A, for the sake of fun and excitement, deliberately slides down my sidewalk in her patent leather shoes. During one of her runs, she slips and falls, injuring her leg. In this situation, there is no question that my inaction exposed A to certain risks, including the possibility that she might fall on my sidewalk. Yet under the circumstances described above her harm seems to be completely self-inflicted. Although I may have controlled the condition of my sidewalk, A, by running across the slippery surface of the walkway, voluntarily placed herself in danger. If she had walked rather than slid, or if she had taken another route, she surely would not have succumbed to the inert hazard presented by my nonfeasance. Because the risks posed by my inaction were completely avoidable, I should bear no causal responsibility for the consequences of A's self-destructive diversion.[11]

Summary

Having now scrutinized the concept of causal responsibility in a variety of transactional contexts, we can appreciate its prominence in our theory of rights. It not only delimits the scope of one's affirmative action, it also delineates the circumstances where the passive must act. At the same time, it both identifies a discrete class of individuals who may enforce these duties and empowers them to take some preventative or remedial action of their own. In so doing, the idea of causal responsibility commits parties to unique, moral relationships in which the rights of one are counterpoised against those of another. In cases where only a preemptive response is sought, it goes even further by providing invaluable assistance in determining how such rights are to be reconciled. Yet in certain scenarios, its influence is often not conclusive. Especially where one party seeks to exercise her corrective rights, she must also show that her harm resulted from the wrongful act of her adversary. Given the importance of wrongdoing in the dialogue of corrective justice, we must next examine this concept.

Chapter 5

Wrongdoing

If causal responsibility is the chain which links risk-creators to their prospective or actual victims, then wrongdoing is the force which activates the victims' power to take hold of these chains and restrict the autonomy of those that threaten them. While in some cases the mere appearance of wrongdoing will suffice for this purpose, in most others the risky conduct actually must turn out to be wrongful. As was mentioned in the previous chapter, corrective rights operate on this latter premise. For such rights, the concept of wrongdoing gives the victim a moral license not available to other individuals. Remember that ordinarily one may not intentionally interfere with the rights of her neighbors. This is because we all possess a negative liberty to be free from unsolicited intrusions upon our interests. When this liberty is compromised by an officious intermeddler, the invasive act may be wrongful, even if its perpetrator commits it with the best of intentions. Such an adverse moral conclusion does not follow, however, where the "injured" party is herself a wrongdoer. Unlike the rest of us, wrongdoers possess no absolute right to prevent others from interfering with their interests. Absent such a protective right, a party who wrongfully causes another harm is vulnerable to the corrective action of her victim, and the victim is justified in taking such action against her.

So we know that wrongdoing plays a key role in the determination of rights. But we do not yet know which acts are wrongful and which are not. While the answer may seem obvious, maybe even intuitive, the quesion is more beguiling than first appears. Are we concerned with morally opprobrious acts, politically irresponsible acts, or conduct that is wrongful in each sense? By what standard are we to evaluate the propriety of one's behavior? According to Divine Law? By some intuitive inclination? Possibly through some socially constructed norm? In making this determination, are we to look only at the effects which these actions produce, or is the answer to be found in the nature of the action itself? Perhaps we shall not discover the truth in either of these extremes, but in some combination of the two? Finally, is conduct failing such a standard universally wrongful, or is its illicit character limited to some group or individual? One simply cannot understand the concept of wrongdoing without grappling with these most difficult issues.

Types of Wrongdoing: Moral and Political

In my view, there are essentially two types of wrongdoing: one moral, the other political. Moral wrongdoing is conduct that not only lacks virtue, but is repugnant to it. Acts of this sort are bad because they fail to conform to some natural or objective good—like truth, knowledge, justice or charity—or because they deviate from the actor's own subjective conception of goodness—for example, by wasting her unique talent or aptitude for teaching. Such conduct can be as seemingly trivial as shouting vulgarities at a sensitive person, or as serious as committing an act of murder. In each case, the actor violates some behavioral standard that she uses both to define a good life, and to achieve its fulfillment. To some extent, the actor's standard of evaluation will be shaped by her social environment, including her family, her community, her culture and the prevailing legal system. One's religious upbringing and psychological intuitions, no doubt, are influential factors as well. In fact, depending on the individual, the standard may be considered externally imposed or internally manufactured. For the religious zealot or the civic republican, only God or country may prescribe appropriate behavior. For the liberal individualist, on the other hand, rational reflection provides the sole means for making such an assessment. Whatever its source, the applicable behavioral standard operates much like a personal moral compass, informing its holder whether her conduct has placed her on the path to virtue or depravity, to self-esteem or psychosis, or to heaven or hell. The lost souls who stray from the high road are wrongdoers in the limited moral sense that they may never find happiness or salvation.

Political wrongdoing may or may not require a different type of behavioral evaluation. In a civic republican regime, like that which prevailed in ancient Greece, political and moral wrongdoing are virtually inseparable. By commanding acts of courage and temperance, laws in such a state are designed to make its citizens virtuous. Those who violate such laws are not simply antisocial, they also display a meanness of character which demonstrates their moral weakness. The same is not necessarily true, however, in more liberal states. Granted, liberal governments often regulate or prohibit many of the same activities that would be condemnable in a civic republic. The act of murder mentioned above comes readily to mind. However, most liberal democracies, including our own, do not endorse any particular vision of an ideal life. Accordingly, they typically do not enact laws for the purpose of attempting to improve the moral character of their constituents. Remaining relatively value neutral, they merely secure the freedom necessary to allow people to choose their own life plans, and to take whatever steps are necessary, consistent with the plans of others, to act on their interests. Laws in such a state have a distinctly pragmatic, political purpose: to establish the conditions for human fulfillment by maintaining order, securing property rights, establishing rules for exchange, and providing a means for resolving disputes. Here, the standards for evaluating conduct are not personal, but social. Indeed, if wrongdoing in the moral sense is doing that which is not good (or inhibiting the realization of a good), then wrongdoing in the political sense is doing that which is not right, or more accurately, that which is contrary to a socially constructed right of another. Political associations simply cannot survive unless each individual agrees to obey the rules of the group. Thus, citizens incur duties to the state, and the state accrues certain rights of action (like the right to tax or to criminally punish) against its citizens. To preserve order, and to secure property interests, each person also must respect the holdings of her neighbor. Such respect is memorialized in a complex web of duties and rights which extend from person to person. Violation of either form of behavioral standard is, it would seem, immoral at least in the weak sense that good people should abide by good laws. Also, insofar as autonomy itself is an objective good which is indispensable to any life plan, conduct which unlawfully impairs another's liberty is sure to carry at least some moral significance. Yet many acts which are socially proscribed do not seem particularly culpable. For example, one who carelessly leaves a roller skate on the sidewalk in front of her home hardly fits the description of an immoral monster. Nevertheless, if a passerby slips on the skate, the property owner's neglect may fairly be characterized as socially or politically wrongful. By failing to pick up the skate, she not only has created a hazard for the pedestrians in her community, she also has inflicted injury upon one of her neighbors, whose life will be temporarily disrupted and perhaps even permanently impaired. This act, though not morally reprehensible, is certainly socially irresponsible. It is wrongful, therefore, in its own unique way.

The Consequentialist View of Wrongdoing

But just what is it about such politically wrongful conduct that makes it condemnable? Are acts of this nature wrongful standing alone or does their wrongful character depend in whole or in part on the impact they have upon the world? Judging conduct by its effects seems to be an attractive possibility. After all, we often feel shame or regret for the injurious consequences that our actions produce. If I borrow a friend's car, and the car is rear-ended while I am driving it, I am likely to feel some sense of guilt or responsibility even if the incident was in no way my fault.[1] Nevertheless, this consequence-based approach hardly seems to serve as a reliable barometer of our sense of moral outrage. Some acts which have a devastating effect upon the lives of others may be completely innocent. My previous example of dropping a nail in the street illustrates this point. In that hypothetical, my act initiated a chain of events which caused the driver to lose her job, her marriage and her children. Yet because my conduct showed little disrespect for the rights of others, few would view it as morally depraved. On the other hand, some acts which seem morally opprobrious have no impact upon anyone. Suppose I throw a rock at a baby who sleeps peacefully in an unattended stroller. My sole purpose is to strike and harm the infant within. By some saving grace, however, the stroller rolls away and my destructive missile falls harmlessly to the ground. Even though I have failed in my perverse mission, my decision to throw the rock still seems to have both moral and political implications.

The Deontological View of Wrongdoing

If a result-oriented approach thus fails adequately to describe our conception of political wrongdoing, an agent-oriented approach appears to do no better. Let's reconsider the rock throwing example above. While my conduct appears unseemly, it certainly is not as bad as if I actually had succeeded in striking and injuring the sleeping baby. I doubt anyone would recommend that I be punished the same regardless of the outcome of my actions. If one *were* to favor this option, it must be because of some aspect of my demeanor which remains the same whether or not I cause harm to the child. I can think of only two possible reasons why my conduct alone might spark this response, and neither in my view provides a satisfactory justification for condemning my actions as politically wrongful.

The Creation of Risk

One reason is that my act of throwing the rock threatened to cause harm to the baby. Here, the creation of risk, rather than the infliction of injury, becomes the yardstick for determining whether certain activities are good or bad. To some extent, this seems both logical and helpful. If harming others is a social faux pas, then threatening such harm is only slightly less disturbing. But does it really explain our sense of political wrongdoing? I think not, at least not entirely. Although almost every human activity produces some risk for those other than the actor, we would not consider a good many of these wrongful. For example, by taking out my trash can and leaving it by the curb, I expose adult passersby to a dangerous obstacle and children to an attractive but possibly deadly hiding place. Nevertheless, few would fault me for committing this desirable and even necessary act. Perhaps, then, it is not the creation of just any risk which makes my conduct blameworthy, but the transgression of some baseline level of social acceptability. Could it be that, in leaving my trash can on the sidewalk, I simply have not exceeded this threshold? Maybe so, but if this potentially hazardous activity doesn't cross the line, it is not clear which ones will. In fact, there are many activities far more dangerous than taking out the trash that still are not considered wrongful. Most of us would agree that it is not wrong for people to drive cars or for manufacturers to produce and sell ladders. Yet car and ladder accidents are among the most common causes of harm in our society.[2] Even if these activities were considered wrongful, I suspect that most of us would not find them wrongful per se. Rather, they likely would be viewed as wrongful only in relation to those persons they endanger.[3]

"Bad" Intent

The other reason why conduct might be condemnable notwithstanding the effect it has on the world is that it is performed with an evil motive or intent. Such was the case when I launched my rock in the direction of the stroller. My design was not to tease or frighten, but to inflict harm upon the child. Besides being morally odious, this intent is extremely dangerous to a political system founded on the notion of equality. Still, we would not want to vilify or castigate any individual simply because she possessed such a mental state. Indeed, once we separate intent from conduct and consequences, and make it the sole criterion for our moral judgments, we proceed down a very dangerous path. How many of us have harbored evil thoughts that we never acted upon? Some frustrated race car driver cuts you off on the freeway. Your blood boils for an instant or two while you fantasize about how you might subject her to the most painful forms of torture known to mankind. This impulse soon passes, however, and you go on with your life, making the accommodations necessary for social survival. If having such thoughts invited damnation, then everyone would be a sinner. Fortunately for us all, this is not the case. Until you actually act upon this urge, no one considers you a bad individual. Likewise, you certainly would not be adjudged guilty of any social wrongdoing, for if nothing else, that term clearly requires some act in furtherance of your deleterious purpose.[4] And even if you decided to act on your bad intent, your conduct would not likely meet with reproval unless it actually produced some adverse consequence for the inconsiderate driver. Indeed, while our moral instinct tells us that laying on the horn for a few seconds might be an appropriate response to her indiscretion, it also instructs us that running her off the road would not.

The Binary Nature of Political Wrongdoing

If the foregoing discussion teaches us anything, it is that political wrong-doing simply is not understandable as a unary concept. As separate ideas, both conduct (including intent) and consequence fail to explain why some deeds are socially appropriate and others are not. This does not mean, however, that each is irrelevant to making this determination. On the contrary, each concept is indispensable for this purpose. In fact, the two notions are complementary, and when combined are capable of distinguishing between good and bad behavior. How is this possible? Because in conjunction, conduct and consequence establish the relational balance inherent in our sense of justice.

Owing and Entitlement

Justice, you may recall, is a virtue which we practice towards others. In its simplest form, it ensures that each individual receives her due from everyone else. This requirement is founded on the interdependent ideas of owing and entitlement. Indeed, these concepts are but flip sides of the same coin. An entitlement is merely something that A has a right to expect from B. Such an expectation, on the other hand, is possible only if B has a duty to provide A with whatever she claims is rightfully hers. Each concept is thus part of the definition of the other. I owe only to those who are entitled to receive; and others may expect to receive only what I am obligated to give.

Up to this point, we have focused primarily on entitlements. In Chapter Three, for example, we concentrated on the nonrelational aspect of that concept. That is, we looked not at who owes the holder her entitlement, but at which of her interests are worthy of such protection. We saw that members of a liberal democratic society may not expect to enjoy complete freedom or security. Indeed, in a world of constant conflict, there are simply some interests which must be sacrificed for the common good. Relatively speaking, these unprotected interests tend to be trivial and insignificant. There are some interests, however, which are not so expendable. Some of these attributes of autonomy are, in fact, so important for pursuing a life plan that political association would be pointless without them. These interests, which are guaranteed by law, constitute our political entitlements.

In the last chapter, we saw how such entitlements connect their holders to those that threaten or cause them harm. Remember that entitlements do more than merely identify our most prized political holdings, they empower us to secure our protected interests, either by compelling others to bestow them upon us, stopping others from interfering with them or requiring others to compensate us when they are curtailed. Still, we may not exercise this enormous power haphazardly; rather, we may use it only against those who, because of their causal responsibility, are obligated to show us respect. Such an obligation, or duty as I have previously called it, inextricably intertwines the concepts of entitlement and owing. It not only tells the duty-bound party what she must give, it also identifies what her right-holding counterpart is entitled to receive. The whole concept of an entitlement, in fact, would be nonsensical without the existence of a duty. After all, the only thing which separates an entitlement from a mere unprotected interest is the existence of a duty securing it.[4]

Once this is understood, it is easier to see how our notions of justice and political wrongdoing depend on both the nature of one's activity and the consequences it may bring about. Because an entitlement is always secured by someone's duty to respect it, one who acts in violation of a duty necessarily deprives another of such a right. Likewise, since a duty requires one to hold harmless another's protected interests, any denial or desecration of an entitlement will always entail someone's breach of a duty to keep it secure. Given this fact, we can appreciate how the political assessment of such exchanges is inescapably relational. An antisocial act is not bad simply because it involves some personal moral failing, but because it has the unavoidable effect of violating someone else's entitlement to be free from such behavior.

Defining Political Wrongdoing

With this in mind, it is finally possible to define what we mean by political wrongdoing. If justice requires that duty-bound individuals respect the entitlements of those to whom they are obligated, then wrongdoing is nothing more than the breach of a duty owed to another. When we break down this definition, a few simple elements emerge.[6] In addition to the existence of a duty, there must be some privileged individual who is entitled to receive the benefits it affords. The beneficiary status of this party not only ties the parties together in a morally significant relationship, it empowers her to take corrective action against her adversary. This power may not be invoked, however, unless or until the duty owed to that beneficiary has been violated. When these three elements coalesce, the interests of the wrongdoer give way to those of her beneficiary in a way that allows a political and moral equilibrium to be restored between them. To see exactly how this works, these elements—of duty, beneficiary status and breach—will each be examined in turn.

Duties and Autonomy

Human beings are subject to two types of duties. One duty type is moral or natural. Moral duties, we have seen, are fundamental obligations required for human fulfillment. The other type of duty, which I shall call political or positive, arises from, and is necessary for, political association. As noted above, such political duties emanate from legal rules which place abstract restrictions on our freedom of action.

Although these moral and political duties have different derivations, they are not mutually exclusive. In fact, they share a common purpose: to secure a measure of autonomy for all individuals.[8] As Aristotle observed, the way to virtue is by exercising one's freedoms of choice and action. These freedoms, however, do not exist in a state of nature, but can be guaranteed only in a political association where the strongest individuals are prevented from subjugating the weakest. Such a political association, in turn, can exist only if its members agree to obey its laws. Obedience of this sort will not follow unless the rules of the association leave most individuals better off than they would be on their own. The essential benefit of association—one that can never be assured in a prepolitical community—is the freedom to act, and protection from the acts of others. Thus, without rules which secure autonomy, there would be no incentive for individuals to form political associations. And without the protection afforded by such organizations, human beings would lack the freedom necessary to flourish as moral agents. This is the overlapping concern of both moral and political duties.

As was noted in the last chapter, duties do not just secure autonomy, they also take it away. Indeed, every duty which protects your rights restricts the freedom of someone else who otherwise might seize what you possess. The main concern of justice is to ensure that the liberty preserved by such duties outweighs the freedom which they deny. Duties which effect this balance are fair, and thus are entitled to respect. Those that do not are unjust, and so are destined for oblivion or rebellion.

General Duties

In our political system, duties take one of three forms: general duties, special duties or duties founded on mutual restriction.[9] General duties are created and imposed by the state against all individuals. The most common of these are the duties to be honest and truthful and not to harm others.[10] Both such obligations help to secure individual autonomy. The proscription against inflicting harm is the most obvious in this regard. It provides a measure of independence to all citizens by protecting them from coercion or compulsion. The duty of honesty may actually be viewed as a more specific aspect of this larger obligation. It shelters individuals from the harm which comes from deceitful manipulation. The requirement of truthfulness may also be considered integral to our positive freedom to interact with others. Indeed, unless individuals deal honestly with others, social intercourse would be impossible. This not only would subvert the purpose of political association, it would preclude the interpersonal exchanges of knowledge, goods and fellowship which give meaning and value to life.

Although both types of general duties restrict the liberties of those that are bound by them, not all general duties are equally inhibiting. Some duties are simply more onerous than others. For example, one who engages in an extremely risky operation, like building demolition, bears a much heavier burden to look out for the interests of others than does one conducting a less dangerous activity. On the other hand, a party who acts under an emergency, like the cabby in the *Cordas* case, has a much weaker duty, and far greater autonomy to protect himself, than others not facing such an exigency. In Chapter Seven, we will consider more closely the way in which risk and need influence the duties that are assigned to certain actors. At this point, it is sufficient merely to note that general duties are not monolithic or static, but may vary depending upon the circumstances to which they apply.

Special Duties

Besides general duties, individuals may also be bound by special duties. Special duties are different from general duties in that they are not created by the state. Rather, they arise from an individual's own voluntary action.[11] Thus, only a party who voluntarily assumes the obligation can be bound by it. There are various ways in which such duties can be created. Ordinarily, they derive from promises.[12] Suppose, for example, that I assure an injured motorist that I will procure and/or provide medical treatment for her wounds. Although I normally would have had no obligation to intercede on her behalf, I incur such a duty once I pledge my assistance. Even without an express promise, however, a duty of care might be implied from an expression of consent or an undertaking to perform a particular action.[13] So in the previous scenario, if I start but then discontinue a rescue attempt without ever making a promise to do so, I still may be responsible for failing to save the injured motorist. In this situation, the voluntary obligation I assume is enforceable because it has important ramifications for individual autonomy. Whether by promising or undertaking, I have made a representation which restricts the autonomy of another by inducing her to act or forbear from acting. In addition, by making a choice to undertake action, I have exercised my own autonomy. For my actions to have any moral meaning, they must be given effect, and I must suffer their consequences.

Mutual Restrictions

The final type of duty, which may be denominated "mutual restrictions,"[14] is a hybrid between the two discussed above. Unlike general duties, mutual restrictions are created by voluntary action. Yet it is not the same kind of specific choice characteristic of special duties. And, unlike special duties, mutual restrictions of the variety I have in mind are not borne episodically, but are assumed by all who enjoy the benefits of a particular cooperative association. They operate on a simple premise. When individuals enter such an association, they mutually agree to obey the rules of that enterprise. This commitment serves two purposes. For the entrant, it allows her to join the association and enjoy its benefits. For the association itself, it ensures the cooperation necessary for its survival. Because each participant must make this commitment, every member of the association becomes duty-bound to all others to play by the rules. When one party breaches such a duty, she exercises a freedom forsaken by her peers. Such conduct is unfair, and thus wrongful, because it affords the breaching party more than her share of autonomy.[15]

Public and Private Duties

It is important to remember that each of these duties apply to public and private relationships alike. The state relates to its members by promulgating, or failing to promulgate, duties of the sort mentioned above. If the law is deficient in this regard, the harm it causes to its citizens may be more severe than any inflicted by human agency. Indeed, such a dereliction may breach the implied promise of political association that all individuals will be afforded the freedom necessary to pursue a life plan. Only by holding the state to these duties can we judge whether the law it creates is either just or unjust.

Beneficiary Status

The second component of wrongdoing—that the duty in question be owed only to a specific beneficiary—limits the scope of an actor's responsibility and gives it some, albeit uncertain, direction. Because duties pose a constant threat to liberty, they rarely will have universal application. For one to have the freedom to pursue a life plan, some reasonable parameters must be given to her social obligations. The beneficiary requirement attempts to stake out these boundaries by loosely defining the limited class of individuals empowered to expose her to corrective action. But while it is certain that this concept places some restrictions on the bearer's duty, it often is uncertain just what these boundaries are. Indeed, because these limitations usually are so volatile and amorphous, one frequently cannot predetermine how large or small her designated group of duty-beneficiaries will be. This will depend, among other things, upon the type of duty in question and the circumstances under which it is to be enforced.

Beneficiaries of Special Duties

Special duties seem to present the easiest case for delimiting the ambit of the bearer's responsibility. The promisor makes a definite commitment to a specific promisee to perform some task which will inure to the latter's benefit. Here, it is clear that the promisee is the direct, intended beneficiary of the promise. The same is true in cases of consent. The consenter gives another an unambiguous license to invade her interests. The licensee is singled out a person who enjoys a freedom of action toward the consenter that is available to no one else.

Express Promises and Third Party Beneficiaries

Still, there are promissory duties whose beneficiaries are not so precisely delineated. Using a frequent example, suppose that A promises to take care of B's mother until her death.[16] In this situation, the promise is made directly to B. Yet the acts which are the subject of the promise are to be performed for B's mother. Who has the right to enforce the promise? Clearly, B does. That A made the commitment to B manifests A's intent to bestow some benefit upon him—whether it be simply to ease B's mind or to relieve him of the actual burden of caring for his mother himself. But what about B's mother? Here, the answer isn't so obvious.[17] We do not know whether A intended to benefit B's mother by his promise. On the one hand, A may have given the promise merely to satisfy a preexisting debt he owed to B. In this event, A may not care whether it helps B's mother, so long as it extinguishes his debt. On the other hand, A may care deeply for B's mother and fully intend that she be comforted by his promised service.[18] The point is, the promise alone does not define the right to enforce it. To clarify its scope, we must examine all of the surrounding circumstances. Even then, the answer may not be forthcoming. In such cases, resort must be made to other factors, including the importance of the duty and the severity of its breach, plus the magnitude of the interest which it invades.

Undertakings

The analysis of the above hypothetical would be more determinate if A actually undertook caring for B's mother. As noted in the previous discussion, such action alone may create a special relationship between the parties which would create a right in B's mother to continued care.[19] Under these circumstances, A's actions, if not his words, communicate his commitment to benefit B's mother. B's mother, in turn, may justifiably rely on this service by foregoing other opportunities for assistance.

As a general rule, however, it is far easier to find a right in a promise than it is in an undertaking. Words are usually far more precise than actions. And, while promises tend to identify their beneficiaries, actions often do not. Consider, for example, a railroad company which places a monitor at one of its crossings.[20] Does it intend to benefit only itself by ensuring the safe and speedy passage of its cargo? Or does it seek to assist the municipality in controlling traffic problems? Or is it really meant as a measure to ensure the safety of motorists who traverse the crossing? This is a difficult question which usually will require consideration of some or all of the extrinsic factors mentioned above.

Beneficiaries of General Duties

There are similar problems in correlating rights with general duties, although for different reasons. Unlike special duties, general duties are not created by voluntary action. Rather, they are imposed by the state as fundamental protectors of autonomy. Thus, the limitations placed on responsibility are premised not on express consent,[21] but on the implied power of the government to fashion rules which reflect society's sense of morality. Here, the state must determine for the parties how best to secure their freedom. This is not an easy task. In a young and diverse nation like ours, where community values may vacillate over time and geographical location, it is often especially difficult to develop, articulate and circumscribe these general standards of behavior.

Intentional Autonomy Invasions

Of course, this is not always true. There are some principles so basic to our moral nature and political survival that they have become a permanent and identifying feature of our culture. Liberty and equality are two notable examples. Because these values are essential to social living, we can never allow them to be torn asunder by those who deliberately calculate to cause harm to others. Unless excused or justified, no one enjoys the freedom to dominate others through force or deception. To prevent this type of personal oppression, the state imposes upon us the obligation to refrain from such intentionally harmful behavior. This duty is not qualified, but unbounded. Just as everyone bears the weight of its burden, so we all enjoy the benefits of its protection. This means that if I intentionally and unjustifiably set out to cause harm, I am responsible to anyone who actually suffers loss because of my action, even if I may not have anticipated this consequence.[22]

Acts with Greater Utility

Many, if not most, general duties, however, are not so expansive. Where one's conduct has some legitimate personal or social value, limits must be placed on the scope of the actor's moral and political liabilities. The difficulty is in knowing when such duties may be invoked and who may enforce them. Take the duty to refrain from inflicting harm upon others. This duty, in essence, imposes certain restrictions on one's freedom of action. But certainly it does not give a right to any individual who may sustain injury as a result of the conduct of another. As with special duties, there must be some identifiable persons, or class of persons, who are to benefit from the protection of this general obligation.

This was the lesson in the famous (or infamous, depending upon your view) case of *Palsgraf v. Long Island Railroad Co.*[23] There, a woman waiting on a train platform was injured when a free-standing scale fell on her head. The scale had been knocked over by the percussive blast of fireworks which had been dropped by a passenger being assisted onto a departing train. Judge Cardozo, speaking for the majority, held that the actions of the railroad employees who had dislodged the package from the passenger's hands, although perhaps careless, were not wrongful toward the injured woman. Because she stood outside the zone of risk created by the employees' conduct, she was not a beneficiary of their duty to exercise care.

Risk and Beneficiary Status

As *Palsgraf* teaches, the slippery concept of risk delineates the duty bearer's responsibility in the only way morally feasible. The beneficiary status conferred by risk supplies the moral adhesive which bonds wrongdoers to their victims.[24] Without this bond, an actor's responsibility could extend indefinitely in time and space. Indeed, even those engaged in primarily self-regarding activities might be held to protect the entire world from the possible harmful consequences of their endeavors. To prevent this from happening, one's responsibility must be confined to those foreseeably threatened by her conduct. Only these endangered parties fall within the actor's power of influence. And through the stimulus of risk, only these parties possess active secondary rights which authorize them to respond with some defensive or corrective action of their own. So, if a risk-creator fails to satisfy her duty of care, her dereliction is wrongful only as against those within this select group. As against all others, her conduct is of no moral consequence.

Beneficiaries of Mutual Restrictions

Unlike general duties, and some special duties, duties of mutual restriction contain a built-in mechanism for defining the scope of their reach. These duties, we have seen, arise from one's joint participation in an activity where all agree to abide by certain rules. This creates a double layer of obligation. While the rules require the participants to behave in a particular manner, the duty of mutual restriction directs them to obey the rules. Because of the controlled universe in which such duties are created, they extend only to those cooperating within this context. For those involved in the joint endeavor, the mutual restriction thus functions much like the absolute general duty which prohibits intentional misconduct. Not only are all participants bound by the restriction, all are beneficiaries of its prescriptive obedience.

Private Beneficiaries

Duties of mutual restriction may be as extensive or restrictive as the cooperative institutions from which they derive. One of the smaller scale usages of mutual restrictions is in sporting activities. Every sport has certain rules which regulate the conduct of the participating athletes. Most, like football, basketball and hockey, also impose sanctions for behavior which exceeds those rules. The duty of mutual restriction justifies such sanctions. If one player acts in an unpermitted fashion so as to gain some tactical or strategic advantage, she cheats the others who have foregone the same opportunity. Besides athletic contests, mutual restrictions often can be found in larger clubs and organizations. Your local bar association is a good example. The entire legal profession benefits from the strict code of ethics to which all attorneys are bound. When a lawyer violates this code, she harms the whole association, and so may be held accountable for her indiscretion.

Public Beneficiaries

Despite these illustrations, one should not get the impression that mutual restrictions apply only to private enterprises. Indeed, they hold an even grander purpose. They are, in fact, the moral force which compel us to obey the law. As we enter society, we incur certain general and special duties. Each type of duty requires that we give up our capacity for unencumbered action and agree to respect the interests of others. These duties would be unenforceable, however, unless everyone was committed to honoring them. The social duty of mutual restriction fulfills this necessary political function. Under it, each party elects to accept her general and special duties only because everyone else has acknowledged the same responsibility. From this mutual commitment, every citizen becomes the beneficiary of her neighbor's obligation to refrain from breaking the law. Unlike general or special duties, however, this duty is not owed to any specific individual. Rather, it is owed to the state, which represents our collective will. When any one of us break this social compact, therefore, the transgression is not just personal, it is a wrong to us all.

Active and Passive Forms of Wrongdoing

So we see that duty-beneficiary relationships may come in a variety of different forms. Some are created by individual choice, while others are imposed by state fiat. Many are limited to a few private parties, though a few extend to the public at large. Aside from these differences in origin and scope, however, there is another important dimension to such bilateral associations which we have yet to consider. Specifically, we must examine the moral content of these relationships, for the obligations they inspire are as different as action is to inertia.

As we saw in Chapter Two, secondary rights empower their holder to interfere with the freedom of another in a number of possible ways. They may entitle her to some corrective remuneration, they may authorize her to regulate the other's risk-creating activity, or they may even allow her to demand protection from an impending harm. In the last chapter, we saw how these entitlements become aligned with correlative duties which impose the burdens of the right-holder's prerogative on certain specific individuals. Such duty-bearers do not enjoy unfettered freedom, but may be required to bestow some positive benefit upon the right-holder, to refrain from exposing her to certain risks, or to compensate her for the privilege of doing so.

Duty-rights packages which restrict the kind or amount of risk that may be produced and imposed upon others establish parameters for affirmative actions. They do not compel action; they merely tell those who elect to act what they can, or more often, cannot do. Any individual who violates such constraints commits an act of wrongdoing known as misfeasance, which in turn activates her victim's right to initiate some preventative or corrective response.

Other duty-rights packages do not simply regulate activity, they actually compel those who would prefer to remain passive to leave their inert state. For example, when a right-holder's entitlement to protection coalesces with the duty-bearer's obligation to secure her interests from harm, a special moral relationship develops between them. This relationship requires the duty-bearer to undertake certain affirmative measures to ensure the safety of her counterpart. Such measures may range from a parent's duty to supervise her mischievous child, to a store owner's obligation to eliminate dangerous conditions on her property. Should a duty-bearer of this sort fail to discharge her responsibility to act, her passivity or nonfeasance, though perhaps less causally potent, is considered every bit as wrongful as an action gone awry.

Breach of Duty

In cases of misfeasance and nonfeasance alike, it is clear how one's breach of a duty amounts to a type of political wrongdoing. To violate a duty means both to exercise for one's self an excessive degree of autonomy and, in so doing, to deny another her entitlement. Although every duty imposes a certain measure of freedom-limiting responsibility (either to act or to refrain from acting) upon its bearer, most duties are not absolute. Thus, they generally afford their bearers at least some amount of liberty. This realm of permitted action constitutes the bearer's social "due" of autonomy. So long as her conduct remains within this realm, whether by acting in a particular manner or by remaining passive, she does no wrong to anyone, even if someone may be injured by her behavior. In fact, under these circumstances, further inhibiting the bearer's activities or compelling her to act in the first place would itself be a wrongful intrusion upon her freedom from unfair restraint.

However, once the duty-bearer's conduct crosses that fine line between freedom and responsibility, both the political and moral tides turn against her. At that point, she begins to exercise more autonomy than has been allotted to her or to others who must engage in the same or similar activity. In taking for herself that which others have foregone, the duty-bearer violates the rules of social organization. She identifies herself as one who places her interests above all others, and who cannot be trusted to cooperate. By the same token, she dishonors a more specific obligation which she owes to certain right-holders. These right-holders may be personally entitled to expect either that the duty-bearer will affirmatively protect their interests, or at the very least, that she will not subject them to unreasonable dangers. Either way, if she fails to conform her behavior to the dictates of her duty, she also defeats the others' entitlement to be secure from harm. In such a case, the repugnance of the duty-bearer's self-indulgence is surpassed only by the injustice that it holds for her victims.

Motive and Breach

To some, this conclusion may at first appear exaggerated if not simply wrong. Indeed, many people seem to think that wrongdoing includes only those actions committed with malice. Such conduct alone, they feel, demonstrates the ill will and wickedness necessary to receive this pejorative label. Later on, we shall see that this understanding of wrongdoing is, in fact, consistent with our sense of injustice. But it is not the only sense in which conduct may be viewed as inappropriate. Indeed, as will be demonstrated in the next chapter, certain activities may be unjust if they are unfair. In that event, the actor's behavior need not be malevolent; it must simply be designed to garner for the actor some advantage to which he is not entitled. If that is established, the injustice resides not in the mind of the actor, but in her deeds.

Part II

The Forms of Justice

Chapter 6

Two Senses of Justice

So far, we've seen that justice requires receiving one's "due" from another. This means that one has a right to expect a certain kind of treatment from her neighbors. When someone violates such a right, we know that injustice invariably results. Yet this does not end our moral inquiry. Activities which infringe rights may be unjust for different reasons, and may be of varying degrees of culpability. This was certainly true for the rock throwing and trash can examples from the last chapter. You do not have to be a moral philosopher to recognize the distinction between deliberately attempting to maim or injure another and merely engaging in some desirable and primarily self-regarding activity which incidentally exposes others to risk. To properly assess each act of wrongdoing, we still need to know exactly why it is unjust and how this impacts the relationship between the actor and her victim. These are the issues that will be explored in this chapter. Specifically, we shall see how rights violations may be unjust in two different senses. The first, which Aristotle referred to as justice in the "wide" or "broad" sense, consists of cases in which the right is denied deliberately or voluntarily, contrary to the dictates of law.[1] The second, denominated by Aristotle as justice in the "particular" sense, involves rights violations which are wrongful because they secure for the transgressors some unfair measure of autonomy.[2]

Justice in the Broad Sense

Aristotle describes the broad sense of justice as a complete virtue or virtue entire because it encompasses all possible excellences of character in one's dealings with others.[3] It requires individuals to assume a dispositional mean between excess and deficiency. For example, they should be friendly, not self-absorbed or officious. At a minimum, they are to accord others the respect due to them as human beings. The repudiation of these virtues is injustice. It is a wickedness of character marked by an internal imbalance in dispositional humors, and includes such traits as self-indulgence, cowardice and anger.[4]

Aristotle's conception of justice in the broad sense is not just moral, but decidedly political as well.[5] In Aristotle's view, people cannot become truly virtuous outside a political association.[6] The polis secures the order necessary for all to pursue a life plan. Moreover, it assists in the realization of such life plans by enacting laws dedicated to the common good of all.[7] These laws mandate virtuous acts and proscribe wicked ones, including those likely to affect others. As Aristotle notes,

> the law bids us do both the acts of a brave man (e.g. not to desert our post nor take to flight nor throw away our arms), and those of a temperate man (e.g. not to commit adultery nor to gratify one's lust), and those of a good-tempered man (e.g. not to strike another nor to speak evil), and similarly with regard to the other virtues and forms of wickedness, commanding some acts and forbidding others[8]

Accordingly, Aristotle concludes that justice in the broad sense is that which is lawful, and injustice that which is unlawful.[9]

Broad Injustice and Volition

Does this mean that any act which happens to violate the law is morally wicked and unjust? Aristotle clearly did not embrace such a vision of justice in the broad sense. According to Aristotle, virtue depends upon volition. Only voluntary acts are worthy of praise or susceptible to blame.[10] A voluntary act is one controlled by the actor (and not compelled by anyone else) and done with knowledge of the person acted upon, the instrument used and the end to be attained.[11] Aristotle divided such voluntary injustices into two subcategories. Those performed voluntarily but not after deliberation (i.e., acts caused by anger), were described as "act[s] of injustice."[12] When an act was committed voluntarily *and* deliberately, however, the actor was deemed "an unjust man and a vicious man."[13]

The Broad Sense of Justice Today

Thus, in Aristotle's day, an actor who voluntarily (and perhaps with deliberation) violated the law committed an injustice in the broad sense. But would the same be true today? After all, unlike in ancient Athens, laws in our justice system do not always track moral principles.[14] Thus, it might be argued that violation of the law today does not necessarily suggest a wicked disposition. Yet there is an important area in which contemporary law and morality do overlap. As has been previously discussed, both require a fundamental respect for the freedom of others. This freedom is secured by laws which prohibit the infliction of harm. If valid, laws which ensure this negative liberty promote the common good of all within the association, for without them, nobody could flourish. Just as in the time of the ancient Greeks, one who deliberately harms another not only fails to display the virtue of a "good-tempered man," he repudiates the law and, in so doing, demonstrates a disregard for the well-being of all others. Today as back then, any such act is wicked and therefore unjust in the broad sense.

To update Aristotle's political conception of justice in the broad sense, then, we might say that an actor is unjust if he voluntarily inflicts harm upon another in violation of the law. But perhaps this definition can be refined even further. Earlier, harm was defined as the invasion of an autonomy interest. If the interest is significant enough, it is accorded legal recognition through the designation of a right. Thus, our main concern is with rights—as these represent the only interests which are protected by law. With this understanding, our definition of injustice in the broad sense may be reformulated as follows: any unexcused or unjustified act which is deliberately or knowingly calculated to interfere with a right of another.

Types of Broad Injustice

There are a couple of ways in which such an injustice may be committed. One way is to fail to accord rights to deserving parties. Because rights in political association are created (or at least articulated) by the state, it alone has the power to commit such an injustice. It may consist of a deficiency in the state's laws or its mechanisms for implementing and enforcing them. If a group of individuals requires or otherwise deserves special protection under the law, all of its members should enjoy a right to prevent others from frustrating this security.[15] If this right is voluntarily denied by the state (either by failing to recognize the right entirely, or by failing to ensure its protection),[16] then the state has acted "wickedly" and the aggrieved parties have suffered an injustice in the broad sense.

The other way that such injustice may be effected is by voluntarily disregarding an entrenched right. This impropriety may be perpetrated by individuals and governments alike. Here, the aggrieved party possesses a right to restrict the performance of certain types of activities by others. If an actor subject to this right knowingly proceeds to engage the aggrieved party in the prohibited fashion, she commits an injustice in the broad sense. For the state, this might involve, for example, taking private property without providing just compensation. For an individual, it may consist of any intentional act designed to violate the victim's right.

How the right is violated will depend upon the obligation owed to the right-holder. Broad injustice may derive from the breach of any of the duties mentioned in the preceding chapter. Thus, any act intended to inflict harm upon another is wicked and unjust because it demonstrates a fundamental disrespect for the right of all individuals to be free. Similarly, one who knowingly lies to another, or deliberately breaches a promise (of either private performance or mutual restriction), undermines the trust required for political cooperation and social exchange. These acts, too, restrict or inhibit autonomy and so are condemnable as unjust in the broad sense.

Intentional Crimes and Torts

Aristotle's conception of unjust acts and unjust persons comports with our contemporary ideas about willfulness and intent. In criminal law, this idea is expressed as part of the actor's mens rea. Where she desires to harm another, or knows that such harm will follow from her actions, her intent is condemned as antisocial.[17] Those harboring such intent are punished by being stripped of their liberty. A similar idea underlies all of our intentional torts. If the tortfeasor commits an act designed to harm another, or does so with knowledge to a substantial certainty that a harmful consequence will follow, she may be forced to pay for any loss caused by her willful conduct.[18]

Abstract or Political Injustice

When we speak of harm in this way, we refer not just to physical injury, although certainly this will often accompany a wicked act. Indeed, as we observed in Chapter Three, in some circumstances it is not even necessary that the victim have suffered an actual impairment of autonomy. Rather, what we are describing is a kind of abstract, moral and political injury. Every act designed to violate the right of another evinces a basic disregard for the well-being of others. This is not only morally reprehensible, it is socially dangerous. Political society cannot exist, let alone thrive, without cooperation. While this may not require acts of altruism, it does necessitate respect for the freedom of others. This freedom includes the right to be left alone when so desired. It is this mutual respect which allows us to live by a rule of law. Acts which repudiate this essential form of cooperation undermine the rule of law and threaten to cast us back into a world where only the strongest survive.

This explains why in cases where an actor intentionally violates the rights of another, our primary concern is in punishing the wrongdoer. Retributive justice, as I shall discuss later,[19] requires that the wrongdoer be given her "due" castigation. Indeed, it is in such cases that our instinct for retribution is at its peak. Because of the gravity of the act, the wrongdoer may be subject to sanctions even if she has caused no actual loss to another.

Corporeal Injustice

Where such an intentional act succeeds in producing actual damages, the need to punish the wrongdoer remains prominent, though it is no longer the only concern of justice. Here, something has been taken from the victim. It may be as tangible as a piece of property or the use of a limb, or as intangible as a lost business opportunity. There are thus two harms in this situation. One to the principle of according all individuals an equal right to be free, the other to the actual autonomy interests of the victim. The former is an injustice in the broad sense which requires a special kind of annulment. Thus, in tort cases, the victim may recover punitive damages from the wrongdoer, sometimes far in excess of her actual loss. The latter harm, however, requires correction not simply because it resulted from a wicked act, although this supplies at least some justification. Instead, the loss must be rectified because the wrongdoer has unfairly ignored the rules others must obey, and the victim has been unfairly deprived of an interest others have not. This is an injustice in the particular sense of inequality. We turn to this idea next.

Justice in the Particular Sense

Aristotle recognized that some acts are unjust not because they are designed to cause harm to another, but because they create an inequality in goods among individuals.[20] "Goods" as used here, can mean any tangible or intangible object of human desire.[21] The inequality in the allocation of such goods is synonymous with our notion of unfairness. It means individuals come to hold more or less of such goods than they deserve.

The Relational Nature of Particular Justice

Conduct of this sort is unjust because it exhibits the characteristics of excess and deficiency. Yet the imbalance in this situation is unlike that displayed by acts which are unjust in the broad sense. These, it will be recalled, are identified internally by some extreme dispositional humor. Where goods are concerned, however, the character flaw of the actor is determined not internally but externally. That is, whether an actor is wicked or virtuous depends upon the consequences of her actions. Only if, as a result of the act, someone holds a share of goods inconsistent with her entitlement, is an injustice done.

Distributions and Transactions

Such an injustice may be created in either of two ways. One is through an unfair distribution of goods. This may occur where one party must allocate goods between at least two others who assert some basis for possessing all or part of them. If the goods are allocated in a way that fails to accord each party her "due," the distribution is unjust. The other way for effecting an inequality of goods is through a bilateral transaction. Here, one party, whom Aristotle characterizes as grasping, takes goods directly from another. The result is an unfair exchange. The taker has gained more than she is entitled, and the other has lost some of what she deserves. No doubt, the party who acts graspingly displays a wickedness of character antithetical to virtue. But it is not the general ill will characteristic of injustices in the broad sense; rather, it is unjust in the "particular" sense of being unfair.

Distributive and Corrective Justice

To avoid such injustice, distributions and transactions must follow an ideal form. There are separate forms for each type of relationship. Each model consists of certain immutable principles with which the relation must comport in order to be fair to the parties involved. The paradigm for distributions is established by distributive justice, while corrective justice determines the fairness of transactions.

Particular Justice and Tort Law

All tort cases involve both distributions and transactions. Laws generally, and tort law in particular, possess the characteristics unique to a distributive pattern of allocating goods. As we shall see in Parts III and IV within, the state, through tort law, distributes to all individuals both duties to refrain from harming others, and rights to be free from such wrongful conduct. Distributive justice requires that such rights and duties be allocated fairly.

Tort claims arise when such duties are violated. Invariably, this entails one party interfering with the right of another without her consent. Such encounters are actually private bilateral transactions. These transactions may be voluntary, arising out of a contract or planned relationship, or involuntary, consisting of an unexpected and unwanted interaction. Each type of transaction results in one party sustaining a wrongful loss at the hands of another. This deficit represents an unfair imbalance created between the parties. The notion of corrective justice requires that such a loss be rectified.

Corrective justice is not just a means for evaluating the fairness of private interactions. Like the requirement of distributive justice mentioned above, it also may be used to evaluate the state's treatment of the private parties involved in the dispute. In a political association, the victim may not correct the wrong herself. Rather, she must seek her recourse in the legal system, which is created and operated by the state. By taking away the victim's ability to exact private vengeance, the state assumes the responsibility for settling the conflict fairly. To satisfy this obligation, it is beholden to the constraints of corrective justice.

To critically evaluate tort law, then, one must look to see whether it meets the dual requirements of particular justice. Distributive justice determines whether the law itself is fair; and, if the law is violated, corrective justice determines the manner of fairly redressing the resulting wrong. Each form of justice will be examined in detail in the next two chapters. For the sake of analytical continuity, I will begin with distributive justice.

Chapter 7

Distributive Justice

As was noted briefly in the last chapter, distributive justice is simply a blueprint for determining the fairest way to pass out things that many people desire. For this scheme to apply, there must be at least one party who holds the coveted objects, and two or more others who can state some valid claim to receive them. When all such players are present, fairness dictates that the goods be disseminated to the claimants in equal shares.[1] "Equality," as used here, does not mean that everybody is entitled to the same amount of the distributed goods. Rather, it requires only that the shares be allocated according to a geometric proportion.[2]

Such a formula, which is founded upon the equality of ratios,[3] operates in the following manner. Suppose it is determined that A should receive five out of every twenty widgets, and that B should receive fifteen. Here, a one quarter to three quarter ratio exists between A and B. If one hundred widgets later become available for distribution, A would receive twenty-five and B seventy-five of these goods. Should one thousand more widgets become available after that, two hundred and fifty would go to A, while seven hundred and fifty would be given to B. Even though A and B receive objectively unequal shares in each distribution, justice is done so long as the goods are allocated in conformity with the predetermined ratio.

This assumes, of course, that there is good reason why A always should be entitled to more widgets than B. For a distribution to be just, the ratio used to allocate the goods must itself be based on some fair criterion. Obviously, the criteria one might adopt for this purpose may vary from society to society, or even from community to community. Aristotle acknowledged that although a "distribution must be according to merit in some sense,"[4] the definition given to this term is not always the same. Ordinarily, the criteria selected will reflect values shared by all those participating in the distributive enterprise. Thus, as Aristotle observed, democrats might base their allocations on one's status as a freeman, while supporters of oligarchy might choose wealth or nobility for this purpose, and supporters of aristocracy might select a standard based upon excellence.[5] If the criterion selected is fair, distributive justice requires only that each individual receive her designated proportion every time a new distribution is made.

Applications of Distributive Justice

This relatively simple scheme for distributing goods can apply in a variety of different contexts. In fact, to anyone who has children, or has ever been around them, the demand for distributive justice is probably all too familiar. With good intentions you present a bag of candy to a group of youngsters. Much to your dismay, however, you learn that the number of grasping fingers exceeds the sum of your confections. You must either withdraw your bounty, and endure the inevitable whining that will follow, or come up with a persuasive reason why certain children must receive fewer treats than others. If you choose the latter alternative, you are held to the demands of distributive justice. This means that your reason for denying a few pieces of candy to some children must be premised upon some criterion which they hopefully will find fair, like age, temporal priority or prior good behavior. If you fail to articulate such a justification, your distributees undoubtedly will be quick to remind you of your unfairness.

Perhaps the more familiar usage of distributive justice is in the area of political policy. In fact, when most people think of distributive justice, they probably think of welfare plans and tax schemes. Indeed, state welfare laws provide a classic example of how a public regime of distributive justice is supposed to operate. In such a system, the government holds a limited fund of money which may be used for the public welfare. This endowment is subject to the demands of many citizens who wish to improve their station in life. To distribute this fund fairly, the state must establish some legitimate criterion for determining who is entitled to a share of this money and how much they will receive. In most cases, welfare laws permit the state to allocate these funds to financially strapped individuals in accordance with their need.[6] To the extent that need provides a socially acceptable reason for making these distributions, such a scheme comports with our sense of justice.

While welfare rules dispense social benefits to their distributees, income tax laws disburse social burdens. That is, instead of giving resources to citizens, tax schemes take resources away. Nevertheless, they too are beholden to the constraints of distributive justice. In order to implement a progressive tax scheme, the state must offer some valid reason why certain individuals must assume more financial burden than others. Just as for welfare, the determining factor in one's tax liability is her financial circumstance. Thus, it is not unfair for the wealthy to pay a greater mathematical share than the poor, as long the amount of their burden represents a fair proportion of their income.

The Distributive Justice of Law

Though welfare and tax programs may be the most prominent illustrations of public distributive justice, they certainly are not the only ones. Indeed, they are but a microscopic crystal at the tip of an enormous iceberg. The truth is that *all* laws fit the paradigm of distributive justice and so must answer to its moral imperatives.

To understand why this is, we must go back briefly to the seminal point in any civilization when individuals move from a state of nature to an organized political system. In making this transition, individuals give to the state all of their natural freedom. The state holds this freedom like the caretaker of a limited community resource.[7] To preserve this precious resource, the state must ration it out very carefully. It does this by promulgating laws. Some laws, like the Bill of Rights and the Civil Rights Act of 1964, affirmatively recognize rights which imbue their holders with positive liberties. Other laws, however, establish protective duties which tend to restrict autonomy by prohibiting or regulating certain types of conduct. Criminal codes and tort rules fall into this category. Because rights and duties are correlative, all of these laws both enhance the freedom of some individuals and reduce the freedom of others.[8] It follows, then, that every law represents a distribution of autonomy by the state to some or all of its constituents.[9]

As would be expected, laws are far from uniform in the way they allocate liberties to members of the public. For one thing, some laws are simply more restrictive than others. An ordinance which limits the height of shrubbery on corner properties, for example, is far less inhibiting than a criminal murder statute which carries the ultimate penalty of death. Moreover, often the same law affords different degrees of autonomy to those individuals subject to it. This typically is true for parties engaged in the same transaction. Thus, while the murder statute mentioned above decreases my positive freedom to harm my neighbor, it also increases my neighbor's negative freedom to remain safe from my conduct. Even where the same law applies to two *different* transactions, there is no guarantee that the parties in each encounter will be extended an equivalent measure of autonomy. Consider the familiar tort doctrine that one must act as a reasonably prudent person under the circumstances. For me, this certainly would require that I remain securely within the confines of my car while I proceed to drive it down a busy city street. Yet, as we saw in Chapter Four, the same restriction did not apply to the cab driver in the *Cordas* case. He, you will recall, was permitted under the law to dive from his taxi in order to save his life.

Distributive Criteria

That laws often distribute autonomy in an uneven fashion, however, is not necessarily indicative of their moral shortcomings. As part of a scheme of distributive justice, laws need not treat every individual the same way. Rather, they need only treat them fairly in accordance with some predetermined geometric proportion. Thus, laws which give some parties more freedom than others are not necessarily wrongful. If there is good reason for such preferential treatment, the demands of distributive justice will be satisfied nevertheless.

Merit

In our political system, there are three criteria which governments often use to distribute autonomy through law. One of these criteria is merit. As employed in this context, merit means a type of personal accomplishment which is attributable to one's own action, and is not dependent upon someone else's disability. Laws generally tend to acknowledge such merit-based actions by awarding their authors greater autonomy. The basic idea is that, if actions are the means to virtue, then every act must have moral consequences. Just as bad behavior should be punished, good behavior should be rewarded. Arguably, any conduct which advances one's life plan without harming others is good, and so deserves special consideration.

Although the laws which rely upon this criterion are far too numerous to catalogue, a few familiar examples come readily to mind. Intellectual property laws, like those involving copyrights, patents and trademarks, reward unique creative or intellectual efforts by affording their authors certain protections not available to others less ambitious.[10] In the area of real property, the law of adverse possession grants special rights to interlopers who, by their persistence, demonstrate an unusual commitment to the land.[11] And, of course, the laws of contracts and sales empower shrewd enterprisers to use their business acumen to secure for themselves the best deals that fairness will allow.[12] In each case, the latitude extended to the actor, though perhaps greater than that enjoyed by others, is justified because it is founded upon the merit of her actions.

The Importance of Need and Risk

The remaining two distributive criteria—"need" and "risk"—are perhaps the most pervasive determinants of American law. Indeed, one can hardly peruse a statutory code or case reporter without seeing their effects. From criminal prohibitions to the welfare and tax schemes discussed earlier, these factors play a key role in shaping our public laws. And their impact doesn't end here. They also appear prominently in much of our private law. As we shall see later on, these concepts are in fact the key features in the legal landscape of tort law. Thus, they warrant special attention.

Need

The criterion of need is founded on a rather simple moral premise. It is that those who either lack autonomy, or are in jeopardy of losing it, deserve added leeway to secure or protect their interests. If freedom is the sine qua non of virtue, then there can be no greater loss than the denial of autonomy. Of course, some threats against autonomy are more serious than others. The permanent impairment of one's mobility, for example, is far more devastating than the elimination of one among many options which may further the actor's life plan. While the former is virtually indispensable to happiness, the latter is more a matter of personal convenience. Certainly, the law cannot guarantee that everyone will be able to follow the optimal path to the realization of her dreams. But it can, and must, guarantee us those attributes of autonomy which make life worth living, and political association more desirable than going it alone. The criterion of need ensures that it does both.

Material Distributions

Perhaps because of its august moral pedigree, need has proven to be a versatile catalyst in the distribution of autonomy. One of its primary functions is to allocate material resources. Indeed, we saw an example of this in our earlier discussion of welfare systems. Distributions under these schemes, you will remember, are made entirely on the basis of the financial need of the recipients. Only those unable to secure the staples of autonomy—like food, clothing and shelter—are entitled to receive such payments. Medicaid programs distribute medical services under the same premise.[13] Other laws promote the availability of these primary goods in more indirect ways. Contracts which place burdensome conditions on the acquisition of such goods are always strictly scrutinized and, where adhesive, are routinely invalidated.[14] Moreover, companies which supply essential services such as water, electricity, transportation and communication are often not only subject to extensive governmental regulation, they also are held to higher standards of conduct in our courts.[15] Yet despite the diversity of these different legal doctrines, the effect of each is the same: to ensure that no one is denied fair access to the basic necessities of life.

Abstract Distributions

Besides distributing such material resources, the need criterion also frequently determines how laws allocate more abstract aspects of autonomy. For example, where an individual suffers from an incapacity that is either internally or externally imposed, her freedom of action is generally enhanced. In such a scenario, the incapacity deprives the individual of rational choice and so renders her vulnerable to the injurious actions of others.[16] Because of this vulnerability, the incapacitated party requires more freedom to protect her interests. Under the need criterion, the law is justified in extending her this accommodation.

Internal Incapacities

Internal incapacities are those found within the mind of the individual. They derive from lack of experience, as for children, or from some psychological or organic deficiency, like that found in the mentally ill. In either case, those possessing an internal incapacity are unable either to assess the riskiness of a transaction, or to freely choose whether to participate in it. Because of this, we do not require the mentally infirm to abide by their contracts. In fact, they are permitted by law to revoke their agreements without suffering any legal consequences.[17] Likewise, we do not expect children to behave with the same circumspection as adults.[18] Free of this responsibility, children have open to them a greater range of alternative courses of action. Thus, while a child of tender years might be excused for running into traffic or playing with matches, an adult surely would not.[19]

External Incapacities

Unlike internal incapacities, external incapacities are not intrinsic, but are caused by outside forces. Nevertheless, they may be just as debilitating. Indeed, even an individual possessing all her mental faculties might be incapable of making a knowing, voluntary choice under some conditions.

Where such conditions arise, the disabled parties are entitled to as much extra liberty as is necessary to protect their interests.

Relational Incapacities

External incapacities are created in two ways: through relations with others, and through extenuating circumstances. Relational influences exist where the parties to an interaction possess unequal power and opportunity to know of and control the risks of their association.[20] Such incapacities arise in numerous common relationships, including those between doctor and patient, employer and employee, landlord and tenant, invitor and invitee, common carrier and passenger, innkeeper and guest, and product manufacturer and consumer. In these relationships, the party who lacks the power to control the risk environment is at the mercy of her counterpart. Not knowing what the dangers are, or when they might materialize, she lacks the ability to protect herself from harm. As a result, she must depend on someone else to provide such protection. In recognition of this, the need criterion turns the incapacitated party's dependence into a right not shared by others outside the subject relationship. Indeed, as we learned in Chapter Four, only she and others like her enjoy the power to force the risk-creator to take some action which will secure their interests.

Circumstantial Incapacities

Although circumstantially created incapacities are more episodic than those arising out of relations, they too create the kind of unusual need which justifies more generous distributions of autonomy. We've already considered a couple of circumstances where such incapacities commonly develop. Earlier on, I described a confrontation between two gun-toting individuals, one of whom gets the draw on the other without notice or provocation. Because of the need to protect her life, the surprised party is likely to lose the capacity for rational thought. Nevertheless, the law permits her to react instinctively in order to protect herself. In this regard, she is granted a freedom almost unknown in a civilized society: the right to take the life of another. Pretty much the same license was extended to the cabby in *Cordas*. Although he did not actually kill anyone when he abandoned his vehicle, he almost surely would have been exonerated for doing so if he had. The reason is that he too faced a life or death struggle which placed him in grave need of an extraordinary remedy. This same need might arise even if the threat to life is not imposed by human agency, as it was in both of the preceding illustrations, but by some natural sequence of events. So if a horrendous storm threatens my ship and its cargo, I am empowered under the law to moor it at the dock of another without her permission.[21] Just as in the other cases of externally created incapacity, the necessity of the circumstance affords me the liberty of undertaking special measures to protect my interests.

Autonomy-Reducing Effect

If all of these incapacities have one thing in common, it is that they tend to increase the debilitated party's autonomy. This, however, is not the only way in which the need criterion operates. In certain circumstances, it may actually diminish one's freedom by heightening her responsibility. To be sure, some parties are better able to protect themselves from harm than others. For example, individuals possessing superior skill, intelligence, experience or training may appreciate dangers that others less gifted cannot. Such persons would be expected to make use of their faculties to avoid obvious hazards. Thus, even though a weekend tinkerer might be forgiven for failing to safely operate a power tool, the law would not extend the same leniency to a skilled carpenter. Because of her abilities, the carpenter is less in need of protection by the state and so must temper her behavior accordingly.

Risk

Like this latter aspect of the need criterion, the distributive criterion of risk operates to reduce one's autonomy. Unlike need, however, the effect of risk is *exclusively* negative; that is, if it is to be a factor at all, risk will always decrease the autonomy of the risk creator, and will never enhance it. Why is this so? Because when directed at others without their consent, risk itself becomes a threat to the idea of freedom.

The Legitimacy of Risk as a Distributive Criterion

People form political associations to secure the liberty which eludes them in a state of nature. With this liberty, each person is able to take the necessary steps to fulfill her life plan. These individual paths to virtue, however, do not all run parallel or on different planes. On the contrary, they often merge or intersect. Indeed, one usually does not act in isolation, but in a closed social environment where the interests of others are almost always affected in some way. In such an environment, risk is an inescapable fact of life.

Living in a such an interactive world is not necessarily a problem; in fact, it offers some definite advantages. Chief among these is the opportunity to receive from others what one cannot acquire alone. Instead of viewing others as a threat, I may see them as providing a means of furthering my objectives. Thus, it may behoove me to permit another to appropriate some of my interests if I am to receive an equal or greater benefit in return. Here, everyone gains from the transaction and there is neither need nor justification for restricting the autonomy of my counterpart. Indeed, such voluntary associations may create the type of special duties which, we noted previously, the state would be obligated to respect and enforce.

In other circumstances, however, the risk of interaction may present real moral concerns. If I do not consent to suffer the consequences of another's action, then it is not a benefit to me, but a menace to my interests. Likewise for my counterpart, without consent her conduct ceases to be just a self-directed attempt at aggrandizement and becomes more an act of misappropriation. By repudiating my negative liberty to be left alone, the actor's exercise of autonomy exposes me to harm both in a political and moral sense. To prevent this injustice, the state must have the power, either before or after the offending conduct takes place, to diminish the freedom of the wrongdoer in proportion to the risk she imposes upon others.[22]

Risk Regulation

Any political organization considering such a distributive restriction, however, faces a dilemma. A harm may be inflicted not only by individuals, but also by public agencies. Thus, states regulating risky activities tread a fine line between justice and injustice. This is because any regulation of a risky activity necessarily impacts the freedom of both risk-creators and those they endanger. If the regulation is more burdensome than necessary, then its superfluous aspect is itself a harm to the party regulated. On the other hand, if the distributive regulation does not go far enough, it is unjust to the party unwittingly subject to the excess danger of the risky conduct.

Balancing Interests

As is apparent, the only way to address this dilemma is by balancing the respective autonomy interests of the parties to a harmful interaction. In this regard, the state, in formulating its distributive rules for risky conduct, must rank in importance and compare the potential conflicting interests. On the one hand, it must consider the importance of the activity to the actor (is it an essential welfare interest or designed to secure the same, or is it more of a convenience or luxury?), the degree to which the interest furthered by the activity can be satisfied in other ways (is it indispensable to one's life plan, or are there reasonable alternatives which will permit the actor to achieve her goals?) and the moral quality of the act (is it one of virtue or debauchery?). On the other hand, the state must consider the degree to which the risky behavior will impede the autonomy interests of others. This requires consideration of several factors, including the probability that the act will affect others, the ability of others to avoid such harms through the exercise of their own autonomy, and the expected magnitude of the harm if it cannot be avoided.[23]

Intentionally Imposed Risks

Where an activity presents a danger that everyone would consider harmful, and the risk of its realization is great, justice would permit severe restrictions on its performance. So it is for acts intended to cause harm to another. Because of the deliberative mental state of the actor, and the power of her will to carry out her intentions, these acts are the riskiest and thus most socially deleterious. Take, for example, the miscreant who discharges a firearm at a crowd with the express purpose of striking and killing one of its number. Because the probability of harm is high, and its likely effect substantial, she would enjoy no freedom to engage in this suspect activity. Here, the grave risks posed by this conduct justify the state in distributing to her an absolute responsibility either to refrain from it entirely or to bear all the consequences for failing to do so.

Unintended Risks

For other acts which pose more remote dangers, and possess more personal or social value, a greater distribution of autonomy to the actor would be warranted. This is often the case with unintentionally risky conduct. Now divorced from the power of the actor's will to bring it about, the consequence of such behavior is strictly fortuitous. For instance, instead of shooting a gun into a crowd, suppose the actor drives an automobile with bald tires close to the scurrying masses occupying a busy city street. When one of the tires explodes, the vehicle rolls toward the throng on the sidewalk. Here, the probability of harm created by the driver's action is certainly less than that of the sniper. And, the act of driving, even with bad tires, is far more desirable. Thus, the actor is afforded at least some freedom to engage in this activity. Nevertheless, because the danger of driving with worn tread is significant, and within the operator's power of control, her liberty of action is not unlimited. In fact, it is seriously restricted by a distributive responsibility to avoid exposing the crowd to such excess risks.[24]

Distributive Justice and Secondary Rights

From this discussion, we see that one's distribution of autonomy is inversely proportional to the hazards posed by her conduct. The riskier her endeavor, the less her freedom of action will be; on the other hand, as the danger in her conduct becomes more self-contained, her right to autonomy increases in kind. But just how is this proportion implemented in real life? What measures does the state use to ensure that those conducting the riskiest activities are denied the autonomy to do so, while those engaged in benign ventures are permitted to act more freely? To a large extent, we have already answered this question, albeit in a different context. The restriction of an actor's freedom depends upon the cluster of secondary rights which others are allowed to exercise against her.

These rights, we have seen, come in two forms. One form is preemptive. Rights in this category impose ex ante restrictions on the autonomy of the actor. That is, they preclude the subject activity either from being performed at all, or from being performed in a particular manner.[25] The other type of secondary right is corrective in nature. It cannot be used to alter the actor's conduct. However, if the act results in harm to another, the victim may rely upon her corrective right to force the actor to compensate for any resulting loss. Although this sanction is imposed ex post rather than ex ante, its financial impact may be just as damaging to the actor's autonomy.[26]

Which of these secondary rights an actor must face is determined by the dangerousness of her behavior. The most ominous activities ordinarily are subject to the inhibiting force of *both* preemptive *and* corrective rights. This is true of most intentional torts, like battery, which display an utter contempt for the interests of others. Thus, in the sniper example above, anyone in the crowd who was in danger of being shot would have been justified in stopping this illicit behavior in any way reasonably necessary. Moreover, if such a defensive measure failed, or the opportunity for its use did not arise, anyone actually harmed in the incident could have required the shooter to pay a sum of damages commensurate with the wrong done. In combination, these rights, and the duties they create, obstruct the actor's autonomy to a degree directly proportional to the hazards her conduct creates.

As the risk of the offending activity recedes, however, so too do the rights which cloak her in restrictive garb. Consider the previous example of the driver who operated her vehicle without checking her tires. While this conduct is not excusable, neither is it as dangerous as shooting at a pond full of sitting ducks. Thus, unless there existed some specific statute to the contrary, no one on the street would be empowered either to force the driver to inspect and change her tires, or to prevent her from using her car in that condition. If the driver's autonomy can be restricted at all, this can be done only after she has completed her act and caused someone harm. At that point, the victims of her neglect could require her to pay compensation for the loss she has inflicted.

The analysis here is more complex than stated, and I will return to it again later on. For now, however, it is sufficient to see how the correlation between risk and autonomy effectuates the delicate balancing of interests adverted to above. The greater the risk posed by the activity, the lower the autonomy right of the actor, and the stronger the state's distributive restriction may be. However, when the other-directed risk of an action is lowered, the actor's freedom of action increases. Accordingly, the state must implement a less onerous distributive restriction of that activity.

Aggregating Criteria

This analytic scheme, though beautiful in its symmetry, is disturbingly irresolute in many situations. The reason is that risk frequently is not the only distributive criterion which influences the scope of our legal doctrines. In fact, either the merit or the need criterion, or both together, also could apply to the same transaction. Depending upon the particular permutation of relevant factors, the autonomy of the interacting parties might expand or decrease. Especially when the doctrine appears in the form of a standard, which balances many considerations in determining the distribution of autonomy, the swings in either direction can be substantial. In such situations, based as they are on a case-by-case analysis of circumstances, it is difficult to predict in advance how much autonomy the law affords. About the only thing certain is that the quest for justice will be far more complicated, and its object far more equivocal.

The *Cordas* case demonstrates just how tricky this analysis can be. In *Cordas*, you will recall, a desperate taxi driver leaped from his cab after being accosted by a would-be kidnapper. For the cabby, and for the court deciding his fate, the distributive concerns of risk and need clearly pulled in opposite directions. The riskiness of the cabby's flight was all too apparent. Indeed, it would be hard to imagine an act more dangerous than abandoning a moving vehicle in the midst of a hectic city intersection. Under ordinary circumstances, such rash behavior would be absolutely forbidden. But the cabby here did not abandon his vehicle on a whim. Nor was he inspired by an evil motive—like wanting to see whether human beings fall like bowling pins when struck by a large rolling object. Instead, he dove from the cab to save his life. At that instant, the cabby faced an emergency situation which required that he take some extreme measure. The need criterion afforded him this opportunity. Despite the serious danger inherent in jumping out of the vehicle, he was nevertheless entitled to exercise the extra autonomy necessary to protect his most basic welfare interest. In this way, the need criterion seems to have superseded the distributive criterion of risk. Yet it surely did not eliminate it entirely. To see how close the competing concerns really were, assume that as the cabby exited, the car was headed for a troop of girl scouts, many of whom perished from the ensuing collision. Would the cabby still be exculpated for saving his skin? I don't think anyone could answer this question conclusively or with much conviction. For here need and risk are not mutually exclusive, but are almost perfectly counterbalanced.

Summary

This is just one of the difficult issues presented by the concept of distributive justice. We will come across yet others when we examine its application to the law of torts. At that time, we will investigate alternatives for resolving these dilemmas. For the time being, however, it will suffice to understand what distributive justice is and how it works. Remember that, despite common perception, it is not just concerned with welfare systems and tax programs, though certainly these are included within its purview. Indeed, as we have seen, it is a far more complex and important concept. It is, in fact, the sole yardstick by which we may measure the fairness of *all* our laws, at least in the abstract. Accordingly, it necessarily will have a central role to play in any theory of legal justice, including the one for tort law which I will propose in the chapters to come.

Given the importance and complexity of this concept, it may be useful to briefly review its fundamental aspects before proceeding to the next form of justice. The core idea of distributive justice is that any formal state decree represents a distribution to its citizens of certain material or abstract entitlements. The entitlements received by citizens need not be perfectly equal to be just, so long as the differences are premised on some fair criteria for distinguishing them.

In essence, all of these criteria are designed to provide a minimum level of autonomy to make social living preferable to a state of nature. Thus, the state rewards individuals, who by the merit of their autonomous action, strive to attain the elusive goal of virtue. To facilitate this pursuit, the state also ensures that each citizen possesses the basic necessities of life. "Need" determines how much of these resources the state is required to give to each individual. Finally, the state guarantees citizens a certain measure of protection from the acts of others, without unduly restricting their autonomy. To balance these interests, the state distributes freedoms to act (rights) and restrictions upon action (responsibilities or duties) on the basis of "risk"—that is, the likelihood that it will cause harm to others.

Such a scheme of distributions still is not just, however, unless it is implemented in some fair way. Secondary rights are created to ensure that they are. By empowering actual or prospective victims to take action against their aggressors, these rights both enhance and restrict the autonomy of the parties to such transactions. Depending upon the degree of risk posed, secondary rights may be used to prohibit some acts entirely, to regulate others in their manner of performance, and/or to compel wrongdoers who perform them to pay for the harm they engender.

Chapter 8

Corrective Justice

As the preceding discussion suggests, distributive justice plays an important role in establishing the social duties which are necessary for political association. It also determines what rights we enjoy as citizens of such a cooperative enterprise. But this is as far as it goes. It does not tells us what is to be done when such rights are violated. What does fairness require then?

The answer to this question is provided by the concept of corrective justice. As was noted in Chapter Six, corrective justice requires the rectification[1] of wrongs[2] that follow from private, bilateral transactions. In such transactions, one party interferes with the preexisting distribution of rights afforded another by distributive justice. She does this by doing something which she should not have done in the first place, or in her failing to make reparation afterwards. Such conduct may be as innocent as breaching a simple promise or as unconscionable as committing murder.

All of these transactions share a common feature. They create an imbalance between the parties involved. In such cases, one party suffers a loss which produces a deficiency in a good. This deficiency is produced by another party who, by so acting, acquires an excessive "gain" of some sort.[3]

Loss

The deficiency which follows from a wrongful transaction may be either abstract or tangible. An abstract loss is not one that can be perceived or objectively verified. Rather, it occurs when one's primary right to be free from intrusion is violated. Correlative to this right, it will be recalled, is one or more duties which safeguard the right-holder's interests. Such a duty is owed to the holder by any party whose conduct places her in danger. This synergism of right and duty forges between the parties a special relationship. From this relationship, the right-holder becomes entitled to a certain degree of respect which she would not otherwise enjoy. This respect may be manifested in a number of ways: it might require that the duty-bound party desist from engaging in the risk-creating activity, or that she alter the particular manner of her behavior, or that she pay for whatever damages her conduct may engender. When an actor violates her duty of care, either by proceeding with the dangerous activity or refusing to suffer its consequences, she repudiates one of these entitlements. Even if no physical harm results, this breach reeks of injustice. Besides disavowing the special bond between the parties, it inflicts upon the victim an injury which is both political and moral. In short, it creates a deficiency in the bank account of rights that is conferred upon her not only as a citizen, but as a human being as well.

Frequently, however, such transactions do result in one party suffering a tangible loss. A loss in this context may include any actual impairment of autonomy. As we learned in Chapter Three, such losses may take many forms. They may be as serious as bodily injuries or as remote as foregone business opportunities. Still, not all restrictions of autonomy create deficiencies which require correction. Such a deficiency exists only if the autonomy interest invaded is important enough to be placed under the aegis of a secondary right. Thus, while my interest in bodily integrity generally is protected by a right, my interest in receiving cordial greetings from passersby usually is not. Even where such rights are recognized, they are not absolute, but presumptive only. Thus, their power often will depend upon the circumstances of their invocation, including the culpability of the injury-producing conduct which threatens them, and the extent to which that action impedes the victim's life plan.

Gain

Like the deficiencies described above, the gains subject to corrective justice may assume different forms. Aristotle believed gains to be a product of one's "grasping" motive.[4] To be grasping, an individual must seek to acquire goods which she does not deserve. According to Aristotle, such goods could be corporeal or ethereal.[5] For example, he explains that one who intentionally wounds another may "gain" by that act, "even if it [i.e., the gain] be not a term appropriate to [that] case[]...."[6] Here, the intentional actor may be said to gain in three different senses. First, the actor accomplishes what she had set out to do, in this way "gaining" the personal satisfaction of some deliberate end. Second, she enjoys a relational benefit by asserting her will over her unsuspecting victim. Finally, in acting in a forbidden manner, she exercises more autonomy than those of her neighbors who obey the law, and so acquires a distinct political advantage.

Gains of this sort are not unique to intentional acts like the assault described by Aristotle. Indeed, even in Aristotle's time, corrective justice was applied to far less cognitive forms of conduct. For example, injuries caused by accident or misadventure did not go without rectification under Greek law. On the contrary, carelessness and indiscretion were punishable if they resulted in the death of another. Thus, if one committed an accidental homicide which was not "perfectly excusable" (i.e., committed in self-defense), the family of the decedent often was required (where so instructed by the decedent before his death) to bring a claim against the responsible actor.[7] If "convicted," the convict could be expatriated for a term of years and required to expiate his crime by engaging in certain religious rites.[8] In addition, he could be required to "appease" the family of the decedent by giving "gifts" or by "humble submission."[9] In some sense, then, even the perpetrator of an unintentional act might accrue enough of a "gain" from her conduct to subject her to corrective justice.

This type of gain is neither material, as it is for the thief, nor psychological, as it is for anyone who desires to subject others to the power of her will. Rather, here the gain is almost exclusively political. Earlier, you will recall, we saw that all who enter a political association agree to abide by its rules, so long as they are fair. This ensures that no one enjoys more autonomy than she deserves (as determined by the legitimate distributive criteria upon which the rules are based). If an individual violates this mutual restriction by committing an act denied to others, she assumes for herself an unfair measure of autonomy. Exercise of this self-ordained prerogative is a political "gain," even if it is unintentional and produces no other demonstrable benefit for the actor.[10]

Implementing Corrective Justice

Once the gains and losses which are the concern of corrective justice have been identified, it remains for determination how this imbalance is to be reversed. Aristotle provides some guidance in this regard. In short, he tells us that corrective justice is done by a judge who restores the equality between the parties by taking away the gain of the wrongdoer and annulling the loss of the victim.[11] Subsumed within this description are two requirements—one procedural, the other substantive.[12]

Procedural Trappings

The procedural aspect concerns the structural mechanism by which such disputes are to be resolved. Although the transactions which create such disputes are bilateral, Aristotle suggests a triadic structure for adjudicating them. This structure includes the two disputants and a judge to whom "they take refuge."[13] Why this structure? As for the parties, only they have experienced the gain and loss unique to their transaction. Thus, both must be present to restore the preexisting equilibrium. With respect to the judge, she fulfills both a practical and symbolic role. She serves as a metaphor of corrective justice, acting as the intermediate between the gain represented by the defendant and the loss embodied in the plaintiff.[14] But she also is the mediator of the parties' dispute; one who possesses the impartiality to see clearly the gain and loss of the parties, and is able to return them to the status quo.[15]

Substantive Content

How the status quo is to be restored is determined by the substantive component of corrective justice. As was noted above, it requires annulling the wrongful gain and repairing the wrongful loss produced by the transaction. But this cannot be accomplished arbitrarily. Here, too, there is a definite structure. Aristotle states that this must be done according to an arithmetic proportion.[16] That is, what was taken as a gain must be returned in the same amount to the one from whom it was appropriated.[17]In this respect, "corrective justice is the intermediate between loss and gain."[18]

This formula works fairly well where the wrongdoer has appropriated from the victim something of definite value, like a piece of personal property. Here, the gain of the wrongdoer and the loss of the victim are embodied at least partially in the stolen property. To correct the imbalance, justice may require simply returning the stolen object to the victim.[19]

In other cases, however, Aristotle's arithmetic proportion is easier to state than to apply. For example, in many situations, the wrongdoer accrues no tangible gain from her act. The gain, we saw above, may be merely psychological or political. Take Aristotle's example of the villain who intentionally slays or wounds another. How do we measure the value of whatever perverse benefit she may derive from such behavior? Even worse, what if the act is not intentional, but only careless? In such a scenario, the wrongdoer does not desire the injurious consequence of her conduct. In fact, she may well wish that she had acted differently. Here the act produces no overt psychological advantage for its author. It is a gain only in the sense that she has behaved in a way not allowed of others. Finally, even if the wrongdoer's gain is susceptible to valuation, there will be cases where that gain will not mirror the loss suffered by the victim. This would be true, for instance, where a careless actor causes catastrophic loss to one or more others. In such an event, how are we to find the intermediate between the loss and the gain?

Weighing Conduct and Harm

These are difficult issues which are not amenable to clear-cut solutions. Yet they are not insoluble. In each case, they require a close examination and comparison of the wrongdoer's conduct and the victim's lost interest.[20] We considered these factors earlier in analyzing how duties and rights are created; we must do the same in determining how their violation is to be redressed.

Highly Culpable Act—Insignificant Harm

Where the wrongful act is intentional, and thus extremely culpable, but the victim has suffered little or no real autonomy restriction as a result, a small award may be all that is needed to repair the actual damage. Consider a case of attempted murder where the wrongdoer fires a bullet at the prospective victim. Unbeknownst to the victim, however, the bullet passes harmlessly through her hat. Here, the prospective victim has suffered little physical harm. Besides the hole in her cap, she is no worse for having endured the wrongdoer's behavior. Yet the wrongdoer's conduct has injured her in a deeper sense. It has both repudiated her equality as a free moral agent, and undermined the rule of law which keeps her safe. On the other hand, the wrongdoer's conduct remains culpable whether or not she caused her target physical harm. Although she did not succeed in accomplishing her purpose, she was able not only to subordinate her victim's will to her own, but also to engage in an activity from which others must abstain.

To eliminate this gain, and repair the loss of the prospective victim, some remedial measure must be imposed. If it were to be based solely upon the victim's injury, the damages probably would not exceed the cost of the hat. After all, the abstract harm which she sustained is difficult to evaluate and is shared by others in society. If it were to be premised only upon the wrongdoer's conduct, however, the award would have to be large enough to reflect its egregious immorality. And yet, it also must take heed of the rather insignificant consequences of the wrongdoer's act. Indeed, while firing the bullet at the victim was surely reprehensible, it was not nearly as bad as it would have been if the wrongdoer had achieved her nefarious objective. To arrive at an appropriate sanction, one must find the intermediate between these extreme positions. This would seem to entail a modest compensatory recovery for the physical harm done, and a sizable though not oppressive corrective award to neutralize the political and moral benefit which the wrongdoer hoped to derive from the act.

Marginally Culpable Act—Enormous Harm

Similar problems of analysis arise where the severity of the action and its consequence are simply flip-flopped, such that the actor's conduct now is virtually blameless, but its effect upon another's autonomy is enormous. In this regard, let's revisit an earlier example in which I accidentally dropped a nail on a roadway after leaving a hardware store. Suppose for the purpose of this discussion, that an unfortunate driver comes along and runs over my nail, causing her tire to explode and her car to crash into a tree. In the accident, the driver is rendered a quadraplegic. Here, my behavior seems to lack any moral repugnance. Although perhaps I shouldn't have removed any nails from the bag before arriving at my destination, doing so would not seem to expose others to grave danger.[21] On the other hand, the driver has sustained one of the most calamitous injuries possible. Because of this incident, her life will be permanently transformed. Many options formerly available to her will be completely foreclosed, while others will be made more elusive.

Just as in the last illustration, corrective justice here requires a remedy that finds the mean between the gain of the wrongdoer and the loss of the victim. The political and personal gain which accrues from my actions seems minimal at best. I derive no personal satisfaction from the consequence whatsoever; if I benefit at all, it is only in doing that which others should not. Conversely, the driver's injury is so devastating that even the payment of money cannot begin to restore what she has lost. Given the gulf between the culpability of my act and the seriousness of her injury, it seems unfair to hold either party wholly accountable for the loss. Although my action has had a profound effect on the life of another individual, effectively destroying much of her autonomy, it displayed no bad faith or ill will. Yet, before we call the driver's injury merely a bizarre outgrowth of an unfortunate accident, it is important to remember that it is directly attributable to an action which possessed no intrinsic value, even for its author. If corrective justice requires that the driver in these circumstances receive some compensation for her loss, it also appears to favor mitigating this amount in view of the rather innocuous nature of my behavior.

Summary and Synthesis

As the foregoing suggests, corrective justice is not a panacea for properly resolving all interpersonal disputes. Still, it is a necessary and able complement to the concept of distributive justice. Whereas distributive justice provides a means of judging the fairness of the rights and duties provided to us by the state, corrective justice ensures that such distributions of autonomy are fairly enforced. When a duty has been breached, it requires that the injured party have a right to redress the wrong. This right affords her a fair and impartial procedural structure for hearing the dispute, and an equitable substantive formula for settling it. By neutralizing unfair gains and losses, it not only ensures that each party receives her due from the other, but in so doing, it also secures the idea of abstract equality central to free political association.

Chapter 9

Justice in Exchange

Up to this point, we have sketched out an image of justice in rather broad strokes. From this account the rough contours of our most basic moral concept should now be more or less apparent. In a general sense, justice requires that we practice virtue towards others by showing them the respect due any rational agent. In its particular sense, it commands us to be fair, according others a share of goods to which they are entitled.

Nevertheless, our picture of justice still requires some finishing touches. Indeed, there remain certain lingering questions which simply must be answered before our portrait will be complete. For example, how are we to assess the justice of *special* duties assumed voluntarily by individuals in their private interactions with others? Distributive justice cannot tell us because it applies only to general duties created and imposed by the state. And why should wrongdoers be required to face their victims in civil court? Couldn't the state just as fairly rectify the gain and loss of the parties by dealing with each one separately? Although corrective justice supports the bipolarity of the adjudicative process, it may not compel it.

For the answers to these questions, we must consider two additional aspects of justice which do not fit neatly into the "broad" and "particular" taxonomies described previously. One such concept, retributive justice, directs our indignation towards those that wrong us, and ensures that they receive their due castigation. We will examine this instinct at length in Chapter Ten. The other missing piece to our sense of justice, known as reciprocity or justice in exchange, specifically evaluates the fairness of special duties arising out of voluntary relationships. Because of its close affinity with the preceding forms of justice, this concept will be considered first.

Relevance to Voluntary Transactions

So far, we have focused primarily on the requirements of justice in nonconsensual transactions. As noted above, one of the main objectives of distributive justice is to protect citizens from such unsolicited interferences with their autonomy. It does this by distributing duties to those conducting risky activities and rights to those they endanger. Once these functions have been performed, however, distributive justice gives way to the concerns of corrective justice. Thus, if such an actor exceeds her distributive share of autonomy, corrective justice determines whether and to what extent the victim may recover compensation for the harm she has sustained.

But what if the interaction of the parties is not accidental and thus forced upon them, but is planned as part of an agreed-upon exchange of interests? Here the taking by one party of the other's interest is not a harm because it was effected through consent. Accordingly, such behavior falls outside the ambit of the general duty to refrain from harming others. Still, this does not necessarily mean that the actors enjoy complete autonomy to exchange interests however they please.

We've already encountered one restriction upon such transfers. Where the relationship of the parties is such that one party lacks the capacity to give effective consent (because of an imbalance in the parties' respective knowledge of and ability to control the risks of their interaction), the concept of need may empower her to walk away from the relationship or compel her counterpart to provide her with protection. Here, justice forbids the dominant party to simply contract away her responsibilities. By enveloping others in a risk environment of her own creation, she is held accountable for all the foreseeable consequences that may befall them.

The other restriction upon such transfers is imposed by the idea of justice in exchange. It provides a means of assessing the fairness of duties created and exchanged by parties in voluntary associations. Aristotle mentions this form of justice in his *Nichomachean Ethics*.[1] He attributes this idea to the Pythagoreans, who defined it as "reciprocity."[2]

Comparability

Reciprocity, as described by Aristotle, has two different nuances. In one sense, it means that the interests exchanged by the parties to a transaction must be comparable.[3] This is especially important in a barter economy where parties exchange different types of commodities or commodities for services. In this regard, Aristotle notes that "it is not two doctors that associate for exchange, but a doctor and a farmer."[4] Thus, there must be some way of equating the value of the goods exchanged.

As Aristotle observes, in more sophisticated economies, money provides the means of comparison. It is a standard that permits all commodities to be evaluated for their relative worth.[5] Aristotle gives the following example:

> Let A be a house, B ten minae, C a bed. A is half of B, if the house is worth five minae or equal to them; the bed, C, is a tenth of B; it is plain, then, how many beds are equal to a house, viz. five. That exchange took place thus before there was money is plain; for it makes no difference whether it is five beds that exchange for a house, or the money value of five beds.[6]

In this scenario, the minae provide a frame of reference for comparing a house to a bed. Unless such goods are commonly exchanged, there is no way to know how or when such a swap will be fair. Each item is unique and has its own intrinsic value. The only way they can be equated is by subjecting them to a common criterion of evaluation. The minae supply such a standard. This currency represents a quantum of value which everyone is familiar with. When the house and the bed are assigned a value under this standard, a means of comparison is established. So if a house is worth five minae, and a bed is worth one, then as Aristotle concludes, it will take five beds to equal the value of one house.

Commensurability

Once this standard of comparison is established, reciprocity also requires that goods exchanged be of roughly equivalent value. That is, given the designated money value of the commodity, the seller must receive an amount of money which approximates the labor and materials expended in constructing it. To explain the importance of proportional equality in exchange, Aristotle hypothesizes an exchange of shoes for a house. He notes that "[t]he number of shoes exchanged for a house [or for a given amount of food] must therefore correspond to the ratio of builder to shoemaker. For if this be not so, there will be no exchange and no intercourse. And this proportion will not be effected unless the goods are somehow equal."[7]

Aristotle suggests that demand in the marketplace usually will ensure that the exchanged commodities are equivalent in value.[8] Indeed, this may have been true in Aristotle's time when the market was small and relatively simple. In such a market, there is likely to be at least a modicum of competition and the parties will possess about the same bargaining power. Under these perfect conditions, a buyer will only pay what an item is reasonably worth. Justice in exchange would thus appear to be a "natural law" implied in every transaction. There would be no need to recognize this value as an independent source of positive law.

This is not true, however, in our modern American society. In our culture, few individuals create the means for their own survival. Most of us purchase our necessities from others who specialize in making them. Thus, we buy our foods from remote processing plants. Our houses are constructed by building specialists. Clothing manufacturers keep us insulated from the harshness of our environment. Yet many people who live at or below the poverty line have trouble acquiring even these basic goods. These individuals have very little ability to bargain for a fair price. Indeed, given the concentration of economic and legal power in the hands of today's large corporate sellers, very few ordinary consumer transactions involve any sort of actual negotiation over terms. In most cases, goods are offered on a take or leave it basis. And even where dickering is possible, often the goods or services in question are so complex or esoteric that few laymen will know what questions to ask or what terms are fair. Under these imperfect market conditions, the value of justice in exchange may have a more significant role to play in our legal system than it did in Aristotelian Athens.[9]

Distributive and Corrective Justice Distinguished

What might that role be? Well, the idea of justice in exchange fills an important void left open by the concepts of distributive and corrective justice. Distributive justice, we have seen, deals only with duties imposed by the state. It does not apply to special duties assumed by the parties themselves. The notion of reciprocity plugs this gap by providing a test for determining whether such privately created duties are fair in relation to each other.

Corrective justice, on the other hand, concerns both involuntary and voluntary transactions. Aristotle listed several voluntary transactions which would be subject to corrective justice, including "sale[s], purchases[s], loan[s] for consumption, pledging, loan[s] for use, depositing, [and] letting."[10] These all have the elements of exchange which also seem to characterize the associations covered by the concept of reciprocity.

Nevertheless, the two concepts are notably different. Corrective justice is primarily a scheme of *redressing wrongs*. Reciprocity, by contrast, determines which voluntary transactions are *wrongful in the first place*. Proof of this point lies in the application of corrective justice to voluntary exchange transactions.

As mentioned previously, Aristotle considered conduct wrongful in the particular sense if it emanated from a grasping motive.[11] In involuntary interactions, graspingness may be manifested by an intent to satisfy a desire at the expense of another. Voluntary transactions, however, are defined by this very intent. People exchange goods because they desire to obtain what the other possesses. Both parties, in this sense, are "grasping." But "grasping" to Aristotle meant more than just a desire for aggrandizement; it meant attempting to get more than one's due.

There is little difficulty in determining if this line is crossed where an actor unilaterally inflicts harm upon another without consent. Since, even in Aristotle's time, most everyone was owed the courtesy of being left alone,[12] an actor who violated this right denied the other her due.

What one is "due" in a voluntary exchange transaction, however, is not self-evident. Here, each party has agreed to forego the right of being left alone in order to enjoy the bounty of the other. Thus, one's due can only be determined by reference to some standard of entitlement. The concept of reciprocity establishes this standard. It requires that the parties to an exchange receive in return something roughly equivalent to what they had given up. Where one party knowingly takes more than she gives, either by extorting a lopsided deal from her counterpart in the first instance or by failing to fulfill her end of the bargain, she has acted graspingly and may be forced to make reparation under the dictate of corrective justice.

Transactions within Voluntary Relationships

So reciprocity is relevant, indeed indispensable, both to establishing the fairness of voluntary reciprocal duties and to resolving claims arising from their transgression. But what relevance does it have to tort law, which, though manifesting the procedural formalities of corrective justice, deals primarily with what appear to be *involuntary* interactions? Well, the fact is that many if not perhaps most tort cases *do* involve at least some form of voluntary interaction, and thus *do* implicate the concerns of reciprocity.

I will discuss this point at length later.[13] Presently, however, I will simply share a few probative examples. Voluntary relationships exist in many forms. They can be very general as to their form, or very specific, describing in great detail the scope of the parties' exchange. They also can be express, as in a written contract, or implied. Examples of general-implied voluntary relationships are legion. Consider the patient who receives treatment from a doctor, or the licensee who visits her social host, or the invitee who makes a trip to the local store, or the passenger on a bus, train, ship or airplane, or even the guest in a hotel. All of these individuals have formed voluntary relationships, and have exchanged interests, without specifying many of their expectations. Yet expectations *do* exist on both sides. Often, in specific-express relationships, these expectations are spelled out in detail. Today, one cannot purchase even common household items without signing some form which clarifies the parties' rights and duties within the relationship.

The concept of justice in exchange helps us evaluate the fairness of these relationships, and the consequences they create when things go wrong. In all of the relationships described above, one might sustain some unanticipated (involuntary) interest loss. Or, where the parties anticipate the possibility of harm, one may suffer an injury different in degree or kind from that expected. Injuries to bodily integrity usually are of this ilk. In such situations, neither distributive justice nor corrective justice, alone or in combination, is adequate to assess the fairness of the resulting exchange. Invariably, one must consider the equivalence of the special duties owed by each party to the other. This is the imperative of reciprocity.

Chapter 10

Retributive Justice

Knowing that people should exchange goods of equal value is, no doubt, helpful in constructing a system of justice, but it does not take us far enough. How do we know who to hold responsible if this type of justice is not done? Corrective justice may require that the imbalance of an exchange be rectified, but does it conclusively designate the appropriate person to bear this burden? Consider the following set of facts. A fraudulently induces B to trade several valuable gold coins for fake pearls. The exchange is unequal and therefore unjust. This is all that the concept of reciprocity tells us. While B may have a claim in corrective justice to remedy the imbalance, it is not clear what he is to receive (the return of his gold coins or something of equivalent value?) or from whom. On this latter point, couldn't one reasonably argue that justice would be served if the state, in separate proceedings, both punished A for his fraudulent act (say, by requiring him to perform rites of expiation, by exposing him to public humiliation, by restricting his liberty, or by taking away the coins he wrongfully acquired from B), and provided compensation to B from a general fund for the value of his lost coins?[1]

Perhaps, but perhaps not. There is something very sterile and impersonal in such a scheme of rectification. It may correct the imbalance in accordance with an arithmetic proportion, but it might seem strangely unsatisfying to B nevertheless. B never has an opportunity to return the inconvenience and embarrassment thrust upon him by A. Nor will A see the injurious fruits of his mischief. While B has been made whole by the monetary award, has he been given his "due"?

Before answering this question, consider a less serious, though I think instructive, example of the same phenomenon. Imagine being extremely hungry and having a craving for Italian food, but being forced to settle for some other type of cuisine, say Chinese. The Chinese food may be sumptuous and filling; still, you leave the restaurant unfulfilled. Though your need for food has been satisfactorily extinguished, your instinctive culinary desire has not.

There must be a myriad biological and psychological reasons why our appetites are so fickle. But there is only one explanation for B's need to confront A. It is the natural human instinct of retributive justice. Retributive justice gives some direction to the feelings of anger, pain, embarrassment, frustration, envy and disappointment we feel when we are treated unfairly or otherwise wrongfully. It points the finger of blame at some wrongdoer who, we believe, has caused us to experience such suffering. This is important to any system of justice, because it is something no other form of justice can do quite as well.

The Nature of Retribution

If retributive justice is thus an instinct directed at another, we still need to know what that instinct is, when it arises, who specifically it operates against and what function it may have in a formalized legal system. The first question need not long detain us. Retribution is a type of recompense for a wrongful act. It should be emphasized that the focus of this instinct is on the act, not necessarily on the consequences it produces.[2] This is an important distinction because it helps distinguish the idea of corrective justice, which requires also that the act inflict some sort of loss upon another.

The Unfairness and Humanitarian Views

Answering the second question—when is the retributive instinct triggered?—is more difficult. It is clear that it derives from some sense of "wrongfulness." But there is no clear consensus as to what this term means. Herbert Morris has argued that conduct is wrongful, and is thus subject to retribution, if it violates the duty of mutual restriction referred to earlier.[3] Under this view, which I shall define as the "unfairness" interpretation of retribution, recompense is sought against the actor because he has acted unfairly, enjoying the benefits of disobeying the rules without paying the costs endured by all others.[4] Jean Hampton, on the other hand, has contended that wrongfulness is an affront to another's value or dignity.[5] Under this interpretation, which I shall call the "humanitarian" view, the retributive instinct derives from the disrespect the actor shows for the moral worth of the victim.[6]

The Affinity of the Approaches

At first glance, it seems to matter which interpretation we choose. The unfairness approach offers a broad vision of retributive justice. It would justify a retributive response to any illegal activity, regardless of its moral quality. The humanitarian view, on the other hand, appears to advocate a more modest role for retribution in a system of justice. It would not apply to all illegal acts, only those in which the wrongdoer has diminished the humanity of the victim. Yet, upon considering all the activities that might fall into this category, it is clear that the humanitarian view is not as restrictive as one might think. Indeed, there are a great many acts of disrespect—

like shouting obscenities, cutting into a supermarket line or talking over another who is speaking—which are not prohibited by law. Inasmuch as the humanitarian view can be read to apply to these pervasive forms of misconduct, it may be every bit as expansive as that held by the unfairness school.

"Fault-Based" Conduct

The similarity between the two approaches may not be limited to their scope. As a practical matter, many of the acts deemed wrongful under the humanitarian view also will seem manifestly unfair. Intentional and reckless acts, for example, not only evince a disregard for the moral worth of others jeopardized by such conduct, they also display a flagrant disregard for the injunctive prerogative of the law. Even careless conduct may demonstrate the kind of indifference for others that incites both legal *and* moral condemnation.

Strict Liability Activities

These approaches may appear to diverge in their assessment of strict liability activities. Such activities, while not prohibited and sometimes not even regulated, are "restricted" by secondary rights of correction. That is, the party engaged in the activity is privileged to proceed only if she is willing to pay for the harm she may impose upon others. Where she fails to do so, her omission is clearly unfair. She enjoys the benefit of imposing unacceptable risks upon others without bearing any of the burden of her activity. But is conduct of this sort morally reprehensible or inhumane? In many cases, the subject activity is both personally fulfilling and socially desirable. Upon closer examination, however, we see that even such "permissible" conduct may have moral overtones. When one participates in a strict liability activity, she often makes a deliberate choice to inflict certain injury upon a large, though unidentified, group of victims. Here, the voluntary nature of this decision renders it vulnerable to moral attack. Even without this voluntary aspect, however, conduct which exceeds a community's tolerance of risk, and causes harm in the process, is wrongful in the sense that it subordinates the community's interests to the grasping will of the actor.

The Relativity of Retribution

Perhaps the surest likeness between these theories is their relativity. Under each, the retributive instinct is not absolute, but will intensify and diminish with different types of behavior. As was noted earlier, the most powerful retributive inclination will be directed toward intentionally wrongful behavior. Besides unfairly repudiating the duty of mutuality, such conduct, we have seen, is unjust in the broad sense of being wicked. At the opposite end of the spectrum are activities involving simple carelessness and those subject to strict liability. These may or may not be unfair or morally blameworthy, depending upon the actor's knowledge or state of mind. If they invite any indignation, it is in a sense far different, and far less severe, than that engendered by intentional acts.

Private and Political Applications

These similarities aside, there is one critical distinction between the two views which may obviate the need for comparison. Each appears to apply to a different aspect of retributive justice. Recall that in any political association there are two primary levels of justice—private justice between interacting individuals and the political justice of the individuals' relationship with their government. This is the starting point for our consideration of the third question posed—against whom is the retributive instinct directed?

Private Justice and the Humanitarian View

The humanitarian interpretation seems to better describe the sense of private justice we employ in our relationships with other individuals. When we are shown disrespect by another, it ignites the retributive instinct inside us, regardless of the legality of the action. Intuitively, we desire both to restore our dignity and to deflate the asserted superiority of our tormentor.[7]

In a natural setting, we would satisfy this instinct by doing something "bad" to the actor ourselves or, if we were not strong enough, with the help of some of our friends. However, in a political setting we are not afforded this latitude. The state prescribes the legitimate means for our exercise of this retributive instinct. If we want retribution, we must get it through the courts. In this way, the judicial system serves the ends of private justice. It allows us to receive the cathartic release of doing something "bad" to our wrongdoer, albeit in a controlled manner with strict limitations.

Thus, the mere fact that the courts are accessible to all serves to temper our private retributive instinct. However, it seldom is sufficient to satisfy that urge completely. To restore the equality between the wrongdoer and the wronged, private retributive justice seems to require that the wronged party be able to hold the wrongdoer responsible for her actions. There must be some gesture which shows that the victim is human, and thus entitled to a minimum of respect, and that the actor is no more than human, and thus not entitled to subjugate others. This is a bilateral adjustment which can only be effected by and between the parties concerned.

One way of accomplishing this objective is to force the wrongdoer to give something of value to the victim.[8] In ancient Greece, we have seen, the wrongdoer presented gifts to the family of a decedent or made "humble submission."[9] In our civil judicial system, the wrongdoer usually must pay compensation to the victim for the loss she has sustained. This remedy has two consequences. It provides a symbolic gesture of the restoration of the moral equality between the parties. In turn, it helps to disgorge from the wrongdoer any gain from her act, and rectify any harm sustained by the victim.[10]

Public Justice and the Unfairness View

Still, there are some moral indignities for which there is no formal remedy. How is it that a society can tolerate such indignities without affording some measure of private retributive justice? The answer is two-fold. One reason is that few if any acts of serious moral disrespect will escape the prohibitive command of the law. Because acts which are intentionally harmful to others threaten the rule of law, and thus the very basis for social living, they are routinely subject to criminal prohibitions. Other acts which evince a serious disregard for human life will also have a direct or at least indirect effect upon the autonomy interests of others, thus subjecting them to civil regulation or restriction. Of those indignities excluded by the law, few are likely to inspire a strong retributive reaction. Thus, they are unlikely to incite breaches of the peace against others, or outright rebellion against the state itself.

This might not be true, however, if the state failed to address wrongful behavior fairly and effectively. Indeed, the other reason why a certain amount of moral disrespect may be socially acceptable is that usually everyone enjoys the same benefits and burdens of the rules. So long as the law secures the respect necessary to protect basic autonomy interests, it should make no difference which immoral acts are permitted and which are prohibited. If someone ridicules or embarrasses me, I may not have legal redress against her, but I do have the same private retributive right under the law to return the insult.

Once my victimizer crosses the line and violates the law, however, I may not do the same. In this case, the wrongdoer has enjoyed the benefit of acting in a way that I may not, and she has freed herself of a societal restriction to which I am still bound. As Morris postulates, the unfairness of this state of affairs may evoke my retributive response. The question is, against whom is this response going to be directed? In a social system where wrong-doers are routinely caught and punished, they have received little real ben-efit from flaunting the rules in the first instance. Thus, it is unlikely that others would envy the wrongdoers' brief moment of rebellion. Where, how-ever, the state is ineffective in capturing and punishing wrongdoers, others may feel some resentment toward the free rider who has beaten the sys-tem. More likely, they will resent the system for failing to treat all citizens equally.

This is the sense in which the "unfairness" interpretation of retribution has validity. It is not a matter of private justice between those who obey the rules and those who do not; instead, it is a matter of political justice between law-abiding citizens and their government. Any government which fails to afford its citizens a modicum of private retributive justice may itself become the object of a violent retributive response.[11] The recent riots in Los Angeles, sparked by a felt inequality of retributive justice, is powerful evidence of this fact.

Retribution's Role in a Scheme of Justice

From the foregoing discussion, we now have the means to answer the final question of retributive justice: What function is it to serve in a mod-ern legal system? The most common response is that it is to punish wrong-doers. We have seen, however, that it does much more than that. In its private aspects, it also helps to explain the face-to-face, bilateral format of modern civil litigation, and to justify, along with corrective justice, the preeminent status accorded to the concept of causal responsibility. In its moral sense, it serves to promote the basic respect for others necessary to secure rights to autonomy. Apart from these functions, it plays an essen-tial part in holding together the fabric of our social quilt. By permitting the state to punish wrongdoers, it cultivates a healthy respect for the law which makes social living possible. Perhaps more importantly, by estab-lishing the threat of civil disobedience, it provides a formidable incentive for the state to be ever vigilant in its pursuit of justice.

Assembling the Pieces

This brings us to the end of our general survey of justice. As we have seen, this concept, although familiar to us all, is both more complicated and multifaceted than first appears. While its many aspects alone are instructive for their moral insights, together they form a normative paradigm for all laws to emulate. In the next three Parts of this book, we will examine the law of torts to see how well it fits this model. Before doing so, however, let's take a last look at how the many pieces of justice combine to comprise our standard of evaluation.

In a political association, justice operates on two levels: one private, the other public. In the private realm, justice causes us to evaluate our relationships with others; in the public sphere, it helps us assess our relationship with our government. In each case, it demands that our most basic autonomy rights be respected by those with whom we interact. As we saw, there are two senses in which such respect is owed: in a general sense of refraining from wicked conduct, and in the particular sense of treating others fairly. With regard to the latter connotation, distributive justice ensures the fairness of duties imposed upon us by the state, while reciprocity ensures the fairness of duties voluntarily created and exchanged by private parties. When such duties are violated, corrective justice requires that the wrong be fairly redressed; retribution, on the other hand, requires punishment for the wrongdoer.

When all of these aspects of justice are assembled, we have the framework for evaluating our laws and the manner in which we apply and enforce them. The most important question for any political society is whether the state secures for its citizens the autonomy necessary to pursue a virtuous life plan. If the state fails in this regard, by deliberately denying this essential right, then it is wicked in the broad sense and deserves no obedience from its members.[12] If, however, the state through law protects the autonomy of its citizens, the next question is whether these protections have been fairly distributed among individuals within the association.[13]

Distributive justice serves this end. It requires that each citizen be afforded a proportional equality of material and abstract entitlements. The distribution of abstract entitlements contains two important components: a right to autonomy and a responsibility not to exercise that autonomy in a way that interferes with the same right in others. This right bestows upon each individual the opportunity to possess, use or transfer her abstract and material resources as she sees fit. Where the distribution of such rights and responsibilities is not founded on some acceptable criteria, both the deficient laws and their creator are unjust in the particular sense of being unfair.

Of course, individuals may restrict their own autonomy by assuming special duties in private transactions. Under the concept of reciprocity, such exchanges or transfers must be fair, reflecting an approximate equivalency of value. If a transfer lacks reciprocity, or if consent is not obtained, the autonomy of the unwitting party is violated and a harm is sustained.

The party inflicting the harm, in turn, has violated her social responsibility and so has committed a unjust act. It may be unjust either in the broad sense of being intentionally wicked, or in the particular sense of securing an unfair advantage for the actor.

In any event, the concept of corrective justice requires rectification of the wrong. In a political association, this task is assumed by the state. Rectification must be performed by a judge or neutral arbiter who is entrusted to restore the preexisting balance between the parties. This is done by removing the wrongdoer's gain and repairing the proportional loss to the person wronged. Both corrective and retributive justice demand that this adjustment be made only by the wrongdoer, who stands uniquely positioned to restore the equality between the parties. If justice in any of these forms is denied, the social aspect of retributive justice may justify forcing the system to change, or eliminating it altogether.

Part III

Justice in the Structure of Tort Law

In the last two Parts, we have explored the many forms of justice. In this Part, and the two that follow, we shall examine how these concepts apply in a tort case. As we shall see, the justice of tort law is not limited to compensating injured victims; instead, it permeates the entire litigation process—from the formal mechanisms used to process such disputes to the substantive principles used to resolve them.

A tort is a civil wrong which arises from a transaction and/or relation. Typically, tortious encounters are involuntary—one party impairs an interest of another without her consent. However, there are a great number of cases where all or part of the parties' interaction is voluntary, as where they act in accordance with a contract or special relationship. In these transactions or relationships, the interests exchanged by the parties often lack reciprocity. One party acquires something she does not deserve, and the other is deprived of something she is due. Because of the inequalities created by these encounters, their effects are a matter of private justice between the parties involved.

Private justice requires that the wronged party have an opportunity to settle the score. To accomplish this, the gain and loss of the transaction must be eliminated and the parties returned to the status quo. Effecting this adjustment, we have seen, is the concern of corrective justice. In our legal system, corrective justice is not merely a private matter. It is implemented through the tort litigation process administered by the state. This process makes the dispute also a matter of "public" justice between the parties and the state.

In accordance with the principles of corrective justice, the dispute of the parties is heard by a neutral arbiter—typically, either a jury or a judge—who corrects the inequality by requiring the wrongdoer to pay damages to the victim for losses she incurred in the transaction. Where the offending conduct is extremely culpable, evincing an utter disregard for the autonomy of the victim, a retributive penalty also may be assessed against the wrongdoer.

To recover tort damages, however, it is not enough for the victim to demonstrate that she has suffered some sort of loss. She must prove, in addition, that she possesses a right to compensation from her wrongdoer. This is where tort *law* comes in. Tort law creates the secondary claim-rights which permit such recovery. Here, too, the noble face of justice is evident. Just as tortious *actions* are subject to private justice responses, and the tort litigation *process* is accountable to the demands of corrective justice, tort *law* is susceptible to justice concerns of its own. Justice in the broad sense requires that the doctrines of tort law recognize those rights, mentioned previously, which are morally and politically indispensable to the well-being of all individuals. Justice in the particular sense, especially distributive justice, ensures that such rights are fairly allocated to those exposed to harmful behavior.

These latter aspects of justice will be the central focus of the remainder of this book. That is to say, I will not consider the propriety of the tort *system* generally; instead, I will limit my inquiry to the justice of tort *law* and its implementation in modern tort litigation. The obvious place to begin this investigation is with the structure of tort law itself. Indeed, if the law's foundational pillars are unsound, the doctrinal edifice they support surely is destined to fall. Thus, in this Part, I will examine each of tort law's intrinsic elements—specifically, the notions of wrongdoing, causation and damages—to determine if they can withstand the moral pressure exerted upon them by the concept of justice.

Chapter 11

The Anatomy of a Tort

Rights and Justice Revisited

We saw earlier that our sense of justice derives from the notion of rights. All primary rights—that is, those rights which passively identify protected interests—share a basic tripartite structure.[1] First, someone must be bound by a duty to refrain from impairing a particular interest of another. Second, the interest-holder must be a direct, intended beneficiary of the duty. And finally, the interest itself must be significant enough to warrant invoking the legal machinery of the state to secure it.

This triadic structure serves to balance the autonomy interests of citizens in liberal democratic states. Each individual possesses both the freedom to act (to pursue a life plan), and the freedom to be secure from the harmful acts of others. These interests are inherently antagonistic: every exercise of positive liberty presents risks of harm which threaten the negative liberty interests of those around them, and every assertion of a right to be left alone threatens to restrict the activities of those pursuing their life plans.

The components of a right ensure that neither interest is accorded undue weight over the other. The duty requirement defines the scope of an actor's positive liberty interest; the beneficiary element delimits a discrete class of individuals who may have the power to restrict this interest in certain circumstances; and the significant interest factor determines the extent of that class's negative liberty in being free from the actor's exercise of autonomy.

By balancing these interests, the three-pronged rights analysis noted above facilitates our quest for justice. Justice, we have seen, depends on the interrelated notions of "owing" and "deserving." What one owes to another is a function of her political or moral duties (the first element). One's just desert, on the other hand, is determined by her entitlements. To have an entitlement, one must be the beneficiary of another's duty (element two), and have some meritorious basis for receiving it—in this case, a significant interest worthy of legal protection (element three). Only where these components are present can we determine whether one has received her due.

The Elements of Tort Law

Is tort law faithful to this triadic structure for dispensing rights? One need not look far to find the answer, for it is evident in every tort claim. Although torts come in many varieties,[2] there are certain common features which all tort actions display. As a general rule, all torts are founded on some conduct considered to be wrongful.[3] And in each case, the wrongful conduct has produced some foreseeable (or proximate) consequence that harms a protected interest of another.[4] For our purposes, then, we may say that wrongful conduct, proximate causation and a legally recognized harm are three inherent features of any tort claim.

Each of these elements correlates to one of the essential components of a right. Wrongful conduct is simply the breach of a general duty distributed by the state. Proximate cause and other duty limiters identify the beneficiary of the violated duty, thus establishing the moral bond between the parties. And the damage requirement confirms that the interest invaded is worthy of legal redress. Seen in this way, the elements of a typical tort claim are but a metaphor for what it means to have a right.

Still, this metaphor seems incomplete. It would be sufficient for primary rights which merely declare that the holder's interests are protected by the law. But tort law does not simply identify primary rights; rather, it establishes secondary rights of action, or as they are sometimes known, claim-rights. These rights are more than descriptive. They actually authorize the holder to interfere with the autonomy of some other person. This may be done in two different ways: either by preemptively inhibiting her conduct, or by compelling her to pay damages for the injuries she inflicts. In either case, the holder's secondary right is not activated unless and until a prospective wrongdoer threatens her interests. Once this causal agency is introduced, she may interpose reasonable preemptive measures to defend herself. Or, if the wrongdoer succeeds in causing her harm, she then may exercise her corrective right of redress.

In tort law, this additional requirement is known as factual causation. By activating secondary rights, and identifying the parties against whom they may be asserted, it would appear to have a key role to play in the allocation of claim-rights to victims of tortious wrongs. And in the past it has. Yet, unlike the other three requirements noted above, there is now some question whether factual cause is indispensable to this end. Indeed, in recent years, even parties unable to identify their wrongdoers have been permitted to use their corrective secondary rights to receive compensation for transactionally induced harms. Given this trend, it is necessary to reconsider whether factual cause deserves the premier moral position which it traditionally has held in tort law's scheme of rights.

The purpose of Part III of this book is to take a closer look at each of these structural components of tort law to see how well they satisfy our sense of justice. I shall begin in this chapter by examining the concepts of duty, proximate cause (plus other duty limiters) and damage. Together, these components establish the core of an individual's legally protected right to be free from the harmful acts of others. In Chapters Twelve and Thirteen, I shall consider whether the notion of factual cause is necessary to transform this protection into an affirmative claim-right, or if justice may permit recovery even in its absence.

Wrongfulness and Irresponsibility

"Wrongfulness" in tort law has always been the source of some confusion and consternation. In early trespass actions, liability was imposed against anyone who committed an affirmative act which directly caused harm to another.[5] Although the actor's conduct may have been blameless, it was considered at least wrongful enough to hold the actor legally accountable. This changed, however, around the mid-nineteenth century. In *Brown v. Kendall*,[6] the Massachusetts Supreme Court added the requirement that the actor have acted unreasonably. No longer was the mere infliction of injury sufficient to characterize the act as wrongful; the conduct also must have displayed some degree of culpability. Still, even as the idea of fault was gaining prominence in American tort jurisprudence, there remained a distinct category of actions for which it was not required. Identified by their abnormal or ultrahazardous dangers, these activities were deemed wrongful if they simply caused harm to others.[7]

How can these very different types of conduct all be considered wrongful? Certainly, moral fault is not the key, since past and present versions of tort law have imposed liability without it. Likewise, if the outcome-responsibility of causation were alone sufficient,[8] the requirement of fault or ultrahazardousness would be superfluous. The answer to this enigma is that these activities are all wrongful in the political sense of being irresponsible.

To be irresponsible in the manner I propose, three conditions must be met. First, there must be a duty or responsibility to perform or refrain from performing a particular activity. Second, the responsibility must be just—that is, it must not be unduly restrictive of freedom. Finally, the responsibility must be breached by the act or omission of the party subject to it. If these conditions are met, the offending conduct is wrongful, even if it did not proceed from an evil motive or wanton demeanor.

The Centrality of Duty

Tort law satisfies all three of these conditions. Consider first the notion of duty or responsibility. When one thinks of "duty," ordinarily negligence cases come to mind. There, duty is overtly recognized as a central element of proof. By contrast, this term, and the concept it embraces, rarely finds expression in cases of intentional torts and strict liability. Nevertheless, all tort actions, whether they acknowledge it or not, are premised on the notion of duty or responsibility.

Primary and Secondary Duties

Indeed, tort law contains a veritable plethora of general duties, each with the same purpose: to secure important autonomy interests by imposing upon each individual the responsibility not to harm her neighbor. These duties are of two sorts. One type of duty, which I shall call primary or normative, lays down rules of behavior like those mentioned above. Thus, intentional tort duties command us, among other things, to refrain from touching others in a harmful or offensive manner, or from confining them against their will. On the other hand, negligence duties direct us to act in a reasonable and prudent fashion. And strict liability duties require that we avoid engaging in activities that expose our communities to locally uncommon or unusually egregious risks. When these rules are breached, or it at least appears that they are about to be, tort law often empowers those endangered by the wrongdoer to take appropriate defensive action. In some cases, such a response either is not warranted or is not possible, and harm inevitably ensues. Here, the other type of tort duty comes into play. This secondary or corrective duty permits the state to enforce the primary, normative duty, and restrict the wrongdoer's autonomy, by requiring that she pay compensation to the party wronged.

Although both primary and secondary duties assist in distributing autonomy interests, their workloads are far from equal. Secondary duties have only one job—they enforce primary duties by compelling breachers to pay compensation to those they injure. This function remains the same whether the normative rule violated is one sounding in negligence, strict liability or intentional tort. In each case, transgression of the underlying duty activates the secondary duty to correct the wrong. Primary or normative duties, on the other hand, must supply rules to regulate all forms of human behavior which may be considered socially unacceptable. These duties come in a variety of forms, each specifically tailored to address a particular type of conduct committed under a certain set of circumstances.

Types of Primary or Normative Duties

On a broad level, one can sort such normative standards into two categories. The first group is the one most commonly associated with tort law. It consists of those rules which either restrict certain kinds of potentially harmful activities—like punching another in the nose, driving too fast or exploding dynamite—or require someone to undertake measures to protect another from harm—say, by covering an exposed excavation hole or picking up a banana peel. The other group of primary duties actually enforce special duties created by the parties themselves. Thus, if a landlord promises to repair some loose floorboards in a tenant's apartment, tort law may enforce her express obligation to eliminate this dangerous condition by holding her liable if she fails to do so. For each of these duties, the moral challenge is to ensure that the restrictions imposed are not so onerous that they unduly burden the actor's exercise of autonomy, but yet are not so weak that they fail to protect others from harm.

The Reciprocal Relationship between Duties and Rights

Since transactions are by nature bilateral, duties imposed upon or assumed by one party will necessarily affect her counterpart. Special duties provide the simplest example of this effect. Earlier, I described special duties as those created by the parties themselves either through a promise or undertaking. Where one commits such an act, she agrees to behave in a particular way toward another. This could involve providing some good or service, or merely refraining from interfering with the other's interests. In any event, the promisor assumes certain responsibilities toward others, and forgoes certain freedoms. This responsibility, in turn, inures to the benefit of her relational partner. It gives the latter the exclusive power to control or restrict the autonomy of the promisor in the designated way, a privilege she would not otherwise enjoy. In many cases, it also induces the promisee to rely in a way that impairs her autonomy, as by committing to some future action or by foregoing other opportunities.

The bilateral effect of general duties is much more complicated. While special duties arise from consensual transactions, general duties usually do not. Here, the state must determine for the parties how much freedom and responsibility each will receive. As a general rule, the party initiating the interaction possesses some measure of autonomy necessary to pursue her life plan; however, she also bears the general responsibility not to harm others. The recipient of such action, on the other hand, possesses some responsibility to protect herself[9] (or at least to not exacerbate her injury),[10] and the autonomy to be free from the harmful acts of others.

As we observed previously, for each individual engaged in a risk-bearing activity, autonomy and responsibility are inversely proportional. So as an actor's responsibility increases (on the basis of some justified distributive criterion), she loses the freedom to act in the prohibited, regulated or restricted way. For example, a property owner generally owes a greater duty of care to invitees than she does to trespassers. Regarding the trespasser, she may use or maintain her property however she likes so long as she does not willfully or wantonly harm her uninvited guest.[11] Her freedom of action is greatly diminished, however, where an invitee is involved. For this entrant, she must act or refrain from acting in a variety of ways—from fixing potentially dangerous conditions (as by salting an icy walkway) to discontinuing hazardous activities (like spraying pesticides)—or risk having to pay damages in a tort suit.[12] The greater the number of these additions to the property owner's obligations, the more serious the corresponding reduction in her autonomy will be.

Such is the predicament of all risk-creators. But what about their relational opposites—i.e., those parties who are exposed to danger? Are their rights and responsibilities subject to the same see-saw effect? It appears that they are. While ordinarily individuals enjoy the right to be left alone, this freedom is diminished, if not extinguished, when one agrees to interact with others. Back in Chapter Four, we saw that a party who consents, by word or deed, to endure the consequences of another's action is herself causally responsible for the resulting encounter. So it was with our tattoo recipient. Once she decided to subject herself to the procedure, she assumed full responsibility for the painful pricking that would follow. In so doing, she also gave up the right to keep her bodily integrity, including her skin, free from the intrusive needle of the tattooist.[13] Thus, even for such risk-receivers, responsibility and autonomy ebb and flow with a reciprocal fluidity.

We see, then, that both risk-creators *and* risk-receivers bear a complement of rights and duties. When individuals transact, so that a specific risk-creator engages a particular risk-receiver, each party's cluster of rights and responsibilities becomes linked to the other. This linkage, in turn, creates a reciprocal relationship between them. Thus, if the actor's responsibility is increased, and her freedom to act is thereby diminished, the responsibility of the recipient to protect herself is usually lowered, and her right to be free from the acts of the other is enhanced.[14] For example, in the case of the property owner discussed above, an inverse correlation develops between her rights and duties and those of the individuals who come upon her land. Because the duty of a property owner to a trespasser is negligible at best, the trespasser is under a greater responsibility to look out for herself. Conversely, since invitees are owed the highest duty possible, they are permitted to exercise less care for their own safety than their uninvited counterparts.

While the risk-creator's conduct often determines how such inverse reciprocal responsibilities are allocated, this is not always the case. In certain situations, the actions or status of the risk-receiver drive this determination. If the risk-receiver is aware or should have been aware of an obvious hazard created by another, or if she possesses greater knowledge, skill or training than the average individual, then she may be held to a heightened responsibility to prevent her own injury, even if the risk-creator ordinarily would have been duty-bound to protect her from harm. In such a case, the risk-receiver's expanded duty reduces her own right of protection and, concomitantly, diminishes or even extinguishes the risk-creator's duty of care. So if a homeowner jumps head first into three feet of water contained in an above-ground swimming pool, her decision to encounter this obvious hazard both enhances her own duty of self-protection and alleviates the pool manufacturer's responsibilities as a product seller.[15] Likewise, an experienced industrial worker who operates a hand drill near a leaking natural gas line (knowing of the risk of an explosion) is expected, by virtue of her expertise, to exercise greater caution than a novice. The more she is required to look after herself, the less others—including the manufacturer of the drill and the owner of the natural gas line—are expected to act as her caretakers.[16]

Duties and Distributive Justice

In a perfect world, where all parties are equal in ability, resources are abundant, and everyone is respectful of the rights of others (by not engaging in activities likely to harm others), everyone would share the same equal distribution of responsibility and autonomy. However, in our imperfect world, where parties lack equal economic and political power, where resources are restricted or scarce, and where some have the inclination and means to engage in acts potentially harmful to others, there is a need to protect some individuals more or less than others. Thus, where parties interact, and one is harmed, the state may impose upon the actor a greater or lesser responsibility than the recipient, or others in society who perform activities of a different sort.

The duties of tort law demonstrate this relativity. As shall be discussed later on,[17] tort law assigns different levels of responsibility to individuals depending upon the circumstances. What is permissible for a child often is not appropriate for an adult. And what an ordinary adult may do, one with greater skill, knowledge and training sometimes may not. Where the subject matter of a transaction is vital to human welfare, we find greater restrictions on its performance than when it is merely a luxury. Finally, greater care must be exercised in the performance of some high-risk activities, like transporting highly combustible chemicals, than is demanded for less dangerous endeavors.

As "unequal" as these allocations of responsibility may seem, they are not unjust. Distributive justice does not require that all individuals be treated the same, only that there be some good reason for treating them differently. In other words, distributions may be quantitatively unequal so long as they are made in accordance with an accepted proportion. Such a proportion, in turn, must be founded on criteria deemed just by the society in which they are to be applied.

Distributive Criteria and Tort Duties

Earlier, we identified at least three such general criteria. Recall that they all share the common purpose of securing a minimum degree of autonomy for all citizens, thus making political association seem preferable to taking one's chances in a state of nature. One criterion, that of merit, generally affords greater liberties to those who use their autonomy for constructive purposes. The need criterion, on the other hand, protects those who are unable to protect themselves. It does this in a couple of ways. Where a transaction concerns a necessity, you will recall, the state heightens the autonomy of the party in need by facilitating her abilitiy to acquire it. Here, not only are the welfare interests of the needy party at stake, the indispensability of the good deprives her of meaningful choice in the transaction. For similar reasons, greater freedom is extended to parties suffering from internal or external incapacities. Because the incapacitated party lacks the volition to consent to the interaction, any injurious consequences of that encounter are wrongful. The final criterion, that of risk, also helps to safeguard the unwary, but it does so in a different way. Instead of enhancing the rights of those in need of protection, it limits the freedom of those engaged in risky activities in accordance with the degree of danger they impose upon others.

These criteria, especially need and risk, lie at the heart of almost all tort duties. I hope to demonstrate this in the next Part, where I shall examine the justice of tort law's various theoretical bases of liability. For now, however, it is enough to recognize the interrelationship between tort law and distributive justice. By premising duties on criteria considered to be fair, tort law satisfies the second condition mentioned above. That is, it ensures that tort rules, and the distribution of autonomy they effect, are fair and therefore just. It also explains why the state, through its courts, is authorized to create these rules and impose them on its citizens.

Distributive Duties and Wrongdoing

Now we can understand how, under the third condition listed above, acts which violate these distributive duties may be wrongful. Laws that are just are entitled to respect.[18] Only by respecting law may we lift ourselves above the depravity of our natural state. Any act which violates a distributive responsibility founded on fair criteria, therefore, is repugnant to political association. And if it is politically condemnable, it also is unjust. For as Aristotle observed, since just laws are created for the good of all individuals, any unlawful act is an act of injustice towards others.[19]

It follows that any tortious act is unjust, and thus wrongful, if it violates a properly promulgated distributive duty. Where an actor breaches a responsibility intentionally or with knowledge of the likely consequences, the act is unjust in the broad sense because it evinces a basic disrespect for human life and directly repudiates the most fundamental condition of political association. Still, conduct need not be so flagrantly blameworthy to be wrongful. Where a distributive duty is violated, even negligently or innocently, the actor exercises more autonomy than is permitted of others who have remained faithful to its mandate. In this case, the action may not be wicked, but it is unjust nevertheless in the particular sense of being unfair.

Duty Limiters, Proximate Cause and Beneficiary Status

To establish a right, it is not enough that the aggrieved party sustain harm from an action which violates a general or special duty. It also must be shown that she was an intended beneficiary of the applicable duty. The beneficiary status of the claimant establishes her unique entitlement to affect the actions of the duty-holder, and thus links the parties in a special relationship.

Tort law contains a similar requirement. One seeking redress for the harmful effects of a transaction may not prevail simply by showing that the alleged perpetrator acted wrongfully. She must also show that the action was wrongful as to her.[20] To meet this burden, it must appear that she was owed a duty not to be subjected to the injury-producing conduct. In essence, the claimant must be one of a class of individuals who were to enjoy the benefits of the duty's protection. Where this connection is established, the claimant possesses a distinctive power to sanction the perpetrator's exercise of autonomy by forcing her to pay compensation for the harm it has caused.

Devices Limiting Tort Duties

The duties of tort law originate from many different sources. Special duties, it will be recalled, are created by the parties themselves. General duties, which are imposed by the state, may be promulgated either by the legislature through statutes, or by the judiciary through common law doctrines. Regardless of how such duties arise, all are subject to the limiting principle described above.

Privity

The doctrine of privity has long served as an effective tool in limiting the scope of special duties. Ordinarily, where two parties exchange special duties by contract, the beneficiaries are clearly delimited. The promisor agrees to assume a responsibility to benefit the promisee in return for the promisee's commitment to undertake some duty towards the promisor. Here, the promisor and promisee are in privity of contract. Under the privity doctrine, only the parties to the transaction are considered beneficiaries of the special duties created between them. No others enjoy the benefit of this protection, even if they are directly affected by the contract's performance.

For example, in the famous case of *Winterbottom v. Wright*,[21] the United States Postmaster General contracted with Wright to service several mail coaches. As a result of Wright's negligence, Winterbottom, an employee of the Post Office, was injured when one of the coaches broke down. The court there held that, under the privity limitation, Wright's duty to repair the coach was not owed to Winterbottom, only to the Postmaster General.[22] Winterbottom, in short, was not a direct beneficiary of the repair contract, and thus had no right to sue for its defective performance.

Since the time of *Winterbottom*, the privity concept has undergone substantial erosion.[23] Still, its vestiges are visible in the law of torts. It may preclude recovery for a breach of warranty where only economic damages have been sustained.[24] It continues to limit the liability of utilities whose negligence threatens a broad group of consumers.[25] In malpractice cases, too, it often precludes recovery to those outside the professional relationship.[26] Even where the privity doctrine has been abandoned, the limiting principle it embodies lives on. Often it is replaced with other doctrines, to be discussed below, which effect the same circumscription of responsibility, but with less precision.[27]

Statutory Limitations

Where the duty is supplied by statute, the search for direct beneficiaries of the enactment is overt. Statutes are not ordinarily drafted for the purpose of resolving transactional disputes. Most are prohibitive rather than corrective. Thus, it often is unclear whether and to what extent such legislative directives may apply to civil proceedings. To clarify this uncertainty, courts routinely examine the statute and its legislative history to determine who it was meant to benefit. Only if a claimant falls within the class of individuals the statute was designed to protect will she be permitted to invoke it as a duty of care.[28] A claimant who satisfies this test is a beneficiary of the statute and so is entitled to sue for its violation.

Proximate Cause

Finally, if the duty imposed upon the wrongdoer arises from the common law, the concept of proximate cause serves to restrict its application. Proximate cause is premised on the idea that in modern political associations, where lives are so interconnected, one act may have vast repercussions.[29] Indeed, even the most trivial indiscretion can produce nearly endless consequences. Take the case of careless driving which results in a run-of-the-mill traffic accident. If this act causes injury to another motorist, it also surely will affect that person's family. It probably will affect her employer and her friends as well. It may even affect the witnesses to the collision and their family and friends. In fact, all those trapped in their cars during the ensuing traffic jam will have been touched by this single act.

The limiting principle of proximate cause determines which of these effects the actor may be legally accountable for. This happens in one of two ways. One way is to trace the connection between the act of the alleged wrongdoer and the resulting injury.[30] If the injury is a direct and natural outgrowth of the action, it is proximate, and the aggrieved party is a beneficiary of the wrongdoer's duty to refrain from inflicting harm. If, however, the connection between the act and injury is remote, separated by time, space or the intervening actions of others, the wrongdoer owes no responsibility to protect the aggrieved party from the effects of her actions.

Alternatively, the duty may be limited by the notion of foreseeability. Here, the critical question is whether the harm caused by the actor was one of the foreseeable risks of her conduct.[31] The list of foreseeable risks delineates a "zone of danger" for which the actor is responsible. Those whose harm falls within this zone of foreseeable risks are beneficiaries of the actor's duty. Those outside this protective realm, however, are not.

By placing parameters on the general duties of tort law, each of these concepts helps to define the specific class of individuals for whom these responsibilities are conceived. In so doing, they operate to secure the precarious balance of positive and negative liberty vital to the well-being of individuals and political associations alike. Indeed, without such limiting

principles, prospective actors would be paralyzed by the specter of catastrophic liabilities for seemingly trivial gaffs; and the claims they elicit
would inundate a justice system already taxed beyond its means of redressing more serious wrongs.

Damage and Autonomy

Such fears no doubt also account for the final element of our trilogy.
Every human endeavor poses risks. And every human transaction affects
someone's interests. Were we to provide redress for every interest invasion, resulting from any type of conduct, we could not maintain a formal
system of justice. We simply do not have the resources necessary for such
a mammoth task. Accordingly, we must be more discriminating in the
manner in which we create rights. This is why a right will not exist unless
the interest affected is significant enough to warrant invoking the legal
machinery of the state to protect it.

Tort rights contain the same requirement. Every tort requires that the
claimant show that she has sustained some sort of harm. There is no set
list of injuries which are deemed substantial. Nevertheless, some injuries
are unquestionably compensable. All torts permit recovery for physical
damage, including bodily injury and loss to property. Many jurisdictions
now allow compensation for psychological harm, even when unaccompanied by physical injury.[32] Other torts redress loss of reputation,[33] loss
of business opportunities[34] and reliance costs.[35] There are also several torts
which require no "actual" loss. These are actionable if the claimant has
suffered some consequence which the law presumes to be injurious. For
example, an assault need not frighten the victim to cause her harm.[36] Nor
is it necessary that a libelous remark be shown to have damaged the reputation of its subject.[37] In either case, the mere commission of the act is
sufficient to sustain a cause of action.

The Essence of Damage

What is the base value which makes each of these harms compensable?
There are several different criteria by which interests may be judged significant, depending upon the society creating the right. In communities
where honor is a paramount value, freedom from embarrassment or humiliation may be an interest worthy of protection. In other civilizations, where
goods are scarce, efficiency may be an important social objective. Here,
there would be a strong interest in discouraging wasteful behavior.

The Deontological View

One view of tort law is that it is concerned with repairing moral injuries or "dignitary" harms.[38] The idea here is that all individuals, because of their humanity, have an interest in being treated decently by others. Presumably, this interest would entitle everyone not only to be left alone when so desired, but also to be treated with respect in all social encounters. In short, it suggests that tort law is founded on some deontological base value, the primary object of which is to enforce general principles of morality.

This view, however, finds little support in the law, and much to undermine it. Unlike public law,[39] private law theories such as tort and contract have never embraced a uniform standard of moral virtue.[40] In tort law, the two most prominent illustrations of this fact are the good samaritan doctrine and the doctrine of intentional infliction of emotional distress. Under the good samaritan doctrine, a bystander is under no obligation to aid an individual in distress absent a special relationship.[41] Thus, although the virtues of altruism and benevolence might impose a moral duty to act, at least where assistance could be rendered without great personal risk, the law has not endorsed the same responsibility. Likewise, under the theory of intentional infliction of emotional distress, actors whose affirmative conduct clearly manifests a lack of respect for others may escape the prohibitive ambit of tort law. Insulting or threatening remarks are not actionable, even if intentionally offensive, unless some other interest has been affected.[41] In each case, the standards employed for judging the propriety of tortious interactions display little concern for moral correctness.

The Liberal View

A better explanation for the damage requirement of tort law is that it is premised on the desire to protect individual autonomy. In our culture, we have observed, autonomy is the base value which determines what interests will be accorded the status of a right. This same deference for autonomy interests is reflected in the remedies of tort law.

Autonomy interests take two forms: actual and abstract. Actual autonomy interests are those which support an individual's independence and/or her opportunity for choice. They are tangible for the most part, and their impairment is ordinarily demonstrable. They include essential attributes of autonomy like bodily integrity and property, along with more nebulous interests in freedom of movement, an unblemished reputation, and an expected range of business options. These interests are not always substantial, however. To assess their importance, one must consider the extent to which they have been impaired. In some cases, the invasion of an actual autonomy interest may be so inconsequential, or so avoidable by the holder, that it requires no legal redress.

Abstract autonomy interests, on the other hand, are always protected from encroachment, and their infringement is always significant. They are not tangible, but ideal—embracing the positive liberty to act as one chooses, and the negative liberty to be free from the harmful advances of others. Such interests may be violated only by voluntary actions, for only these evince the contempt indicative of repudiation. Where this contempt is shown, the harm is both moral and political, since it undermines the freedom essential for association and fulfillment.

Each of these types of autonomy interests finds protection in tort law. As was noted earlier, physical injury, mental distress, reliance and reputation costs, economic damage and even loss of privacy all impair the victim's independence and/or freedom of choice. Each is a form of actual loss which, if appreciable, justifies holding the actor accountable. No less significant is the harm which follows from acts intended to injure. Here, the autonomy restriction does not have to be actual, like those above, but may be abstract. It consists of a direct rejection of the ideal of equal freedom for all. Insofar as such harm threatens the victims' rights as a moral and political agent, the harm is dignitary. Yet it satisfies this definition in a way far narrower than supposed by the deontological view. It is immoral only in the sense that it repudiates the victim's abstract entitlement to autonomy.

Chapter 12

The Question of Factual Cause

While duty, beneficiary status and harm are important features of tort law, they alone are not sufficient to state *any* tort claim. In addition to these elements, one must also prove factual causation. Factual cause has been a prerequisite to bringing a tort action since the inception of the common law. In fact, during this formative period, causation was practically all that the plaintiff had to prove in order to recover.[1] Under the early trespass form of action, it will be recalled, any individual whose affirmative act directly caused injury to another was liable even if his conduct was in no way culpable. Yet despite the prominence of causation in these early cases, its use seemed more intuitive than calculated. Medieval opinions made little attempt to explain what factual causation meant or why it was important to establishing the defendant's liability. Because of this silence, the legal concept of causation has always been shrouded by a cloud of ambiguity.

To pierce this foggy veil, a multitude of descriptions and definitions have been proposed over the years by jurists and legal scholars alike. For example, many jurisdictions have employed a "but for" or sine qua non test for factual causation. According to this definition, an action or condition is a cause of an event if the event could not have happened without it.[2] Richard Wright, H.L.A. Hart and Tony Honoré have taken this test one step further. In what has been called the "NESS" test, an action is not a cause unless it is a necessary element in a set of actual conditions which were sufficient to bring about the resulting occurrence.[3] Troubled by the all-or-nothing approach of such tests, the drafters of the Restatement (Second) of Torts offered yet another definition of legal cause. According to section 431 of the Restatement, a condition is a legal cause when it is a substantial factor in producing harm to another.[4] Arno Becht and Frank Miller were not satisfied by these or any other explanations. Echoing the exasperation of many in the tort field, they have concluded that causation is an indefinable concept that is understandable only through common sense and experience.[5]

Needless to say, the inscrutability of this concept has made it less than endearing. It has become like an acquaintance who never speaks, withholding from all others her most personal thoughts and emotions. After a while, the effort of getting to know this silent stranger becomes more trouble than it is worth, and whatever fidelity is felt toward her soon disappears. So it is with factual causation. Within the last few decades, those disaffected with this concept have given it the cold shoulder. In a variety of contexts, the factual causation requirement now is either lightly brushed aside or completely disregarded. The doctrine of *Ybarra v. Spangard*,[6] the lost chance doctrine,[7] actions for increased risks[8] and medical monitoring,[9] and the theories of alternative,[10] enterprise,[11] and market share liability[12] are all indicative of this trend. Under some of these approaches, the injured party cannot demonstrate that the conduct of the defendant caused her any actual harm; in others, she is unable to identify the causal agent who produced her loss. Either way, the burden of the loss is lifted from the victim and allocated to others whose causal responsibility is at best conjectural.

Such loss shifting measures may be good or bad. If they rid the law of useless historical baggage, and by so doing perpetuate more equitable results in tort cases, then they are undoubtedly good. If, on the other hand, they strip tort law of its moral backbone, thus depriving it of any legitimacy, then they certainly are bad. Because we do not yet understand the concept of causation and its role in resolving tort disputes, we currently have no way of knowing which fate the law faces. Under these circumstances, any further erosion of the causation requirement would be foolhardy if not socially dangerous. Before continuing this trend, therefore, we must fill the epistemological void that deprives us of sound judgment. To do this, we must confront, and hopefully answer, three critical questions: 1) What is factual causation, at least as applied in tort law, and under what circumstances will it be found to exist?; 2) Does factual causation help to further the end of justice in tort law, and if so, in what way?; and 3) If it does serve this end, is it a necessary part of justice in tort law? These questions will form the basis of our discussion in the next two chapters. I shall begin in this chapter by attempting to determine the true nature of factual cause.[13]

Definitional Ambiguity

Part of the problem in defining factual causation is that the general concept of cause and effect appears in so many other contexts where it possesses different meanings and uses. There are medical causes, scientific causes, sociological causes, economic causes and philosophical causes, among many others. This definitional uncertainty presents two problems for our legal system. One is that the term says too much. Because most people are familiar with the concept, they have preconceived ideas about its meaning. These preconceptions, which often conflict with our legal definitions of causation, become ingrained in our psyches and are difficult to alter or overcome. But as bad as this problem is, the other definitional problem is worse. Rather than saying too much, the term "causation" may actually say too little. It seems incapable of describing adequately most of the juridical relationships which are the subject of contemporary tort cases.

Misfeasance and Nonfeasance

In general, tortious conduct may be characterized as either misfeasance or nonfeasance. Misfeasance is a direct, affirmative act, while nonfeasance is a failure to act. An act of misfeasance alone may produce a harm, or it may operate in conjunction with many other forces.[14] Because nonfeasance is a passive state, it alone cannot produce harm; rather, it can only prove injurious if it creates a condition which allows one or more other causal agencies to intervene.

Sine Qua Non and Simple Misfeasance

The idea of causation may explain how a single act of misfeasance may be related to a tortious injury. In such a case, the "but for" or sine qua non test previously referred to allows us to see the connection between the two. Take, for example, a routine traffic accident where a speeding motorist strikes a pedestrian in a crosswalk. Here, it is easy to recognize the relationship between the action of the motorist and the harm it has produced. We can perceive the event, seeing and hearing the auto make contact with the victim's leg. From common experience, we can judge the impact which the motorist's excessive speed must have had upon her ability to stop the car or take evasive action, and on the pedestrian's ability to jump out of the way. Scientifically, we can reconstruct how the bones of the victim gave way from the force of the car's bumper. In this type of case, the idea of causation is reasonably clear. If the pedestrian would not have been injured without the driver's negligence, as would appear, than we can say that the driver's conduct caused the resulting harm. Here, the sine qua non test proves to be an effective device for pointing the finger of blame at the motorist.

The Problem of Nonfeasance

There are many other tort cases, however, where the sine qua non version of causation is neither so clear nor so efficacious. Few tort actions today are founded on purely affirmative conduct which directly brings about harm to another. On the contrary, many if not most such actions are based on someone's nonfeasance, or failure to act. Consider the police agency which fails to respond to a domestic violence call. Or the landlord who fails to provide adequate security for her tenants. Or the business invitor who fails to inspect for and correct dangerous conditions on her premises. In all of these cases, the actor charged with wrongdoing has not, in a traditional sense, "brought about" or "effected" injury to another. Instead, she has failed to take appropriate precautions to protect the injured party from the acts of others, or even from the victim's own misconduct. For these types of cases, the concept of causation seems unequipped to provide any meaningful basis for connecting the injuries to the alleged wrongdoers.

The reason is that the term itself possesses nothing to distinguish one omitter from another. To prove this, consider the previous hypothetical where a negligent driver runs down a helpless pedestrian. For purposes of this discussion, suppose further that there are many individuals in or near the crosswalk as the vehicle approaches, but none take any action to prevent the collision. How do we know which, if any, of these bystanders is a "cause" of the pedestrian's harm? Without knowing more, it would be absurd to find that any of the bystanders caused the collision in the prevailing sense of having brought it about. And what if we *were* to determine that one of these onlookers was a cause? Would not all the onlookers in the vicinity then be causes? Surely such a conclusion would follow from the sine qua non test, since if any had acted to save the pedestrian the collision probably would not have occurred.[15]

Passive Causation and the Duty to Act

To narrow the field of potential tortfeasors, the law must develop some criterion independent of the "but for" concept of causation. There must be a legitimate basis for distinguishing certain omitters from others. Tort law has developed such a criterion. Under current doctrine, one who fails to act may be liable only if she and the victim are conjoined in a "special relationship."[16]

Special Relationships

As we saw earlier, special relationships derive from either undertakings or imbalanced associations. In the case of undertakings, an uncompleted action of one party induces a prospective victim or her potential rescuers to forego opportunities for assistance. By triggering such reliance, the "undertaker" indirectly controls the circumstances which will determine the endangered party's fate. A similar kind of power is exercised by the dominant party in an imbalanced association. You will recall that in such relationships one party is aware of the risk of the parties' association and possesses the wherewithal to control it. The other party, however, lacks these abilities and so is in need of protection. To eliminate this imbalance, the dominant party incurs an obligation to safeguard her charge. The latter, on the other hand, becomes entitled to expect such protective action.

The Overlap between Normative and Causal Responsibility

For both undertakings and imbalanced associations, the omissions of the party in control are "causes" of another's harm only because she possesses a duty to act that most individuals do not. Suppose, in our crosswalk example, that the pedestrian was a child being escorted home by her baby-sitter. Thus, the baby-sitter is among the bystanders in the crosswalk at the time of the collision. Here, the failure of the baby-sitter to protect the child from the oncoming car may be a "cause" of her harm not because her omission in some way effected that result, but because she possessed a special preexisting obligation to take some preventative measures.

In cases of omission, like this, the scope of the omitter's duty defines the extent of her causal responsibility. Obviously, the baby-sitter is not accountable for the child's welfare every minute of every day. There are simply some risks which fall outside the purview of her occupation. For instance, unless she had some advance notice, the sitter would have no obligation to protect the child from an errant bullet fired during a drive-by shooting. Such a duty is excluded from the realm of her responsibilities both because the child's parents do not rely on her for such protection, and because preventing such an occurrence is beyond her power of control. Still, there are some tasks so central to the job of baby-sitting that those engaged in this endeavor are expected and thus obligated to carry them out. The most obvious duty in this regard would be to shield the child from risks which *are* within the sitter's power to repel. This certainly would include making a reasonable effort to ensure the child's safe passage across a major thoroughfare. Such a duty is founded on the assumption that if the baby-sitter takes appropriate action, she is capable of protecting the child from traffic hazards in the area. It follows from this assumption that if the sitter satisfies her duty, the child could never wind up in harm's way.[17] Conversely, should the sitter fail in her undertaking, we must infer that her omission facilitated the very injury she was sworn to prevent. Thus, by allowing the child to enter the danger zone of the crosswalk, the sitter not only breaches her duty of protection, she also automatically establishes her causal responsibility for the mischief that occurs within it.

When viewed in this way, we see that the notion of causation—at least insofar as it applies to omissions—is like an empty balloon. By itself, the balloon has little form or content. If it is to have any definite shape, it must be filled with some substantive matter like air. This air, in turn, must be delivered with a force strong enough to expand the balloon's rubber shell. Usually a compressor is necessary to supply such force. Finally, the amount of air discharged by the compressor must be regulated by an operator who controls the ultimate size of the balloon. Passive causation, like the balloon, is a vacuous vessel with no discernable shape. It has no meaning unless infused with some other substantive concept. As we saw above, risk, like the air in a balloon, is the essential material that makes the causal shell come to life and gives it a definite form. That is, as foreseeable risks increase or decrease, the scope of one's causal responsibility will inflate or deflate as well. Of course, risk in itself is not important; there must be some impelling force which gives it moral significance. Like the air compressor mentioned above, the duty requirement in tort law provides the force necessary to expand the rubbery parameters of one's causal balloon. It does this by defining the types of risks which one must counteract, inflating or deflating the size of this responsibility depending upon the circumstances. This adjustment is not made spontaneously, but by some catalyst which sets the whole process in motion. In the inflation of our balloon, the compressor operator serves this purpose; in defining the breadth of one's duty to act, it is the power of autonomous action which provides this catalytic burst of air. As we saw above, one has a duty to protect others only as against those risks which are within her sphere of influence. Any risks beyond her power of control simply are not her responsibility. From the foregoing, we can say that the potential of one's autonomous action establishes her duty of care; that this duty, in turn, delimits the risks which she is bound to protect others against; and that the scope of these dangers determines her causal responsibility if she fails to control them. With this, our balloon analogy becomes complete. Like the compressor operator, the power to control dangerous conditions is the catalyst which releases the compressive force of duty. This force impels the substantive gas of risk into our vacant causal balloon, thus giving it a definite shape and defining the reach of its flexible boundaries.

The Multiple Sufficient Cause Conundrum

If the concept of sine qua non causation does a poor job of identifying culpable omitters, it does an even worse job of distinguishing between multiple causal agents. One of the best illustrations of this deficiency appears in *Anderson v. Minneapolis, St. P. & S. S. M. Ry. Co.*[18] There, two fires, one sparked by the defendant, the other of unknown origin, combined to burn the plaintiff's property. Either fire alone would have been sufficient to produce this result. Under these circumstances, application of the sine qua non test would compel the rather unjust and counterintuitive conclusion that neither fire starter was casually responsible for the destruction of the plaintiff's structure. Indeed, even if one of the blazes had not been set, the property still would have been burned by the other. Because the defendant's fire was not indispensable to the result, she could not be held liable under the "but for" test of causation. This would mean not only that a culpable party would escape legal sanction, but also that an innocent victim would be afforded no relief for his losses.

Toward the Substantial Factor Test

Recognizing the inequity of such an outcome, the court discarded the sine qua non test in favor of a substantial factor test of causation. Under this test, it was not required that the defendant's negligence have been a necessary element in the destructive formula which consumed the plaintiff's property. Rather, the plaintiff was obligated to show only that the effect of the defendant's fire upon the result was substantial. With little discussion, the court found that the plaintiff had satisfied this burden. Accordingly, the defendant was held liable for the entire loss sustained by the plaintiff in the conflagration.

Although the substantial factor test offered a more palatable solution to the *Anderson* case than its counterpart, it also created some problems of its own. By reducing the plaintiff's conceptual burden from a necessity to a substantial factor, it invited fact finders to apply a lower evidentiary burden to the plaintiff's case in chief, at least on the element of causation. In addition, it rejected the all-or-nothing approach of the "but for" test and offered an alternative view in which causes were indeterminate at best. Finally, and perhaps most importantly, it relied on the vague notion of substantiality which, by itself, lacked any intrinsic meaning.

The Restatement Approach

Nevertheless, following the decision of the *Anderson* case, the drafters of the Restatement (Second) of Torts adopted the "substantial factor" test for determining causation.[19] Despite its deficiencies, this test promised to do what the barren sine qua non view of causation could not—i.e., provide a means for evaluating degrees of causal agency. Using this test, it was hoped that one might make the kind of comparative assessment of causes which would justify distinguishing one from the other. Still, before the "substantial factor" test could be a desirable alternative, the drafters of the Restatement had to ameliorate some of its inherent ambiguity. They attempted to do this by delineating several criteria to be used in its application.[20]

As it turns out, the criteria set out by the Restatement do not really explain what a "substantial factor" is; instead, they provide a comparative basis for selecting from among a group of causal agents the party whose exercise of autonomy has most likely controlled or influenced an outcome. They do this by focusing attention not only on the target wrongdoer, but also on the other human and nonhuman causes which may have contributed to the result.

At least one of these considerations directly examines the action of the target wrongdoer to evaluate the power which she has exerted over a particular event. Specifically, it asks whether the actor has created either "a force which remains in active operation until the time of injury," or "a situation harmless unless acted upon by others."[21] Obviously, affirmative acts of misfeasance represent a clearer expression of one's liberty, and are more likely to have a direct impact on an outcome, than would a decision to remain in a passive state. This same criterion also facilitates a comparative analysis among the target wrongdoer and other possible causal agents. Because acts of misfeasance are direct, they usually preclude outside influences on the result; failures to act, on the other hand, are wrongful simply because they permit some other agent to produce the injurious consequence.

The remaining criteria also help to assess the relative impact which such other causal agents may have had upon an event. In fact, one of these considerations serves this function overtly. It evaluates "the number of other factors contributing to the result and the extent of their effect in producing it."[22] The final consideration does this more subtly, but no less effectively. It examines "the lapse of time" between an act and an injury.[23] This, of course, has no independent significance, but is important only insofar as it suggests that other causal agents may have had an opportunity to influence the outcome with their own actions.[24]

Causation as Factual Responsibility

It should be apparent from this discussion that the substantial factor test is far less important than the individual parts which comprise it. Because of its nebulous dimensions, the test itself is unlikely to serve as an efficacious tool for mining the craggy depths of causal complexity. Yet the considerations upon which it is founded together support a theory of legal causation which is truly momentous. Stated in brief, this theory imposes causal responsibility upon those who, by act or omission, either have or could have exercised such control over an event that it represents a clear expression of their autonomy.

This analysis is not strictly (nor even predominantly) a matter of causation, but is more appropriately viewed as a question of "factual responsibility" for harmful outcomes. Tort litigation, after all, has primarily one purpose—to determine who is responsible for injuries which result from an interpersonal interaction. Responsibility, in this sense, has two components. As I have indicated previously, one of these components establishes conduct as wrongful or normatively irresponsible. This, we determined, means nothing more than that the actor has exceeded her state-distributed share of autonomy. By contrast, the other aspect of responsibility, which we are considering here, forges distinctive moral bonds between interacting parties. Unlike its normative counterpart, its purpose is not to cast judgment upon the parties, but merely to determine which autonomous agent(s) is/are subject to the victim's claim-right.[25] As we have just seen, this is done by identifying the actor whose conduct has so influenced an outcome that it can said that she has placed upon it her distinctive signature. Because only such a factually responsible party violates the social trust of cooperation and respect necessary to political association, only she may be subject to the ex post distributive restrictions of tort law.

Factual Responsibility and Misfeasance

Understood in this way, factual responsibility may expedite our analysis of both misfeasant and nonfeasant behavior. The causal effect of affirmative, misfeasant actions is clearest, and thus easiest to assess. The more control such conduct has over a consequence, the more likely it is that that consequence is a product of the actor's exercise of autonomy. And the more definite this connection is, the greater will be her responsibility for the harm. So in my original hypothetical where the negligent driver struck the pedestrian in the crosswalk, we can say without hesitation that the driver was factually responsible for the collision. It was her act, and her act alone, that displayed the controlling force necessary to determine the fate of the hapless pedestrian.

Factual Responsibility and Nonfeasance

Although it is more difficult to connect omitters to injurious occurrences, the reasons for doing so also are better explained by the concept of factual responsibility. Omitters misuse their autonomy not by committing harmful acts, but by neglecting to protect others from harm. Accordingly, for these individuals, we need not determine whether they *actually* influenced some injurious outcome; rather, we must speculate about whether they possessed the *power* to prevent it. We confronted this problem earlier in the baby-sitter example. There we saw that the baby-sitter's causal responsibility for failing to protect the child was determined by her duty to act. This duty, you will recall, arose both from the sitter's undertaking to serve as the child's caretaker, and from the parents' reliance upon her to perform the tasks normally associated with this occupation. Once the sitter assumed this obligation, she distinguished herself as one of only perhaps a handful of individuals who were responsible for the child's well-being. Because only members of this exclusive group had the duty to act on the child's behalf, only their omissions could account for any harm the child might sustain. For all others who remained passive around the youngster, inaction was both a predictable and legally acceptable reaction. With these bystanders eliminated from the field of possible causal agents, the sitter stood out as a conspicuous candidate. The only remaining question was, among the few others who may have had some obligation to look after the child, who had the delegated power to safeguard her from the particular hazards of the intersection? Because only the sitter possessed both the obligation *and* the ability to escort the child safely across the street, her failure to exercise such caution alone may be viewed as a factual predicate to the resulting collision.

Factual Responsibility and Multiple Causes

Whether one's conduct is characterized as misfeasant or nonfeasant, it is clear that the assessment of her legal liability cannot be made in isolation, but must take cognizance of all other causal agents and their relative contributions to the plaintiff's loss. The reason is that harmful occurrences seldom are the product of a single autonomous action. Indeed, many autonomous acts, either separately or in combination, may significantly influence such events. The idea of factual responsibility allows one to consider all these causal agencies and their contribution to the injury. It also acknowledges that such responsibilities can have varying degrees. Some acts may be more or less potent than others in the effects they produce. The concept of factual responsibility invites a comparative weighing of these disparate influences in assigning liability. Where the actions of one individual display an overwhelming power over an event, the injurious results may be solely attributable to her, and the inconsequential actions of others may be disregarded. On the other hand, where multiple actions operate to produce a harm, and all have been influential both in its occurrence and in its distinctive character, then the actors may share factual responsibility for the resulting loss.

Multiple Acts of Misfeasance

We saw an illustration of this in our previous discussion of the *Anderson* case. There, it will be recalled, the confluence of two fires destroyed the plaintiff's property. That each fire alone was independently capable of causing the blaze, however, is of little relevance. In the first place, such a conclusion is not factual but hypothetical. It is premised on the speculation of what might have occurred if there were not, in fact, two fires. While the law of probabilities may support such a view, we will never know for sure whether the defendant's fire alone would have reached the plaintiff's property, or whether it would have petered out or been extinguished some time before. Perhaps more importantly, despite whatever uncertainty that may exist concerning the manner in which the fires merged, two things are beyond dispute: the plaintiff's property was destroyed by a single force—fire—and only the defendant and the unknown source had a hand in creating it.

In this way, *Anderson* is like some Dickensian tale where a father and mother each actively teach their child how to steal and cheat, and alas, she grows up to be a thief. Is there any doubt that the child's corruption is directly attributable to her parents, and to no one else in the world? Would anyone deny that each parent individually is to blame for the child's delinquency? Clearly not. Here, bad parenting is the sole cause of the child's downfall, and both the mother and father were indistinguishable co-participants in determining her fate. As in the *Anderson* case, therefore, each actor has had a controlling, though indeterminate, influence over the outcome.

Still, one might argue that *Anderson* and my Dickens hypothetical are different in at least one key respect. Whereas *Anderson* involved only one known culpable cause—i.e., the defendant—both parents in my hypothetical were clearly blameworthy. While this may be true, it has absolutely nothing to do with determining the factual cause or causes of the respective incidents in question. Instead, for the *Anderson* case, it raises a purely normative dilemma: should we hold a marginally culpable actor liable for the complete destruction of a structure even though we are not sure to what extent his conduct contributed to that result? As far as I am concerned, this question must be resolved either in the determination of normative responsibility (is the defendant's breach of his duty egregious enough to warrant such a sanction?) or in the allocation of damages (should the defendant only be held liable for a percentage of the plaintiff's loss?). It has no place in the search for factual responsibility. For so long as the defendant's action helped to create the destructive force which alone consumed the plaintiff's property, he is factually responsible for the resulting loss, even if he shares this responsibility with someone or something else.

Multiple Omissions

Both of the above examples involved multiple acts of misfeasance which combined to produce a single result. But what happens if two or more parties fail to act, and their omissions together lead to some injurious consequence? Does the notion of factual responsibility still assist in determining who should be held liable for any harm that may have been done? I believe that it does, although its efficacy in this regard still remains to be seen.

A Hypothetical Dilemma

The best way to test the mettle of this theory is by subjecting it to one of the most perplexing, yet stimulating fact patterns ever to grace the pages of a torts book. It goes like this:

> C, an automobile rental company, negligently fails to discover and repair the defective brakes on one of its cars. C rents the car to D who negligently fails to apply the brakes in time to avoid an accident in which Pedestrian is injured.[26]

In this scenario, both C, the rental company, and D, the driver, are omitters. Although the omissions of each separately seem to have been sufficient to produce the accident with Pedestrian, neither alone was necessary to that result. So under the sine qua non test, both parties would escape liability. This intuitively seems wrong since, in conjunction, C and D appear to have played a big part in causing Pedestrian's injury. Likewise, the substantial factor test, by itself, seems no better equipped to resolve the thorny question of causation presented here. Indeed, if the notion of substantiality was vague as applied to affirmative acts, it is practically incomprehensible when applied to omissions. Because all omissions involve the same exercise of autonomy—i.e., passivity—how do we know which inactions are substantial and which are not? Without any means for answering this question, the substantial factor test compels us to find that *both* omitters are casually responsible for the accident. This conclusion, although directly opposed to that suggested by the sine qua non test, may be no less specious.

The Need for Comparative Analysis

By dropping the search for "substantiality," and focusing instead on the parties' respective powers of control, it may be possible to assign factual responsibility to one omitter and not the other, or to allocate different degrees of factual responsibility among them. To do this, we must make a comparative assessment of the conduct of all possible causal agents. Only by implementing such an approach may we determine which parties have so indelibly etched their mark on an outcome that it represents a clear expression of their autonomy.

Examining Each Omission Separately

This analysis must proceed on two levels. On one level, we must look at each target defendant individually, examining the nature and scope of her conduct. A couple of questions would be important in this regard. One question is whether the conduct under scrutiny was really nonfeasance. In many cases, behavior which appears passive may be part of a more general, affirmative activity. For example, the driver in our fact pattern did not just fail to apply her brakes, she also affirmatively operated the rental car in a negligent manner. Viewed in this way—that is, as a kind of misfeasance—her conduct seems to bear a clearer connection to the resulting collision with Pedestrian.

Whether the defendant's behavior is classified as affirmative or passive, it also would be crucial to determine her state of mind just prior to the occurrence. Did she deliberately disregard a known danger or merely fail to perceive a foreseeable risk? This is important because when a party knows of and appreciates an obvious danger facing another, she possesses enormous power to forestall the impending harm. If she consciously refuses to protect the potential victim, fully aware of the consequences of her inaction, the loss which follows may be seen as an unequivocal expression of her will. Of course, as the certainty of the threat decreases, so too does her power to prevent the potential harm. Nevertheless, even where the risk of harm is lower, and the omitter's complacency is less than intentional, her passivity still may reflect her autonomous choice to ignore the interests of others.

Examining Other Causal Agencies

The second level of analysis concentrates not on the target defendant, but on the other causal agencies which may have influenced the injurious event. Here, too, several questions would be critical to the evaluation of factual responsibility. For instance, were any natural (i.e., nonhuman) forces in operation at the time of the occurrence?[27] Besides the target defendant, did the conduct of any human beings contribute to the outcome? If so, what was the form of such conduct? Was it an affirmative act which impacted the plaintiff in a direct way, or only an omission with a more tenuous connection to the plaintiff's injury? In what temporal sequence did these acts or omissions occur; or more specifically, who had the last and perhaps best chance to avert the accident? How many of these additional causal agents are there, and what was their mindset at the time of the event? When these questions are answered, we will have a more complete picture of the circumstances surrounding the injurious occurrence. Indeed, not only will we have expanded our field of possible causal influences, we will have evaluated the strength of each party's contribution to that unfortunate consequence. Equipped with such knowledge, we now may undertake the type of comparative analysis intrinsic to the concept of factual responsibility.

Resolving the Dilemma

Returning to our example involving the rental car company, the careless driver and the pedestrian, let's compare the conduct of our two omitters using the criteria mentioned above to see if we can find some basis for distinguishing them. The most noticeable distinction is the sequence in which C's (the company's) and D's (the driver's) omissions occurred. D's failure to apply the brakes obviously came after C's failure to inspect them. This temporal fact is important because it affects the parties' respective abilities to control the outcome. Assuming the worst—that is, that the brakes did not work at all—there still existed a few conditions under which the accident would not have happened. For example, if the pedestrian was not present, and no one else was on the street, a collision would have been impossible. Moreover, if the pedestrian was cautious and alert, she probably would have been able to jump out of the path of the car. Finally, if the driver had operated the car in a prudent fashion, remaining attentive and minding her speed, there is a substantial likelihood that she could have taken some action, besides applying the brakes, to avoid striking the pedestrian.

All three of these conditions were beyond the control of C. Certainly, C had no power to determine who walks the streets, where they do so or when. Likewise, C had neither the authority nor the opportunity to demand that the pedestrian take evasive action to protect herself. And, unless C had some specific knowledge of D's bad driving habits, C could not control how D operated the car.

The same is not true, however, of D. Although D could not control the pedestrian's whereabouts, D's driving could affect the pedestrian's ability to get out of the way. If, for instance, D was speeding or steering erratically, the pedestrian's chances of avoiding the oncoming car would be greatly reduced. And regardless of how D's actions affected the pedestrian's ability to defend herself, one thing is certain: D alone possessed the power to control her own actions behind the wheel. Even without brakes, D had the last, best opportunity to avoid a collision by steering clear of the pedestrian. By failing to take advantage of this opportunity, D seems to have had a far more significant factual influence upon the outcome than C.

Further analysis of the nature of each party's behavior confirms this conclusion. Unless operating a rental car agency which occasionally fails to inspect its inventory is considered an affirmative act, which seems to be a stretch, then C's negligence in this case is a classic omission. C presumably did not create the brake problem, nor was it in C's business interest to consciously disregard the well-being of its customers by renting such seriously defective cars. Thus, their failure to repair the brakes in no way appears willful. More likely, it was the result of time or money constraints common to the industry. Moreover, C's control over the car and its brakes, at best, was nominal. If C is a reasonably successful enterprise, most of the time its cars will be in the possession of its customers who may abuse them badly. If a defect does develop from such use, it is reasonable for C to expect that it will be discovered and reported by a customer. Assuming C had received no such complaints from D or anyone else prior to the accident, C may have lacked the knowledge necessary for it to exercise greater control over the car, either by keeping it off the road or submitting it to more frequent inspections.

D, by contrast, had both the opportunity and the ability to change the result in this case. For D's failure to apply the brakes to be negligent, she must have acted in one of three ways: either she was aware of the pedestrian's presence and deliberately or recklessly decided to wait before applying them; or she was inattentive, and so deprived herself of the opportunity of applying them sooner; or she was driving so fast that it was impossible to apply them in time to avoid the collision.[28] If the first alternative were true, then D's conduct would be willful, and the injury to the pedestrian would be a clear expression of her autonomy. If either the second or third alternatives were true, then D's conduct is more properly viewed as misfeasance. By speeding or driving inattentively, D created risks that did not exist before she got into the car. Thus, unlike C, which merely failed to discover dangers produced by others, D had greater awareness of both the risks facing the pedestrian and the need to control them. With this knowledge, she had the power to ameliorate these risks merely by conforming her behavior to the dictates of the law. If she had done so, we noted earlier, both she and the pedestrian might have taken evasive action and escaped without incident. By opting not to proceed in this fashion, D exercised her autonomy in a way that was almost sure to compromise the negative liberty of the pedestrian. Thus, both alone and in comparison with C's conduct, D's behavior stands out as the predominate, if not sole factual determinant of the accident.

The Advantages of Factual Responsibility

If this discussion proves anything, it is that the term causation is hopelessly inadequate to describe why we hold certain wrongdoers liable and others not. Especially in cases of omissions and multiple agents, it is simply incapable of establishing any meaningful distinctions among parties who, for one reason or another, find themselves linked to an injurious event. I have suggested that the concept of factual responsibility, as defined in this chapter, may serve as a worthy replacement. In fact, it already appears, albeit rather inconspicuously, in the factors underlying the Restatement's substantial factor test. While the comparative and relativistic approach condoned by this concept may not resolve all vexatious issues currently handled by the notion of causation, it offers several advantages over traditional dogma. For one thing, it openly acknowledges that the sine qua non test is confusing in some contexts, and counterintuitive in others. Additionally, by adopting an analysis which is highly relativistic, it provides a more propitious vantage point from which to sort out the many forces operating simultaneously on any given occurrence. Third, as has been indicated above and shall be discussed in greater detail in the next chapter, it ascribes some moral relevancy to the search for causal responsibility.[29] Beyond all this, it appears to be the only theory which can explain all of our current notions of causal responsibility while still retaining its conceptual purity.

Chapter 13

Factual Cause and Justice

Now that we have a clearer understanding of factual causation, at least within the context of tort law, we may proceed to a consideration of the remaining two questions posed at the beginning of the last chapter. Specifically, we must decide whether factual causation is relevant to the pursuit of justice in tort cases, and if so, whether it is indispensable to that end. Only in so doing may we determine whether it has any chance of surviving the recent assault that has been mounted against it both from within the smokey trenches of our courts and from the ivory tower of academia. If factual causation serves the end of tort justice, it may not be discarded without undermining the law's legitimacy; but if it is merely incidental to this objective, it might give way to more compelling concerns. In this chapter, I hope to uncloud the crystal ball which will help us tell its fortune.

The Tort System's Defining Features

Before we may analyze the connection between causation and tort justice, however, we must first briefly review the attributes of the tort system which make it morally distinctive. Stated simply, the tort system is a publicly operated institution of private dispute resolution. The state provides both the rules and the fora for deciding such conflicts in a peaceful fashion. These aspects of the system create a relationship between the state and its citizens which is subject to the demands of political justice. This means that the rules must be based on criteria which fairly distribute autonomy among the disputants, and that the procedure for applying these rules is evenhanded. The dispute itself is a matter of private justice between the parties involved. It provides an orderly means for one party to seek retribution against another, and to correct any ill effects arising out of their interaction.

These retributive or corrective measures generally may not be invoked unless the aggrieved party proves two things at the very least: first, that she has suffered some actual or presumed impairment of her autonomy; and second, that she received this harm at the hands of a wrongdoer.[1] When these conditions are satisfied, it may be argued, justice requires that the injured party be compensated for her loss, and that the wrongdoer be punished for her indiscretion. But what is it that authorizes the injured party to receive her compensation *from her particualar offender?* And what compels the wrongdoer to make her penance *only to her particular victim?* The answers to these troubling questions can be found in the concept of causation, for without it our notions of political wrongdoing and corrective claim-rights would simply be incomprehensible.

Causation and Wrongdoing

At first, the suggestion that wrongdoing derives from causal principles may seem misguided. There is no question that some forms of behavior may be considered wrongful in the general sense of being wicked. Acts of greed, for example, would be adjudged morally culpable in almost every society. Such conduct is wrongful because it displays a mean dispositional humor which is completely at odds with the concept of virtue. As we saw in Chapter Five, however, this connotation of wrongdoing is not the only one possible. In fact, most of our laws, including tort law in particular, are not founded on this view. With few exceptions,[2] conduct is not deemed politically wrongful simply because the party committing it is less than virtuous. Rather, to be wrongful in both a moral *and* political sense, it must affect the autonomy of others.

Acknowledging this truth, we earlier defined wrongdoing as the breach of a duty owed to another. Such duties, we saw, may be owed to the state, to private individuals or sometimes to both. For example, the criminal proscription against drunk driving benefits *all* members of society, *not* any *one* individual in particular. Thus, when a person drives while intoxicated her conduct *is* wrongful, but it is wrongful only to the state. This all changes, of course, if the driver crashes her car into that of another motorist. Her behavior is still wrongful in a public sense, but it now takes on a distinctly private character. Why? Because an additional duty is invoked in this situation. Under the law of torts, individuals are obligated to behave in a reasonable fashion, or pay for the loss they cause if they fail to do so. This duty, unlike the criminal law forbidding DUI, is owed to specific private parties who are placed at risk and ultimately harmed by the actor's unreasonable conduct. Thus, when the driver injures another motorist, she does not just violate the state's DUI law, she also breaches a private duty of care. Here, the transgression is wrongful not only to society generally, but to the actual victim of her recklessness as well.

What distinguishes these two types of wrongdoing is the notion of causation. Conduct may be socially wrongful with or without causation. That is to say, we might condemn an action on its own terms without regard to the effect it has upon others. As we saw in the above illustration, driving under the influence was criminal behavior regardless of whether a crash occurred or anyone was injured. In either case, the conduct of the driver was politically and morally intolerable because she exercised a degree of autonomy denied to everyone else, and in so doing, violated the duty of mutual restriction which makes social living possible. For private injustices, on the other hand, causation is not so incidental. In fact, it is an essential attribute of any private wrong. This is because private duties are concerned as much with the injurious effects of an action as they are with the propriety of the actor's conduct. Indeed, the whole purpose of such duties is to protect the interests of specific parties from the causal influences of those who endanger or impair them. Thus, we saw that drunk driving was not wrongful to any particular individual until it culminated in harm to the other motorist. At that point, the private duty of tort law was violated, and a personal wrong was inflicted upon the victim.

The Connective Role of Causation

We see, then, that causation is inherent in our notion of tortious wrongdoing. Yet its influence does not end here. Causal responsibility also plays a fundamental role in determining the victim's right of redress. It does this by activating the victim's secondary rights and giving them appropriate moral direction. Although we considered this function generally in Chapter Four, it is worth taking a few moments here to see exactly how this works in tort cases.

When one engages in risky conduct that appears tortious—say, by threatening another with a gun—she activates the secondary rights of any party in reasonable apprehension of harm. Because the need for action is great, tort law bestows upon the endangered party a privilege of self-defense. This entitles the prospective victim to take any preemptive action reasonably necessary to end the danger. Unless she finds herself in an extreme emergency situation, she may direct her defensive response only against the party creating the risk. The reasons are twofold. On the one hand, if appearances are correct, the protagonist will also be a wrongdoer who enjoys no right to expose others to such risks. On the other hand, to permit the prospective victim to react against innocent third parties might entail violating *their* rights.

This analysis changes only slightly where the risk-creator's activity actually results in another's harm. Since the victim's interests already have been compromised by the actor, there no longer is a need for defensive measures. Instead of protecting her interests ex ante, the victim in this situation seeks to replenish them with an ex post award of damages. Her object, therefore, is correction, not preemption. Unlike preemptive secondary rights, which are triggered by the mere appearance of misconduct, corrective secondary rights are activated only if the actor's conduct actually was wrongful, and even then, only if it had some harmful effect upon her legally recognized interests. Without wrongdoing, there is no justification for subjecting the actor to an ex post restriction of autonomy. Without harm, there is simply nothing to correct. And without causal agency, there is no basis for allowing this particular victim to invade the coffers of this particular wrongdoer. Indeed, it is the latter concept alone which links the actor to her victim in a completely unique way. It assigns the actor's duties of care and reparation exclusively to the injured party, and in turn, imbues the victim with the sole power to enforce them. As a result, only the wrongdoer bears the moral responsibility for the loss flowing from her actions, and so only she becomes vulnerable to the victim's corrective rights.

Causation and the Determination of Rights

In light of all this, it would be hard to exaggerate the value of causal principles in reconciling the competing rights of parties involved in tort disputes. In every case, the court must balance the defendant's prima facie right of action or inaction against the plaintiff's prima facie right both to be left alone in the first instance and, where this right is violated, to receive compensation for any resulting loss. The concept of causation facilitates this analysis. Remember that duties and entitlements are relative and circumstantial by nature. They remain abstract and undefined until the lives of their holders intersect. Only when one's interests come into conflict with those of another will her actual rights become apparent. At that point, the actor's interest in behaving in the injury-producing manner becomes counterpoised against the interest of the claimant in being free from harm. Where one party's interests exceed those of her counterpart, she may be said to have a right of action—for the protagonist, the right to engage in a particular activity; and for the claimant, the right to redress the loss incurred. But even this determination does not declare a universal entitlement in the victor; rather, it merely identifies the party with the superior right in that particular transaction. This assessment could not be made by comparing the interests of the claimant to some innocent third party, or by weighing the protagonist's stake in acting against the abstract rights of others not threatened by her conduct. It is possible only by analyzing the relative positions of the parties who are causally responsible for that encounter.

Advancing the Goal of Political Justice

Using the concept of causation to mediate tort disputes in this way appears to further the ends of both political and private justice. From a political standpoint, we know that the state, to satisfy the demands of distributive justice, must do two things. First, it must create fair rules which recognize people's important rights. That is, it must give individuals freedom where they absolutely need it, and it must protect these freedoms by restricting certain activities which might endanger them. It does this by establishing laws, including tort laws, which are founded on the fair criteria of need and risk. Second, a just state must make sure that its rules are fairly implemented and enforced. In our system of government, rights and duties are implemented in a variety of ways. The state restricts the most socially dangerous conduct—i.e., acts intended to cause harm to another—by subjecting them to preemptive action (like criminal arrest), regulatory action (like agency review) or corrective action (as in a tort suit). Behavior which is inherently risky, though less so than intentional misbehavior, is subject to fewer restrictions—perhaps only regulation and corrective sanctions. Finally, activities that pose danger only when performed in the wrong way, like acts of negligence, are generally limited only by the ex post corrective restriction of tort law. Given the low risk and high value of the latter activities, the state does not enforce such rules directly; rather, it requires private citizens to monitor such behavior and to bring the wrongdoers to justice when they are personally aggrieved.

Distributive Justice Implications

Relying on causal principles to identify these wrongdoers serves the state's interest in fairly distributing autonomy among those engaged in voluntary and involuntary social transactions. This is because parties who have been causally impacted by the conduct of others are in the best position to determine whose use of autonomy is either excessive or deficient. By doing what others are prohibited from doing—most particularly, inflicting harm upon others—wrongdoers exercise more than their share of autonomy. Victims of such behavior, having personally experienced its effects, can thus pinpoint the cheaters in a way no one else can. Likewise, the fact of their injuries gives these victims both first hand knowledge of their own autonomy deprivations, and the best possible incentive to correct them.

Causation and the Balancing Analysis of Rights

Once the wrongdoers are hauled into court, the element of causation affords the bilateral setting necessary for the state both to declare the rights of the parties and to correct whatever imbalance of freedom exists between them. Unlike ex ante autonomy restrictions, which are premised on the nature of one's conduct, the corrective sanction of tort law may not be implemented without an act *and* an injury. And not just any combination of acts and injuries will do. It is simply impossible to ascertain whether the actor exceeded her allocation of liberty, or if her victim, through her loss, suffered some deficiency, without considering the precise circumstances of the transaction in which both occurred. Indeed, as we saw in the *Cordas* case, even the most deliberately harmful act may be appropriate if it is born of some compelling exigency and it produces little actual injury to others. Conversely, even the most serious injury may be debited as a social sacrifice if the actor causing it lacked the power to prevent it from happening. So, to evaluate the actor's conduct we *must* know not only the need for her action, but also the danger it posed to *her particular victim*. Similarly, we cannot properly assess the victim's loss *unless* we weigh it against the risk created by and the value inherent in the actions of *her particular wrongdoer*. The concept of causation facilitates this balancing process both by bringing together the necessary parties—i.e., those involved in a specific injurious encounter—and by promoting the comparison of their respective interests. In doing this, it assists the state, through its courts, in ascertaining which individuals *actually* received more or less than their share of autonomy. Only when this is established may the state fairly distribute the restrictive ex post sanctions of tort law.

Public Retributive Implications

By advancing such a scheme of distributive justice, the concept of causation fulfills an equally important political function. You see the state has a practical retributive interest in holding causal agents responsible for the harms they inflict. To survive, any society must inculcate in its citizens a respect for law.[3] For if the law is not respected, the bonds of political association will disintegrate, either through direct threat or through uncontrollable chaos. Just as the convention of promising is necessary to the peaceful and productive exchange of rights (thus strengthening the relation between and among citizens), the convention of obedience to law is indispensable to social living (thus ensuring the citizens' bond to the state). Accordingly, when one party violates a state-created distributive regulation of autonomy by violating the autonomy interest of another, the state has a right and duty to punish the act which violates this convention. The law supports this convention in two ways. It requires the specific wrongdoer to make reparation to the victim, thereby encouraging her future respect. And it also makes public the determination of disrespect through open proceedings and published opinions, thereby encouraging others to respect the law by refraining from the sanctioned act.

Causation's Influence on Private Justice

If commanding obedience were the sole object of the law, however, there is no reason why the wrongdoer should be forced to pay compensation *to the injured party*. The same punitive effect could be achieved by requiring the actor to pay a fine to the government.[4] Indeed, compensation might not be necessary at all. Respect for the law might be better instilled through more stringent forms of punishment. The fact is that obedience to law cannot be ensured only through state-imposed sanctions. People must want to obey the law. Without this cooperation, even the most powerful political system could not survive for long. How is this measure of voluntary submission achieved? By affording citizens a realistic opportunity for private justice.

Where one has inflicted harm upon another, the victim is likely to harbor a powerful retributive instinct. This instinct, in turn, usually impels the victim to take corrective action to undo the wrong done. In nature, these inclinations could be extinguished privately by an act of vengeance. In political society, however, the state provides the sole means for obtaining retributive or corrective justice. It does this by allowing the victim to seek redress in the public institution of the courts. In these political fora, as in nature, causation plays a key role in determining the direction of the victim's response. In both contexts, the victims' relief comes neither from the state nor from some innocent third party, but from the wrongdoer who caused her harm.

Private Retribution

As part of a public system for resolving private conflicts, tort litigation is our modern counterpart to private vengeance.[5] It allows a victim to face her wrongdoer and vindicate her rights in a formal, nonviolent manner. The concept that makes this possible is factual cause, or as I have called it, factual responsibility. It identifies the wrongdoer and makes her directly accountable to the injured party. In so doing, it helps such injured parties vent the anger and frustration which follows from tortious acts. This, in turn, exorcises the retributive demons that lurk in all of us. Political systems which remain responsive to this need meet the demands of social justice, and so are willingly obeyed. Those that do not are destined for anarchy or rebellion.[6]

Causation and Corrective Justice

Holding causally responsible actors liable for their actions is not just a matter of good politics. It may be the only way of vindicating the private wrongs they create. If one incurs a harm at the hands of another, there is no one besides the wrongdoer who can completely undo the damage of the invasion. In so acting, the wrongdoer has not just inflicted corporeal harm, she has invaded the moral space enjoyed by the victim as a human being. This a personal wrong. It is one uniquely experienced by both its creator and its recipient. And it can only be righted between them.

If this sounds familiar, it should. It is an articulation of corrective justice, and it too is reliant on the concept of causation. As will be recalled, corrective justice requires the rectification of wrongful losses and wrongful gains. Such an adjustment is accomplished through an arithmetic formula—that which is taken from the victim must be returned by the wrongdoer in the same proportion. Invariably, a gain and loss will be sustained in every wrongful transaction. The wrongdoer benefits by exercising more autonomy than her distributive share (that is, by committing an act which creates socially unacceptable risks). The victim, on the other hand, sustains both a reduction in her physical, emotional or economic well-being and a more ethereal impairment of her right to be left alone. The wrongdoer must pay to the victim something to correct this imbalance. If nothing more, this payment symbolizes the restoration of normative equality between the interacting parties. Because the inequality is unique to *these* parties in *this* particular transaction, rectification generally must come solely from within this relationship. The concept of causation ensures that it does.

The Relativity of Private Justice

So it appears that causation is not just a relevant concern of justice in tort disputes, it is a requirement. It not only facilitates the political distribution of autonomy to members of society, it quenches their thirst for retribution and allows them to undo the harmful effects of transactions in the only way morally acceptable. Still, this does not mean that only parties who have caused harm to another may be subjected to a financial penalty; nor does it suggest that parties who have sustained harm may receive compensation only from those inflicting it. Justice is not a monolithic or static concept; rather, it is multifaceted, flexible and relativistic. Private justice in interpersonal disputes may vary according to the interest invaded, the riskiness of the offending activity, and the relationship of the parties. And the demands of private justice might give way at times to the public fairness concerns of the state. Where conditions are ripe, therefore, it might be permissible to impose liability upon a noncausally responsible actor, or to allow an injured victim to receive compensation from someone, perhaps anyone, who may better absorb the loss.

Above I have tried to show how retributive and corrective justice justify holding a factually responsible wrongdoer accountable for injuries she inflicts upon others. Nevertheless, they do not necessarily compel such a result.[7] The reason is that the force of these normative instincts diminish with the culpability of the offending conduct.

Where a wrongdoer acts intentionally or willfully to interfere with the rights of another, the private retributive instinct is greatest. The wrongdoer has asserted her will over that of her victim, failing to accord her the respect due a rational agent in a liberal democratic society. In addition, a strong retributive response may follow from less deliberate conduct which imposes upon the victim a severe autonomy restriction like death or serious bodily injury. Even where the harm does not rise to this level, however, there still may be a strong need for personal rectification by the causal wrongdoer if she has violated a trust cultivated by her special relationship with the victim.

Where the wrongdoer acts merely carelessly, the slight to the victim's rights of personhood is far less. Thus, the resentment and indignation caused by the act is bound to be reduced, and the need for face-to-face vindication will become more remote. The same is true where the victim suffers only a modest restraint of her autonomy. An intangible or insignificant indiscretion is more easily forgiven than invasions which are physical and permanent. These too may be excused if they are caused by a good-faith interloper, rather than a neglectful caretaker.

As this private retributive instinct fades, the necessity and practicality of corrective justice also wane. Where the neglectful actor involuntarily harms another, she enjoys only an abstract benefit in exercising the autonomy to create unacceptable risks. It is unlikely that any actual advantage accrues from this behavior. Thus, for purposes of corrective justice, the imbalance between the parties may be difficult or impossible to calculate.[8] Or, where the victim's harm is great, it may cause the wrongdoer to be held accountable for loss far in excess of her culpability.[9] In these types of cases, it may be unfair to require the wrongdoer to make complete reparation.

When the individual's need for private justice recedes to this extent, the state's interest in sanctioning such behavior is also less compelling. While an intentional act amounts to a direct and unequivocal repudiation of the rule of law, an inadvertent mishap shows very little of this disrespect. And, given the involuntary nature of such acts, it is unlikely that a sanction could force the actor to alter her behavior in the future. Under these circumstances, the need for the state to punish *this* individual wrongdoer for *this* particular act diminishes. In turn, there is less of a need to subject the act to public condemnation.

Competing Aspects of Justice

Whatever the magnitude of these private justice concerns, there are always countervailing justice requirements which also must be met. On occasion, these competing concerns may be so important that they take precedence over all others. First and foremost among these alternatives is the need for social justice. Social justice requires that the state protect society against forces which threaten its general health and welfare.[10] Under this form of justice, the state may take extraordinary measures to curtail activities which pose serious and pervasive risks across a broad range of the population. Or, when an epidemic of disease or injury affects large segments of society, the state may implement steps to ensure that the victims are treated and their losses redressed. In these situations, the need for wide-scale, immediate action may be so compelling that it outweighs any competing requirement that the tactics used conform to the paradigm of causal responsibility.

The demands of procedural and factual justice also may support the use of such extreme measures. Because justice is a limited commodity in a society, "perfect" justice can never be guaranteed. There are times when the substantive demands of corrective and retributive justice must give way to the exigencies of procedural justice. Thus, an otherwise meritorious claim might go unsatisfied if, for example, the cause of action is pleaded improperly or filed in an untimely manner. On other occasions, the normative purity of the law might succumb to the need for factual justice in a broader spectrum of cases. This accounts for the notion of jury nullification in many criminal cases. In all of these situations the dictates of justice are relative, and so must be weighed on a case by case basis.

The Justice of Noncausal Theories
of Products Liability

In recent years, product-related accidents have begun to create the type of need that would seem to justify such desperate measures. Today, manufacturers create hundreds of thousands of products which they market throughout the country. Because of exacting specifications and sophisticated manufacturing processes, each product bears the same design characteristics. If the design turns out to be unsafe, the threat posed by the product is not isolated, but is nationwide. If enough individuals are injured by the product, are unable to work and are required to seek financial assistance from the government, this societal risk may itself be a public harm. In these scenarios, the public nature of the danger may appear to outweigh the normative dictates of private justice.[11]

Because of the need for social justice in cases involving product-related injuries, courts throughout the country have responded by weakening or eliminating the causation requirement. As noted earlier, market share, enterprise and alternative liability theories all hold manufacturers accountable for such injuries even where there is no evidence that their products were factually responsible for the consumer's injury.[12] At the same time, these theories compensate consumers who suffer such injuries despite their inability to identify the source of their harm. Here, the widespread nature of the conduct, and its potentially devastating effects, purportedly warrant punishing those marketing such products regardless of the actual harm they cause. Likewise, the social cost of the resulting injuries is considered so great that there is justification for shifting it to noncausal, yet financially secure parties who, by raising the price of their goods, can spread the loss to the public.

Compensation Systems

There is nothing necessarily unjust in the results achieved by this approach. In fact, the same tradeoffs in justice are exemplified by modern worker's compensation schemes. The relatively simple and expeditious claim system of worker's compensation may seem preferable to the cumbersome and complicated procedure of the tort system, even though in the former the victim's recovery is neither obtained directly from her wrongdoer nor premised on the fair distributive criterion of risk. Moreover, it may appear better to ensure that injured workers receive some compensation for their injuries even if this means requiring reparation from employers who are neither normatively nor factually responsible for such losses. And, the advantages of worker's compensation in keeping employers in business, reducing their operating costs, and ensuring some quick and sure recovery for injured workers may outweigh the unfairness of denying such workers the ability to vindicate their rights fully under the tort system.

In comparing such worker's compensation systems with the more recent product liability doctrines mentioned above, we see that each endeavors to assure some measure of social justice for its beneficiaries. What distinguishes the two, however, are their different political derivations. In every jurisdiction, worker's compensation is a pure distributive scheme developed and promulgated by a legislature responsive to the electorate. It compensates workers in accordance with their need as determined by the severity of their injuries. The novel theories of manufacturer liability, on the other hand, do not give rise to an independent scheme of distributions. Rather, they represent a unique hybrid between distributive and corrective justice. The problem is, these theories are not true to either form of justice, but constitute a corruption of both. Because the terms of liability are determined by a court rather than a legislature, and are conditioned upon criteria removed from the distributee (i.e., compensation is not premised solely on the claimant's need, but requires additional proof of someone else's wrongdoing), true distributive justice is illusory. Alternatively, although such sanctions arise from transactional disputes, the absence of causation makes corrective justice impossible. The manufacturer may be punished in proportion to the degree of risk she created, and the consumer may receive compensation commensurate with her loss, but without proof of causation the wrong existing between them, if any, can never be righted.

While such causation-free theories are not offensive to the notion of justice, they still give good cause for concern. In a system of government founded on a separation of powers, we need to be ever mindful of the proper role of each branch. Allowing courts to punish wrongdoers and to compensate injured parties, though perhaps not undesirable from a moral standpoint, gives them a power normally reserved for our legislatures. This is bad on one level because it tends to take away authority from the body best able to investigate the wisdom of such broad social measures, and concentrates it in the hands of a few individuals who are less informed. What makes this bad situation even worse, however, is that the few officials invested with this new power are not accountable to those of us who must bear its consequences. To the extent that this usurpation of prerogatives threatens the delicate system which protects us from tyranny, it may be not only politically misguided, but socially suicidal as well.

Summary and Conclusion

So we see that causation *is* indispensable to the private justice of tort *law*. Not only does it facilitate the distribution of autonomy among parties engaged in social intercourse, it also helps to satisfy our retributive instincts, and ensures the bipolarity intrinsic to corrective justice. Still, we have learned that the private justice concerns of tort law must at times give way to more pressing social priorities. Where this is the case, causal principles may be discarded and resort may be made of other forms of justice, like pure distributive schemes which dispense penalties and entitlements. This shift cannot be made within the realm of tort law, however, without either seriously weakening its distributive effectiveness or undermining its corrective identity. That the moral framework of tort law cannot accommodate all cases, like some involving product-related injuries, does not mean that it is suffering from some terminal infirmity; rather, it merely suggests that some other political solution must be found to complement it. For the true test of justice is not whether it can be done the same way in every case, for it never will. Rather, the question is whether the system of justice in use is normatively and factually fair enough that, on balance, it is preferable to some other system or to a state of nature. If the answer is affirmative, justice is being served, albeit imperfectly.

Part IV

Justice in the Content of Tort Law

Chapter 14

Intentional Torts

While the foregoing structural considerations ensure that tort claims are founded on valid claim-rights, they do not determine what the content of those claims should be. Granted, they must incorporate the notions of duty, beneficiary status, factual responsibility and damage. But the substantive interpretation of each element may vary greatly from case to case. Duties may be onerous or negligible; beneficiary classes may be expansive or severely restricted; significant interests may be tangible or intangible.

Such variations are not antithetical to justice so long they are fair. Every tort claim pits the autonomy interests of one party against another. On the one hand, the defendant may have a positive liberty interest in performing acts which further her life plan. The plaintiff seeks to restrict this liberty ex post by forcing the defendant to pay damages for the injuries caused by her actions. The plaintiff, on the other hand, possesses a negative liberty interest in protecting her autonomy from invasion by the defendant. The defendant attempts to justify restricting her autonomy as a cost of social living. Tort claims are fair if the rights they afford fairly balance the defendant's freedom to act and the plaintiff's freedom from harm.

Tort law protects these respective interests in different ways, depending upon the nature of the offending activity involved. Intentional torts sanction all actions committed either with the desire to cause another harm, or with knowledge to a substantial certainty that such harm will follow. Negligence claims are founded on conduct which is not intentional but unreasonable or "faulty," meaning that it was committed in disregard of an avoidable risk. Finally, the theory of strict liability restricts supposedly "fault-free" activities which create abnormal dangers for others in the same community.[1]

The object of this Part is to determine whether the rights created by these bases of liability fairly distribute autonomy interests among the parties affected. I will begin in this chapter by broadly examining intentional torts. In the next two chapters, the focus will shift to the fault-based theory of negligence and the "no-fault" theory of strict liability.

Political Aspects of Intentional Misconduct

Intentionally harmful acts are the nemesis of political associations. Such associations are founded on the rule of law. Although laws may have numerous purposes, they must, at a minimum, protect all citizens from the harmful advances of their neighbors. Without such protection, political associations are no better than a state of nature where only might makes right. Acts designed to harm others threaten this protection by repudiating the rule of law necessary to secure it.

To maintain the peace, states are empowered to place severe restrictions on such intentional acts. These restrictions, we have seen, may be either preemptive or corrective. Preemptive restrictions, like criminal laws, forbid the performance of such acts entirely. Almost all intentionally harmful behavior is subject to some type of preemptive restriction. Most of these acts are also covered by the corrective restrictions of tort law. While preemptive restrictions provide all citizens with the primary right to be free from such conduct, intentional torts create claim-rights which permit victims to receive compensation for the damage it produces.

The Elements of Intentional Torts

To recover under an intentional tort theory, the claimant generally must show four things: that the defendant committed a voluntary act; that the act was intentional (i.e., made with a desire to produce a particular consequence or with knowledge to a substantial certainty that it would occur); that a forbidden consequence resulted; and that the defendant's act caused the forbidden consequence. In some respects, this litany seems to deviate from the core elements of a tort claim discussed above. There is no mention of "duty," nor is a specific class of beneficiaries defined. Yet upon closer scrutiny, one can see subsumed within this analysis all that is required to fashion a claim-right.

Duties, Rules and Injustice

Intentional tort theories are premised on the general duty to refrain from inflicting harm. In fact, the duty here applies in its purest sense. As noted above, the most basic requirement for political association is the forbearance from asserting one's will over someone else. If individuals were permitted to invade the interests of others at their whim, there would be no law; and without law, political association would be impossible. Thus, except for unusual circumstances (like self-defense, necessity, etc.),[2] the duty to refrain from intentional misconduct is absolute. This means that the actor has no autonomy right to engage in such activity, and bears an unconditional responsibility to abstain from it.

The duty here takes the form of a rule. A rule is a legal command that specifies either (or both) the type of activity that may (or may not) be performed or the manner in which it may (or may not) be conducted. Where a rule obtains, the focus is entirely upon the circumstances of the actor's behavior. If it conforms to the rule it is benign; but if it deviates from this requirement, it is subject to sanction. For intentional torts, the rule is to forebear from deliberately inflicting harm upon others. In such cases, only three questions need be decided:[3] did the actor voluntarily commit the forbidden act?, did she possess the requisite mental state?, and did her act produce the prohibited consequence? If the answers are affirmative, the duty has been violated, and both the actor and her act are wrongful.

When a general duty is intentionally disregarded, the dereliction of the actor is unjust for a couple of reasons. First and foremost, it is unjust in the broad sense of being wicked. It evinces a character marred by meanness or intemperance. At worst, it may display a fundamental disrespect for the humanity of others. It seems to regard victims not as moral agents valuable as ends in themselves, but as objects to be used for the actor's own gain. Besides these shortcomings, the action also is unjust in the particular sense of being unfair. As a cost of social cooperation, all individuals must give up the freedom to act however they please. This means that they must at least agree to respect the rights of others. One who commits an intentionally harmful act, however, fails to make this sacrifice. Instead, she unfairly hoards a disproportionate share of autonomy by reserving for herself the privilege of unbridled action.

The Beneficiary Status of All

As bad as this is, the injustice of an intentional harm will not alone sustain a private right of action. As we saw above, it must also be shown that the victim was an intended beneficiary of the duty violated. Who enjoys the protection of the general duties inherent in intentional torts? All of us. Because such duties are vital to the success of political associations, they inure to the benefit of all their members. This is why one need not be an intended victim to recover for harm occasioned by an intentional act. The commission of any intentionally harmful act is antisocial, and thus politically dangerous, regardless of who it winds up injuring. Under the doctrine of transferred intent, therefore, the state is justified in requiring the wrongdoer to make reparation even to one who is harmed by mistake.[4]

A Broad View of Causal Responsibility

For the same reason, intentional wrongdoers may be held responsible for consequences causally remote from their offending conduct. Again, because of the pernicious nature of the activity, the public good may require that the tortfeasor, rather than her innocent victim, bear the cost of her misdeed. In such cases, there is sufficient reason to take a more expansive view of factual cause. Thus, the actor may be accountable for harms following only indirectly from her actions, as where she pollutes the stream of a neighbor after dumping hazardous substances in a water source a short distance away.[5] Or, she might be liable for the unexpected consequences of her direct action, as where her spiteful kick produces extensive injury to the leg of the recipient.[6]

Abstract and Actual Harm

The implications of such conduct are in fact so pregnant with political significance that no actual injury need be sustained by the victim. To satisfy her claim-right, the plaintiff must show only that the consequence defined by the tort has occurred. In many cases, the consequence causes no tangible autonomy restriction to the victim. It may be as trifling as "apprehending" the impending action of the tortfeasor,[7] or bearing the brief passage of another across one's property.[8] Still, in these cases, a significant interest of the victim is harmed. It is the peace of mind of being free from the intentional intrusions of others. This is an abstract harm which threatens the notion of autonomy itself.

Doing Private Justice

It is this abstract injury which entitles the claimant to both corrective and retributive justice. Recall that corrective justice requires both a wrongful gain and a wrongful loss. The gain of the tortfeasor, we have seen, is at least a political one. By acting in a way forbidden to others, she assumes for herself an excess of autonomy. But she also denies her victim the freedom owed to all rational moral agents. Such conduct undermines the principle of political cooperation, and so indirectly threatens everyone who enjoys its benefits. More than this, it creates a moral chasm between the wrongdoer and her victim, expressing the superiority of the former and the inhumanity of the latter. Corrective justice requires the negation of this imbalance; our retributive instinct justifies punishing the wrongdoer for creating it.

Promoting Distributive Justice

Besides furthering these private justice concerns, the common law scheme of intentional torts satisfies the rigorous demands of distributive justice.

Where there is no justification for behaving in a deliberately harmful manner, the actor may be subject to both preemptive or corrective restrictions. Thus, one who actually or apparently engages in such conduct may be stopped from doing so by anyone reasonably in fear of being harmed by it. Or, she may be made to change the manner of carrying out her activity. And if she succeeds in harming someone else, she may be required to pay damages for the loss sustained by her victim. In combination, this battery of sanctions presents the most onerous restriction of autonomy possible in a liberal democratic state. This is appropriate, however, because deliberately harmful conduct poses the greatest danger to the stability of such a society. Not only does it threaten the health and welfare of individual citizens, it breaks the bonds of cooperation necessary for political association. Given the high risk of such activity, distributive justice dictates that individuals conducting themselves in this manner receive far less autonomy than those involved in less dangerous enterprises.

Privileged Intentional Behavior

The same would not be true, of course, for intentional acts which are performed out of a grave necessity, as where one's life or bodily integrity are in jeopardy. The law of intentional torts accommodates this need by bestowing upon the endangered party greater autonomy with which to protect herself. Indeed, those threatened by the acts of others or by natural forces are privileged under tort law to respond with some reasonable, though deliberately harmful, defensive measures of their own. Such a reaction is justified so long as it does not exceed the necessity which prompted it. Thus, while it would be permissible to shoot an approaching armed robber, it would be unreasonable to drop her as she runs away. Because the prospective victim's liberty of action is tied to the criterion of need, the law of intentional torts again comports with the requirements of distributive fairness, and so remains true to the ideal of justice.

Applying the Abstract Principles

This all sounds fine in theory. Now let's see exactly how these abstract principles play out in each of tort law's seven traditional intent-based theories of recovery. Intentional torts come in two varieties: those committed against persons—namely, assault, battery, false imprisonment and intentional infliction of emotional distress—and those committed against property—including trepass to land, trespass to chattels and conversion. Although the elements for each type of tort differ significantly, both display the unmistakeable structural characteristics outlined above. Indeed, even one with only a casual familiarity with this area of the law cannot help but notice the clear pattern of symmetry and proportionality which runs throughout it. Especially evident in these torts is the delicate way in which notions of wrongdoing and harm are inversely correlated and counterbalanced. In each case, three rules of justice predominate: 1) the more culpable the conduct of the tortfeasor, the less onerous the victim's proof of damage will be; 2) on the other hand, as the intrusion into the victim's interests (both qualitatively and quantitatively) recedes, the more egregious the tortfeasor's behavior must be to hold her civilly liable; and 3) the greater the threat to the victim's interests (both in terms of the imminence and magnitude of the prospective loss), the more justified she is in taking defensive action, and the more force she may use to protect her rights.

Intentional Torts Against Persons: Assault and Battery

Because harms against persons are generally considered far worse than those directed against property, intentional torts of this type are usually both easier to prove and harder to excuse. The tandem torts of assault and battery are good examples. Battery consists of any act intentionally designed to inflict a harmful or offensive contact upon another.[9] The tort of assault is but an inchoate battery. It applies to any act that intentionally places another in apprehension of such an impending contact.[10] In either case, the conduct in question represents both a serious attack upon the personhood of the victim, and a direct threat to the peace and tranquility of the community. Thus, such a tortfeasor may be held liable for her actions even where she causes no actual damage to her intended victim,[11] and even where she is mistaken about her victim's identity.[12] Only when the actor employs such tactics defensively (i.e., to evade the onslaught of another) is she justified in wielding this kind of force. Even then, she may not use the opportunity to punish or torture her attacker, but must measure her response to match the threat, and must cease the counterassault when her interests are no longer in jeopardy.[13]

False Imprisonment

Acts intended to restrict liberty are a little trickier. Under the tort of false imprisonment, one may be held liable for intentionally confining another against her will.[14] Confinement, in this sense, may be actual or apparent. That is, the victim may be physically unable to leave a location because of some obstacle which prevents egress (like a fence or locked door), or, even where no such boundaries exist, she may feel compelled to remain at a site because of some external inducement, like fraud, coercion or duress. Either way, the effect upon the victim's liberty is typically less severe and direct than the application of force required for battery. Rather than inhibiting the victim's physical capacity for locomotion, the confiner's act merely interposes a temporary impediment to the victim's range of options for exercising her mobility. Thus, the liberty interest at stake in a false imprisonment, although important, is generally less fundamental than the dignitary interests covered by assault and battery. This explains why one who claims to be wrongfully detained, in addition to proving intent and confinement, generally must prove either that she was aware of the imprisonment, or that it caused her to suffer physical harm.[15] Whether or not she is aware of her predicament, the victim typically retains greater control over her own destiny than in other intentional torts. For example, unless her body is bound or otherwise immobilized, she remains free to search for a means of escape. Since the tortfeasor's restriction of her liberty is not complete, the victim bears some responsibility to find a safe route to freedom.[16] If she fails either to look for or to use such an outlet, the resulting loss of liberty is less the fault of another than it is a voluntary relinquishment of that right. This is especially true in cases of apparent confinement, since the victim's immobility proceeds from her own fear or imagination and not from any external barrier. Here, it may be the victim's choice among bad alternatives, rather than any direct coercion, that keeps her in her place.[17] Where this is so, the intentional act which precipitates her decision, if culpable at all, is far less wrongful than an assault upon her bodily integrity, and thus is less deserving of state sanction.

Intentional Infliction of Emotional Distress

The injury protected by the tort of intentional infliction of emotional distress (IIED) is even more uncertain than that covered by false imprisonment. Because of this ambiguity, the connection between act and injury in this tort is stronger and even more apparent than in any of the preceding theories of recovery. Under section 46 of the first Restatement of Torts, an actor could be held liable for intentionally inflicting emotional distress upon another if and only if the resulting psychic injury was severe.[18] Unlike other intentional torts which could be sustained without proof of actual loss, the new theory of IIED not only required evidence of harm, it demanded that the harm achieve an aggravated magnitude of seriousness. The rationale for this heightened evidentiary burden was manifest: since emotional injuries occur frequently, are often trivial or insubstantial and are always highly subjective, some convincing proof of psychological trauma was indispensable to establishing the veracity of the victim's claim. For many jurisdictions, this meant that an IIED claimant could not recover unless she was able to show that her emotional distress was accompanied by some objective physical consequences, like vomiting, hives or insomnia.[19]

By the time the Restatement (Second) of Torts was published, courts had begun to recognize that there was another way to verify speculative emotional injuries. Instead of requiring proof of physical consequences, IIED could be authenticated by the inhumanity of the tortfeasor's actions. Under the new version of section 46, an actor who engaged in extreme or outrageous conduct which exceeded the bounds tolerated in a civilized society could now be held responsible for causing others to suffer severe emotional distress.[20] In contrast to the first Restatement, the behavior required by the second Restatement was considered so offensive and depraved that any reasonable person exposed to it would likely be shocked or disturbed. Thus, such reprehensible conduct served an authenticating function which practically eliminated the risk of rewarding trivial or fraudulent claims. Recognizing this fact, those implementing the tort of IIED decided to change it in two significant ways. First, the drafters of the second Restatement reduced the claimant's burden of proof on the element of intent by also accepting proof of the tortfeasor's recklessness.[21] Second, many jurisdictions which formerly had demanded objective physical evidence of the claimant's emotional injury soon abandoned that requirement, confident that the new wrongdoing element would provide sufficient confirmation of the claimant's harm.[22]

Both of these changes, while directed at different aspects of the claimant's prima facie case, display the relativity necessary for such a sensitive moral analysis. This should not be surprising since the tort of IIED, from its inception, has consistently endeavored to flexibly interplay the notions of wrong and wrongdoing. As we have seen, at the core of this tort is the honest acknowledgement that misconduct and harm are not really separate and independent concepts; rather, each consists of a complicated admixture of acts and injuries, duties and entitlements, and responsibilities and rights. These connected ideas operate much like opposed pulleys in a sophisticated moral machine. Just as you cannot adjust one without affecting the burden of the other, you cannot change either without impacting the integrity of the whole system. To the extent that the tort of IIED embraces this inverse reciprocity, it helps to keep our scales of justice in a precarious state of balance.

Intentional Torts Against Property: Trespass to Land

Intentional torts directed at property interests share this same conceptual interdependence. Take the tort of trespass to real property. As a general rule, one who without consent interferes with another's ownership or possessory interest in real estate may be held liable for actual or nominal damages.[23] Like assault and battery, an unsolicited intrusion upon someone else's land was deemed early on to represent a serious personal and social wrong. This sentiment arose from the medieval system of feudalism in which one's security and social status were determined solely by the boundaries of his real estate holdings. Yet even today the breach of one's property line often is viewed as a prelude to violations far more serious. Indeed, if your home is a sanctuary to which you take refuge, then any unexpected invasion of your dwelling is both a desecration of your privacy and an immediate threat to your survival. Thus, as with other actions which directly repudiate the dignity of others, trespasses to land are subject to an onerous restrictive duty of preclusion. One who breaks the close of her neighbor's property, without permission to do so, simply must be prepared to bear the consequences of her actions. Neither a good faith motive nor an absence of harm will excuse her from liability.[24] On the other hand, the property owner/occupier may not serve as judge, jury and executioner against all those who enter her land surreptitiously or in defiance of her will. Rather, she may protect her property only with a degree of force likely to repel the intrusion.[25] So while the odiousness of the trespasser's conduct eliminates the property holder's burden of proving any actual loss, the ethic of proportionality prohibits her from responding in a vindictive or retributive fashion. This is because, like the rest of us, the property holder remains beholden to the demands of justice. She may exercise her autonomy in a way that secures and promotes her own interests, but she may not use it to trammel the freedom of someone else, even if the object of her response has made the unfortunate mistake of trespassing against her.

Trespass to Chattels and Conversion

If trespass to land is analogous to assault and battery, at least insofar as the concatenation of its substantive requirements is concerned, then trespass to chattels and conversion bear some striking similarities to false imprisonment and IIED. Like their personal injury counterparts, the property-protective torts of trespass to chattels and conversion cover interests that are of only modest importance. In fact, of all the interests secured by our intentional torts, the personal property rights addressed by trespass to chattels and conversion are clearly the least significant. Where harm is questionable on one end of the moral spectrum, we have seen, the law typically requires greater proof of wrongdoing on the other. This was true for false imprisonment, and especially so for IIED. It also holds true for the property-based theories of trespass to chattels and conversion.

Trespass to chattels and conversion are actually complementary concepts that track the wrongfulness of personal property invasions at different points along a continuum of severity. Trespass to chattels covers interferences that are mild to moderate, while conversion applies to those that are serious or worse. The most benign form of trespass is an intermeddling or misappropriation which displays no defiance of the owner's possessory interest. Because of the rather innocuous nature of the misconduct, the aggrieved party may not recover presumed or nominal damages, but must prove any actual loss that the invasion has caused her to suffer.[26] Where the claimant is dispossessed of her chattel, however, there is reason for greater concern. Here, the taking is of longer duration and is effected with an utter disregard for the owner's rights.[27] Thus, damage is presumed. Even so, because the dispossession does not amount to a serious interference with the property, the claimant may recover only for the decreased value of the good and/or for her lost opportunity to use it.[28] However, once the property is seriously damaged, destroyed or dispossessed for an extended period of time, the wrong moves from the realm of trespass and into the domain of conversion. In this theory, liability is premised on both the nature of the tortious conduct and the severity of the invasion. Regarding the wrongdoing, section 222A of the Restatement (Second) of Torts requires consideration of the extent and duration of the tortfeasor's exercise of dominion and control over the chattel, her intent to assert a right inconsistent with the claimant's right of control, and any possible good faith motivation she may have harbored while committing the act.[29] In evaluating the harm to the property owner, the Restatement looks at the extent and duration of the interference with the owner's right of control, any damage that may have been done to the chattel, and the inconvenience or expense which the interference caused the owner to endure.[30] Under this analysis, those who commit egregious acts of wrongdoing may be held liable for conversion even if the chattel they misappropriate is only partially damaged or is later returned. Similarly, an actor whose behavior is less repugnant may nevertheless be found responsible if she renders the good a total loss. The result in either case is that the tortfeasor is required to pay for the entire value of the subject property at the time it was converted. This scheme seems eminently fair since it reflects the ideals of balance and proportionality that are so central to our conception of justice.

Indeed, it is hard to imagine how a moral system of rectification could accommodate the interests of actors and right-holders any better than the syndesmotic processes that have been used to define and implement these property-based torts.

Summary and Segue

It seems, from the preceding discussion, that the law of intentional torts has been artfully crafted to serve a number of ends simultaneously. First, it helps to promote the public objective of establishing some measure of social control. Besides declaring rules of unacceptable social behavior, intentional torts provide the public with a peaceful means of resolving disputes which otherwise might result in vengeance and violence. Second, these causes of action further the more intimate goal of ensuring private justice. Torts like battery, false imprisonment and IIED allow victims who have been degraded or dehumanized to repair such personal and moral indignities by obtaining a public declaration of wrongdoing, even where they have no physical scars to show for their misery. Finally, and perhaps most importantly, our intentional torts employ a highly relativistic and interdependent scheme of analysis that significantly advances our search for distributive and corrective justice. Indeed, by counterpoising conduct against harm, and proportioning responses to actions, the law of intentional torts ensures that each party to a harmful transaction receives the appropriate complement of both rights and responsibilities. The question now is, does this symbiosis continue when the clash of interests is not intentionally initiated, but results accidentally from some external risk created by an otherwise self-regarding activity? We shall take up this question next.

Chapter 15

Negligence

Instinct alone tells us that a different scheme of justice will be required for actions which are not intentional, but merely faulty or fault-free. These latter forms of conduct may display an unwitting disregard for danger, or they may reflect a desire to take a calculated risk, but they do not demonstrate the contempt for autonomy characteristic of intentional wrongdoing. In fact, such benignly culpable behavior may actually hold great personal or social value. Because the risk of harm presented by faulty or faultless conduct is lower, and its effect is at least marginally self-directed, those who create such dangers retain some right of autonomy to conduct these activities. To afford actors this greater freedom, tort law generally reduces their duties of care towards others. This means not only that their range of available activities is expanded, but also that it is more difficult to hold them financially accountable for the injuries they may produce.

Such is the nature of both the fault-based theory of negligence and the "no-fault" theory of strict liability. Unlike intentional torts, these theories contain strict causation and damage requirements which reduce the actor's exposure to liability. For these theories, the actor's duty does not extend to the world at large; rather, under the element of duty or proximate cause, she is responsible only to those endangered by the foreseeable risks of her activity. Even where the injured party falls within the scope of this duty, the actor may not be found factually responsible for the resulting loss unless her actions substantially controlled or influenced that outcome. If this connection is established, the defendant's liability still is not complete, but will be limited to such losses as reflect some *actual* impairment of the claimant's autonomy.

While the causation and damage requirements of negligence and strict liability are more stringent than those found in intentional torts, they remain responsive to the demands of private justice. Besides ensuring that the injured party has a complaint worthy of legal redress, the damage element serves to activate her right of corrective action. Once this right is triggered, the causation requirement takes her corrective instinct and directs it at the only party who can undo the wrong—the factually responsible tortfeasor. By channelling the victim's rights in this way, the notion of factual cause not only furthers the goal of corrective justice, it also helps to quell any retributive desires which she may harbor against her wrongdoer.

By and large, these private justice principles apply in much the same way under both negligence and strict liability. That is, regardless of the theory being used, proximate cause will still embrace only foreseeable risks, factual cause will continue to focus on the actor's control over the incident, and the damage requirement will entail some showing of tangible harm.[1] Even within each theory, it is unlikely that there will be any significant change in the application of these requirements from one situation to the next. Because the principles themselves are practically invariable, and their implementation relatively simple, I will address them no further here.

Instead, I will focus exclusively upon the duties imposed under each theory. As we shall see, there are a great number and variety of duties used to hold an actor negligent or strictly liable. These duties are not uniform, but restrict the autonomy of certain individuals in vastly different ways depending upon the circumstances. Given both the complex and mercurial nature of such obligations, there is cause to wonder whether they satisfy the concerns of distributive justice. Specifically, do they allocate autonomy in a way that seems fair, according each party her due? The answer to this question is quite complicated and will consume both of the next two chapters. I shall begin in this chapter with the duties of negligence law.

Standard-Based Analysis

Unlike intentional torts, negligence claims are determined by standards rather than rules. Negligent acts pose foreseeable, though not necessarily substantial, risks towards others (and usually will have some private or social benefit). In such cases, the underlying act itself may not be dangerous; it presents risk only when performed in the "wrong" way.[2] Thus, the actor will have some autonomy right to participate in the subject activity. This right must be balanced against the actor's duty to refrain from inflicting harm upon others. Both the autonomy right and the duty of the actor may vary from case to case, depending upon the type of activity in question, the particular manner in which it was conducted and the circumstances surrounding its performance. Because the propriety of the action changes with the situation, there is no bright-line rule which defines the actor's duty in each case. To evaluate such conduct, one must employ a flexible standard of care which can adapt to the particularities at hand.

In negligence cases, the standard commonly applied is that of the reasonably prudent person.[3] As the preceding discussion suggests, at the heart of this standard is a duty of care which can be either heightened or relaxed. An individual who complies with her duty of care, at whatever level it is set, acts in a reasonable fashion and so may be said to satisfy the standard. Where this is the case, her exercise of autonomy may not be sanctioned.

However, if the actor behaves unreasonably, thus breaching her duty of care, she fails the standard and may be liable for any resulting loss.

Duty and Autonomy

Although one cannot apply this standard without balancing many factors—like the actor's right of action and the interests of her victim—it is the concept of duty which emerges as the driving force in determining how the balance is to be struck. We earlier observed this catalytic influence when considering the inverse relationship between duty and autonomy. Remember that when the duty of the actor is increased, her autonomy to engage in the subject activity is restricted; likewise, when the duty is decreased, she enjoys greater freedom to pursue it. In many cases,[4] the actor's duty also determines the responsibilities and liberties of those with whom she interacts. Thus, where the actor bears a heightened responsibility to avoid causing harm, the recipient of her action is granted greater negative freedom from such conduct, and is relieved of at least some of the responsibility to look out for danger.

Special and General Duties

The duties underlying negligence law are created in two ways. One way is through the private agreement of consenting parties. These "special duties" are morally legitimate because they reflect uncoerced expressions of the parties' autonomy. The other source of tort duties is the state. As we have seen, the state has a political and moral responsibility to provide protection to citizens in return for their submission to the law. Such protection is secured by "general duties" which restrict harmful conduct.

These general and special duties impose both positive and negative limitations on the autonomy of their subjects. Either type of duty may require a passive party to take action to aid or protect another. If this positive command is not followed, the omitter's inaction is wrongful and may expose her to liability. On the other hand, both duties may direct individuals to refrain from engaging in certain dangerous activities. Where this duty is breached, the actor may be made to bear the financial consequences of her dereliction. In each case, the burden imposed by such duties is not fixed but fluid, changing along with the circumstances. Thus, the duty of precaution one owes when handling explosives may far exceed that imposed in a less volatile setting. Likewise, the obligation to act cautiously might differ depending upon whether a gun was fired or a ball of yarn was tossed. These sundry permutations of duty are fair so long as they are based on some acceptable criterion like need or risk. When we look closely at the many duties of negligence law, we see that they satisfy this central tenet of distributive justice.

Special Duties and Failures to Act

Consider first the special duties which may ground one's duty to act. Previously, we saw that duties of altruism are not highly favored in political systems, like ours, which are premised on the notion of autonomy. Indeed, liberal governments are formed to *guarantee* individuals certain basic liberties—such as the freedom to speak, assemble and worship, and the negative liberty of being safe from the harmful acts of others—not to *force* citizens to act on behalf of their neighbors. In recognition of this fact, tort law generally imposes no duty upon individuals to aid others. Nevertheless, we have seen that such a duty may exist where the parties are in a special relationship.[5] Special relationships, you will recall, arise either when the parties possess unequal abilities to control the risks of their association,[6] or when one party undertakes to aid the other but, because of her intervention, leaves the vulnerable party in a worse position.[7]

In each of these situations, the special relationship may be founded upon a special duty. Where the parties interact in a imbalanced relationship, there seldom is a written document guaranteeing the weaker party protection by the stronger. Nevertheless, such relationships often are longstanding, creating in the participants certain expectations about the other's actions. For example, suppose a landlord and tenant enter a lease agreement and, at the time the lease was executed, both parties were aware of a local custom whereby landlords provide security for their dwellings. In such a situation, the parties' relational status may tacitly delimit their respective responsibilities.[8] Or, assume the tenant has no legal right to alter the physical structure of the building or to license someone to patrol it; where this is known to the parties, both landlord and tenant may understand that the former bears the responsibility for securing the premises. In each case, the parties' relationship may create an implied, voluntary agreement which is sufficient to establish the landlord's special duty to protect the tenant.

Such a special duty also would accrue to one who, by undertaking to act, worsens the condition of another. This might occur if the undertaking is performed badly, thus directly affecting the victim's autonomy.[9] But it might also result from an undertaking which simply causes the party in distress to rely on its completion by foregoing other opportunities for assistance.[10] It may even include discouraging other potential rescuers from intervening on her behalf.[11] In any of these situations, the undertaker's behavior may express a voluntary commitment to assume a duty which she would not otherwise have.

Such special duties are just, and thus enforceable, for a number of reasons. The most obvious reason is that even the simplest transactions would be impossible without them. In order to interact, we must be able to predict the outcome of our exchanges with others. Such predictability is supplied by the special duty that one will do as she has agreed. Another important reason for enforcing special duties is that they hold serious consequences for the concept of autonomy. This is because someone who promises or undertakes to act on behalf of others does not just make a benevolent gesture, she insinuates herself into the lives of her proposed beneficiaries by inducing their reliance. It follows that when such a special duty-bearer fails to follow through on her appparent commitment, she does more than withhold a benefit, she often works irrevocable changes in the destinies of those with whom she interacts. But perhaps the best reason for enforcing special duties is that they provide the foundation for political association. Political unions derive from an implied arrangement between the state and its members: the state secures the basic attributes of autonomy for all individuals, and in return each citizen agrees to obey just laws which make this security possible. To ignore the binding effect of voluntary commitments, then, would be to deny the legitimacy of this association.

General Duties and Failures to Act

Despite their importance, special duties do not constitute the only basis for imposing on individuals an obligation to act on behalf of others. Such an obligation also may be created by general duties. Unlike special duties, which are formed voluntarily, general duties are handed down by the state.[12] This is significant because it makes them more difficult to justify. All duties represent some restriction on the bearer's autonomy. Where this restriction is voluntarily assumed, as with special duties, it cannot be considered a harm to the bearer for it emanates from her own exercise of autonomy. Where the restriction is forced upon the actor by some outside source, be it an individual or a political institution, it may be wrongful unless justified.

The state walks this tightrope when it uses general duties to require individuals to protect those with whom they transact. As we saw above, not all omitters are required to provide assistance to others—only those who are parties to special relationships have this responsibility. To legitimate this distinction, it must be shown that imposing greater duties on those in special relationships is objectively fair.

Earlier, I noted that the need which derives from a relational incapacity may be a valid basis for distributing responsibility. Where one party possesses superior knowledge of the risks associated with a transaction, and is in a better position to reduce or eliminate them, the other party's consent to the relationship and its consequences may be vitiated. If, during such an association, the vulnerable party sustains an injury at the hands of the other, the resulting loss presumptively would constitute a wrongful invasion of her interests. Under the need criterion, therefore, the state would be justified both in imposing upon the dominant party a heightened responsibility to protect her relational counterpart from such harm, and in enhancing the reliant party's autonomy by entitling her to such protection. This explains why it is fair to require those in "special relationships" to undertake preventative measures not asked of others. The relational need of the more vulnerable party renders involuntary any loss she sustains in the transaction, and so justifies the wrongdoer's tort duty to rectify it.

The General Duty to Act Reasonably

The general duties of negligence theory do not just require action where none would otherwise be demanded; they also place restrictions on the manner in which we carry out our activities once we undertake to perform them. Here, too, some may be expected to exercise more caution than others. Public utilities and medical practitioners, for example, must take greater care in their endeavors than those pursuing less essential vocations.[13] Children, on the other hand, can get away with misjudgments adults cannot.[14] All of this is fair, of course, if there is a convincing justification for treating these groups of actors differently.

Adjusting the Standard

When determining liability for affirmative negligent acts, tort law adjusts the defendant's responsibility up or down in five situations. In the first two, there is something special about the actor. For children and persons with physical disabilities, the reasonableness standard is modified, and the duty reduced. Neither is required to act as a "normal" adult; rather, they need only exercise the care demanded of a reasonable person with the same attributes.[15] The other special actors are individuals who possess superior skill, knowledge, training or experience regarding the activity in question. The responsibilities of these individuals is increased.[16] They are not judged as ordinary folk, but are held to the reasonable limit of their capabilities.[17] This is true for defendants and plaintiffs alike.[18] In two other scenarios where the duty is altered, the transaction rather than the actor is special, either because of the danger inherent in the included activity, or because of the importance of the good or service involved. Thus, when the activity poses high risks, those who engage in it bear a heightened responsibility of care towards those it endangers.[19] And if the subject good or service is essential to human welfare, the individual providing it to the public owes a greater responsibility to protect those who seek it.[20] Finally, one's duty of care may be modulated where the circumstances are special. We simply expect less of those in exigent circumstances than we do of those with time for rational deliberation.[21]

The Autonomy of Special Actors

All of these variations can be explained, and justified, under the distributive criteria identified and discussed previously. The special duty for children and those physically impaired is based upon the need created by their intrinsic incapacity. Both are afforded more freedom of unrestricted action than others. It is apparent why this privilege is extended to children. The experimentation which comes from such freedom is an indispensable step in the development of a child. It allows children to learn, sometimes by their mistakes, the basic physical and social principles expected of adults. Although this rationale is less persuasive for the physically disabled, it is not without merit. Unlike children, the attribute which incapacitates these individuals cannot be changed. Still, they stand to benefit from their added freedom. With lighter responsibilities, the physically challenged are encouraged to engage in the same activities open to everyone else. This not only helps them to overcome the limitations of their disabilities, it allows them to make substantial contributions to society in a variety of important occupations.

Mental Incapacities Distinguished

People with mental incapacities may seem to require the same privilege of unrestricted autonomy. Like children and the physically disabled, often they are incapable of conforming their behavior to the dictates of society. Nevertheless, there is an important distinction to be drawn between the mentally disabled and all others. The extra autonomy afforded to minors and the physically challenged benefits both the actors themselves, who gain experience, and society, which will someday harvest productive citizens. Except in rare situations, however, those suffering from intrinsic mental disabilities are unlikely to reap or bestow the same benefits from the extension of such a privilege.

No matter how much liberty is extended to such individuals, it is doubtful that they will come any closer to formulating or realizing some definite life plan.

Special Victims

The distinction between each of these types of individuals dissipates where they are acted upon, rather than acting themselves. Here, tort law extends greater protection to all types of incapacitated parties. In such cases, the actor imposing the risk owes each special victim a heightened responsibility to prevent harm,[22] and each in turn enjoys greater freedom of action. For example, a motorist bears a greater responsibility when driving past a location where children are likely to be present than she would where they are not.[23] Conversely, children may exercise greater abandon around a roadway than we would permit of adults. In cases like this, an unusual allocation of responsibility and liberty is justified because of the incapacitated party's vulnerability and need for special care.

Advanced Actors

A different sort of incapacity arises where persons of average abilities transact with those who possess superior mental attributes.[24] In such cases, the "special" actor holds an advantage over her transactional partner because she possesses the knowledge and ability to control the risks inherent in the parties' relationship. For example, she may supply a dangerous instrumentality for the other to use, as where a chemical manufacturer markets a toxic pesticide for use by the general public. Alternatively, she may have the power to determine whether and to what extent risks not of her own creation may enter the environment of the parties' transaction. Landlords who provide security systems for their buildings stand in this position. In these situations and others like them, the disparity between the parties creates a "special relationship"[25] in which the less knowledgeable party suffers from a relational incapacity.[26] Such an incapacity, we have seen, establishes a need which justifies extending the more vulnerable among us a generous cloak of protection.

Within relationships of this sort, the dominant party incurs a duty to protect her reliant counterpart from dangers which the latter's less developed faculties could not discern. This is especially true where the dominant party explicitly or implicitly induces the other to depend on her expertise.[27] Under these circumstances, there is good reason to doubt the vulnerable party's willingness to encounter the danger or ability to avoid it. Accordingly, any injury resulting to that party from the interaction may be presumptively wrongful. At the very least, it justifies tipping the scales of comparative responsibility decidedly against her "superior" counterpart.

Special Activities and the Criterion of Risk

In many of the relationships described above, the parties' underlying interaction involves some significant risks. Where such risks are substantial, this alone might justify imposing a greater duty of care upon their creator. Under the risk criterion of distributive justice, the state has the right, indeed the obligation, to protect citizens from such potential harms. The greater the risk, the greater is the state's authority to regulate the activity. It does this by distributing weighty responsibilities to those engaged in these endeavors.

The risk criterion permeates much of the law of negligence. It sometimes is expressed overtly. For example, where one hires an independent contractor to perform an inherently dangerous activity, or to correct a dangerous condition, she bears a nondelegable duty to ensure that the danger is not realized in harm.[28] Likewise, when children engage in "adult" or "dangerous" activities, they lose the special protection of the law, and are held to the higher standard of a reasonable adult.[29] Even where it is not acknowledged, the risk criterion surreptitiously influences the decision of negligence cases. Risk is part of the balancing process intrinsic to applying the reasonable person standard. The greater the likelihood that an action will produce harm to another, and the more devastating the magnitude of the loss, the greater her responsibility will be.[30]

Special Goods and Services and the Need Criterion

While the risk criterion protects individuals from harmful conduct, the need criterion ensures that they receive what they must to survive. There is ample evidence that the law of negligence seeks to protect persons bargaining for necessities in consensual exchange transactions, or those deprived of necessities in nonconsensual interactions. This is accomplished by imposing stricter duties against the purveyors of such goods and services, and by making these commodities more accessible to those who need them most.

As a general principle, an individual seeking to obtain a necessity cannot be forced to waive an important right in return. For example, tort law usually precludes a medical practitioner from securing a waiver of liability for personal injuries resulting from malpractice.[31] Moreover, providers of important public services, such as utility companies, public carriers and innkeepers often carry a heightened responsibility to protect their patrons.[32] Although the privity barrier protected many early businesses, providers of bad food have long been subject to heightened duties (under tort or warranty theory) for injuries caused by their products.[33] Even home builders and landlords, who supply us with our means of shelter, are often delegated added responsibilities to ensure that the structures they provide are reasonably fit and habitable.[34]

In each case, the necessity of these goods deprives the needy party of meaningful choice in the transaction. Thus, any injury which she sustains while attempting to acquire such goods is presumptively harmful. Under the need criterion, the state may preempt such harmful exchanges, and facilitate the acquisition of necessities, by requiring their providers to exercise greater care in the preparation and dissemination of these goods.

The Special Circumstance of Exigency

In our final example of special negligence duties, the distributive criterion of "need" again plays an important role. As a general rule, those forced to act under exigent circumstances are less accountable for their actions. Since the most basic requirement of autonomy is self-preservation, we all possess a substantial interest in taking whatever steps are necessary to ensure our own survival. The law of negligence affords us this latitude by lowering our duty of care in potentially life-threatening situations. This explains why the unlucky cabdriver in the previously discussed *Cordas* case was permitted to abandon his vehicle as it careened toward a city sidewalk. His responsibility would have been far greater, no doubt, if no gun had been held to his head. Where the need for desperate action is apparent, it is fair to allocate the party in distress a disproportionate share of autonomy. With the vicissitudes of life such as they are, we all stand to benefit from this practical dispensation at one time or another.

The Relativity and Aggregation of the Criteria

Although each of these distributive criteria may justify altering the defendant's responsibility, they do not always have the same weight in effecting this change. They admit of innumerable variations, increasing or decreasing in significance depending upon the circumstances. An incapacity may be trifling or enervating. Some goods are absolutely vital to existence, others less so. And risks may range from the substantial to the trivial. In each case, a fact finder must determine the extent to which these factors influenced the outcome. The greater the effect, the more burdensome will be the actor's duty to avoid harming others.

It should be noted that these distributive criteria, while activated in different ways, are not mutually exclusive. Indeed, often more than one may apply to a given interpersonal dispute. We have already seen an example of this in the *Cordas* case. There, the cabdriver engaged in the high risk activity of abandoning a moving taxi. This, of course, would ordinarily increase his duty of care. In this case, however, he acted out of a dire necessity—i.e., to save his life from a gun-toting carjacker. This need tended to decrease his responsibility to those on the street. Although the court exonerated the cabby of any liability, the interrelationship of these countervailing factors made this a difficult case to decide. Why? Because there are no set patterns for blending such distributive criteria. In this case and others like it, responsibility cannot be predetermined in accordance with some definitive rule of behavior, but must derive from the unique circumstances of the parties' entire transaction.

So we see that the many species of negligence duties all conform to the ideal of distributive justice. Through the flexible reasonable person standard, the state allocates an uneven array of liberties to its citizens. This discrepancy in treatment is morally and politically acceptable because it is premised upon criteria considered to be just. These criteria—of need and risk—explain why omitters can be commanded to help their neighbors, why children and the physically disabled can act in ways others cannot, why certain goods and services are made more accessible and why stricter restrictions are placed on dangerous activities. Just as the needy require greater autonomy to protect their most basic interests, those who are socially irresponsible require greater restraint to prevent them from imposing their will upon others. By balancing these concerns of freedom and safety, the negligence standard facilitates the ad hoc determination of responsibility in the interpersonal disputes of tort law.

Determining Breach

Once a fair duty of care has been established, it remains for decision whether this obligation has been breached. Here, too, the concerns of justice are evident. Because the breach culminates the wrong, and thus invokes the corrective sanction of the law, there must be some reasonably fair means of determining whether the alleged tortfeasor exceeded her distributive share of autonomy. Although the reasonable person standard provides a general framework for this analysis, it seldom yields easy or clear-cut answers. This is because the standard, by itself, has no positive or normative force. To have meaning, it must tap into the moral instincts of the community deciding the dispute. It is no wonder, then, that the difficult task of applying the standard normally is assigned to our civil juries. By examining the unique circumstances of the parties' encounter, the jury in its common wisdom determines what is reasonable and what is not. In this manner the allocation of responsibility remains responsive to the intuitive dictates of justice in each particular case.

How does the jury make this determination? As we saw earlier, the reasonable person standard requires that the actor's responsibility be balanced against both her own autonomy interests and those of her actual or prospective victim. There are at least three considerations relevant to this task. One is whether the actor's autonomy would be restricted by performing in another, safer way, and the extent to which that alternative would reduce the attendant risks to others. In addition, it is important to determine whether changing the performance of the act would affect the expected gain (i.e, would it destroy the personal virtue or common good which the original act was designed to achieve, or was the manner of that act not necessary to achieving the desired good?). Last, one must assess the value which the activity had for the actor in her pursuit of virtue. In other words, how indispensable is it to her life plan?.[35] As a general rule, if there are alternatives to the intended action which would not unduly restrict the actor's autonomy or the "goods" which she seeks to achieve through the exercise of her autonomy, and if such alternatives significantly reduce the risk that her action will harm others (to the extent that the act then would seem more self-directed than other-directed), then the actor may be negligent for failing to take those alternative measures.

Breach as Injustice

In what sense are such negligent acts wrongful and unjust? As we saw earlier, it is not necessarily because they are morally blameworthy. If they are "faulty," it is only because they are unfair. Remember that when individuals enter political associations, all mutually agree to restrict their autonomy by obeying the law. The only precondition is that the law be just. Where the law is unjust because it is wicked, denying essential rights, or unfair, distributing those rights unfairly among citizens, then those cheated by the law are justified in rebelling against it. However, where the law is founded on accepted distributive criteria, all are bound to respect and follow it. One who violates a just law is herself unjust because she breaches the duty of mutual restriction essential to political association. She exercises a degree of autonomy that others, through their own self-restraint, may not. This is the case with those who act negligently. As we saw above, the duties of negligence are fair insofar as they are founded upon legitimate distributive criteria. By failing to comply with such duties, the negligent actor enjoys a freedom of carelessness forbidden to others in society. Her breach is unfair, and thus wrongful, because it disturbs the proportional equality created by the law of torts. But it also is unjust in a far more personal sense. Beyond usurping an unfair share of freedom, the negligent tortfeasor invades a superior right of solitude held by her victim. This is a distinctively private wrong experienced only by the sufferer of such misconduct.

Chapter 16

Strict Liability

Like negligence, the theory of strict liability is founded upon the general duty to refrain from harming others. And, as in the former area of the law, the duties in strict liability are not absolute. The acts subject to this theory are not intended to cause harm; instead, they are designed to further some legitimate purpose of the actor. Thus, while the actor bears a responsibility to avoid causing harm, she also enjoys an autonomy interest to act in accordance with her life plan. For a court to strike the appropriate balance between the actor's responsibility and autonomy, therefore, it must employ a flexible standard of care rather than a rigid behavioral rule.

Unlike in negligence cases where the reasonable person standard reigns supreme, there is no single uniform standard for assessing strict liability. The concept of strict liability has been applied in a wide variety of contexts involving a number of different causes of action.[1] The two most prominent uses of this concept are in the areas of abnormally dangerous activities and product liability. Except for using the descriptive theoretical term "strict liability," however, these theories have never had much in common. Indeed, the substantive bases of assigning responsibility under each theory are, and always have been, considerably different. While a multifactor analysis is used to declare an activity abnormally dangerous, standards ranging from consumer expectations to balancing risk and utility often determine the defectiveness of a product. Even within each theory, these standards have not remained constant, but have undergone substantial transformation throughout their troubled histories. Given the rather schizophrenic personality of strict liability, both within and between these theories of recovery, the moral identity of that concept remains uncertain. Just what are its central features and what is it supposed to accomplish? Does it satisfy the requirements of corrective and distributive justice, and if so, in what sense are the diverse activities it regulates wrongful? To answer these questions, we must examine more closely the two main forms of this concept, beginning with it earliest incarnation in the theory of abnormally dangerous activities.

Nonnatural Uses of Land

Although strict liability in some form has been part of tort law from its inception, that theory is most often associated with the seminal English case of *Rylands v. Fletcher*.[2] There, a coal mine being leased by the plaintiff was flooded when the defendant-mill operator's water reservoir collapsed. In the ensuing lawsuit by the plaintiff to recover for the damage caused to the mine, the defendant initially prevailed on the ground that he had not been negligent in the construction or maintenance of the reservoir. On appeal to the Exchequer Chamber, however, the decision was reversed and judgment was entered for the plaintiff. There, Lord Blackburn ruled that the mill operator was responsible for the damage to the mine even though he had exercised due care in his operations.

Although Lord Blackburn's opinion was somewhat cryptic, he seemed to premise the defendant's liability on two grounds. One ground appears to be the mill operator's misfeasance. Indeed, in several places throughout the decision he noted that the water for the reservoir did not naturally rest on the defendant's property, but was brought there by the defendant's own affirmative act.[3] Unfortunately, Lord Blackburn did not explain why he found this fact important. Nevertheless, one can reasonably surmise his reasoning. In earlier times, and even up to the time of this case, an actor could be held liable simply for committing an affirmative act which caused injury to another. While this rule played an important peace-keeping function in medieval England, by the mid-nineteenth century it had become more a matter of personal responsibility. Under such a principle, Blackburn might have felt compelled to hold the mill operator accountable for asserting his autonomy both over the natural landscape, which was transformed by the reservoir, and over his neighbors, whose own property interests could have been affected by that structure. Yet Blackburn clearly did not premise his decision solely on the fact that the defendant had affirmatively constructed an "unnatural" object on his property; rather, what sealed the miller's fate was the extraordinary danger which he had thereby created. Looking only at the characteristics of the reservoir itself—i.e., as a large body of standing water—Blackburn concluded that this condition was intolerably hazardous because it was "likely to do mischief" if the structure were ever to break.[4]

The House of Lords later affirmed the Exchequer Chamber, but on grounds seemingly different from those articulated by Lord Blackburn. Writing for the House, Lord Cairns eschewed any direct discussion of the affirmative nature of the defendant's construction and maintenance of the reservoir, or the danger posed by that activity. Instead, he focused exclusively on whether the mill operator's use of the land was natural or non-natural. This choice of terms was unfortunate because it obfuscated the underlying rationale of Cairn's decision to affirm. On the one hand, "natural" could be taken to mean any condition comprised of natural elements, such as water, trees, soil, rocks and so forth. Cairn's finding that the reservoir at issue was not natural, however, undermined this interpretation.

On the other hand, "natural" could include those conditions which exist without human intervention, like hills, lakes, streams and forests. If this were the case, then a "nonnatural" use would be very much like Lord Blackburn's conception of misfeasance. But a closer look at Cairn's opinion reveals that he had a different understanding of the terms "natural" and "nonnatural." He described a natural use as one "in the ordinary course of the enjoyment of the land." Under this connotation, community custom would seem to determine which activities are natural and which are not. Because the miller, in erecting the reservoir, had used his land in a way that was not common for his locale, he was required to bear the financial burden of the losses that that activity had caused others.

Ultrahazardous Activities

Because of its uncertain English heritage, the *Rylands* doctrine of strict liability was destined to face an identity crisis here in America. Relying on Lord Blackburn's view, the drafters of the first Restatement of Torts adopted in section 520 a theory of recovery for "ultrahazardous activities."[5] The clear emphasis here was on the inherent danger posed by the activity itself. Indeed, section 520 defined an ultrahazardous activity as one that "necessarily involves a risk of serious harm to the persons, land or chattels of others which cannot be eliminated by the exercise of the utmost care."[6] As so defined, this theory was designed to include such activities as dynamite storage and blasting which pose high levels of risk no matter where they are carried on.

Abnormally Dangerous Activities

By the 1960s, however, the foundational underpinning for this theory had shifted. No longer was risk the only factor important in establishing the actor's liability. Having slowly become aware of Cairn's decision in the House of Lords, many courts began to require that the defendant's activity also be inappropriate for the location in which it was conducted. With this shift in focus, the salient inquiry now was not whether the activity was ultrahazardous, but whether it was abnormally dangerous.

This new vision of strict liability was endorsed by the Restatement (Second) of Torts. Specifically, section 519 established liability against those engaged in abnormally dangerous activities.[7] This conception of activity-based strict liability is the one currently in use by most jurisdictions.[8] Although no definition of an abnormally dangerous activity is provided, the drafters of the Restatement, in section 520, did list several factors to assist in determining which activities fall within the purview of this theory, including:

(a) [the] existence of a high degree of risk of some harm to the person, land or chattels of others;
(b) [the] likelihood that the harm that results from it will be great;
(c) [the] inability to eliminate the risk by the exercise of reasonable care;
(d) [the] extent to which the activity is not a matter of common usage;
(e) [the] inappropriateness of the activity to the place where it is carried on;
(f) [the] extent to which its value to the community is outweighed by its dangerous attributes.[9]

Clearly evident in this multifactor standard are both the risk concern of Lord Blackburn and the custom concern of Lord Cairns. The first three factors—which examine the probability of harm posed by the activity, the likely magnitude of any resulting injury and the possibility of reducing the activity's inherent risks—together help to demonstrate just how dangerous the conduct in question really is. On the other hand, the remaining three factors—focusing on the common usage of the activity, and its appropriateness and utility in the community in which it is being conducted—provide some yardstick for determining whether the risks created by that enterprise are tolerable or intolerable to the people who must put up with it. Although all of these factors need not be satisfied to find the actor liable,[10] it seems essential that at least one or more of the considerations from each category weigh in the plaintiff's favor. Indeed, it would be difficult to imagine imposing liability against one engaged in a high risk endeavor unless that activity were either uncommon to or frowned upon by the community where it takes place. Consider the act of driving an automobile. Everyone knows that it is sure to bring death and destruction to thousands of people each year, yet no one would argue that drivers should be held strictly liable for all injuries that may result from this activity, no matter how unavoidable they may be. In fact, it would be virtually impossible for an activity to be considered high risk if it did not exceed those hazards normally created by other members of the community. Presumably, then, before an activity can be defined as abnormally dangerous, not only must it present an extraordinary hazard, the danger it creates must also be considered unacceptable to the surrounding community.

The Justice of Activity-Based Strict Liability

We see from this brief survey that, at different stages of historical development, activity-based strict liability has been justified on three grounds: risk alone, community disapproval alone, and a hybrid of these two. Our task now is to determine which, if any, of these views comports with our notions of justice.

Reliance on the Distributive Criterion of Risk

As we already have observed, our society recognizes risk as a valid basis for distributing autonomy. Since the fundamental task of the state is to protect individuals from harm, it must take preventative action to curb injurious conduct. The greater the risk of an activity, the more likely it will cause harm to another, and thus the stricter the state's regulation of that enterprise may be. Activities which are intended to harm others, and which have no other intrinsic value, may be prohibited entirely. Other enterprises, which pose less danger and/or possess greater personal or social utility, must be subject to less stringent restrictions. Strict liability activities generally fall into this category. Such activities not only advance the interests of those that conduct them, they also generate goods or services which benefit others as well. Given the risk posed by these enterprises, it is fair that they be regulated; yet because of their virtuous aspects, they must not be preempted. Subjecting such activities to the ex post sanction of tort law appears to strike a fair balance between these competing concerns of safety and liberty. It allows the public to enjoy their social benefits without absorbing all of their private costs. Just as important, it affords those who engage in these enterprises the freedom necessary to pursue their own life plans while assisting others in achieving theirs.

There are a couple of problems, however, in relying upon risk alone to distribute autonomy in the adversarial context of a tort case. One is that doing so obviates the need for such an adversarial setting in the first place. To determine the riskiness of an activity, one is required to examine only its inherent characteristics. This, you will recall, was the approach of Lord Blackburn in *Rylands*. Under his view, a reservoir is dangerous because of the large volume of water it contains. Other activities, like blasting or operating a nuclear power plant, could be analyzed in a like manner. Once it had been determined that the enterprise's danger level crossed the line of ultrahazardousness, it would make no difference who was affected by the activity or in what way. This is because the wrongfulness of the conduct simply would not depend upon the nature of the effect it had upon others. If it were ultrahazardous it would be considered wrongful, and the actor would be responsible for whatever harm followed from it. Thus, there would be no need for a bilateral comparison of the rights of the parties; both the wrongfulness of the activity and the veracity of the injury could be determined independently of each other in separate proceedings. Here, a legislatively created scheme of distributive justice would appear to be the most efficacious means of allocating autonomy to those conducting such activities and those who involuntarily bear their consequences.

The other problem with using risk as the sole criterion for imposing strict liability is that it may promote autonomy restrictions which are overly broad. Unlike negligence, which merely condemns the minute details of one's behavior, strict liability determinations apply to entire categories of human endeavor. Instead of saying that one should not drive a gasoline truck ninety miles an hour on a crowded highway during a stormy night, it says that one should not drive such a truck at all unless she is willing to pay for any injuries which may be caused by that activity. No limits are placed on this rule by the concept of risk alone. If an activity's danger is solely a function of its intrinsic propensities, then it is just as ultrahazardous when conducted in a bucolic country setting as when it is carried on in the biggest metropolis. Supposedly, it will be objectionable whether it is carried on in Death Valley, California or in Los Angeles. Under this view, a determination that an enterprise is ultrahazardous would not just subject its purveyor to liability for one past, completed act; instead, it would conclusively establish her responsibility for all future harms which might arise from her ongoing operations anywhere within the same jurisdiction.

The Importance of Community Norms

To avoid placing such undue burdens on activities of this sort, the assessment of liability must be based on more than just risk. It must also consider the demographic characteristics of the locality in which the enterprise is being conducted and the predilections of the people who live there. Indeed, risk itself is not understandable in a vacuum, but has meaning only in relation to some discernable context. Thus, even though the propensities of blasting are the same in Death Valley and Los Angeles, the risk posed by that activity will vary markedly in these locations depending upon the number of buildings, power lines, water mains, gas pipes, and most importantly, people nearby. So an activity which is ultrahazardous in one geographic area may not be dangerous at all in another. Even where the danger of an enterprise is comparable in two different locations, the desirability of that endeavor to the inhabitants of each community may vary greatly. In farming communities, for example, crop dusting might be an acceptable risk; the same would not be true, however, for those who live in a suburban residential neighborhood.

We see, then, that the only way to ensure that the regulation of this or any other activity is not overly broad is to consider the context in which it is carried on. On a private level, this consideration serves to protect the actor's autonomy by ensuring that her activity is restricted only in those locations where its risks are unacceptable. From a social standpoint, it also helps to secure a place of importance for the adversarial system in evaluating such conduct. While legislatively enacted distributive schemes are good at establishing broad policy objectives, they generally are incapable of making fine distinctions to suit specific circumstances. It follows that such a scheme would be ill-adapted to assess the social value of particular activities in a wide array of different locations. This can be achieved only within the more flexible parameters of civil litigation.

The Role of the Judge

Even in this setting, determining whether an activity is *excessively* risky can be a difficult assignment. In negligence cases, this job is performed by the jury. In fact, only juries, who represent a cross-section of the community, are deemed capable of deciding what conduct is just in that locale. Yet in strict liability cases, the burden of identifying abnormally dangerous activities falls on the judge.[11] As a policymaker for the state, the judge decides which endeavors may operate free of the ex post restrictions of tort law, and which must pay their way. Handing this responsibility to a judge seems reasonable since the imposition of liability does not just limit isolated instances of misconduct, as does negligence, but places restrictions upon entire categories of potentially valuable human activity. And, while the judge is afforded enormous power in doling out this responsibility, her discretion in this regard does not go unchecked. The community custom factor ensures that her determination of duty remains responsive to the sense of justice pervasive in the locale where the activity is conducted. Only where the activity and its attendant risks are inappropriate for *that particular* community, such that its risks exceed its value, will the actor bear the heightened duty of strict liability.

Activity-Based Strict Liability and Negligence

Viewed in this light, the theories of negligence and strict liability for abnormally dangerous activities seem strikingly similar. Both employ standards which help to balance the actor's autonomy right to act and her responsibility to refrain from harming others. For each, responsibilities are founded, at least in part, on the distributive criterion of risk. And both require that these duties be underwritten by community values of justice and fairness. The only apparent difference between these theories is their focus. In negligence, we concentrate on the *manner* in which the activity is performed. In strict liability, on the other hand, the spotlight is on the desirability of the *activity itself*. Yet despite this analytic distinction, both theories yield a similar conclusion. If either an activity or the manner of its performance exceed a community standard of acceptability, the actor's conduct is in some sense unreasonable. While negligent acts are unreasonable in themselves, abnormally dangerous activities are unreasonable because of their ill-advised conception or location, and/or because the parties conducting them fail or refuse to pay for their consequences.

Strict Products Liability

In product liability actions, any semblance between negligence and strict liability is often strenuously rejected. In fact, one of the primary reasons why product-based strict liability was developed was to avoid the onerous burden of proof required under the theory of negligence. Even so, strict products liability always has been more than just an attempt to side-step a few outdated evidentiary requirements. Indeed, those who ushered in this new concept did so with lofty ideals and grand purposes. More than anything else, they attempted to guarantee justice to the forgotten victims of the industrial revolution—consumers. Nevertheless, throughout the years, justice in this area has been an especially elusive commodity. Consumer groups have complained that strict products liability does not go far enough in protecting them from the hazards of modern gadgetry. Manufacturers, on the other hand, have decried the deleterious effect which such liability has had upon product development, insurance costs and competitiveness in the international market. While we cannot hope to consider all the nuances of this debate in the following discussion, we can at least touch upon the most fundamental question underlying it: Is the theory of strict products liability sufficiently grounded in principles of justice to give it enduring moral credibility? To answer this question, we must go back to the nineteenth century where the seeds of products liability law were sown.

Phase One: The Elimination of Privity

As we saw in Chapter Eleven, the doctrine of privity shielded early manufacturers from liability for injuries suffered by remote consumers of their products. Under this doctrine, the manufacturer's duty of care extended only to the immediate purchaser of the good, in most cases a distributor or retailer. This meant that, if a consumer were later harmed by the good, her only recourse was against the entity who sold her that item. In many cases, this seller was a small merchant who either knew the consumer personally, and thus was not an attractive target of litigation, or lacked the financial resources to pay for her loss.

To alleviate the harshness of this doctrine, it soon became riddled with exceptions. The most prominent exception, and most long-lasting, permitted injured consumers to recover damages against the manufacturers of inherently dangerous products. Originally, this exception applied only to products—like poisons and guns—whose sole function was to injure or destroy.[12] Later, it was expanded to include other items which were intended for intimate bodily use, such as food and drugs.[13] Finally, as was noted earlier, Judge Cardozo in *MacPherson v. Buick Motor Co.*[14] eliminated the privity rule entirely. His rationale was that *any* product, if unreasonably made, presented an intolerable danger to an innocent consumer. Thus, after *MacPherson*, the manufacturer's duty to use care in the construction of the product was owed not just to its immediate purchaser, but to any reasonably foreseeable user or consumer of that good.[15]

The demise of the privity doctrine around the turn of the century marked the end of product liability law's first phase of development. During this formative period, two interrelated trends were apparent. The laissez-faire freedom previously enjoyed by manufacturers was now dramatically reduced, and the power of consumers in protecting their interests was substantially enhanced. What was the force behind these changes? The answer lies along the road to *MacPherson*. Both the gradual erosion and eventual elimination of the privity doctrine were justified by the extraordinary risks posed by the increasingly lethal products of that era.

The Centrality of Risk in the First Phase

By the late nineteenth century, most products had begun to pose dangers incomprehensible just a few decades before. The use of electricity, in particular, endowed even the most common products with awesome destructive potential. Examples now are all around us. Consider the power saw which can dismember its user in the wink of an eye; or the programmable coffee maker which can short circuit and start a fire in the dark of night. The combustion engine, too, was rapidly working its share of mischief. Indeed, by the time of *MacPherson*, injuries caused by cars were so frequent that they practically went unnoticed. If these inherent dangers were not bad enough, they were compounded further by the complexity of most products then coming onto the market. The advent of interchangeable parts had begun to make products so intricate that they posed insidious dangers which could not be detected by casual, untrained inspection. In fact, because of the use of mass advertising campaigns, which not only extolled the virtues of the product but of the manufacturer as well, consumers frequently felt no need to subject their products to examination. Instead, they entrusted their safety to those who seemed to readily guarantee it. Besides intensifying consumers' dependency on the manufacturer, and in turn increasing their need for protection, such tactics served to increase their vulnerability to hidden product dangers. The amplified risks which arose out of all these factors gave good reason for expanding the responsibilities of those that marketed such products.

The Second Phase: Toward Strict Liability

If the doors to the courthouse had been opened to consumers during this preliminary phase of product liability law, the pathway through that portal remained cluttered with some imposing obstacles at the beginning of the second.[16] While consumers could sue manufacturers for product-related injuries, they often were incapable of proving that the manufacturer did anything wrong. There were many reasons for this, but of these two were especially determinative. First, in cases where the product contained no visible flaws, most consumers lacked the sophistication either to investigate for latent defects or to second-guess the manufacturer's design specifications. Second, even where there was an obvious defect in the product, it was usually impossible for the consumer to pinpoint exactly how it got there. With new modes of distribution, it was not uncommon for a product to be handled by two or three intermediaries before it was purchased by the consumer. Frequently, the consumer had no way of knowing which of the parties within the chain of distribution actually caused the defect. Certainly, given the realities of mass production, no one in the manufacturer's plant would have first-hand knowledge of how any particular unit on the assembly line was treated. The only evidence available in this regard were the manufacturer's own quality control records, and these more often than not were less than helpful to the prospective claimant.

To the keenest observers, it soon became apparent that the cause of these problems was the relational imbalance which had developed between manufacturers and the people buying their products. Only manufacturers possessed the expertise necessary to understand the complicated inner-workings of their wares. They alone had access to the morass of scientific and technological information commonly relied upon by those in the same or similar industries. And it was they who exercised exclusive control over the myriad files of secret trade practices actually used in the design and construction of such goods.

One of the first to recognize this widening gulf between manufacturers and consumers was Justice Roger Traynor of the California Supreme Court. In the seminal case of *Escola v. Coca Cola Bottling Co.*,[17] Justice Traynor relied upon this relational imbalance as a justification for applying strict liability principles to cases involving product-related injuries.[18] In what is one of the most memorable passages in his now famous concurring opinion, Justice Traynor described the nature and origin of this imbalance as follows:

> As handicrafts have been replaced by mass production with its great markets and transportation facilities, the close relationship between the producer and consumer of a product has been altered. Manufacturing processes, frequently valuable secrets, are ordinarily either inaccessible to or beyond the ken of the general public. The consumer no longer has means or skill enough to investigate for himself the soundness of a product, even when it is not contained in a sealed package, and his erstwhile vigilance has been lulled by the steady efforts of manufacturers to build up confidence by advertising and marketing devices such as trade-marks. Consumers no longer approach products warily but accept them on faith, relying on the reputation of the manufacturer or the trade mark. Manufacturers have sought to justify that faith by increasingly high standards of inspection and a readiness to make good on defective products by way of replacements and refunds. The manufacturer's obligation to the consumer must keep pace with the changing relationship between them. . . . [19]

The Centrality of Need in the Second Phase

This preoccupation with leveling the commercial playing field soon became the central characteristic of product liability law's second phase of development. While the first phase made it possible for consumers to recover for product-related injuries, the second phase, driven by the perceived inequality among parties in the marketplace, justified alleviating the consumers' burden of proof. Great strides were made toward this end during the early 1960s. In the 1960 opinion of *Henningsen v. Bloomfield Motors, Inc.*[20] the New Jersey Supreme Court eliminated the privity requirement in warranty cases and cast doubt upon the enforceability of broad disclaimer provisions. Three years later, in *Greenman v. Yuba Power Products, Inc.*[21] the California Supreme Court, with Justice Traynor now writing for the majority, formally adopted strict liability as a basis for recovery in cases involving product injuries. This movement reached its apex in 1965 when the drafters of the Restatement (Second) of Torts endorsed the *Greenman* decision and recognized the nascent theory of strict products liability.[22]

Just like the first phase, the second phase in the development of product liability law seems to have been inspired by sound moral instincts. As we have seen, this stage was designed primarily to remediate the distinct relational imbalance which had existed between manufacturers and consumers during the early part of the twentieth century. It was this disparity in expertise and bargaining power which had begun to render consumers powerless to protect themselves from product-related injuries. Indeed, because most consumers were unaware of most product risks, and lacked the know-how to find them, they were effectively incapable of avoiding product injuries. This vulnerability was further enhanced by manufacturers who, through advertising and marketing campaigns, attempted to win consumers' trust and confidence and assuage their concerns about safety. As we have seen before, the reliant parties in such imbalanced relationships are in special need of protection. Unlike others who are free of constraining relational bonds, these parties lack the autonomy to secure their most basic interests. Where this is the case, the distributive criterion of need allows the state to afford them the protection they lack. This has been done in the product liability area by holding sellers strictly accountable for the losses caused by their goods. Using need as a legitimating factor, the state, through the doctrine of strict products liability, had both heightened manufacturers' duty to make safer products, and bolstered consumers' right to redress for product-related injuries.

The True Nature of Strict Products Liability

Of course, it doesn't take a theory of strict liability to accomplish either of these objectives. We've already seen how, under the theory of negligence, certain actors may have greater responsibilities and their relational opposites greater rights. Providers of public necessities, for example, are under a heavier burden to ensure the safety of those that must use their services. Yet despite this potential overlap between negligence and strict liability, those who helped to usher in product liability law's second phase vehemently denied any such connection. In fact, the drafters of the Restatement (Second) of Torts openly declared the separate identities of the two theories. In this regard, section 402A provides that a product seller may be held strictly liable even if she has exercised all possible care (i.e., acted nonnegligently) in the construction of that good.[23] Many courts have echoed the same theme. In explaining the difference between the two theories, courts frequently are heard to declare that the focus in negligence is on the reasonableness of the manufacturer's conduct, whereas in strict liability the focus is on the condition of the product itself.[24]

These protestations aside, there has always been, and still is, serious doubt about the alleged distinction between strict products liability and negligence for making dangerous products. The source of this uncertainty is the analytical standard that has been used to apply the product-based version of strict liability. Under section 402A of the Restatement, the critical inquiry is whether the product, at the time of sale, was in a "defective condition unreasonably dangerous to the user or consumer."[25] If it was, then strict liability attaches, and the manufacturer is responsible for all injuries caused by that item. If it was not, then the plaintiff is relegated to using some other theory of recovery.

The Ambiguity of the Defectiveness Standard

Before section 402A was even adopted, it was apparent to the drafters that this "defectiveness" standard lacked the substantive content necessary to stand on its own. Indeed, because the term "defect" connotes little more than that something must be wrong with the product, it served more to signify the objective of the law than to provide a workable test for applying it. To ameliorate this weakness, the drafters of the Restatement created the consumer expectation test.[26] Under this test, a product is deemed defective if the risks it poses exceed those that would be expected by a reasonable consumer of that good. Given strict liability's roots in warranty law,[27] such a test was a logical choice. It was more concerned with whether the consumer received what she had bargained for in the sale than it was with the inherent safety of the product.

Manufacturing Defects and Consumer Expectations

The consumer expectation test worked well in cases involving manufacturing defects, like the adulterated food cases from which it emerged.[28] There, the product deviated from the manufacturer's own specifications for the product. Because the "bad" unit was unlike almost all others sold by the manufacturer, the danger usually would be a surprise to any consumer familiar with that type of item. So if a mouse were found in a soft drink bottle, the consumer's expectations about the product would be violated, and the offending unit would be considered defective. Under these circumstances, the manufacturer's liability truly would be strict. Once the consumer satisfied the consumer expectation test, she would recover even if she were unable to show exactly how the mouse had gotten into the bottle.

The Design Dilemma

Despite its success in manufacturing defect cases, the test proved to be far less efficacious in cases where the design and labeling of the product were called into question. In such cases, the product does not deviate from other like units sold by the manufacturer. Indeed, the product is marketed exactly as planned. Here, the conception of the product itself comes under attack. The problem is that most consumers have little idea as to how most products could or should be designed. Without such an expectation, the consumer-oriented test of the Restatement is of no use.[29] To define defectiveness in such cases, therefore, some other standard had to be created.

The "Risk-Utility" Solution

Although many alternative tests have been proposed, almost all rely in whole or in part on some form of risk-utility analysis.[30] Under such an approach, a product is deemed defective if the risks it presents exceed its utility with that design. Several factors must be weighed to make this determination. These include the probability and magnitude of harm posed by the product, the economic and technological feasibility of implementing alternative designs which are safer and no less desirable, and the ability of the consumer to discover and avoid the product's dangerous aspects.[31]

While more enlightening than the consumer expectation test, the risk-utility standard is not so much a definition of defectiveness as it is a means for second-guessing the manufacturer's design efforts. Indeed, most of the factors incorporated into the risk-utility test tend to divert attention away from the product and direct it back toward the manufacturer. The level of harm in a product is important only because it shows what information *the manufacturer* could have used in producing a better product. Likewise, economic feasibility indicates the increased cost which *the manufacturer* would have to bear in order to make the product safer. And technological feasibility establishes what alternatives *the manufacturer* could have used to improve the product's design.

Product-Based Strict Liability and Negligence

In its cumulative effect, this analysis bears two unmistakable hallmarks of negligence. First, it reinstitutes the reasonableness of the manufacturer's conduct as the touchstone for liability. It does this by requiring the fact finder to balance the same factors necessary for a determination of negligence under Judge Learned Hand's familiar B<PxL formula.[32] While the feasibility factors focus on the manufacturer's burden of changing the product design (B), the risk factors consider the foreseeability and magnitude of danger it poses to consumers (PxL). Second, to the extent a feasible alternative design is a prerequisite to liability, the concern here is not over the *activity* of manufacturing the product at all, as would be expected under strict liability, but over the particular *manner* in which it was designed

and constructed. As we saw earlier, this latter concern is unique to the theory of negligence. So while strict liability serves as a theoretical basis of responsibility in design cases, in practice, we see, it almost invariably gives way to its fault-based counterpart.

Product Category Liability

There is one situation, however, where the two theories seem to remain distinct, at least in theory. It arises in cases in which the manufacturer is held liable simply for engaging in the activity of producing an undesirable, though not necessarily defective, product. Such was the case in *Kelley v. R.G. Industries, Inc.*[33] There the court imposed liability against the manufacturer of a handgun for the injuries which resulted from the criminal use of that product. In this case, the plaintiff, who was victimized by the shooting, attacked the product not for malfunctioning, but for working exactly as it was supposed to. That is, she challenged the one feature that gave it functional utility—its ability to discharge a bullet at a velocity great enough to injure or kill a living thing. Other products also have been held actionable not because their purpose was undesirable, but because they created an incidental hazard which could not be discovered or removed. Asbestos has been attacked on this ground.[34] In both types of cases, there is nothing wrong with the way in which the manufacturer constructed the good; rather, it is the fact that she made and sold the product at all that is condemned. Such a reaction typically is premised on a finding that the risks posed by the product, even if designed as well as possible, simply exceed whatever utility that good may hold for society.

Product Liability and Abnormally Dangerous Activities

This activity-based form of strict products liability, also known as product category liability,[35] bears some facial similarities to the theory of strict liability for abnormally dangerous activities. The most obvious of these is the categorical nature of the standard being applied. Under each theory, the actor may be held liable simply for engaging in the enterprise itself, notwithstanding the care she uses in pursuing that endeavor. Another important likeness between the two theories is their reliance upon a balancing test for determining which activities to sanction and which to leave alone. Thus, regardless of whether the activity in question is the general operation of a dynamite factory, or the specific process by which the dynamite is manufactured, it will be necessary to weigh both the risk posed by the enterprise and its attendant benefits for the public.

Product Category Liability and Negligence

Given the close nexus between these forms of recovery, we can see the roots of negligence even in the activity-based version of strict products liability. As with abnormally dangerous activities, product category liability indirectly examines the reasonableness of the manufacturer's decision to engage in her chosen enterprise. In addition, it openly employs the familiar distributive criteria of risk and need to raise the manufacturer's responsibility for causing product-related injuries. Finally, just as in its alter theoretical ego, product category liability ultimately requires a determination of the social acceptability of the conduct in question.

Moral Deficiencies of Strict Products Liability

Despite the apparent congruity between negligence and product category liability, one should not become too optimistic about the political and moral integrity of the latter theory of recovery. Indeed, the painful truth is that *any* form of strict liability which focuses upon the conception of a product is more politically controversial, and certainly more morally suspect, than either negligence or the theory of abnormally dangerous activities.

Corrective Justice Concerns

For starters, design-based strict products liability is inimical to the concept of corrective justice. Why? One reason is that it seldom will merely eliminate the gain and loss of the parties to the transaction. In fact, most of the time it will result in a disproportionate appropriation of the manufacturer's interests and/or a windfall to the consumer. This becomes apparent when strict products liability is compared to other theories of recovery. As we've seen, negligent conduct and activities which present abnormal dangers generally are conducted on a local level. One who drives negligently usually doesn't make it a point to take her carelessness all over the country. Likewise, those who crop dust normally do so over a very limited geographical area to advance local economic concerns. When such an actor is held liable for engaging in one of these activities, the judgment neatly matches her wrongdoing—that is, it condemns that part of her conduct which is bad and leaves unrestricted that which does not offend. It also permits her to change her behavior, or relocate to another community, in order to avoid further liability. On the other hand, many product manufacturers distribute the same type of product all over the world. When the design of one product is found defective, the entire product line is called into question. Such a determination often will force the manufacturer to change her product specifications or means of production, especially in class actions and cases where compensatory or punitive damages are unusually high. When this occurs, the judgment of liability is over-inclusive. It does not just undo the gain of marketing the one product unit which injured the plaintiff, it effectively changes the way the defendant must do business. Extracting a concession of this magnitude in a single lawsuit does more than correct the imbalance existing between the defendant and any particular plaintiff, it actually attempts to adjust the defendant's moral ledger with society generally.

Even if the manufacturer does not feel compelled to alter her product, the doctrine of strict products liability is likely to cause her to absorb losses out of kilter with her responsibility in specific cases. One of the reasons for this is the tendency of courts to hold manufacturers accountable not only for the hazards which their products imposed upon individual consumers in particular transactions, but for any and all risks which the same product line presented to the public at large. For example, in applying the risk-utility test for defectiveness, courts often consider how widely distributed the product is, and thus how broad a range of potential victims it might injure.[36] Similarly, one of the relevant criteria used to award punitive damages is the extent of the risk created by the manufacturer in distributing the offending good.[37] In each case, the larger the number of people endangered by the manufacturer's product, the greater her potential liability in any given case may be. This means that in cases involving design defects, where the same product frequently is marketed all over the country, the defendant-manufacturer's financial responsibility necessarily will exceed her actual gain. It also means that, over a broad range of cases in which such damages are recovered, the defendant's cumulative liability will transcend whatever social wrong she has committed. On the flip side, because each plaintiff will receive compensation for conduct that was not wrongful *as to her*, all such claimants will enjoy a windfall.

What makes all of this even harder to palate is that, unlike the determination of an abnormally dangerous activity, a finding of design defectiveness is not usually based on a clear community custom or norm. In every community there will be individuals who disagree about the social value of just about any type of product—from cigarettes to lawn mowers to cosmetics. What is worse, in most cases involving design defects, the fact finders have no normative basis whatsoever for evaluating the propriety of the product. Whether a punch press should have an interlock instead of a sweeping guard or dual hand buttons, for example, usually will be beyond the ken of most laymen. As a result, those asked to make this determination are required to judge the item on scientific and technological principles supplied to them by experts. When this happens, there appears little point in using our jury system as means for achieving corrective justice. Because manufacturers' gains cannot properly be comprehended by our civil intermediaries, the litigation process seems woefully ill-equipped to undo the private wrongs arising from such product-induced transactions.

Distributive Justice Concerns

The weaknesses in this system do not just inhibit the attainment of corrective justice; they also serve to undermine the state's ability to fairly distribute autonomy among its citizens. As we have seen, states allocate rights and responsibilities in different ways. The most socially dangerous conduct is completely prohibited by criminal sanctions. Activities posing less risk, and possessing greater utility, usually are subject to regulatory restrictions. And modestly risky though desirable enterprises are inhibited, if at all, only through ex post determinations of financial liability. This system of distributions is disrupted, however, in cases involving defective product designs. Strict products liability is supposed to help implement the last, and least restrictive, form of regulation—the ex post payment of damages. But instead of requiring manufacturers to pay their fair share of private losses, this theory often forces them to pay merely for creating a certain level of social risk deemed unacceptable by members of one particular community. Indeed, as indicated above, the extent of a manufacturer's liability usually will depend not upon the injuries actually caused by its products, but upon the number of people potentially endangered by them. Invariably, the social magnitude of the product hazard will inflate the manufacturer's financial responsibility above that necessary to eradicate the losses of individual plaintiff-consumers. Because of this, manufacturers frequently must either change their whole mode of operation or go out of business. The end effect is not one of piecemeal ex post regulation, but of an indirect preemptive restriction of the entire enterprise. Besides unduly inhibiting the autonomy of those engaged in such useful endeavors, this type of public regulation is beyond the province of judges or juries. Indeed, it would be unfair, to say the least, to permit the fact-finders in one particular proceeding to dictate to consumers in other communities what goods they will have the freedom to use and how much they must pay to enjoy them. If such a determination is to be made, it must be undertaken only by those public entities—like legislatures or administrative agencies—which are more directly accountable to the people who must endure its consequences.

The Wrongfulness of Strict Liability Conduct

So we see that strict liability is terribly ill-suited for cases involving product-related injuries. Besides compromising both the private notion of corrective justice and the public ideal of distributive justice, it fails to offer any real alternative basis for determining the rights and responsibilities of manufacturers and consumers. This is because in every product liability case, the manufacturer's conduct is actually negligent—either in the manner of constructing the product or merely in the decision to ever put it on the market. In this latter, categorical sense, the idea of strict liability resembles that used to evaluate abnormally dangerous activities. For each theory, the actor's responsibility is determined by distributive rules which allocate autonomy on the basis of the criteria of risk or need. Viewed in this light, it should not be surprising that when a strict liability duty is violated, the breach is every bit as wrongful as a negligent act. Although it may not be as culpable in a pure moral sense,[38] it is "faulty" nevertheless in the political sense of being unfair.

As one might expect, this political form of wrongdoing, though still legally suspect, is generally more subtle and variegated than other types of faulty conduct. Indeed, strict liability activities may be considered unreasonable in at least three different respects. First, where the activity in question imposes upon the relevant community an ultrahazardous and uncommon risk, such that the risk exceeds whatever utility the activity holds for that community, the activity-operator not only exercises a privilege her neighbors do not share, she exposes them to risks that they do not, and often cannot, reciprocate. Here, as in negligence, the risk-creator's behavior is doubly offensive: besides clearly transcending a firmly fixed baseline level of tolerable danger, she instigates a forced appropriation of her neighbor's property and health while refusing to pay for her pilferage. Conduct of this sort is unreasonable, and thus wrongful, not just because it does more harm than good, but because the one externalizing these risks reaps the benefits of her self-serving, destructive enterprise without incurring any of its social costs. Second, even where the dangers posed by the activity are outweighed by its social utility, such a venture still may be considered wrongful if it is conducted in an irresponsible fashion. Thus, if an inherently hazardous enterprise could be operated more safely by implementing a few simple and inexpensive remedial measures—like using different materials, changing its physical plant or operating procedures, relocating certain instrumentalities, or providing adequate warnings—it surely would be condemned for its dereliction if it failed to do so. In this situation, the overall design of the enterprise appears unreasonable because it creates risks that are both unnecessary and easily avoidable. Third, if the danger posed by the activity is serious, involving a high probability of causing potentially catastrophic harm to many people, and if the financial burden of compensating for this damage would not significantly impair the viability of the venture or diminish the general availability of its goods or services, then it would be wrongful for the activity-operator to refuse to compensate her victims, even if the enterprise otherwise provides some important benefit to the surrounding community.

A simple analogy makes this latter, seemingly paradoxical, truth more obvious. Imagine that your neighbor continually comes upon your property without your consent and strips away lumber from your home in order to build an airplane that others in your community might use to purchase supplies, receive medical treatment or visit distant relatives (for the sake of strengthening the analogy, you may assume as well that the neighbor dismantles the homes of many other local residents). Because there are no other towns or airports within three hundred miles, the airplane seems like a good idea. Nevertheless, after several planks of your roof disappear, you decide to ask your neighbor to pay for the confiscated lumber so you might patch up the gaping holes that now ventilate your home. Although your neighbor is modestly wealthy—possessing enough money and resources not only to pay for your lumber, but also to construct and operate the airplane at low cost to the community—she declines your request. Is there any doubt that her rebuff is unreasonable? Even if one were to concede that the social value of the airplane exceeded the risk posed by your neighbor's actions, it seems manifestly inappropriate for her to take your property and jeopardize your physical well-being without at least agreeing to compensate for your loss. Besides intruding upon your seclusion, your neighbor forces your participation in a grossly imbalanced redistributive enterprise. What makes this compulsory gambit especially distasteful is your neighbor's unabashed unwillingness to share any of its costs. Perhaps her obduracy would be understandable if the burden of financial accountability would send her to the poor house. But under the assumed facts, it clearly would not. In fact, if she were to pay reparations, everyone, including your neighbor, would receive at least some benefit. Your house would get repaired, your neighbor would get her plane, and the community would receive an affordable and valuable service. Far from suffering a monetary hardship, your neighbor actually would make out much better than anyone else. In addition to using the plane for her own private purposes, your neighbor, in effect, would receive a special licence to take and use your property at her whim, and could earn a profit by leasing the plane to the public. The equities of this situation, though not perfectly balanced, become downright lopsided when no compensation is required of your neighbor. Now you alone are forced to subsidize the construction of the community airplane while others sit back and watch. And your neighbor? Well, she is certainly taking *you* for a ride; but not in the air—all the way to the bank! On top of all the other advantages she enjoys, your liability-immune neighbor also is relieved of the financial burden of paying her own start-up costs.

Strict liability actors are very much like this inconsiderate neighbor. By engaging in activities that inevitably cause injury to those nearby, the demolition company, the combustible substance warehouser and the vicious animal breeder, among others, all "take" the property of their neighbors to advance their own business or personal objectives. Although strict liability takings are not nearly as calculated or functional as those of the neighbor above, they often are an unavoidable byproduct of such activities, and so are just as indispensable to these pursuits as the materials used to carry them out. In either type of case, the risk-creator acts wrongfully in that she shamelessly promotes her own interests at the expense of certain others, yet makes no concession for their physical, emotional and material well-being, even where such protective or restorative measures could be undertaken with little effort or expense.[39] Where this occurs, fairness requires that such wrongdoers disgorge their unjust enrichment by repaying those who have been compelled to sacrifice their freedom. Tort law's theory of strict liability remains surprisingly loyal to this principle, although in the aberrant case of products liability, the theory itself is not always sensibly applied.

Part V

Justice in Three Paradigms of Tortious Interaction

Up until now, we have seen how the structure and content of tort law serve the ends of justice. The elemental components of tort claims ensure that claim-rights are extended to deserving parties. The theories of tort law distribute these rights fairly according to some acceptable criteria. Nevertheless, we have not yet examined the justice of tort law in action. Perhaps this would not be important if the law applied the same way in every case. But it does not. The theories, and their conceptual elements, are dynamic; thus, the demands of justice will vary with the unique circumstances of each particular dispute.

In my view, all interpersonal interactions, including torts, can be categorized as either transactions, relations or some combination of the two. For our purposes, a transaction may be defined as an encounter between two or more individuals in which less than all of the interacting parties are willing participants. Most people probably conceive of tortious occurrences in this way. Indeed, examples of such encounters come readily to mind. Automobile collisions, slip and fall accidents and workplace injuries all seem to fit the description of a transaction.

Although all transactions lack full consent, they actually come in two different forms: random transactions and calculated transactions. Each of the illustrations mentioned above involves purely random encounters. A random transaction is an interactive episode in which *none* of the parties plan on interfering with the rights of the others. In calculated transactions, however, the interaction among the parties is instigated and intended by *at least one* of the participants. Intentional torts, like assault or battery, are the most common examples of these transactions.

Where parties *do* consent to associate with each other, the resulting interaction is called a relation. Relations consist of either long- or short-term associations among individuals willing to exchange their interests. Although relations typically are associated with the law of contracts, many torts arise from this interactive context as well. Indeed, as we already have seen, tortious wrongs often are inflicted by doctors against their patients, by manufacturers against the consumers of their products or by common carriers against their passengers.

Parties bound together in such relationships may or may not engage in underlying transactions. Relations and transactions ordinarily become intertwined when one of the parties to a relation affirmatively imposes an unexpected and unconsented risk upon the other. A good example would be where a doctor sexually molests an anesthetized patient. Although the parties share a special doctor-patient relationship, such an untoward encounter clearly falls outside the parameters of that association. Because this type of perverse touching is neither contemplated by the patient nor required for her treatment, the doctor's behavior culminates a kind of illicit calculated transaction. In cases of nonfeasance, on the other hand, often the only nexus between the injured victim and the omitter is the relationship existing between them. To illustrate, suppose the molestation described above had occurred in a hospital. Unless the hospital either directed or ratified the doctor's act (or is vicariously responsible for its commission), one cannot point to any conduct of the hospital which prompted or promoted the wrongful transaction with the patient. Nevertheless, hospitals normally owe special duties to patients because of the nature of their relationship. As a business invitor, premises lessor and health-care provider, the hospital is required to safeguard the interests of its patients so long as they remain within the institution's four walls. To satisfy this obligation, the hospital is expected to hire ethical doctors, supervise their activities and provide adequate internal security. The hospital in our hypothetical breaches one or more of these duties if it fails to prevent the assault upon the patient. In a scenario such as this, the hospital's liability arises not from its actions, but solely from the neglect of its relational responsibilities.

The distinctions between transactions and relations, and even between the two forms of transactions, carry great moral significance. There is a big difference, for example, between intentionally causing someone harm and fortuitously interfering with her interests. While the former, calculated transaction is wrongful in the general sense of being wicked, the latter, random transaction is unjust only in the narrower sense of being unfair. And, despite their differences, the justice concerns of both of these transactions are far simpler than those involving relations. Because transactions, by my definition, lack the mutual consent of the parties, the state must supply the rules to guide their interactive behavior. As we have seen, it does this both by distributing to the instigator(s) a general duty to exercise reasonable care, and by allocating to the victim the autonomy necessary to vindicate her rights. Here, justice is done so long as the rights and responsibilities assigned to the parties are neither too expansive nor too restrictive. In relations, however, the parties either expressly or implicitly agree to fashion their own rights and obligations. Often, the commitments made by the parties may differ from the duties which would otherwise be imposed upon them by the state. In such situations, the determination of justice will require more than merely identifying and applying the appropriate distributive rule. It also will necessitate examining the effect which the parties' relationship may have had upon that scheme of distributions. Obviously, analysis of these scenarios will be far different, and far more complicated, than those where such relationships do not exist.

We see, then, that there are three discrete paradigms of tortious interaction, each with its own peculiar moral matrix and thus each deserving independent consideration. The first, which I have denominated the paradigm of calculated transactions, will be discussed in Chapter Seventeen. Chapter Eighteen next examines the second transactional paradigm, which consists of random interactions. The third and final paradigm—that of relations—will be considered in Chapter Nineteen.

Chapter 17

Calculated Transactions

Earlier, I defined calculated transactions as those in which fewer than all of the parties consent to the interaction, but at least one deliberately precipitates it. This definition is accurate as far as it goes. Yet it does not tell us much about the cases which fall within this paradigm. Indeed, it is like describing a specific person as a virtually hairless mammal who walks erectly on two legs. While such a description may satisfy an anthropologist, it wouldn't really help us pick that individual out of a line-up. So it is with calculated transactions. Besides being unilaterally instigated, they seem to have little else in common. To properly analyze this paradigm, therefore, we must identify its more detailed, distinguishing features.

A close examination of the cases within this paradigm reveals that it is really a collection of four separate types of transactions: those that are adversarial in nature; those that occur by mistake; those that are inspired by some altruistic purpose; and those that are self-endangering. What links these transactions is the centrality of the actor's motivation to the determination of her liability. Indeed, for each kind of transaction, one simply cannot evaluate the justice of the encounter without examining the protagonist's purpose for initiating it. But just as motivation ties these transactions all together, it also serves to set them apart. In adversarial transactions, the desire is to *inhibit* the autonomy of the other, while in mistaken encounters there is *no* desire to affect the autonomy of the actual aggrieved party, and in altruistic interactions the desire is to *protect* or *promote* another's autonomy. In the remaining subcategory of cases (i.e., those involving self-endangering transactions), the actor intends not to harm anybody else; rather, she willingly exposes *herself* to danger. Here, the apparent motivation is either to confront the risk itself, perhaps for the sake of excitement or self-destruction, or to obtain some greater ulterior benefit. Given the divergent motivations behind these transactions, it should not be surprising that each presents its own distinctive moral concerns.

Adversarial Transactions

Of all calculated transactions, those bearing an adversarial signature seem to be the most condemnable. Unlike the other transactions in this paradigm, only adversarial encounters are specifically designed to interfere with someone else's interests. No doubt, many of the transactions in this subcategory are worthy of disapprobation. These encounters, which I shall call "proactive," are characterized by an unprovoked and unjustified attack by one party against the rights of another. But not all adversarial encounters are the result of such malevolence. Some of these transactions, which I shall call "reactive," are inspired by the rather noble purpose of self-defense. Obviously, justice will not mean the same thing in both types of transactions, but will vary dramatically according to the circumstances of each.

Proactive Form

Proactive transactions are not only the most morally reprehensible form of interaction, they are also the most politically intolerable. As we saw earlier, the autonomy of all individuals may be restricted by the general duty not to harm others. This duty, which is owed to each member of society, can be heightened or diminished depending upon the type of action being performed. Generally, the riskier the conduct, the greater the actor's responsibility will be. Intentionally harmful behavior is the riskiest type of conduct one may commit. Because of the actor's mental state, injury to another is not just possible, it is at least substantially certain to occur. Thus, absent some compelling necessity, the actor possesses no autonomy right to engage in such deliberately harmful activity, and bears an unconditional responsibility not to.

This onerous duty is enforced in a variety of ways. Most proactive transactions are forbidden by criminal laws. Thus, if there is good cause to believe that such an encounter is about to occur, the harmful activity may be preempted entirely. The same preemptive effect may be achieved under the civil law by obtaining a preliminary or permanent injunction. Where the threat posed by the proactive conduct is more imminent, tort law permits the endangered party to take immediate action to curtail the danger. If the actor breaches her duty, and succeeds in causing harm to another, she may be held liable under an intentional tort theory of recovery. Assault, battery, false imprisonment, intentional infliction of emotional distress, trespass to land and chattels and conversion all may fit within the proactive subparadigm. For many of these theories, it is not even necessary that the offending conduct actually result in harm. Because such proactive behavior is so inimical to the concepts of freedom and equality, it produces a political and dignitary harm sufficient to state a cause of action.

Proactive transactions are wrongful in two different senses. On the one hand, they are unjust is the general sense of being morally depraved. Clearly, one who intentionally harms another without any excuse or justification demonstrates a gross imbalance in dispositional humors. She possesses an excess of self-interest, and a deficiency of respect for her peers. On the other hand, such unilateral transactions are wrongful in the particular sense of being unfair. By violating the mutual restriction which requires everyone to obey the rule of law, the proactive instigator exercises a measure of autonomy afforded to no one else. In so doing, she not only takes unfair advantage of her victim, who suffers a direct loss of autonomy, she also cheats all other members of society who have foregone the opportunity to use their natural powers for the same self-serving end.

Given the serious moral deficiencies in proactive behavior, justice in all its forms supports the expansive role which tort law plays in sanctioning it. Insofar as the rules of defensive action and liability are premised on the accepted criterion of risk, the applicable intentional tort theories satisfy the demands of distributive justice. In addition, because such intentional misbehavior alone does harm to the abstract notion of autonomy, corrective justice requires that this political injury be nullified with at least a nominal award of damages, even if no actual loss has been sustained by the claimant. Finally, in cases where such transactions have their worst dehumanizing effects, the imposition of punitive damages against the proactive wrongdoer is not just politically expedient, it is compelled by the moral imperative of retributive justice.

Reactive Form

A notably different scheme of justice applies to calculated transactions which are reactive rather than proactive. In this subparadigm, the actor does not initiate the encounter merely to satisfy some personal desire; instead, she acts to defend her interests. Here, the actor's autonomy is threatened either by the conduct of another individual or by some natural force. These dangers create a need for the party in jeopardy to implement some protective measures. Although the actor's response is calculated to interfere with the autonomy of the aggressor, or of some other individual whose interests are essential for the preservation of her own, the necessity of the situation reduces her duty of care and increases her liberty of action. Under these circumstances, she may employ reasonable efforts to secure her autonomy. This means that she may do what is necessary to eliminate the risk of harm, but may not exploit her special freedom for either personal gain or revenge.

These guidelines for reactive conduct generally are contained within the intentional tort privileges of self-defense and necessity, among others.[1] Under the doctrine of self-defense, for example, a party may use reasonable force to protect herself if it reasonably appears that her interests are in imminent danger.[2] Thus, if some desperate criminal has pointed a gun in my direction, I may employ a proportional amount of force, like pulling out a gun of my own, to end the threat. Here, I have a right to protect my interests; but I also bear a responsibility not to use excessive force. As long as I act within my right—by using no more force than is necessary to shield myself from harm—I cannot be held liable for any injury which I may inflict upon my tormentor.

The same would not be true, however, were the threat to my interests created by someone or something other than the party against whom I asserted my defensive response. This occurs in cases involving private necessities. Under the privilege of private necessity, I am still permitted to take reasonable action to repel an impending danger; however, if in doing so I cause harm to some third party who was not responsible for my predicament, I may be held liable for her resulting loss.[3] We saw this earlier in *Vincent v. Lake Erie Transportation Co.*[4] There, a ship owner seeking to save his cargo kept his vessel moored to a dock during a terrible rainstorm. After the ship collided with the dock, partially destroying it, the dock owner sued the shipper for the damage. While recognizing the ship owner's right to remain at the dock during the storm, the court held that he was liable for the loss. Because the interest in jeopardy involved nothing more than personal property, and because the protective reaction was directed against a completely innocent third party, the ship owner's duty was greater and his autonomy lesser than if he had invoked the privilege of self-defense.

In either of these reactive contexts, the autonomy distributed to the actor far exceeds that enjoyed by those who instigate proactive transactions. Rather than inhibiting such conduct with an unconditional rule of preclusion, the law undertakes the delicate balancing of autonomy and responsibility necessary for implementing a standard of reasonable behavior. This greater flexibility is warranted by the more benign nature of such reactive transactions. Unlike calculated, proactive conduct, reactive measures do not evince a wickedness of character. Indeed, they are used not to denigrate the moral worth of other human beings, as are proactive deeds, but merely to satisfy our most natural instinct for survival. Even where the reactive duty of reasonable care is exceeded, the violation is often more a function of overzealousness than of malice. In such cases, the actor's indiscretion is wrongful only insofar as it unfairly secures for her a liberty not permitted of others.

For conduct of this sort, the requirements of justice will be more evenly balanced between the reactive party and those subject to her defensive response. In accordance with principles of distributive justice, the need for protection entitles the actor to greater freedom of action, while the serious risk posed by her response demands that she retain some responsibility for her behavior. Likewise, the individual subject to this response has a right to be free from such an intrusion upon her solitude; yet, because of the apparent exigency created by her own actions or by some other force, this right to protection is not absolute. To the extent that intentional tort privileges expand and contract the autonomy of the parties to effect this precarious balance of interests, they seem to comport with our sense of distributive justice. Moreover, in cases of private necessity, the notion of corrective justice seems to support the reactive party's liability for harms occasioned by a defensive action. Here, the actor gains protection of her interests only by impairing comparable interests of another. To correct this imbalance, it seems fair to require the reactive party to disgorge part of her benefit by compensating for her victim's loss. Finally, because tort law seldom imposes punitive sanctions against the reactive party, it seems to comply with the weakened retributive appetite usually developed in such transactions.

Mistaken Transactions

The second general type of calculated transactions—i.e., those precipitated by a mistake of fact—share many of the attributes of proactive adversarial transactions. For one thing, mistaken transactions also are proactive. They are initiated by the actor without any provocation or justification. In addition, although they are not necessarily committed with the purpose of inflicting harm, they are intended to affect the autonomy of some other person. And, because neither type of transaction is born of necessity, those initiating them share the same absolute duty of care. So just as adversarial actors are liable for harm they inflict upon their neighbors, those who intentionally, though mistakenly, interfere with the autonomy of others are fully responsible for the injurious consequences of their actions.

These calculated, mistaken transactions fall within the purview of two separate, though conceptually similar tort doctrines. The most obvious one is the intentional tort doctrine of mistake. It holds that, unless a party is reasonably mistaken about the use of a privilege (a scenario which, in my taxonomy, is covered under calculated, reactive transactions), all mistakes of fact are held against the actor and not the injured victim.[5] Thus, in *Ranson v. Kitner*,[6] when a hunter shot and killed a dog in the mistaken belief that it was a wolf, he was liable to the dog's owner for conversion. Here, no exigency compelled the hunter to fire his weapon in a panic; instead, he made a conscious choice to pull the trigger without investigating the identity of his target. Although the hunter's error was made in good faith, he nevertheless enjoyed no right to behave in such a rash and potentially deadly manner.

In other cases within this subcategory, the actor actually does intend to cause harm to someone; but because of bad luck, she mistakenly injures the wrong party. These situations are covered by the doctrine of transferred intent. Under this doctrine, the intent to impair the autonomy of the desired victim is "transferred" to the actual party injured by the actor's conduct.[7] Thus, even though the actor had no wish to harm the injured party, and may not even have known of the latter's presence at the time she committed the injurious act, the law presumes that she possessed the requisite intent. When this legal fiction is applied, the mistaken actor bears the same absolute duty to her actual victim that other proactive parties owe to theirs.

Both types of mistaken behavior are wrongful in at least the narrow sense of being unfair. The hunter who shoots without thinking may not be a contemptible miscreant, but because she exercises an abandon not reserved to others, she is a kind of outlaw nonetheless. In the same vein, one who desires to harm *someone*, and succeeds in injuring *anyone*, violates a norm of social restraint even if her actual victim is not the one she had intended. Besides being unfair, however, this form of deliberative wrongdoing also displays more moral turpitude than actions which are harmful only by mistake. Indeed, because they are designed to flaunt the rules others must live by, they are unjust in the general sense of being wicked.

For each type of mistaken transaction, the relevant tort rules are custom tailored to satisfy the demands of justice. As both transactions involve high-risk activities, and neither is a matter of necessity, distributive justice favors placing onerous restrictions upon the liberty of those who initiate them. Thus, whether the actor is mistaken about the nature of her act or the identity of her victim, tort law holds her responsible for the harmful consequences of her indiscretion. In cases of pure mistake, where the neutrally motivated actor gains no personal benefit from the encounter, the imbalance between the parties may be corrected merely by repairing the victim's loss. Where the transaction arises out of malicious motive, however, both corrective and retributive justice require that the victim be afforded the opportunity to nullify the political gain of the actor. For intentional tort cases premised on the doctrine of transferred intent, this is often accomplished by allowing the claimant to recover from her wrongdoer a substantial award of punitive damages.

Altruistic Transactions

In the next group of cases within this paradigm, the motive for initiating the transaction is neither neutral nor malicious, but altruistic. Like in the reactive transactions mentioned above, the actor here responds to some situational need. The difference is that in altruistic transactions, the action is not designed to advance the actor's own interests, but to protect or secure the interests of someone else. Nevertheless, the distributive duty of the actor in each situation will be considerably alike. In the altruistic subcategory, as in the reactive context, the exigent circumstances increase the actor's right to intrude upon the lives of others. Still, she does not enjoy a freedom of unbridled action, but retains a significant duty to proceed with caution. For if she is mistaken about the need for intervention, the moral prerogative of her altruism will be lost.

These competing concerns of autonomy and responsibility are separately addressed, though evenly balanced, by several unrelated tort doctrines. A couple of legal principles enhance the good samaritan's liberty to provide assistance to others in distress. For example, the intentional tort privilege of defense of others provides the altruist with a license to intervene on another's behalf without fear of legal reprisal. In some jurisdictions, this license is strictly construed, authorizing such intervention only where the apparent victim *actually* was in need of assistance.[8] Other jurisdictions construe this license broadly, empowering the actor to lend aid whenever it *reasonably appears* that there is a need to do so.[9] In either case, the intervenor's interpersonal rights are significantly increased. The same effect is achieved by the rescue doctrine of negligence law,[10] though in a slightly different way. Like the privilege of defense of others, the rescue doctrine strengthens the altruist's rights against a wrongdoer who has placed the prospective victim in danger. But it does not allow such a good samaritan to act upon the risk-creator directly; rather, it simply entitles her to compensation if she is injured while attempting to extricate the victim from a dangerous situation.[11]

Other tort doctrines help to define the limits of the altruist's right to interject herself into another's business. Under either version of the privilege to defend others, the intervenor may not simply throw caution into the wind, but must exercise due care in rendering assistance. So if she uses more force than is necessary to free the prospective victim from harm, she may be liable to any party made to bear the consequences of her excessive action.[12] Similarly, once the altruist undertakes to render aid, she owes the victim a special responsibility to act reasonably. This responsibility usually takes two forms. On the one hand, the actions of the altruist must not be performed in a way that worsens the victim's condition, either by exacerbating a preexisting injury or exposing her to greater danger.[13] On the other hand, the intervenor who induces the victim to rely on her assistance, or who discourages other potential rescuers from providing aid, may not discontinue her efforts without exposing herself to possible civil liability.[14]

Where any of these responsibilities are neglected, the transgression may be considered wrongful even though the actor's motivation is benevolent.

Obviously, such behavior is not morally opprobrious from a deontological standpoint. Yet it still manifests a degree of normative indifference which makes it unfair. Those who overzealously engage in these altruistic missions reserve for themselves a freedom of action forbidden to others resigned to respect the moral space of their neighbors. This is bad in itself because it unnecessarily exposes those in danger to increased risks. Taken to an extreme, however, such liberal interventionism threatens the very principle of autonomy it attempts to secure.

In transactions of this sort, where the communitarian notion of mutual assistance clashes with the value of rugged individualism inherent in the concept of autonomy, special justice concerns are raised. Because the prospective victim in these cases requires special protection, distributive justice affords the altruist greater freedom to intervene on her behalf. Nevertheless, this freedom cannot be unlimited, but must be tempered by a duty which prevents the altruist from exceeding her license. Such a duty is heightened further by the persistent risk that any intervention may be unwanted by the party it is supposed to help. The rules of tort law, which empower and protect rescuers where they act responsibly and hold them accountable when they do not, seem to do a good job of effecting this delicate equilibrium. They also seem to reflect the realities of corrective justice in this context. Although the altruist seeks to give rather than gain by her intervention, she retains an abstract benefit, and one with potentially deleterious social ramifications, by forcing others into transactions without their consent. Thus, in accordance with principles of corrective and retributive justice, tort law generally permits those harmed by the altruist to receive some compensation for their losses, but precludes them from punishing her with an exemplary sanction.

Self-Endangering Transactions

As was noted at the outset of this discussion, self-endangering transactions are different from the three preceding types of calculated encounters in that they usually threaten the actor's own interests and not the interests of others. In this situation, the actor is fully aware of the hazards that await her, yet she deliberately proceeds to confront them. Often, these transactions are initiated by thrill-seekers merely for sport. An example would be a trespasser who hops aboard and then jumps from a moving train for the sheer excitement of the experience. In other cases, the actor does not seek out danger for its own sake, but decides that, on balance, the benefit to be derived from acting exceeds the known risks that such action will engender. This is true of motorists who, for the sake of convenience, drive around railroad crossing barricades and are injured or killed by oncoming trains. In each of these scenarios, the actor makes an informed choice to initiate the transaction either because of or in spite of the danger it entails.

Cases of this sort typically fall within the purview of the tort doctrine of implied assumption of risk.[15] Although often raised as a defense, this doctrine actually operates like a no duty rule.[16] The idea here is that, absent a special relationship between the parties, the defendant is under no obligation to protect the plaintiff against self-inflicted injuries. Why? Because the risk of harm is simply beyond the defendant's power of control. Although the defendant may create a condition which poses some risk to others, the plaintiff alone decides whether or not she will come within the danger zone.

Traditionally, courts have afforded the deliberate risk-taker no protection against the injurious effects of her own choices. Indeed, under the doctrine of assumption of risk, she has been completely precluded from passing her loss onto others. While many jurisdictions still hold this view, it appears to be slowly eroding. Since the advent of comparative fault, many states have begun to temper the harsh effect of this doctrine by permitting juries to determine whether and to what extent the plaintiff should be held accountable for her loss.[17]

As a practical matter, the "no duty bar to recovery" approach seems preferable to the "jury determination" approach for a variety of reasons. Perhaps the most obvious of these is that it provides a clearer normative standard of behavior. When an individual knowingly and voluntarily assumes a risk, there is no need to compare her actions with those of her counterpart in order to determine her responsibility; if she makes such a choice, she is held accountable for all of the resulting consequences. This, in turn, makes it easier both for individuals to predict the ramifications of their actions and for judges to assess their responsibility in a court of law. Given this added determinacy, it is reasonable to expect that, under the no duty approach, fewer claims for relief would be filed by those sustaining self-inflicted injuries; and of those cases that are instituted, an increasing number would be dismissed before they ever reach trial. Besides identifying meritless claims, this filtering process would have the more general effect of easing the dockets of our already overcrowded judicial system.

Yet as compelling as these practical advantages may seem, they do not supply sufficient reason for choosing one approach over another. To make this decision, it is also necessary to determine which of these approaches is more desirable from a moral standpoint. Here, too, the no duty approach appears to come out on top. If the purpose of tort law is to protect people from the wrongful advances of their neighbors, this objective is ill-served by allowing risk-seeking plaintiffs to recover damages for self-imposed injuries. A wrong, we have seen, consists of the nonconsensual blocking or invading of another's interest. Using this definition, it is clear that one who voluntarily chooses to encounter danger sustains no moral injury. Rather than being denied an interest, such an actor advances her interests by pursuing and receiving the object of her desire. Granted, she may sacrifice some of her negative liberty in exercising this choice; but she also enjoys the benefits of unrestricted freedom which make life worth living. Under these circumstances, any injury she may sustain in the encounter must be viewed not as a wrongful transgression of her rights, but merely as a predictable incident of her own expression of autonomy.

In cases of this sort, distributive justice requires that the risk-taker assume complete responsibility for whatever loss she may sustain in the encounter. On the one hand, there is good reason to deny her the right to shift the loss to her transactional counterpart. By initiating the transaction, she alone creates and controls the risk of harm. In addition, insofar as the risk-taker forces the encounter upon another without her consent, she repudiates the latter's abstract entitlement to autonomy, even if she causes the other no actual harm. Thus, if a loss is born of the transaction, though it may be the actor's own, it is fair to hold her accountable for it. On the other hand, there is no just basis for imposing upon others a duty to prevent such transactions from occurring. Short of violating some statutory proscription,[18] these blameless participants do not impose unreasonable risks upon the risk-taker, but are themselves forced to engage in unsolicited encounters. Accordingly, the distributive criterion of risk will not support subjecting them to a duty of care. Neither may such a duty be premised upon the criterion of need. Self-endangering transactions, like all others, are unilaterally initiated. Because there is no preexisting relationship between the parties, there is no special need to protect the thrill-seeker from relational exploitation. And, absent such a need, there is no sound moral basis for holding any one but the risk-taker responsible for the consequences of these unsolicited encounters.

Principles of corrective justice compel the same conclusion. Remember that corrective justice is not a concern unless both a wrongful loss and a wrongful gain arise from the same transaction. Neither are present, however, in self-endangering encounters. No loss is sustained by the risk-taker, even if she is injured, since she receives what she desires, or at least what she should have expected from the transaction. If anything, she gains a superseding benefit by initiating the transaction without the consent of her counterpart. Conversely, the other party acquires no advantage from the interaction, for she receives nothing of value from the actor, and exercises no excessive measure of autonomy. In fact, just the opposite is true. As a victim of the unsolicited overreaching of the risk-taker, she herself sustains a moral deficit. In light of this, it is difficult to justify any award to the actor, no matter how small.

Shared Characteristics

These, then, are our four forms of calculated transactions. While they display several obvious differences, they also share some important similarities. Besides lacking mutual consent, adversarial, mistaken, altruistic and self-endangering transactions all are typically governed by general behavioral rules created by the state. For each, the focus of attention primarily is on the motivation of the protagonists who instigate such encounters and not upon the conduct of their counterparts (except to ensure that the interests violated are worthy of legal protection). And, because of the unilateral nature of such transactions, there usually is little difficulty in determining who is causally responsible for the damage they engender. As we shall see in the next chapter, these characteristics help to set such calculated transactions apart from those which occur at random.

Chapter 18

Random Transactions

Besides belonging to the same species of human interaction, calculated transactions and random transactions are about as similar as Cain was to Abel. Granted, random transactions also occur without the full consent of the parties involved, and so are regulated exclusively by the state. But this is where the likeness between these paradigms ends. While calculated transactions are the primary concern of intentional torts, random transactions are covered by the law of negligence and strict liability. Moreover, unlike calculated transactions, which are primarily other-directed, random transactions are essentially self-regarding. That is, the protagonist acts with the purpose of satisfying some private interest and not with the intent to interfere with the interests of others. As a result, the risks posed by random transactions almost always will be far less than those created by calculated transactions. This distinction, in turn, affects our moral judgment of each type of behavior. Whereas many forms of calculated action are wrongful per se, the nondeliberative conduct of random transactions is wrongful only if it creates an unreasonably dangerous condition. Here, the determination of wrongfulness is premised not upon clear rules of behavior, as it often is in calculated transactions, but upon the standard-based balancing of right and duty. This is significant because it tends to make the normative analysis of random transactions more bilateral. In assessing the actor's liability, the risk and value of her activity must be weighed against the importance of the victim's interests and the extent to which they have been impaired. And, once this is done, it frequently is necessary to compare the actions of both the actor and her victim to establish the party or parties causally responsible for the injurious encounter.

Unilateral-Bilateral Dichotomy

This is not to say that all random transactions can be lumped together and analyzed the same way. Clearly, they cannot. The reason is that there are different varieties of random transactions. The main dichotomy in this paradigm is between unilaterally initiated encounters and those that are bilateral in origin. While each type of random transaction is more complex than calculated transactions, bilateral encounters tend to be more difficult to analyze than those unilaterally instigated. Why? Because unlike unilateral transactions, which raise only the issue of normative responsibility, bilateral transactions also require that we venture into the murky depths of causal responsibility.

Unilateral Random Transactions

By unilateral transactions, I do not necessarily mean that one party commits an affirmative act while the other remains passive. Nor am I suggesting that such interactions are initiated or caused by only one party, though this often may be the case. Rather, I mean that, in the bipolar context of a tort dispute, only the party or parties on one side of the litigation axis is or are normatively responsible for the encounter. Sometimes the plaintiff may be the sole cause of her own injury, as when she carelessly stumbles and falls into the path of the defendant's reasonably operated subway train. More often, however, it is the conduct of one or more defendant that forces the encounter.[1] In these situations, the injured plaintiff does nothing to induce the misfortune which befalls her.

Examples of defendant-induced, albeit random, transactions are scattered throughout the case law of torts. As noted at the outset, these encounters are exclusively the domain of negligence and strict liability actions. Thus, a unilateral transaction might include the collision between a negligent driver who jumps a curb and an innocent pedestrian strolling along the adjacent sidewalk. Or, it might involve the explosive impact of a strict liability blasting operation upon the home of a nearby landowner. Whatever form these transactions take, two things are clear. One is that the defendant will have committed an affirmative act without the intent to inflict harm upon somebody else; the other is that, as a result, the plaintiff will have suffered a loss which she did not bring upon herself.

In such cases, the key issue for determination is the actor's normative responsibility. It achieves this premier status almost by default. Given either the plaintiff's passivity prior to or during the transaction, or the utter blamelessness of her conduct, it normally is self-evident that she bears no responsibility for the transaction. On the other hand, because of the affirmative nature of the defendant's conduct, her connection to the plaintiff's injury usually is not in doubt. What is not so obvious, however, is whether she possessed an obligation either to prevent the transaction from occurring or to pay for its consequences. The answer to this question depends upon four interrelated considerations: was the defendant bound by a fair duty of care; did she owe that duty to the plaintiff in particular; did she breach her duty; and did the plaintiff thereby sustain any legally cognizable harm. If all four of these criteria are satisfied, the defendant is guilty of wrongdoing and is susceptible to an ex post sanction of liability. The plaintiff, on the other hand, acquires a corrective right which allows her to force the defendant to pay for her loss.

Distributive Justice and the Duality of Duty

The random actor's duty of care generally is much less restrictive, and much less plain, than that imposed upon the catalyst of a calculated transaction. Those who act with the intent to cause harm, we have seen, usually are burdened by an absolute duty either to abstain from a particular form of conduct or to suffer the consequences for failing to do so. In such cases, one may be found normatively responsible simply for having committed such an intentional act, regardless of the effect that act may have had upon others. In random transactions, by contrast, the defendant's duty cannot be ascertained without also considering the impact her conduct has had upon the plaintiff. Here, the interaction is not inspired by an evil motive, but is an unexpected outgrowth of the defendant's primarily self-directed activity. Under these circumstances, the state may not restrict the defendant's autonomy entirely; rather, it must balance her interest in pursuing her life plan against the interests of others in being protected from harm.

This can only be done, if at all, by holding the actor's conduct up to flexible standard of care. As we have already seen, both negligence and strict liability theories employ such a standard for assessing the liability of a unilateral actor. In negligence, a reasonable person standard is used. In strict liability actions, different multifactor standards are implemented. Under either theory, and under any such standard, the defendant's duty of care is adjusted according to the circumstances at hand. Thus, where the offending conduct presents extraordinary risks, the actor's duty of care normally is increased. Conversely, if the actor's behavior is merely careless, or she must act under an exigency, her responsibility will be far less onerous. Because in each situation the actor's duty is premised on the socially accepted criteria of risk and need, the standards which afford these adaptations satisfy our sense of distributive justice, at least on a conceptual level.

Of course, no matter how fair such standards are in theory, they would be distributively unjust if they were to be applied in situations where they were not warranted. Such might be the case if an actor's responsibility for a transaction were held to exceed her power of controlling it. Consider again the facts of *Palsgraf v. Long Island Railroad Co.*[2] There, it will be recalled, the employees of a railroad company negligently jostled a passenger as he attempted to board a moving train. Unbeknownst to the employees, the passenger was carrying a package of fireworks. As a result of the employees' conduct, the passenger dropped the package, causing an explosion. The concussion of the blast knocked over a standing scale which fell upon and injured a waiting ticket holder. In this case, the risk posed by the employees' conduct might favor subjecting the railroad to a substantial duty of care. Such a duty would be fair, however, only if it were not absolute. Unlike calculated conduct, providing careless assistance to another does not directly repudiate the rule of law, and so does not pose an imminent threat to society generally. Thus, there is no justification for holding the railroad and its employees responsible to everyone or anyone impacted by the explosion. To afford these parties and others like them the freedom necessary to pursue their own life plans, some reasonable limits must be placed upon their potential liability.

Risk, Harm and the Limitation of Duty

In negligence and strict liability actions, this limitation is established by the concept of foreseeable risk and is implemented usually under the rubric of duty or proximate cause. In the *Palsgraf* case, this concept would confine the railroad's responsibility to the class of individuals who appeared, prior to the explosion, to be threatened by her conduct. This protected group surely would include the jostled passenger himself, or others standing immediately nearby. But it clearly would not extend to the distant ticket holder who was affected by the explosion only because of the highly unusual chain reaction initiated by the conduct of the employees. Here, the railroad was under no obligation to look out for the interests of anyone outside the zone of danger created by the innocuous action of assisting a passenger onto a train.[3] Although such a result may seem harsh to the injured ticket holder, it is the only way of securing a fair share of autonomy for the railroad. It does not exempt the railroad from all responsibility; rather, it makes the railroad's liability coextensive with its ability to predict and control the hazards of its enterprise. Were the carrier liable for risks beyond its power of prevention, the resulting restriction of its autonomy itself would be excessive and thus unfair.

Risk is not the only factor which serves to circumscribe an actor's duty of care in random transactions. Indeed, the concept of foreseeable risk merely helps us ascertain who the eligible beneficiaries of a duty may be. To conclusively establish one's beneficiary status, it is also necessary to consider the additional element of harm. Earlier, we saw that harm generally is not important in defining the duty of care owed by an intentional actor. Such an actor, you will recall, may be held liable even if she causes no actual harm to anyone. For conduct that is less than intentionally injurious, however, no duty of repair arises unless and until the plaintiff suffers some actual autonomy impairment, and even then, the loss must be more than would be expected in ordinary social intercourse.[4] So in the above example, the negligent railroad would owe no duty to passive onlookers who either remained unaffected by the explosion or suffered a psychological trauma too nebulous or trivial to redress. In cases like this, where the actor's behavior is primarily self-directed, she is entitled to greater freedom to go about her business. The harm requirement, by limiting the consequences for which the actor may be held responsible, assures her this latitude.

The Binary Analysis of Breach

Once the scope of the actor's duty has been established, the next question is whether she breached this personal obligation. For most calculated transactions, we saw, the determination of breach is premised on a single factor. If the actor committed one of the forbidden acts enumerated by our tort rules, she could be found liable regardless of whether she actually interfered with the interests of anyone else. For random transactions, however, the breach analysis is not unary but binary. In addition to examining the offending conduct, it also is necessary to evaluate the prospective risk and actual harm which it imposed upon others. So, in deciding if a nondeliberative defendant violated her duty of care, one must consider not only the personal and social value of the activity in question, and the hardship of requiring the defendant to conduct it in a different manner, but also the importance of the interests threatened by that activity, and the potential magnitude of their impairment. Only if it appears, on balance, that the harm sustained by the plaintiff exceeds the utility of the offending act will the defendant be subject to an ex post monetary sanction of tort liability.

This comparative analysis, while expendable in the evaluation of calculated transactions, is the key factor in assessing the morality of unilateral, random transactions. For one thing, it helps to further the end of corrective justice. Unlike intentionally harmful behavior, the conduct which initiates random transactions is not wrongful in itself. It is wrongful, if at all, only because of the effect which it has had or may have upon another. By acknowledging this, the balancing analysis mentioned above allows us to distinguish accidental encounters from those that require some form of corrective action. At the same time, it also tends to satisfy our demand for distributive justice. Indeed, by considering the interests of *both* transacting parties, it ensures that the allocation of autonomy among them is not arbitrary or capricious, but is firmly rooted in the actor-inhibiting concept of risk and the victim-protecting concept of need.

Harm and Corrective Rights

We see from the foregoing discussion that the existence of some tangible harm is indispensable not only in the creation of a duty of care, but also in the determination of whether that standard has been violated. Yet the notion of harm plays an even larger role in the evaluation of random transactions. Besides defining the defendant's responsibility, it is essential for establishing the plaintiff's right of action. Recall that rights may be preemptive or corrective. Preemptive rights, which allow the holder to curtail the activity of another, are activated by the presence of risk alone. Such rights commonly arise in calculated transactions where an unwilling participant must take immediate defensive action to protect her interests. Corrective rights, on the other hand, are triggered only when the claimant sustains a tangible harm. Until this happens, the plaintiff suffers no wrong and has nothing to correct. Once her autonomy is impaired, however, she develops an entitlement that empowers her to extract from her wrongdoer a sum of money sufficient to nullify the imbalance existing between them. In many cases involving purely random transactions, this is her only available remedy, and for good reason. Unlike intentional behavior, which is entirely other-directed, random misconduct is primarily self-regarding and so is entitled to greater freedom from restraint.

Bilateral Random Transactions

The analysis of bilateral random transactions is similar in many respects. The determination of the defendant's duty will require an examination of both the nature of her conduct and the harm sustained by the claimant. Likewise, it would be impossible to ascertain if the applicable duty had been transgressed without balancing the defendant's right of action against the claimant's right to secure her interests from outside intrusion. Finally, the claimant's entitlement to compensation will turn on her ability to prove that she has suffered some legally recognized impairment of her autonomy. Despite these similarities, however, the evaluation of bilateral transactions is frequently far more complicated than those unilaterally initiated.

In unilateral transactions, we saw, the claimant has no control or influence over her fate. In bilateral transactions, however, the plaintiff is not just an innocent victim, but an active malefactor. That is, she engages in some faulty conduct of her own which contributes to the ensuing encounter between the parties. Here, the defendant's wrongdoing is not necessarily the sole cause of the transaction; instead, both parties often share responsibility for the fortuitous intersection of their lives and interests.

The conjunctive aspect of bilateral transactions adds two new levels of analysis to the search for justice. On one level, it necessitates that we undertake a wholly independent examination of the *plaintiff's normative* responsibility for the injuries she sustained in the transaction. Specifically, we must determine both the nature and extent of her moral failing. On another level, it requires that the *plaintiff's causal* responsibility for the incident also be considered. Here, we must determine how much her moral failing contributed to her loss.

These additional concerns, in turn, serve to intensify the binary character of the analysis already needed for random transactions. Indeed, for bilateral encounters, we must scrutinize not only the plaintiff's harm, as we did for unilateral engagements, but the quality of her actions as well. And we may not simply compare the competing interests of the parties, we also must compare their conduct and assign to each some measure of causal influence.

These new issues—concerning the plaintiff's normative and causal responsibility—are not the same in every bilateral transaction. Indeed, they will vary depending upon the circumstances of the case at hand. For example, in some cases the parties' normative responsibility may be virtually commensurate, while in others one of the actors may be more clearly at fault. So too with the question of causal responsibility. Only rarely will the actions of the plaintiff and defendant have an identical, or at least indistinguishable impact upon an outcome. In many cases, one party's causal influence over an incident may either slightly or substantially exceed that of her counterpart. What accounts for these fluctuations in normative and causal responsibility? The answer, we shall see, lies in the temporal sequence of the parties' actions.

Simultaneous Encounters

Where the plaintiff and defendant act simultaneously in precipitating a harmful transaction, the analysis of their rights usually takes on two characteristics. First, the determination of causal responsibility, and to a lesser extent normative responsibility, will almost always require a comparison of the parties' respective actions leading up to the transaction. Second, in most cases, both the normative and causal responsibility for the encounter will be fairly evenly split between the actors who brought it about. While these attributes are not categorical, they help to distinguish such transactions from those that develop in sequential stages.

Defining Characteristics

A simultaneous transaction is one in which the actions of the parties occur at roughly the same time and continue to have operative effect up until the moment they culminate in an injurious encounter. While neither action is completely blameless, likewise neither is intended to interfere with the interests of anyone else. This distinguishes simultaneous random transactions from unavoidable accidents, on the one hand, and calculated transactions on the other.

The following hypothetical is illustrative of such a simultaneous encounter. A, while driving an automobile, is distracted by a storefront window display and so fails to scan the road ahead for pedestrians. B, a pedestrian who is reading a map, steps into the street without checking for oncoming traffic. Because of the actions of each, A's car strikes B and causes her severe injuries.

In this situation, it is clear that both parties will share normative responsibility for the collision. Each party was held to a state-imposed standard of reasonable conduct and each seems to have violated that standard to some extent. By driving inattentively, A breached her duty to safeguard pedestrians and other motorists from the foreseeable risks which such carelessness invariably creates. Similarly, B, by failing to watch where she was going, not only risked involving others in an accident, she also unreasonably subjected herself to physical harm.

Fixing the Parties' Normative Responsibilities

By and large, the determination of whether a particular party is at all at fault for causing the transaction may be made without much concern for the actions of the other. Of course, the defendant's duty will turn, in part, on whether she could have foreseen injury to the plaintiff or others like her. Likewise, the plaintiff's contributory fault will depend on the foreseeability of the defendant's actions. Nevertheless, the normative responsibility of each party is determined primarily by her own behavior. Thus, in deciding if A's driving was reasonable or unreasonable, we need not compare her conduct with that of B; instead, we need only hold it up to an abstract standard of prudence. The same is true for B. Her responsibility will arise from the community norm imposed upon urban pedestrians, and not from the actions of the party who ran her down.

Still, once one reaches the conclusion that each party is at least partly to blame for the accident, the degree of the parties' normative responsibilities cannot realistically be assessed without comparing their respective actions. For example, although the act of walking across a roadway without looking in both directions may seem to be the epitome of foolishness, it probably would appear far less blameworthy were the pedestrian run over by a joyrider traveling at twice the legal speed limit. In such a case, the conduct of the driver helps to color our perception of the pedestrian's behavior, and so assists us in evaluating the moral culpability of both parties to the transaction.

Causal Indeterminacy

If, as is common, the actions of each party are found to be normatively wanting, typically both actors also will be held causally responsible for precipitating the encounter. Indeed, the contemporaneous aspect of these transactions almost necessitates such a conclusion. More often than not, the parties' actions will meld in a way that makes it virtually impossible to trace their independent effects. All that can be determined for sure is that each act was an indispensable factor in setting the parties on a collision course. So it was in our illustration above. If A had kept a proper lookout, she most likely would have been able to stop or steer clear of B as the latter set foot into the street. Or, if B had glanced up from her map, she surely would have refrained from stepping in front of A's oncoming car. Thus, had the conduct of either been different, the accident probably would not have occurred.

While this fact tends to establish the parties' causal responsibilities, it is not conclusive in all cases. For simultaneous transactions, where there are multiple causal agents, it also is necessary to compare the parties' respective actions to determine the extent of their influence upon the outcome. As we saw earlier, the idea of causal responsibility, or as I have termed it, factual responsibility, is not absolute but highly relativistic. Its purpose is to identify the parties whose control over a transaction is so great that it may be said to bear their distinctive signatures. To make this determination, one must consider such factors as the number of causal influences on the occurrence, the directness or indirectness of each cause's impact upon the outcome and the temporal sequence of their initiation and operation. Unlike calculated transactions, where one party deliberately instigates the encounter, simultaneous bilateral transactions always involve at least two possible causal agencies. Thus, for cases within this subcategory, it is especially important that one undertake a more expansive analysis of the circumstances which brought the parties to conflict.

Causal Equivalency

Using this broader approach, the parties' causal responsibilities for a simultaneous random transaction often will appear roughly equivalent. Indeed, the mere nature of these transactions makes this so. First off, both parties commit the same generic type of wrongdoing. There are no random transactions in which one party acts deliberately and the other is only careless. These, we have seen, are included within the paradigm of calculated transactions. Though the parties may engage in substantially different activities—like in the above hypothetical where A drove a car while B walked across the street—they are guilty of an identical sin: disregarding the foreseeable risk of their interaction. Granted, in some cases the derelictions of one actor may be far more serious than that of her counterpart; on these occasions, it might be reasonable to assign different degrees of causal responsibility to the parties. But in most cases of ordinary negligence, such fine distinctions will be all but illusory. Even where there is some discernable difference in the nature of the parties' conduct, it frequently will be next to impossible to tell how much of an effect each act has had upon the outcome. Because the parties normally act under the same circumstances at roughly the same time, neither party is in any better position than the other to avoid the accident. For each, the risk of harm often becomes apparent, if at all, only seconds before their interaction. With both parties acting unintentionally, and with the same limited opportunity to prevent the inevitable, there appears to be no meaningful basis for distinguishing the causal responsibility of one actor from that of her counterpart.

Sequential Encounters

Sequential encounters differ from simultaneous encounters in one material respect. Instead of operating at the same time, the actions of the parties take effect in definite chronological stages. Sometimes the plaintiff acts first and the defendant's action follows. This would be the case where the plaintiff carelessly parks her car in a narrow alley way and it is later struck by an inattentive driver. Other times, the defendant acts before the plaintiff. For example, a construction contractor excavates a hole without erecting proper barriers; thereafter the inattentive plaintiff walks by and carelessly falls in. In each case, one party creates a dangerous condition, and the other unreasonably exposes herself to it, thus culminating the transaction.

Distinguishing Features

To some, this factual distinction between simultaneous and sequential transactions may seem trivial. After all, in each scenario both actors behave in a way that is less than prudent, and both undoubtedly contribute to the resulting encounter. Nevertheless, the analysis of these transactions is unique in two respects. On the issue of normative responsibility, we shall see that the acts of one party may nearly foreclose the duty of the other. And on the question of causal responsibility, our investigation will reveal that there may be great disparity in the degrees of control exercised by the parties over the transaction.

Chronology and Normative Responsibility

As was indicated earlier in this discussion, an actor's normative responsibility for a random encounter cannot be assessed by looking at her conduct alone. One must consider, in addition, the foreseeable risks imposed upon the prospective victim, and the interests actually taken from her in the transaction. When the victim herself is in part causally responsible for the encounter, there is a further need to compare her actions to those of her transactional partner. In most cases, this comparison enlightens the evaluation of, but does not determine, the moral propriety of the parties' respective actions.

In sequential transactions, however, the culpability of one party may all but exonerate the other. What accounts for this is the chronological ordering of the parties' actions. Unlike in simultaneous transactions, where neither party is better equipped to avoid the impending accident, one party in a sequential transaction—i.e., the one acting second—frequently will have the last, best opportunity to circumvent disaster.[5] If she is aware of the dangerous condition and yet deliberately proceeds to confront it, she will have initiated a calculated transaction and so may be held fully responsible for the consequences. In such a case, the intentional misconduct of the actor is considered an unforeseeable circumstance which falls outside her counterpart's duty of care. However, if the actor's mental state is anything less than intentional—either because she is not completely aware of the danger or does not voluntarily wish to expose herself or others to it—the resulting encounter will be a random transaction. While she may not be solely responsible for its occurrence, the blame she is likely to receive for precipitating it will be far greater than if she had acted simultaneously with others.

To illustrate this point, let's reconsider the example mentioned earlier where a pedestrian steps into an open excavation hole. Changing the facts slightly, suppose that the pedestrian actually saw the hole and intentionally attempted to jump over it, say, to test her leaping ability. Before proceeding with this stunt, she made no effort to investigate the size of the hole. As a result, she greatly miscalculated both its diameter and its depth. She did not discover her mistake, however, until she was suspended perilously above the hole, anticipating the injuries which eventually would follow from her folly. Because she lacked full knowledge of the hole's dimensions, we probably cannot say that she deliberately exposed herself to the dangerous condition it presented. Nevertheless, we surely can characterize her conduct as reckless. Aware of the hole, she possessed the power to avoid the danger entirely; yet for nothing more than curiosity or sport, she took a running jump into the black abyss of the unknown. More than mere carelessness, her conduct demonstrated a near complete disregard for her own safety. Although she may not bear the total burden of her loss, clearly she has earned a far greater share of responsibility than the creator of the hole.

Chronology and Causal Responsibility

For similar reasons, one who fails to look before leaping virtually assures herself the distinction of being the primary cause of her inevitable injury. Previously in Chapter Twelve, we saw how the temporal sequence of a transaction may have a profound effect upon the determination of causal responsibility. There, we considered a car accident brought about by two sufficient causes: the failure of a rental company to inspect the vehicle's brakes; and the failure of the driver to apply them prior to the collision. Although both omissions were operative up until the time of the accident, we observed that the driver's failing actually may have had a greater influence on or control over the outcome. Because of the temporal propinquity between her act and the resulting collision, she possessed the last, best opportunity to avert the danger, either by honking the horn or by swerving to the side.

If the chronology in this case is sufficient to tip the balance of causal responsibility against the driver, there can be little doubt that our intrepid hole-jumper must receive an even more lopsided share of this burden. Unlike the brakeless motorist, the jumper enjoyed almost infinite opportunities for avoidance. Her decision to face danger did not arise out of an exigent situation, but was made under favorable circumstances which afforded her unlimited time for thoughtful deliberation. Having observed the hole, she could have eluded the hazard it presented simply by taking some other route. Even though the construction contractor placed no obstacles around the excavation, it was the act of the jumper, more than anything else, that precipitated the transaction. Under these circumstances, justice requires that she bear the lion's share of causal responsibility for the injurious consequences of that encounter.

Although this example may be a bit peculiar, the analysis it evokes is not. Whenever parties act in such a chronological sequence, the actor who confronts a preexisting danger created by another typically will possesses greater power to control her own fate. This power, we have seen, has a significant impact on the determination of her legal status vis a vis her transactional partner. It not only heightens her normative responsibility, it also tends to expand her causal responsibility for any resulting loss.

Random Transactions and Comparative Analysis

Nevertheless, in all bilateral transactions, including those that develop sequentially, *both* parties share at least *some* responsibility for the adverse consequences they engender. Each party has breached her distributive allocation of responsibility (thus establishing her normative irresponsibility), and each has contributed in some way to the outcome. For cases within this paradigm, then, it frequently will be necessary to compare the normative and causal responsibility of each party to determine how to allocate the loss precipitated by their interaction. Although these forms of responsibility tend to become aggregated in the comparison, they do not lose independent significance. It is quite possible that one factor could predominate the analysis. For example, where a defendant's culpability is extraordinary, but her influence over the result is modest, her liability may be minimal if, as in our hole-jumping hypothetical, the plaintiff recklessly chooses to encounter the danger which caused her injury. Here, the plaintiff's causal responsibility for the result might substantially overshadow the other elements of the comparison.

It should be pointed out in closing, however, that the comparative determination of responsibility is not necessarily an all-or-nothing proposition. Most jurisdictions implement this analysis through comparative fault statutes or common law rules.[6] Under these systems, the contributorily responsible plaintiff is not automatically barred from recovery; instead, her damages are reduced in proportion to her "fault." At least insofar as bilateral transactions are concerned, this is as it should be. For even the independent acts of strangers may so coalesce as to be inseparable. Like the ingredients to a culinary recipe, each causal element in an interaction may be prominent, unique and essential; but together they are bound to produce a result truly distinctive in itself. Without any one of these autonomous elements, the result could not be the same. To deny their singular contributions to the outcome, therefore, is to deny their independent value. This is a dangerous prospect in a society founded on the notion of liberty, where every autonomous action reflects the triumph of rational association over brute force.

Chapter 19

Relations

While calculated and random transactions make up a significant portion of contemporary tort disputes, it seems clear that most tortious interactions today arise out of relations. Indeed, because we are a consumer-based society, just about everything we need or want must be acquired from someone else through mutual exchange. Our food, our clothing, our homes, our livelihood, even our entertainment, is obtained from others for a price. Since most of our time is spent interacting with others to obtain these goods, it is not surprising that when mishaps occur, they usually take place in the context of some type of relationship.

The Nature of Relations

Relations, like transactions, may take on any of a wide variety of forms. Some relations are of short duration, as where a consumer purchases a product from a local retailer. Others may last for years, as is frequently the case of salaried or at will employment relationships. Many relations are highly formalized, setting out in detail the terms of the parties' encounter. Lease agreements and other contracts are of this sort. Yet a substantial number of relations are much more casual in nature, often initiated on only a moment's notice. Social visits and shopping excursions might fall within this category.

These disparate relations can be grouped into two general categories: jural relations and consensual relations. Jural relations display two fundamental characteristics. One characteristic, which accounts for the appellation used to describe these associations, is that the relationship of the parties is imposed upon them by law, and is not necessarily the result of their mutual consent. The other feature of jural relations is that they are custodial in nature. Because of either the vulnerability or the misconduct of one party, the state requires that she be relegated to the custody of another. Parent-child relations, relations between prisoners and their jailers, as well as those between mental health institutions and their involuntary inmates all fall within this narrow category of relations.

Consensual relations are far more common. From commercial exchanges to social encounters, the principal attribute of these relations is the consent of all participants. Thus, unlike those in jural relations, or those participating in calculated or random transactions, parties in consensual relations are not forced to exchange their interests; rather, they do so willingly, usually with the hope of acquiring some identifiable benefit.

These differences aside, all relations are joined by a common bond. Unlike transactions which are unexpected by all or some of the participants, relations are formed with full knowledge of the parties involved. Although sometimes the nature or extent of their engagement is not completely anticipated, at least some interaction with another is certain. This is important because it invariably causes each party to develop expectations both about her relational partner and about the details of their interaction.

The Added Complexity of Relational Analysis

Such expectations may develop in one of two ways. The surest way to cultivate expectations is by entering a mutual agreement. In a mutual agreement, the parties decide between themselves how the risks of their relation will be allocated. For example, it is not uncommon for a lessor to assume the obligation of repairing broken fixtures for her lessee; on the other hand, the lessee usually accepts responsibility for the general upkeep of her apartment. Under such an agreement, the lessee may reasonably expect that if her unit suddenly stops receiving heat, the lessor will either fix the problem herself or pay an independent contractor to do the work for her. However, if the apartment becomes extremely dirty through normal use, it is understood by both parties that the lessee bears the burden of cleaning it up.

The other way expectations may be cultivated is through communicative action. One party to a relationship says or does something which seems to express her commitment to assume certain responsibilities toward her counterpart. Aware of this expression, the other party changes her position in some way, usually by foregoing opportunities for protection. Thus, if our lessor from the above example hires a doorman to stand guard over the entrance to her apartment building, a lessee might reasonably, though inaccurately, believe that the lessor has undertaken to secure the premises from all criminal activity. Because of this expectation, the lessee might then refrain from taking measures to protect herself—say by buying a gun or a can of mace. Here, of course, there is no actual agreement between the parties. Although the lessee develops an expectation about how the risks of the relation are to be distributed, this expectation is not shared by her counterpart. Nevertheless, the lessee, as the expectant party, gives up some of her freedom of action by relying on this perception.

Regardless of whether such expectations are formed bilaterally—as in the case of a mutual agreement—or unilaterally—as in the case of communicative action—they invariably play a pivotal role in evaluating the justice of any relational encounter. Indeed, where the parties agree to create and share the burdens and benefits of their relation, they in effect devise their own private scheme of risk allocation. This agreement may either supplement the state-imposed duties of the parties or prevent such duties from arising in the first place. While communicative action does not establish an independent source of responsibility for the parties, it does affect the duties allocated to them by the state. Thus, when one party induces another's detrimental reliance, the state typically holds the reliance-inducer to a more stringent standard of care. In either type of relation, a simple hermeneutical truth emerges: one simply cannot assess the political and moral propriety of the parties' association without first considering how the behavior of one participant may affect the rights of the other. At a minimum, this requires scrutinizing each exchange for evidence of consensual risk assignments, justifiable reliance or both. In combination, the concepts of consent and reliance not only serve to distinguish relations from mere transactions, they also tend to make such encounters especially difficult to analyze. Because of the enormous moral significance of these concepts, and their uniqueness to relational interactions, it is necessary that we examine each more closely.

Consent: The Moral Adhesive of Private Agreements

Consent is the conceptual cornerstone of any agreement. It draws parties together. It justifies their union and allows them to plan their subsequent interactions. When circumstances change, it authorizes them to alter their relationship by modifying the terms of their association. On a political level, it frees the parties of the responsibilities ordinarily imposed upon them by the state. At the same time, it gives each party a power over her counterpart otherwise forbidden in a liberal democratic system.

Given the fecundity of this concept, it should not be surprising that it is the central focus of cases within the relational paradigm. One simply cannot assess the justice of a relational encounter without possessing a full understanding of consent and its effect upon the rights and obligations of the parties. In this regard, several questions are of critical importance. What is true consent and how may it be communicated to others? What is the scope of a party's consent and when does the risk of a particular injury fall within the purview of that concept? Where the parties consensually allocate the risks of their relationship, what happens to their primary and secondary rights if injury actually results from their encounter?

Finally, how is this concept used to shape the corrective remedies of tort law and is this usage fair and just?

Express and Implied Consent

Consent can be manifested through either words or actions. When consent is given verbally—by oral communication or in writing—it is said to be express. Such verbal agreements are normally associated with contract law. In fact, in many cases, the parties' mutual expressions of consent do give rise to a contractual or quasi-contractual relationship.[1] This does not mean, however, that these relations are foreign to tort disputes. On the contrary, many tort cases involve some sort of express verbal arrangement between the parties. Apartment leases are a good example. In many instances, the terms of an apartment lease are incorporated into a formal written contract and often make provision for the safety of the building or unit to be occupied. Similarly, most consumer goods are sold with warranties which delimit the rights and responsibilities of the seller and buyer with regard to certain product hazards.[2] And nowadays one cannot rent a bicycle, run a 10K race or go horseback riding without executing a written waiver or release which exonerates the provider of the service of liability for personal injuries sustained by the user.

Like express consent, implied consent indicates a party's subjective willingness to interact with another. The difference is that, for implied consent, this intent is never verbalized. Instead, the parties' interaction is premised upon a tacit understanding shared between them. In most cases, this understanding arises from a prior course of dealing between the parties or some specific or general community custom.[3] For example, in short-term exchange transactions, the community norm in most places is that when one receives a good or service from another, she is obligated to pay fair market value for it. So if I walk into a barber shop and receive a satisfactory haircut, it is assumed and expected that I will pay a reasonable price for the service, even though neither the barber nor I ever overtly communicated this understanding. Here, my action of sitting in the barber chair and remaining mute while he cuts my locks, when viewed against the underlying social custom, is enough to communicate my assent both to the onslaught of the scissors and to the payment of the barber for his effort.

Because social customs are so prevalent, and the time and expense of contracting so prohibitive, many associations develop informally on the basis of implied consent. Besides exchange transactions—like the barber shop example mentioned above—implied consent may be found in a multitude of other, more stable relationships: from an employer's unstated commitment to keep her premises safe for her employees, to a doctor's assumed responsibility to protect and preserve the health of her patients, to a product manufacturer's silent guarantee to stand behind the quality of her merchandise. In fact, given the number of contingencies that may arise during a relationship, it is doubtful that any relation is ever completely free from such implied understandings. Even parties engaged in contractual relationships often assent to terms which they never reduce to writing. Take the apartment leases mentioned above. It is not uncommon for a landlord to provide security for an apartment building without committing to this responsibility in the lease agreement. Yet, as has been observed earlier, the mere undertaking by the landlord to secure the premises may be sufficient to create in the minds of the tenants an implied obligation to protect them from outside intruders.

The Substance of Consent

Whether one's assent to assume a relational risk is expressly or impliedly manifested, it must bear certain substantive characteristics to be valid and enforceable. First, the party giving consent must possess full, actual knowledge of the risks to be encountered.[4] A general awareness of the risk will not suffice; nor is it enough that a reasonable person would have recognized the danger. For consent to be effective, the consenter must harbor a subjective appreciation for both the magnitude of the relevant risk and the probability of its realization in harm. Second, the consenter must voluntarily elect either to expose herself to the danger or to accept responsibility for the consequence of doing so.[5] This means, at a minimum, that in making her decision, the consenting party is free from any incapacitating or coercive influences. Only where these elements coalesce—so that the choice to accept the risk is both knowing and voluntary—can it be said that the election is truly consensual.

The Epistemology of Consent

In some cases, it is not difficult to determine whether and to what extent a prospective consenter was aware of a risk before agreeing to expose herself to it. Where consent is express, for example, often the risks of the relation are clearly delineated. Indeed, waiver provisions used in participatory sporting events frequently list the dangers inherent in the sport and declare that the signatory is fully aware of them. In other situations, however, the risks of the relationship are not so explicitly defined. This is especially true of relations where the parties' consent must be implied from the surrounding circumstances. Because the risks of such encounters are not overtly catalogued, it usually is much harder to assess whether the consenting party knew of their existence prior to entering the relation. The only way to make this determination is by examining several factors, including the characteristics of the consenter, the circumstances in which such consent was given, the level of risk information available to the consenter prior to the encounter, and the nature of the risk itself.

Characteristics of the Consenter

People acquire and process risk information in vastly different ways. Often, the level of one's knowledge of risk can be attributed directly to certain objective facts about her personal identity. For example, age normally is one of the best predictors of a person's ability to appreciate risk. Except for the occasional prodigy, children generally are less aware than adults of the hazards that await them in the world. Another telling characteristic is one's mental capacity. Even among adults, intelligence levels can vary greatly. Obviously, the more advanced one's mental capacity, the more likely it is that she will be cognizant of dangers that may confront her during her relational associations. For the same reason, one's education, experience and training are fairly accurate indicators of her knowledge and appreciation of risk. Those with special skills—like professionals and tradesmen—are thus expected to know more about the risks of their enterprises than others lacking such attributes.

Regardless of these individual personality traits, there are certain aspects of human nature which shape the way all people perceive or misperceive risk. As a general rule, human beings are poor risk assessors. Risks are so prevalent in our society that we simply cannot accumulate data on all of the dangers that confront us; and even when we are able to collect such information, we often lack the time necessary to ponder these risks before acting. As a result, we develop certain short-hand techniques—known as heuristics—which allow us to make snap judgments about the dangers we encounter every day.[6]

The "availability" heuristic is one of the most important of these risk assessing techniques.[7] Under it, a person's perception of risk will be influenced by her ability to conceptualize the danger from past experience. When a particular risk comes readily to mind, the image of that danger is said to be more "available" for retrieval from the perceiver's memory bank. The perceiver assumes that if examples of the risk are easy to envision, then the danger will arise with some frequency and, when it does, her assessment of it will be reasonably accurate.[8] In many cases, this heuristic serves us well. For those of us who must drive on a daily basis, car accidents are an all too ordinary sight which remind us of the need for caution when sitting behind the wheel. Unfortunately, however, our ability to recall risk images is affected not only by the breadth of our past experiences, but by the salience of those experiences as well. For example, most people are able to remember catastrophic, sensational events—like plane crashes or nuclear disasters—with less effort than more mundane occurrences—like tripping on a stair or falling off a ladder.[9] The problem is that there often is no statistical correlation between how memorable a risk is and how much harm it may cause. Indeed, in the examples given above, one is actually far safer sitting on a plane or living near a nuclear reactor than walking down stairs or standing on a ladder. Nevertheless, for events or activities with such high levels of salience, the availability heuristic often tricks us into overestimating the danger they present.[10]

The heuristic of "representativeness" operates in a similar fashion.[11] People tend to categorize risks in accordance with their salient characteristics. When a new risk appears to possess one of these characteristics, the subject often considers it representative of the relevant preexisting risk category. The subject then equates the statistical probability of each risk without searching for differences which might render the comparison inaccurate.[12] To illustrate, the novice carpenter who has operated an electric saw in the past may associate with that activity certain risks such as electrocution or mutilation. Each time she uses the tool, she remains mindful of these risks. However, because she considers each usage representative of the activity generally, she might fail to consider other possible dangers which may arise when the tool is used in a different environment. Thus, if the saw were operated near a gas duct, the danger of sparking and explosion —which is not representative of ordinary saw usage—may easily escape her comprehension.

Even where information of new risks becomes known, people often are reluctant to alter their preexisting conceptions of danger. The heuristic of "anchoring and adjustment" is one reason for this. Upon confronting a risk, people develop a preliminary estimate of its magnitude and probability. They immediately become "anchored" to this estimate and often are unwilling to change or "adjust" it even in the face of additional information.[13] Those living in hurricane zones, for instance, may downplay the danger of such natural forces despite seeing frequent examples of its destructive effect upon her neighbors. This intransigence is caused by another deficiency in human risk perception—that of overconfidence.[14] The sad fact is that most people are unaware just how inaccurate their estimates of risk actually are. Convinced of their competency, they simply disregard data which might provide them with a more accurate portrait of the risks they encounter.[15]

The Circumstances of Consent

While the characteristics of the consenter give us some insight into her general capacity for comprehending risk, it does not tells us whether she likely perceived a specific danger on any particular occasion. She may have been well-suited or ill-equipped to appreciate the consequences of her risk choice, but did she actually recognize the dangers confronting her before assuming this responsibility? One can only answer this question by examining the circumstances in existence at the time the consenter made her decision.

Perhaps the most revealing consideration in this regard is the temporal sequence of the events which led to the ultimate harm sustained by the consenter. If she consented to accept the risk of harm at the outset of the relationship—before the parties had yet interacted—the chances of her possessing full knowledge of the dangers involved are small. In this situation, the dangers being assumed are both abstract and speculative. Unless the risks are an inherent and unavoidable by-product of the relationship, it would be difficult for the consenter to predict in more than a general way the exact hazards she might later encounter. Where, however, the consenter is confronted with the risky condition and *then* decides to expose herself to it, her knowledge of the danger is likely to be significantly enhanced. Here the risk is real, not hypothetical. Presumably, therefore, the consenter has the opportunity to investigate the risk and discover its precise nature before electing to proceed further with the relation.

However helpful this temporal relationship is in illuminating the consenter's awareness of risk, it alone is not dispositive of her state of mind. To accurately assess her subjective knowledge, it also is necessary to consider the imminence of the danger to be encountered. The closer the proximity between the exercise of consent and the risk-creating condition or activity, the greater the consenter's awareness of the danger is likely to be. This is true even where consent is given before the risk materializes in an actual hazard. For example, one who agrees to engage in an impromptu boxing match with the pugilist standing before her can be fairly certain of the dangers she faces in that bout. She can see the physical attributes of her opponent and can evaluate her agility and stamina. One who agrees to defer such a contest for a couple of months, however, cannot really be sure of the risks she will encounter on the day of the competition. During the intervening sixty days, her adversary may radically transform her body, increasing both her strength and body size. She may train ferociously to enhance her cardiovascular conditioning. She may even sharpen her boxing technique or learn new tactics for pummeling her opponents into submission. The lapse of time makes it nearly impossible for the fighter to appreciate the remote risks she might confront in the distant future.

In other contexts, however, the additional time may actually provide the consenter with a better opportunity to accumulate information about the risks of the relation. As the consenter's data bank expands, so too does her apparent awareness of the consequences of her choice. A good illustration of this is where a race car driver, after agreeing to compete in a particular event, conducts a thorough inspection of the entire race track and its facilities.[16] Here the lapse of time between the driver's exercise of consent and her participation in the race allows her to make a more informed decision about whether to go through with her decision.

A final circumstantial determinant of the consenter's knowledge is the frequency of her exposure in the past to the same or a similar risk. At first blush, it would appear that one who has had extensive experience dealing with a particular danger is far more likely to appreciate its magnitude than another confronting the risk for the first time. Each time the consenter encounters the danger she learns more about its unique characteristics. And, on each occasion, she enjoys a new opportunity not only to process this information, but to reassess the danger and to formulate new ways of reducing or neutralizing the risk of harm. Smoking is an example of an activity in which the participant must make innumerable risk choices over an extended period of time. However, there comes a point where repetitive exposure to a risk becomes desensitizing. After a while, one who is intimately familiar with the risk may begin to underestimate the danger it presents.[17] This is frequently the case with factory workers who must work on the same equipment and perform the same tasks day in and day out.[18] Lulled into a false sense of security, such workers often fall victim to the descending ram of a punch press or the whirling rollers of a conveyor system. Whether the frequency of one's exposure to risk enhances or diminishes her awareness of danger, however, one thing is certain: this factor usually has a critical influence upon her exercise of consent.

The Availability of Risk Information

Experience is not the only way that one may acquire knowledge of the risks she chooses to assume. She may receive such information from external sources as well. These sources may be as general as a law or piece of common community knowledge or as specific as a media report or a formal warning. No matter what the source, the degree of attention paid to the risk undoubtedly increases or decreases our awareness of it.

Laws and regulations provide us with some of our most valuable risk information. There are certain types of products or activities which are more heavily regulated than others. While this may be due in part to political influences, often such regulatory measures reflect the actual or apparent risks associated with the product or activity in question. In any event, most people perceive this to be the case. Thus, when a safety statute is passed or a regulation is promulgated, we tend to view the subject matter of such governmental action as more risky than other types of enterprises. For example, given the extensive regulation of the pesticide industry, the average consumer is generally aware of at least the general dangers presented by such products. The same is true of prescription and nonprescription drugs.[19] Other products which are subject to far fewer governmental standards—like bicycles—often are perceived as significantly less dangerous.[20] Here, the absence of legislation may appear to the consumer to bespeak the product's safety. While this perception may be misguided, there is no question that it is induced, albeit perhaps subtly, by the extent of regulatory activity taken by the government in this area.

Another way people receive general information about risk is from common community knowledge. Conversations among neighbors, word of mouth and gossip all help to establish a tight network of information concerning local hazards. In large and small cities alike, the residents all are aware of the "bad sections" of town where crime runs rampant. In addition, certain distinctive topographical features—like a deep river, steep cliff or a swamp which serves as a haven for snakes—frequently are a matter of common wisdom. Even the unique characteristics of the locale's people, and the property they own, may be known to others in the vicinity. For instance, everyone may know that "old man Jones" is a disturbed fellow given to fits of violent rage. Or, it may be understood that the Smith's dog is a ferocious mutt which will attack anyone who even comes near their property. Although this type of information may not be formally communicated, or even openly discussed, it nevertheless serves as a significant source of one's knowledge of local risks.

There are, of course, more direct ways of disseminating information about specific forms of risk. Often this is done by providing instructions or warnings to those who are likely to face a known danger. Such information may be communicated through a variety of mediums. It may be transmitted verbally—as when an amusement park employee describes for prospective thrill-seekers the hazards to be expected on a particular ride. Or, it might be written—as is the case with traffic signs or product labels. Sometimes the message is presented in the form of a visual symbol, like an orange pylon, a skull and cross bones or a flashing light. Other times, as in the case of emergency sirens, the warning is audible. Risk information may even be received through our olfactory sense, as when we inhale the distinctively pungent aroma of gasoline. But no matter how the message is obtained, each of these communicative techniques helps to expand our awareness of the dangers that may confront us on a daily basis.

Despite the prevalence of such information, probably the greatest external source of our knowledge of risk is the print and broadcast media.[21] Unlike many of the mediums mentioned above, people actively seek out newspapers and television shows in order to get information. Thus, they are likely to be more attentive when receiving the information being conveyed or broadcast. Also, because media officials are generally considered to be objective and professional, possessing an expertise and detachment often not attributed to other information sources, people are more inclined to accept and remember the facts they report. Most of the time, this reliance poses no problem. Individuals accumulate relatively accurate information on the basis of their own fears or interests. On some occasions, however, the public's dependency on the media may backfire. Pressured to "scoop" their competitors, news reporters sometimes exaggerate risks to pique the interest of their readers or viewers.[22]

The scare over the chemical "Alar" is illustrative. In 1989, the television news-magazine show "60 Minutes" called Alar, which was then being used by farmers to keep apples on trees longer, "the most potent cancer-causing agent in our food supply."[23] Following the report several newspapers throughout the country ran articles decrying the health risks of this insidious chemical. As a result, apple sales dropped dramatically and several metropolitan school districts banned from their cafeterias all apples and apple-based products.[24] As it turned out, the risk of getting cancer from consuming trace amounts of Alar was minuscule. By the time the voice of reason was heard, however, much of the public's confidence in our agricultural system had been severely shaken. Like it nor not, the media's impact on our perception of risk had proven to be enormously, even disturbingly, powerful.

The Communicative Nature of Risk

The most overlooked, and in some cases misunderstood, influence on our knowledge of risk is the nature of the risk itself. Certain risks are simply easier to perceive and comprehend than others. Take the risk of electrocution. Ordinarily, electricity is a silent killer. You cannot see it or touch it. It has no smell and seldom makes any noise. Thus, even when one is aware that she is in an area of high voltage, it is easy for her to misjudge or forget about the danger that surrounds her. Now consider the risk of mutilation from the exposed rotating blades of an industrial fan. This risk offers plenty to grab and hold one's attention: the sight of the spinning blades, the whirring of the motor and wind as it rushes from the unit, and the cool but firm feel of the air as it blows by. Given their different characteristics, these risks are likely to leave far different impressions upon those who must endure them.

Even where there are no such obvious dissimilarities, the circuitry in people's brains seems to be prewired so that they will perceive some risks as more or less dangerous than others. There are certain risk attributes that automatically push our hot button for fear. One of these factors is the "newness" of the risk in question.[25] People tend to have the greatest aversion to unfamiliar and uncommon dangers. In most cases, new or unfamiliar risks are the product of modern technology. It was only fifty years ago, for instance, that the world was first forced to confront the dangers of nuclear energy. Still wary of its awesome destructive power, people fear the risk of nuclear disaster perhaps more than any other risk.[26]

This reaction, of course, is not prompted solely by the novelty of this hazard. It also is influenced to a great extent by the gravity and extent of the harm that it poses to the public.[27] The more catastrophic the prospective loss appears, the greater people's suspicion of the hazard will be. This "dread" factor explains why many people are afraid to fly on airplanes. While the risk of a crash is low, the result in most cases is certain death for all those unfortunate enough to be aboard.

This fear, in turn, is fueled by the involuntary nature of such a risk. Indeed, as our control over a particular hazard declines, our trepidation toward that risk seems to grow in kind.[28] This is why most people would rather sit behind the wheel of an auto, where the risk of injury or death is staggering, than entrust their lives to a pilot and ground crew who they do not know and have no power to supervise or instruct.

Finally, the imminence of harm plays a key role in our perception of many risks.[29] In the case of airplane crashes, the risk of death materializes often minutes or seconds after a problem is discovered. The cancer caused by smoking, however, may not develop for twenty or thirty years after the smoker first picks up the habit. As a result, she often underestimates the danger which she surely will confront in the future.

Consent and Volition

Regardless of whether an individual possesses full knowledge of the dangers in a particular relationship, she is incapable of assuming responsibility for these risks unless her decision to do so is completely voluntary. By "completely" voluntary, I do not mean that the actor must possess extraordinary powers of reason. Indeed, even a child is capable of volition. Nor do I suggest that her choice must be made free of all outside pressures. The truth is that every choice we make is influenced at least in part by such considerations as tradition, social norms, familial ties, sexual attraction or simple desire.

There are, however, certain things which not only influence our decisions, they actually prevent us from exercising free will. Mental capacity and age, for example, are two of the most important internal determinants of one's volition. Other pressures are not inherent in the decision-maker, but are exerted upon her by external forces. Need is the greatest of these influences. Whether the necessity arises from the indispensability of a primary good, a relational imbalance or an exigent circumstance, it holds the greatest power over one's freedom of choice.

Internal Incapacities

True volition is seldom evident in certain parties—like young children and adults with mental disabilities—who possess substantially limited intellectual faculties. Such individuals simply are incapable of knowing or understanding the risks to which they are exposed. Even where they may be aware of these dangers, they typically are unable to appreciate the consequences of their actions. For such individuals the disability which impairs their volition is not variable with the circumstances; rather, it is categorical and intrinsic. In recognition of this vulnerability, the law generally allows these parties to void contracts which purport to waive the distributive responsibilities of their counterparts.[30]

There may be situations, however, where the intellectual limitations of such parties do not inhibit their ability to make informed, voluntary choices. For example, a child with special intelligence, experience or skill may possess the same decision-making capacity as an ordinary adult. Because such a child would be able to appreciate the consequences of her decision, her consent to assume the responsibility for that choice would be both valid and enforceable. Likewise, not all of those who suffer from mental infirmities are incapable of volition. Indeed, many possess enough intellectual acuity not only to be self-sufficient, but to lead rather ordinary lives.[31] Although their mental capacity may be less than the average adult, they still are able to recognize danger and to comprehend the ramifications of exposing themselves to it. Like mature minors, these decision-makers should also be held accountable for their actions and their choices.

Instead of depriving these parties of freedom of choice, therefore, the law should do no more than cloak them in the protective shroud of presumptive incapacity. In cases where the suspect party appears to have assumed the responsibility for certain risks, it should be up to her relational counterpart to rebut this presumption. This could be done with either direct or circumstantial evidence. For example, the decision-maker may have made statements about her state of mind before or after the occurrence of the injury-producing event. Alternatively, the nature of the risk itself, the frequency of the decision-maker's exposure to the danger, and the way in which she behaved while around the hazard all would help to determine whether she really knew what she was doing. Where it appears that she fully appreciated the danger and the consequences of accepting it, the presumption would be rebutted and her consent should be enforced to bar her recovery.

External Influences on Volition

There is an inverse correlation between need and choice. Where our very existence is jeopardized, and our need for security is greatest, we generally enjoy little freedom of choice. In such dire circumstances, we have no alternative but to exercise any and all means at our disposal to protect our most basic welfare interests. As the threat to our well-being diminishes, however, so too does the need for desperate action. With less at stake, we may be more judicious and deliberative in the exercise of our choices.

Primary goods—such as food, clothing, shelter, health, transportation, education and employment—are all things that most people cannot live without. Not surprisingly, the state through public law usually affords us access to these most basic staples of existence. Because of the universal need for such goods, their availability generally cannot be altered by private agreement. Thus, parties providing such necessities as medical services, utilities, transportation and housing generally are prohibited from disclaiming responsibility for their actions as a precondition to voluntary exchanges. Such disclaimers are void and unenforceable even if formally accepted by the other party in a contractual agreement.[32] Here, the other party has no real choice; she must have the primary good and will do whatever is necessary to acquire it. Because the apparent consent of the other is invalid, the actor remains bound by the general duty imposed upon her by the state.

Need is not just a matter of acquiring primary goods. It also concerns one's ability to protect herself from the harmful effects of outside influences. The need for protection often arises in many kinds of relations. In fact, some relationships are formed or maintained for the purpose of providing this security.[33] Custodial relations—like those between parents and children or those involving the aged and infirm and their caretakers—are representative of this group. In other types of relations, protection from harm is an incidental, though still a significant aspect of the parties' association. This is true of both fiduciary relationships and relationships established for the exchange of consumer goods and services. All of these relations have at least one thing in common—one party controls the risks of the association and the other relies on the former to protect her from harm.[34] Given the basic nature of the association, there is good reason to question whether the weaker party's apparent consent to assume the risks of the relation is truly voluntary. Thus, as in the case of internal incapacities, a rebuttable presumption of incapacity seems in order in this context as well.[35]

Finally, the need for protection may derive from the circumstances in which the risk choice must be made. Exigent circumstances not only deprive the decision-maker of the opportunity to gather information about the impending danger, they also deny her the time for thoughtful reflection.

Where the time for deliberation is short, it is unlikely that the decision-maker will engage in the type of cost-benefit analysis necessary to make a truly rational choice. Instead, pressed by the compulsion of imminent harm, she will act instinctively and rashly, in some cases exposing herself to greater danger. This could explain why, for example, a tenant whose apartment becomes flooded from a burst water pipe might remain in the unit to recover her personal mementos. Even where the situation is less urgent, the external pressure placed upon the decision-maker can be enough to destroy her volition. Factory workers who must either perform under strict time deadlines and production quotas or risk losing their jobs often have no alternative but to place their limbs in harm's way.[36] Here, the will of the decision-maker is not reflected in the risk choice, but is subordinated to the interests of others. Under any of these compelling circumstances, necessity not volition determines the actor's fate. It follows, then, that risk choices exercised in such a milieu should be looked upon with great suspicion.

Determining the Scope of the Risk Choice

Once it is established that the decision-maker has made a knowing and voluntary choice to assume a risk, it remains to be determined whether the harm resulting from the parties' relation falls within the scope of that risk. This often can be a tricky question. The problem is that risks have no definite parameters. They can be expansively or restrictively conceived, depending upon the mindset of the viewer. What makes this possible are the variety of factors which coalesce to comprise even the most ordinary risks.

The risk of fire provides an apt illustration. Fire itself is an obvious danger. But fire hazards have many aspects which can vary from situation to situation. Part of the risk is the agency which starts the blaze, another part is the manner in which the fire is set, and still another part is the nature and extent of the autonomy interests which the flames threaten to consume. So when an apartment renter assumes the risk of fire damage, does this include a fire commenced by a faulty space heater which was used only after the landlord deliberately failed to supply adequate heat as required by law?[37] Or, does an employee who uses gasoline to clean a machine in the immediate proximity of an open flame assume the risk of injury where a rat which is ignited by the flame takes refuge in the machine, causing an explosion?[38] And when a teenage girl who attempts to make a scented candle pours perfume over a lighted wick, does she assume the risk that the flame will be transformed into a ball of fire which ultimately will cause her severe burns?[39] There are no right or wrong answers to these questions. One who takes an expansive view of fire risks might conclude in each case that the injuries sustained were the foreseeable consequence of the choices made by the decision-makers. On the other hand, those with more conservative inclinations might reasonably find that the risk of fire-related harm did not include either intentionally induced hazards, dangers created through bizarre circumstances or catastrophic physical injuries.

Complicating the interpretation of risk choice is the manner in which such choices are made and expressed. In many instances, it simply is not clear what the decision-maker has consented to. This may be less of a problem where the parties' agreement is reduced to writing. Here, the specific risks allocated to each party frequently are set out in detail. Still, no one possesses the prevision required to predict and assign the responsibility for all contingencies which might develop during a future association. Thus, it sometimes becomes necessary to glean the decision-maker's intent by interpolating or extrapolating from the terms of her written contract. Where no formal explication of consent exists, the task of defining its scope is made even more difficult. In such cases, custom, prior course of dealing and the surrounding circumstances are the only evidence of the actor's intent. Occasionally, these indicia are discrete enough to establish certain limits to the actor's responsibility; other times, however, they are so nebulous that they provide little meaningful assistance in fixing these boundaries.

Waivers and Releases

The broadest assumption of responsibility one may undertake is to waive one's rights or to release her counterpart from liability for her actions. With a waiver or release, the decision-maker often agrees to accept the risk of the other's misbehavior. Except for intentional wrongdoing, it includes all types of faulty conduct—from the commission of negligent acts to the failure to alleviate dangerous conditions.[40] In many cases, there are no limitations of time or place; the decision-maker bears the risk of harm for any activity within the scope of the relation for as long as the relation lasts. It also makes no difference whether the injury sustained is tangible or intangible, trivial or severe. If the harm falls within the generic risk of the waiver or release, any right of recovery for that harm is extinguished.

Because of the expansive nature of such risk choices, they are usually the most closely scrutinized for abuse. After all, there are only two reasons why someone would take on such an onerous burden: either she greatly miscalculated the risks that she would later encounter or she obtained some equal or greater benefit in return. Where the decision-maker assumes the risk of all personal injury, including the possibility of death or great bodily harm, the former alternative often seems to be the most plausible. Indeed, a presumption to this effect is recognized openly in the Uniform Commercial Code. Under section 2-719(3), a contractual remedy limitation clause which prohibits the user of consumer goods from recovering consequential damages for personal injuries is considered prima facie unconscionable.[41] Tort law's treatment of such risk allocation devices is no less severe. A waiver or release which concerns a public necessity—like those mentioned above—or which derives from a contract of adhesion—such that the risks are effectively forced upon the decision-maker by one with far superior bargaining power—is normally found void as against public policy.[42] While there may be occasions where the enforcement of such agreements is justified—as when the other party relies to her detriment upon the decision-maker's expressed consent—for the most part these risk choices lack the free will necessary to establish a private scheme of responsibilities.

Consent to the Risks of a Relation

When one waives a right or releases her counterpart from liability, she accepts the responsibility not only for the risks inherent in the parties' relationship, but also for all additional risks that may arise because of the other's misconduct. One who consents merely to engage in a particular relation, by contrast, assumes the responsibility only for those dangers that are a normal and natural part of that association. Thus, a thrill-seeker who agrees to ride a roller coaster accepts the fact that she may be jostled about or may become nauseous or ill. These, we all know, are the inevitable incidents of that diversion.[43] She does not, however, assume the risk that the coaster operator will have failed to properly construct, inspect or maintain the ride in a reasonably safe condition.

Here, the only difficulty in defining the consenter's responsibility lies in identifying the hazards which foreseeably may arise from the relationship. In the case of highly structured, formalized relations—like participatory games or activities with specific rules of behavior—this poses no great concern. Regardless of who the actual participants are, the relation always unfolds in roughly the same manner. For other relations which are more casual and spontaneous—say, for example, a social visit from a friend—the risks to be encountered may be far from clear. In such a case, the mere agreement to associate may be insufficient to allocate to the consenter full responsibility for the dangers she later encounters.

Consent to a Specific Consequence

An even more narrow responsibility is conferred upon the decision-maker who consents to bear some specific consequence. Here, the consenter does not accept all dangers naturally flowing from the relation, but only those that expose her to a particular type of harm. It is not uncommon, for example, for an individual to gamble with some of her interests but not with others. Thus, if I lend my car to my neighbor, I might reasonably expect that I will not receive it back in exactly the same condition. It may have greater mileage, it may be dirtier, the tires may be slightly more worn, there may be stains on the upholstery or carpeting or it may even be dented or scratched. I do not anticipate, however, that it will be returned in a condition which will jeopardize my life, at least not without some explanation as to what the problem is and how it got that way. So if my neighbor has punctured a hole in my car's brake line, I may or may not have reason to complain of the physical damage to the vehicle, but I certainly do not agree to relieve her of responsibility for the personal injuries I may sustain when my brakes fail.

Likewise, just because one may consent to a minor physical invasion does not mean that she also accepts the responsibility for injuries of the same general type which are far more egregious. A consequence possesses the dimensions of both quality and severity. Where the impairment of an interest is substantially different in degree than could have been expected, the consequence itself seems to take on a different character. To illustrate, suppose that A challenges B to a fist fight. B possesses the same general physical build as A. However, unbeknownst to A, B is an expert in the martial arts whose hands are registered as lethal weapons. Because of B's extraordinary skills, A's neck is broken during the encounter. As a result, she is rendered a quadriplegic. In the bout with B, A could have expected to sustain certain kinds of physical injuries, like bruises, scratches and perhaps some broken bones. The risk of permanent paralysis, however, does not appear to be one of the dangers which A might have contemplated when she issued the challenge to B. It is doubtful, then, that A, by agreeing to engage in the boxing match, automatically assumed the risk of becoming a quadriplegic. Here, the consequence actually sustained by A so far exceeds her expectations that her original provision of consent fails to excuse or justify that result.

Consent to an Act, Defect or Condition

The scope of one's responsibility for a risk choice is smallest when the decision-maker's consent extends only to a particular act, defect or condition. In this situation, the consenter merely agrees to endure a particular hazard without giving any thought to the consequences of her decision. Only if the hazard and the consequence are identical will she be held accountable for the effects of her choice. For example, if the decision-maker consents to engage in sexual intercourse she cannot later complain that her partner touched various private areas of her body, assuming of course the areas are ones normally touched during intercourse and the manner of touching is not excessive. Often, however, one's consent to an immediate danger does not necessarily manifest her assumption of the risks that may follow from it. In the above example, an ingenue may consent to a sex act knowing of the bodily contact involved, but, because of her naivete, still not assume the responsibility for catching a sexually transmitted disease. Similarly, a social guest may decide to encounter a dangerous condition on the property of her host—say, by turning the cracked porcelain handle of a faucet—without realizing that it may sever the tendons in her wrist if it breaks.[44] And a product consumer who knows of the dangers of a defectively labelled pesticide may nevertheless fail to appreciate the risk of sunbathing in a grassy area where the chemical previously has been applied.[45] In each of these cases, the decision-maker's choice is merely to initiate a transaction, it is not to endure the effects of that encounter. While there may be good cause to make her shoulder some or even all of the resulting loss, this may not be done under the pretense of effectuating her will.

The Effect of Consent

Assuming either or both parties actually do consent to allocate the risks between them in a particular manner, what should be the effect of that purely private decision? Often such arrangements are made amidst a complex web of state-created responsibilities. For example, although the relationship between product sellers and their customers is heavily regulated, it is not uncommon for these parties to devise risk-allocation agreements of their own. In situations such as this, what is the interrelationship between the private responsibilities created by the parties and the public duties which might otherwise be imposed upon them by the state? May the two coexist? Do they clash? Or are they mutually exclusive?

In my opinion, public and private duties merely complement or supplement each other, they rarely compete or conflict. One reason for this is that the state devises public duties to secure and facilitate individual autonomy, including the freedom to choose how to live one's life. This purpose would be undermined, however, if private agreements could be replaced by a different scheme of state-imposed responsibilities. In such a case, the choices exercised by the parties would not be enforced, but would be subordinated to some interest deemed more compelling by the state. Although such paternalism might arise from a benevolent motive, it is nevertheless antithetical to the tenets of a liberal democratic system of governance. If liberty is to be anything more than a vacuous concept, the exercise of personal choice must be given preeminent status as a means of determining one's responsibilities.

Another reason for the consistency between privately and publicly created duties is that private agreements prevent the formation or application of conflicting schemes of relational responsibility. State-based duties generally are promulgated to protect us from harm, which may be defined loosely as the nonconsensual interference with the interests of another. Such duties simply do not apply, however, where the right-holder consents to endure, or to take responsibility for, the intrusion of her neighbor. Here, the consenter freely gives up some of her interests in return for the more desirable interests of her relational partner. In such a scenario, the consenter is not harmed, and so is in no need of protection by the state. In fact, insofar as she acquires what she desires in the exchange, her rights are actually furthered by allowing her to establish the terms of her association. In this context, consent operates much like the concept of risk; both serve to delimit the scope of duties imposed by the state. Where the parties to a relation have devised their own scheme of responsibilities, the state's interests end where the parties' consensual agreement begins. Thus, if our social responsibilities are a patch-quilt of public and private duties, then consent is the invisible seam which both separates the different pieces and binds them into a truly distinctive integrated fabric.

In concluding that a consenter suffers no harm from a mutually agreed-upon exchange, we are of course saying that no primary right of hers has been violated. But even if this were not so—that is, assuming harm could follow from such a consensual transaction—the consenter still would not be entitled to protection under a state-imposed duty of care. Why? Because where an interpersonal association is not coerced, a party unhappy with the effects of that relation simply lacks a secondary right of redress.

Earlier, we saw that secondary rights—i.e., those that empower us to interfere with the interests of others—are not activated unless certain conditions are satisfied. Besides the requirement of harm, one must show that she has been the victim of another's actual or apparent act of wrongdoing, and that this wrongful conduct caused her to suffer the injuries of which she complains. Consent, however, prevents each of these conditions from being realized. First of all, consensual conduct is not wrongful. By agreeing to the transaction, the consenter not only relieves the other of a state-imposed duty of care, she actually imbues that actor with the right to intrude upon her interests in some specified manner. In addition, because consent is the catalyst which sets the relation in motion, one who agrees to interact with another bears complete causal responsibility for precipitating such an encounter. Without the consenter's expressed willingness to interact, presumably no relation would ever be formed. Because the consenter alone is normatively and causally accountable for the invasion of her own interests, she stands outside the protective umbrella of the state's scheme of distributive duties.

Be that as it may, the general principle that private agreements take priority over public duties is not absolute. Indeed, in some situations the state may have an interest in holding the parties to public standards of conduct even though they have attempted to delimit for themselves the extent of their responsibilities. This interest reaches its height when the state itself, or at least the principles it is founded on, are placed in jeopardy by an actor's misconduct. Previously, we saw that the right of autonomy is possible only in a political association. By distributing duties of care to all citizens, the state ensures that every citizen also enjoys certain protected liberties. When the state and its laws are threatened, therefore, so is the guarantee of freedom. To preserve this moral requisite, the state may at times be justified in refusing to enforce certain privately created responsibility schemes. Although this may work a temporary denial of autonomy to the parties involved, it operates to safeguard the long-term freedoms of all citizens.

Under what circumstances may the state exercise this prerogative? In this day and age where people are so interdependent, just about any transaction or relation may have significant social ramifications. An individual who sustains an injury in the workplace, for example, is not the only party who suffers a loss. Her employer's productivity may decline, or the cost of that operation may rise. Valuable medical resources will be expended to treat the injuries. The manpower of local police or federal agencies may be needed to investigate the accident. The victim's family will suffer emotional or psychological damage. As a result, one or more of these individuals may lose time from work, thus affecting their employers. The public impact of this one isolated incident seems never-ending. Yet the state may not regulate all human interaction, regardless of the parties' consent, simply because the outcome of that interaction may have a remote rippling effect on society generally. Indeed, if this were the case, no consensual agreement would ever be enforceable. In order to confer appropriate deference to such privately created responsibility schemes, the state may superimpose its own standards of relational behavior only in situations where the public interest is compelling.

One scenario where the state's interests may supersede those of consenting parties is where the conduct in question is intended to cause harm. The problem with such behavior is that not only is it inherently self-destructive, it is socially disruptive as well. Looking again at the boxing match between A and B, suppose each fighter consents to relieve the other of liability for the injuries she might sustain in the fight. Here, A and B have deliberately devised a scheme to subject each other to the risk of serious bodily injury or death. In the event they carry out this plan in public, they also threaten to create a public disturbance. Even if no breach of the peace results from the fight, A and B undoubtedly will pass the cost of their injuries onto society—either by depleting medical or police resources or by suspending their productivity indefinitely. In light of these effects, the state may seek to discourage such bouts of mutual combat. One way of accomplishing this is to disregard the parties' private arrangement and hold them accountable for the losses each inflicts upon her adversary.[46] Here, the public policies of preserving lives, keeping the peace and protecting social resources may outweigh whatever individual interests the parties may have in seeing their agreement enforced.

The other situation where state interests may predominate is when the risks posed by the privately approved behavior are not contained to a particular relationship, but are spread broadly throughout society. Such risks typically are presented by mass-marketed products. When a manufacturer distributes a product with a defective design, for instance, the risk of injury is not peculiar to any particular consumer; rather, it faces every person who buys, uses or even comes near that commodity. Here, the state may refuse to allow the manufacturer to escape liability by consensually allocating to the consumer all responsibility for product-related injuries. To deter the public distribution of unsafe products, it might elect instead to ignore the parties' private risk allocation and hold the producer to some general duty of care.[47]

Consensual Risk Allocation in Tort Law

In discussing this contest of supremacy between privately and publicly created duties we are, in fact, addressing a more specific controversy: the battle between contract law and tort law. It is not unusual for the parties to a tortious encounter to have allocated by consensual agreement some or all of the risks of their relationship. In some cases, this is done expressly in a written contract; in others, the agreement must be implied from the actions of the parties. Often, tortfeasors assume by private assent greater responsibilities than would be imposed upon them by the state; other times, the risk of harm is consensually assigned to the party who ultimately sustains injury in the encounter. In each case, a court must determine whether the protective duties of tort law may be supplemented by, or must give way to, the contract-based responsibilities created by the parties themselves.[48] As we shall see in the ensuing sections, making this determination can be a most confounding endeavor.

Duties Consensually Assumed
by Tortfeasors

The easiest cases are those in which the tortfeasor consents to assume the risk of personal injury. As indicated above, such consent may be given either expressly or by implication. Express assumptions of responsibility by dominant relational actors are relatively rare, though not unheard of.[49] For instance, to solicit participants in scientific or psychological experiments, it may be necessary for the institution doing the research to guarantee the safety of the subjects involved.[50] More frequently, however, such dominant parties use their superior bargaining position to shift risk responsibilities to those with whom they transact.

Still, many dominant actors wind up assuming greater duties because of either their status or their actions. Merely by entering the medical profession, for instance, doctors assume a general, albeit unwritten, obligation to take reasonable measures to ensure the health of their patients.[51] Likewise, common carriers which exercise complete control over the individuals temporarily in their charge take on the responsibility of protecting them from harm.[52] A similar duty is assumed by lessors of residential properties who impliedly warrant the habitability of their premises.[53] Even product manufacturers who place their wares in the stream of commerce are said to back such goods with an implied warranty of merchantability.[54] Given the ability of such dominant actors to monitor and regulate the risks of their relationships, and the utter vulnerability of those with whom they do business, there usually exists between the parties an understanding that the former will use their powers to safeguard the interests of the latter.

Even where such an understanding is absent going into one of these imbalanced relationships, often expectations of this sort will develop once the parties begin to interact. In many cases, the dominant actor cultivates these expectations by undertaking to safeguard her patrons. We've already seen an example of this above—where a landlord installs a security system for the purpose of protecting both her premises and her tenants. Yet there are innumerable other illustrations. A sheriff's department promises to inform a citizen of a dangerous prisoner's release but fails to do so.[55] A police department assigns an officer to monitor a school crossing but then discontinues the service.[56] Or a prospective employer who requires an applicant to undergo a physical examination neglects to inform him of the results.[57] In each case, the parties, by mutual though implied consent, allocate the responsibility for personal injuries to the party who undertakes to prevent them.

Risks Consensually Assumed by Aggrieved Parties

The other operative role which consent plays in tort law—besides establishing the tortfeasor's duty of care—is to bar or at least reduce the plaintiff's recovery. Tort law accomplishes this risk-allocating objective through two doctrines: the intentional tort privilege of consent and the negligence and strict liability defense of assumption of risk. Although both theories tend to hold plaintiffs accountable for their risk choices, they do so for different reasons based upon different conceptual methodologies. In fact, each doctrine itself is often relentlessly subdivided and its more specific forms separately analyzed using a variety of disparate standards. This has been especially problematic for the defense of assumption of risk, which may be categorized and evaluated as either "primary" or "secondary," "express" or "implied," or "reasonable" or "unreasonable."[58] Yet despite this attempt at microanalysis, little effort has ever been expended to reconcile these divergent approaches. The result of this neglect is a jurisprudence of consent that is both confusing and internally inconsistent.

The Privilege of Consent

The consent privilege traditionally has applied in two different contexts. In one context, commonly referred to as objective consent, the plaintiff appears to consent to someone else's act, but in reality either does not desire the action at all or does not prefer its consequences.[59] In the other scenario, usually described as subjective consent, the consenter actually seeks both the act and its consequences. In each case the plaintiff is barred from recovery, but not for the same reasons.

Where the plaintiff's consent is objective only, she does not actually license her counterpart to intentionally invade her interests. Any such intrusion into the plaintiff's solitude, therefore, may be considered a harm. Yet it is not a harm for which the defendant-actor is responsible. Because the defendant here relies upon the plaintiff's overt expression of consent in deciding to initiate the encounter, the plaintiff alone is causally responsible for whatever loss she incurs in that transaction.[60]

The famous case of *O'Brien v. Cunard S.S. Co.*[61] aptly illustrates this point. The plaintiff there boarded a ship bound for Boston. Because of the outbreak of a small pox epidemic, all emigrants were given the option of receiving a vaccination before arriving in port or being detained upon arrival. Written notices to this effect were posted throughout the ship. Aware of these notices, the plaintiff stood in a long line of individuals who she knew were waiting to be vaccinated. When she came within fifteen feet of the surgeon administering the shots, she witnessed several individuals before her receive their inoculations. When her turn came, she held up her arm without objection. After receiving the vaccination, the plaintiff accepted her vaccination certificate and went on her way. Later, however, she sued the steamship owner for battery, alleging that its agent, the surgeon, had vaccinated her against her will. The trial court directed a verdict for the defendant and the Supreme Court of Massachusetts affirmed. The court reasoned that although she did not verbalize her assent, her conduct unequivocally indicated her desire to be vaccinated. By holding up her arm under the circumstances then prevailing, she, not the defendant, served as the catalyst to the parties' relationship. She alone held the power to determine whether such an encounter would occur. If she had remained in her cabin rather than entering the vaccination line, or if she had exited the line once she saw the notices and observed others before her being vaccinated, or even if she had objected to the procedure when it came her turn to be inoculated, she could have remained immune from the conduct of the surgeon. By failing to take any of these measures, however, the plaintiff behaved in a way that induced the surgeon to proceed with the vaccination. If she was harmed by that procedure, the only reasonable conclusion is that she had brought that harm upon herself.

In cases where the plaintiff's consent to the relation is subjective, her responsibility proceeds from an altogether different premise. Consider the weekend athlete who agrees to participate in a game of tackle football, knowing it to be a sport of often violent contact, but then complains when another player grabs her around the ankles. By agreeing to endure the intrusion of other participants, in this example for the purpose of having fun or receiving some exercise, the consenter extinguishes her counterpart's duty of care.[62] Without such a duty, the other player's conduct is completely justified even though it may cause the consenter some physical injury. Moreover, because the consenter receives what she desires or at least expects, it is difficult to see how her autonomy is impaired. Indeed, insofar as her choice has been realized in the resulting transaction, her interests appear to be enhanced. Under these circumstances, then, we see that the consenter suffers neither wrong nor harm.

The Defense of Assumption of Risk

There is a fundamental difference between the privilege of consent and the defense of assumption of risk. A consenter typically agrees to endure an act which is both intentional and imminent. Usually, the act itself holds some immediate benefit for the consenter. Thus, one who agrees to sexual relations receives the obvious sensory pleasures that follows from such intimacy. Or, one consenting to open heart surgery gains the life-saving benefit that only a trained surgeon can offer. One who assumes a risk, on the other hand, agrees to relieve others of responsibility for unintentional acts or conditions either committed or created in the past or which may occur in the future. Ordinarily, the party assuming the risk derives no direct benefit from it; rather, she gambles that the risk will never materialize in harm. Thus, if I deliberately walk in front of a forklift truck at a wholesale warehouse I might assume the risk of being struck by the vehicle even though I do not desire that consequence and derive no direct benefit from it. In such a situation, I seek some ulterior benefit—like convenience or excitement—which outweighs the small, but known risk of the oncoming forklift.

This basic factual distinction between consent and assumption of risk affects the analysis of choice in each scenario. To exercise true choice, one must have full knowledge of the dangers inherent in an option and must enjoy unrestricted volition in deciding to exercise it. In cases involving the privilege of consent, the consenter's knowledge seldom is at issue. Because the parties interact at the same time and place, the risk of intrusion is certain, obvious and imminent. Here, the consenter knows full well what to expect in the ensuing encounter. In cases of assumed risk, however, the party making the choice inevitably faces greater uncertainty. Frequently, the danger lurks in a preexisting condition which may present a multitude of risks, all with varying degrees of intensity, as where one enters a dark, cluttered room without turning on a light. In other situations, the danger may not yet be in existence, but may develop as part of an ongoing relationship involving thousands of different transactions over several years, as where a construction worker is directed by her employer to use a myriad tools to perform an infinite number of tasks on a wide array of projects. Because of the multiplicity and diffuseness of the risks, and their remoteness in time and place, it is often difficult if not impossible to know whether the alleged risk-assuming party was aware of the danger before it resulted in harm. Even where it is clear that she possessed some general knowledge of the risk of harm, there typically is no telling how much information she actually possessed, including most importantly whether she contemplated the exact consequences which were about to follow. Given the uncertain nature of such interactions—both in their occurrence and their consequences—courts traditionally have applied the doctrine of assumption of risk infrequently and with great skepticism.[63]

Express Assumption of Risk

The concept of express assumption of risk has long been a target of tort law's general reluctance to permit such private allocations of responsibility. As has been discussed above, express forms of consent or assumption of risk ordinarily are contained in contractual agreements. In most cases, such contracts are drafted by product or service suppliers who refuse to transact unless and until the agreements are signed by their customers. Overwhelmingly, these contracts protect the suppliers' interests by requiring their customers to assume the risks of their relationship. Where such clauses are enforced, their effect is absolute. The customer either relieves the supplier of a duty to exercise care, or releases her from any liability which may result from her breach. The trouble is, however, that in many cases such express assumptions of risk are *not* enforced, even though they appear to be clear and unequivocal. Why? Because often there is good reason to seriously doubt the authenticity of the customer's consent. Could she possibly have known the dangers that would await her as the relation progressed into the future? Did she have the opportunity to negotiate over the issue of risk allocation, or was it a necessary precondition to the transaction? Was the good to be obtained so fundamental to human flourishing that she had no real choice but to enter the relation and hope that she came out unscathed? Overcome by these and other concerns, many courts, we shall see, frequently ignore such contractual provisions and continue in effect the state's scheme of distributive tort responsibilities.

Where a party enters a written contract agreeing to assume the risks of a proffered activity or to release from liability their creator, the lexicon of assumption of risk very often is ignored. Instead, courts routinely employ a standard contract analysis to determine its enforceability. This includes consideration of the contract's intrinsic fairness, and thus its social acceptability, and its legitimacy as an expression of the "intent of the parties."

Such an analysis invariably proceeds in two steps. The first requires the court to determine as a matter of law whether the assumption of risk or waiver provision is enforceable.[64] To be enforceable, a contract must not offend public policy. The general rule is that exculpatory agreements are valid and binding.[65] However, over the years, this rule has been severely eroded under the weight of a multitude of exceptions.

Many of these exceptions are contained in section 195 of the Restatement (Second) of Contracts.[66] Under section 195, terms exempting a party from liability for intentional or reckless acts are violative of public policy. Many waivers of negligence liability are also deemed unenforceable. These include exculpatory agreements entered into between employers and employees, those protecting purveyors of public services, those between members of a protected class and parties who have a duty to provide such protection, and those exempting product manufacturers from harm caused to their consumers "unless the term is fairly bargained for and is consistent with the policy underlying that liability."[67]

Many courts have expansively interpreted or added to the items on this list, or have created a list of their own. In this latter camp is the California Supreme Court. In *Tunkl v. Regents of the University of California*,[68] the court indicated that an

> attempted but invalid exemption involves a transaction which exhibits some or all of the following characteristics. It concerns a business of a type generally thought suitable for public regulation. The party seeking exculpation is engaged in performing a service of great importance to the public, which is often a matter of practical necessity for some members of the public. The party holds himself out as willing to perform this ser-

vice for any member of the public who seeks it, or at least for any member coming within certain established standards. As a result of the essential nature of the service in the economic setting of the transaction, the party invoking exculpation possesses a decisive advantage of bargaining strength against any member of the public who seeks his services. In exercising a superior bargaining power the party confronts the public with a standardized adhesion contract of exculpation, and makes no provision whereby a purchaser may pay additional reasonable fees and obtain protection against negligence. Finally, as a result of the transaction, the person or property of the purchaser is placed under the control of the seller, subject to the risk of carelessness by the seller or his agents.[69]

Whatever the exact formulation, these exceptions have been liberally employed in striking down exculpatory agreements. And these exceptions have affected a wide variety of prospective risk shifters. Besides employers and product manufacturers mentioned in section 195, the parties denied exculpation on public policy grounds include public utilities,[70] common carriers,[71] innkeepers,[72] public warehousemen,[73] professional bailees, including garagemen,[74] parking lot owners[75] and parcel checkrooms,[76] banks for safety deposit boxes,[77] public housing authorities,[78] telephone companies for yellow page advertising,[79] parents on behalf of their children,[80] school districts for student injuries in organized athletic competitions[81] and charitable hospitals.[82] And this litany is far from comprehensive.

If the exculpatory provision does not violate public policy, the second step of the analysis requires careful scrutiny of the agreement to determine whether it expresses the intention of the parties. Specifically, the court must decide whether the plaintiff was aware that by signing the contract she assumed the risks associated with the activity or waived the right to sue if they resulted in injury.[83] Traditional interpretational maxims of contract law are invoked for this purpose. Under these rules of interpretation, an exculpatory term, to be enforceable, generally must be clear, specific and understandable to a lay person.[84] Courts will construe such agreements strictly against the party seeking exculpation, and will disfavor any such agreement which is too broad or general.

Despite its apparent simplicity, this analytic scheme for express assumption of risk suffers from some very serious theoretical deficiencies. First off, the general bar of the doctrine under this scheme is illusory. Given the incredible number of exceptions which riddle the "rule" of enforceability, it is disingenuous to suggest that the mere reduction of consent to a contractual formality suffices to preclude the promisee's claim.

In addition, by retaining enforceability as the rule, courts have had no need to reexamine its underlying basis. The existence of the rule presumes strength in its normative content. When exceptions are added, the norm is not questioned; rather, the exceptions are explained in a way that satisfies the norm. This is precisely what was done in *Tunkl*. After reaffirming the autonomy and responsibility norms inherent in private, voluntary transactions, the court observed that in the exceptional situations it described, "the releasing party does not really acquiesce voluntarily in the contractual shifting of the risk, nor can we be reasonably certain that he receives an adequate consideration for the transfer."[85]

This type of tunnel vision produces further rippling effects. By concentrating on reconciling the exceptions with the rule, it ossifies the contractual basis for the doctrine. More than this, it prevents courts from searching for other, perhaps more important, norms which may underlie the various exceptions. *Tunkl* is illustrative of this tendency as well. Although the court described the general characteristics of each exception, and tied these loosely to the contract norm of consent, it failed to look for other common normative threads linking them all together. In this way, it failed to provide an adequate test for future cases which may warrant judicial intervention but do not fall neatly within the taxonomy established by the court. Indeed, a closer look would have disclosed how significant relational principles are to this analysis.

Finally, compounding all its other ills, this scheme is inconsistent with the analysis employed for implied assumption of risk. As we will see below, the terminology alone is simply different. But even more importantly, the theoretical perspectives they assume are diametrically opposed. Whereas express assumption of risk is premised on contract principles, the implied version of the doctrine, at least in one of its formulations, bears the distinctively different markings of tort theory. Thus, by failing to formally acknowledge any normative criteria outside the ambit of contract, this strictly unilateral analysis impedes the discovery and development of a uniform approach to private risk allocation questions generally.

Implied Assumption of Risk

If the treatment of express assumption of risk clauses has been harsh, at least it has been internally consistent. In the few cases where consent is true, and the doctrine is applied, the beneficiary of the agreement owes no duty of care, and the party subject to it bears complete responsibility for the injurious consequences of the relationship. Although the treatment of the doctrine of implied assumption of risk has been no less severe, the interpretations of its impact upon the distribution of risk have been far from uniform.

The obvious problem with implied assumption of risk is that, not only is the extent of the alleged consenter's knowledge and choice unclear, as it is for express assumption of risk, the alleged assent is never verbally articulated by either party to the relation. This is troublesome for two reasons.

First, it raises greater doubt as to whether the party to be bound by the agreement ever actually desired or expected to assume full responsibility for the transaction. Such an expression of willingness is not communicated in unambiguous language, but must be gleaned, if at all, from the subtle gestures made by the parties and the context of their association. Second, assuming some understanding was reached between the parties, one would require the talents of a psychic to ascertain its nebulous contours and limits. Indeed, depending upon the frequency of their prior associations and the strength and pervasiveness of the community custom in existence at the time, the parties themselves may have had only a vague and unstable conception of their respective rights and responsibilities throughout the course of their relationship.

Primary Implied Assumption of Risk

Not all instances of implied assumption of risk suffer from these infirmities. In cases of *primary* implied assumption of risk, for example, much of the ambiguity in the underlying agreement is removed. Under this doctrine, the party assuming the risk consents to accept the dangers inherent in a particular relationship, thereby extinguishing her counterpart's duty of care.[86] Consider again the sport of football. Almost everyone even remotely familiar with this athletic endeavor knows that it is both violent and dangerous. It requires that the participants physically contact each other in order to block and tackle. Given the force with which bodies traveling at full speed may collide, serious injuries like broken bones, cuts and abrasions are a foreseeable part of the game. Indeed, these are its primary risks. One might expect, therefore, that absent some attempt at private risk-allocation, the participants in this high-risk activity would owe each other a duty of care. Those who engage in a game of football, however, typically do not expect this protection. Rather, to ensure that the game is both exciting and competitive, each player impliedly agrees not only to accept any contact permitted by the rules, but also to endure whatever injuries may follow from it. In this way, these gladiators of the gridiron relieve each other of the duty to refrain from such potentially hazardous behavior, or to provide compensation if injury actually occurs.[87]

Secondary Implied Assumption of Risk

Cases of secondary implied assumption of risk are far more complicated. Here, the risk which causes the plaintiff's injury is "secondary" in the sense that it is neither a necessary nor an expected consequence of the relationship in question. Instead, it arises only because of the defendant's carelessness or some unlikely sequence of events. Because the risk will not appear in every such relationship, its realization in harm is usually not as foreseeable to the plaintiff. Accordingly, the plaintiff does not consent to the harm merely by entering the relation. If she is to be allocated responsibility for the loss, there must be evidence that she agreed to accept the specific, secondary risk which spontaneously developed during the parties' association.

The need for such a heightened evidentiary showing is compounded further by the defendant's conduct in cases of this sort. This becomes apparent after comparing activities creating primary risks with those producing secondary risks. Where the risk is primary, there is little basis for condemning the risk-creator's actions. One reason for this is the reciprocal nature of the relation in which the activity takes place. In our previous example of a football game, the rules permit each player to block, tackle or otherwise impact another. Thus, all participants impose and bear the same risks of injury.[88] Secondly, even where one party imposes greater risks upon the others—say, by more recklessly hurtling her body towards those of her opponents—her conduct does not necessarily appear more culpable. In fact, such exuberance often is the hallmark of the best players. Finally, the harm produced by such excessive behavior is no different in kind than when the player's conduct is considered more reasonable. In each case, the risk of physical injury is obvious. If this more aggressive play has any effect at all upon the risk quotient, it merely increases the probability that an accident will occur, and perhaps slightly exaggerates the injuries which might follow from it.

Now consider conduct which exposes another to a secondary risk. Suppose the operator of a ski resort leaves a large, mechanical snow plow in the middle of a downhill run. Cruising down the slope, a skier sees the plow in her path a few seconds before she will come upon it. Instead of stopping or steering a different course, she elects to maneuver around the plow. Unfortunately, she fails to negotiate the turn and crashes into this immovable mogul. Here, the risk of injury by collision is secondary to the commercial relationship existing between the skier and the ski slope operator. While one might expect to find trees and other skiers on the slopes, she would not ordinarily expect to find a large piece of mechanical equipment. Avoiding snow plows simply is not one of the risks which makes skiing a dangerous activity. The irregularity of this risk is important for several reasons. First, the spontaneous nature of the risk virtually ensures that the skier will not be capable of making an accurate evaluation of the danger posed. Not only will she have no prior experience with a random risk of this sort, she also will enjoy precious little time to decide whether or how to encounter it. Second, unlike the danger of running into other skiers, the risk of crashing into a misplaced plow is not reciprocal, but is imposed upon the skier unilaterally by the slope operator. Third, in contrast to the primary risks of skiing—i.e., allowing many people to slide down a steep, snow-covered hill at high rates of speed—neither the skier nor the operator is likely to receive any actual benefit from leaving the plow in the middle of a run. Finally, the risk of colliding with a snow plow, which necessarily includes the possibility of death or serious bodily injury, presents a magnitude of harm far exceeding the expectation of the average skier.

The Effect of Assumption of Risk: Current Approaches

Because of such concerns, not only are implied assumptions of risk seldom recognized, but even when they are, courts often have no idea how this defense should affect the plaintiff's claim for relief. Should she bear sole responsibility for her own injury, or should this burden be shared as well by her relational counterpart? Although there have been numerous answers to this question, few are clear, all are substantially different, either in their use of terminology or their mandate, and none is particularly satisfactory.

A Doctrinal Identity Crisis

The defense of assumption of risk was founded on the rationale that the plaintiff's choice eliminates her right to take corrective action against her alleged wrongdoer. As a consequence, the defense traditionally has served as an absolute bar to recovery. About fifty years ago, however, courts and academics began to question whether the defense's preclusive effect was too extreme. Indeed, by the middle of this century, some jurisdictions had recognized the principle of comparative fault as a means of allocating loss among parties to tort litigation.[90] Under this scheme, the plaintiff is not completely denied relief; instead, her recovery is diminished in proportion to her own fault. At first glance, this principle seems to have nothing to do with assumption of risk. After all, consent, not fault, traditionally has provided the conceptual basis for that defense. Nevertheless, assumption of risk has never been completely free of fault-based concerns. Indeed, many courts have long maintained that the decision to encounter danger may be reasonable or unreasonable.[91] Where it is unreasonable, they concluded, the plaintiff is negligent and her claim falls within the purview of comparative fault. In such situations, a sticky dilemma arises: to apply the preclusive bar of assumption of risk or to adopt the mitigating principle of comparative fault. Responding to this conundrum, many courts were moved to reconsider the entire concept of assumption of risk.

The Elimination of Assumption of Risk Approach

The most drastic approach has been to eliminate entirely the defense of implied assumption of risk.[92] Under this view, all cases of private risk choice are handled under the relevant comparative fault system. Thus, even where the plaintiff knowingly and voluntarily elects to encounter a relation-based danger, she is not necessarily barred from recovery; rather, her recovery is reduced in proportion to either her fault or her causal responsibility.[93] This approach appears to have been motivated by two concerns. One is that the determination of implied consent is so difficult and time-consuming that it is not worth the effort. The other fear is that the policies underlying the principle of comparative fault—i.e., that each party's responsibility should be correlative with her culpability—cannot truly be achieved if the defense of assumption of risk remains intact. Indeed, under assumption of risk, even the most reckless conduct might go unpunished if the plaintiff appears willing to accept its dangerous consequences.

While this rather draconian treatment of implied assumption of risk is both simple and clear, it suffers from several serious infirmities. The most obvious problem is its failure to acknowledge the moral weight of one's exercise of consent. When a risk-taker voluntarily engages in a relation with known dangers, her counterpart owes no duty to refrain from affording her that choice. Absent such a duty, the risk-creator's conduct in offering the dangerous association, though perhaps undesirable in a general sense, is not wrongful *as against the party assuming the risk*. Here, the consenter desires to consummate the relationship, and in return for the privilege of doing so, accepts full responsibility for the consequences of her decision. In this situation, the allocation of risk is not partial, as it often is under comparative fault systems, but total.

Second, the total elimination approach fails to recognize any distinction between primary and secondary assumption of risk cases. Yet important analytical differences do exist. Because primary risks are intrinsic to the relevant relation, the risks of the parties' association are often much clearer than secondary risks which arise spontaneously and unexpectedly. As a result, true consent appears to be more viable, and easier to assess, in cases involving primary risk allocations. In addition, because secondary risks are not an inherent part of the relation, but are ancillary to it, they are or at least should be easier to prevent or avoid. Thus, when an actor fails to take necessary precautions to avert or ameliorate such risks, her conduct may appear more morally (though not necessarily legally) culpable than one who engages in an innately dangerous activity.

Finally, assuming the consenter has made an informed choice in electing to expose herself to the danger, it is difficult to see either how that decision may be called negligent or, alternatively, how its causal influence over the injurious outcome can be anything less than complete. In all cases, the risk-taker weighs the costs and benefits of a relation before choosing to proceed. If she believes that the benefits of the relation outweigh the known risks, she maximizes her happiness by initiating the association. Even if others might not agree with her choice, they have little basis for second-guessing the reasonableness of her motives. While external risks can be evaluated against a community norm of acceptability, there simply is no social standard for purely self-directed risk-taking. For some people, chancy endeavors are the most exciting and lucrative; for the more cautious among us, even slightly risky enterprises may seem foolish and intolerable. Without an adequate yardstick for judging the consentor's risk choice, it is simply impossible to call her behavior faulty or fault-free.

The Duty-Comparative Fault Approach

Other jurisdictions have been equally unkind to the doctrine of assumption of risk, although in a slightly different way. They too eliminate assumption of risk as a defense to a tort claim. But instead of vanquishing the concept in one fell swoop, they first dismember it, shunting its parts off into the bins of duty and comparative fault.[94] California's approach is typical of those in this category. Under the California approach, if the risk which the plaintiff chooses to encounter is primary—in other words, it is inherent in the relation itself—then the defendant simply owes her no duty of care.[95] On the other hand, if the plaintiff voluntarily exposes herself to a secondary risk—i.e., one not naturally arising from the relation—then the defendant's state-imposed duty of care remains intact.[96] That the plaintiff may proceed to assume this secondary risk does not affect this duty. It merely means that the plaintiff herself may have acted in a fashion which will cause her to bear some of the responsibility for her injuries. Accordingly, the doctrine of comparative fault is applied to determine the extent of her responsibility.[97] In such a case, the fact-finder is permitted to compare the defendant's breach of her duty of care with the plaintiff's reasonable or unreasonable decision to subject herself to the danger. Where both parties share part of the blame for the injurious encounter, the financial responsibility for the resulting loss may then be allocated between them in accordance with their culpability.

This approach, while not perfect, is certainly preferable to the one which categorically extinguishes all forms of implied assumption of risk. In it, appropriate recognition is given to the moral effect of one's risk choice. It does not just reduce the culpability of the risk-creator, it completely eliminates her duty of care. It also accords due deference to the power of consent and the autonomy concerns which underlie it. When one exercises her will by choosing to enter a beneficial, though perhaps risky relation, she accepts full responsibility for the consequences of her decision. To give only partial effect to that choice would be to deny the freedom of the consenter and, even worse, to erode the sanctity of that fundamental right.

Still, there is at least one very troubling aspect to the duty-comparative fault approach. Although it recognizes the preclusive effect of primary assumption of risk, it fails to extend the same treatment to the assumption of a secondary risk. In California, for example, a defendant who creates a secondary risk continues to owe a duty of care even when the plaintiff voluntarily exposes herself to that danger.[98] If the defendant breaches that duty, her conduct may be found negligent in spite of the plaintiff's choice. In such a case, the principles of comparative fault are said to apply. The plaintiff is not barred from recovery altogether; rather, her conduct is compared to that of her counterpart and her damages are reduced in proportion to her own fault.

To say that this result is morally misguided would be generous indeed. The critical mistake of this approach is its failure to recognize the relational nature of one's state-imposed duties. Although the creation of an avoidable secondary risk may be socially undesirable, it is not a wrong to any particular individual unless it, first, is imposed upon her against her will, and second, causes her harm. One who consents to encounter a risk, however, may not claim to be the beneficiary of such a duty. This is true whether the risk is inherent in the relationship itself or is offered unexpectedly as the relation runs its course. Once the risk-taker recognizes the danger and proceeds to exercise her choice, any social responsibility which might have protected her simply evaporates.[99]

By disregarding this moral truth, the duty-comparative fault approach promises to vitiate the principle of autonomous choice. If one party to a relation creates a condition that the other finds desirable, at least insofar as she would rather encounter it than not, then the autonomy of each is furthered if the parties are permitted to act without either ex ante or ex post interference. In such a scenario, the risk-creator is afforded the benefit of unrestricted activity, and the risk-taker is afforded the right of unencumbered choice. As in all other cases of consent, the risk-taker here is the sole determinant of her fate. By choosing to encounter a secondary risk which she has the option of avoiding, she assumes full causal responsibility for the consequences of her action. Moreover, to the extent that she makes an informed determination that the benefits to be derived from her decision exceed the possible risks, her interests are advanced by acting on this choice even if doing so may result in injury.

If this sounds implausible at first, consider further the benefits of taking risks. Risk often is the only avenue to financial or personal advancement. Indeed, the biggest risk seekers often are the biggest winners in the stock market or in the world of business. For the rest of us, taking risks may be the only way of putting some excitement in our otherwise ordinary and perhaps rather dull lives. Or, it may help us develop discipline, strength, courage, skill and stamina, which in turn allow us to become more virtuous individuals. Such is the case, for instance, with almost any dangerous sport. Just because risk may sometimes get the better of us does not mean that relations that present us with danger are necessarily bad. On balance, they are not.

Beyond all this, it is difficult to see how the duty of a risk-creator can remain unaffected by another's decision to avail herself of such a dangerous condition. The state creates general duties to protect our most significant autonomy interests. In the case of property owners, for example, an invitor owes a duty to exercise reasonable care to keep her premises safe for her patrons. Where, however, an invitee is already aware of a danger on the premises, but nevertheless makes a voluntary choice to encounter it, her conduct repudiates the need for protection. It is as if she has said to the invitor, "Although I know you generally must refrain from exposing me to dangerous conditions, on this occasion I do not want you to deprive me of the opportunity of facing this hazard, for this is a condition which I freely choose to encounter." While she may feel differently afterwards, at the time she sallies forth into the danger zone, she surely neither expects nor relies upon the assistance of the invitor to safeguard her from the risk of harm.

If there are any reasons for maintaining the invitor's duty of care in this situation, they must concern public matters extrinsic to the private justice of the parties' relationship. For example, had the invitor deliberately constructed the hazard in hopes of injuring anyone coming onto her property, the state might be justified in punishing and deterring her conduct by holding her liable for the loss she ultimately causes. Or, if the *social* ramifications of the activity appear significant—perhaps entailing future incidents which produce unpaid medical expenses and lost productivity—it may be necessary to enforce the invitor's public responsibility of eliminating the danger created by it. To determine if such concerns exist, a case-by-case examination of the parties' conduct and its consequences would have to be undertaken. This, however, is not overtly countenanced by the duty-comparative fault approach, which, at least in regard to secondary implied assumption of risk, categorically preserves and enforces the duty of any risk-creator. Under this approach, an actor may be held liable even if her conduct does not pose any such public risk, and even though the private risk she creates is gratefully accepted by the only party it encompasses.

The Reasonable-Unreasonable Choice Approach

There is yet another strategy for handling cases of implied assumption of risk. While this approach appears to be more discriminating than the one preceding, it suffers from an analytic deficiency of its own. Under this view, the plaintiff is barred from recovery if her decision to assume a risk is considered reasonable. If, however, her choice is deemed unreasonable, her recovery is not precluded, but mitigated in proportion to her own fault.[100] The idea here is that unreasonable conduct is a form of contributory negligence and so falls within the purview of an applicable comparative fault system. For such behavior, the defense of assumption of risk merges into the concept of comparative fault. No such merger occurs where the plaintiff makes a reasonable election to encounter danger. Because this decision is free of culpability, it escapes the reach of such a system entirely. Here, assumption of risk remains an independent, absolute defense.

Application of this approach yields what appears to be a rather anomalous result. The foolhardy plaintiff who negligently places herself in harm's way may still be entitled to some relief, even if her recovery is subject to reduction because of her fault. The prudent plaintiff, on the other hand, is extended no such leniency. Despite exercising due care in opting to expose herself to the risk of harm, this plaintiff is denied any compensation whatsoever.

Appearances aside, this result may actually make good sense. The fact is that "unreasonable" assumption of risk may be an indirect way of describing behavior which is not truly consensual.[101] Although implied forms of assumption of risk are supposed to be founded upon the plaintiff's subjective will, in many cases the plaintiff denies any knowledge of the danger. In order to assess her credibility, it is then necessary for the fact-finder to ask whether a reasonable person in the same circumstances would have recognized and appreciated the risk, and if so, whether this risk was sufficiently outweighed by the benefits of proceeding further. Here, a finding that the plaintiff unreasonably assumed the risk suggests by implication that, given the limited benefits of encountering the danger, no reasonable person would have made the same decision. If one accepts the premise that informed, autonomous individuals ordinarily act in their own best interest—that is, that they will accept a risk only if they believe that they will receive some greater benefit in return—there is reason to suspect either that the plaintiff lacked full knowledge of the danger or that her decision to subject herself to it was not freely made. One way or the other, the plaintiff cannot be said to have consented to relieve the defendant of her duty of care. As the above approach acknowledges, each party should then share at least some of the responsibility for the ill-considered transaction. Where, however, the plaintiff's choice is reasonable—such that a prudent person might have seen the benefit in the encounter and elected to pursue it—there is no occasion to second-guess her knowledge or volition. Having made an informed decision, she now must live with the consequences.

Final Thoughts on Consensual Risk Allocation

Despite their differences, all of these approaches—indeed all of the consent-based doctrines we have examined so far—share a common deficiency: they fail to undertake a thorough investigation of the circumstances surrounding the exercise of a party's consent. Earlier in this chapter, we saw that many factors serve to influence how we perceive and react to different kinds of risk. The characteristics of the consenter, the environment in which the choice is made, the availability of risk information and the nature of the risk itself all affect our awareness of relational dangers. We also examined several factors which can impair the voluntariness of one's decision-making. These range from the disabling effects of internal incapacities like youth or mental infirmity to external pressures like necessity and relational imbalance. Even where consent is authentic, we saw that the state at times may be justified in disregarding the parties' private allocation of risk and imposing its own scheme of relational responsibilities. None of the current approaches to private risk allocation, however, employ an organized or comprehensive strategy for addressing these important considerations. Until they do, the jurisprudence in this area will continue to be fraught with inconsistency, confusion and unfairness.

Beyond these pragmatic concerns, there is one final, critical feature to these cases which courts routinely overlook. It is that whenever consensual risk allocation is an issue in a tort case, corrective and distributive justice cease to be the only moral constraints on the resolution of the dispute. In cases such as these, the determination of liability must also comport with the demands of reciprocity or justice in exchange. Typically, one party accepts certain risks in a transaction in return for some greater gain. Where the risks and gains accruing to one party seem grossly out of kilter with those of her counterpart, the relation may be described as unfair. In most cases, this unfairness is the result of the incapacity of the "cheated" party. Pressured by necessity, or unaware of the folly of her choice, her expression of consent fails to accurately represent her subjective will. Here, the concept of reciprocity often favors ignoring the consenter's assent and holding the risk-creator to a state-imposed duty of care. This may not be justified in all cases, however. As we shall see below, where the consenter's choice induces another to forego more important opportunities, there may be good reason to hold her responsible for the risks contained within the parties' relationship.

Relations and Reliance

Besides placing individuals in a posture conducive to consensual risk allocation, relations virtually guarantee that the interacting parties will rely upon each other in one way or another. Such reliance may derive either from the relative status of the parties themselves or from certain words or actions they may exchange during their association. In each case, the parties develop expectations which may affect their behavior and, in so doing, determine the nature and course of their relationship. Often these expectations concern the question of risk allocation. For example, one individual might objectively communicate her intention of assuming the responsibility for a risk arising in the relation; her relational partner, in response to this manifestation, may then give up certain opportunities to protect herself from this risk. Here, the relying party may expect that her counterpart will provide the security she has forsaken. Where this occurs, justice might require that the apparent risk-taker be held to her expressed consent, even though she may have neither fully appreciated the risks of the relation nor actually desired to assume responsibility for them. In such a case, the reliance she induces may be so damaging that, in spite of her unwillingness, it is fairer that she bear the responsibility for the forbearance of her counterpart.

The Effect of Reliance

How should the existence of such reliance affect the determination of justice when a cooperative relationship goes bad? There is no doubt that reliance in itself is a type of harm. One who relies passes up certain opportunities for action. Each opportunity, in turn, represents a choice that could have been exercised by the relying party but for her faith in the words or deeds of another. When one is denied such a choice, she effectively loses some of her liberty. This loss can be as great as forgoing immediate assistance in an emergency or as remote and ephemeral as delaying an uncertain business venture. But so long as the interests affected are significant, the concept of reliance, with its obvious autonomy implications, is worthy of moral consideration.

The extent to which this kind of harm tips the scales of justice in favor of one party or the other cannot be predetermined, but invariably will depend upon the circumstances in existence during the parties' relationship. Where the relationship is imbalanced, the more vulnerable party typically relies upon her more knowledgeable counterpart for protection. Here, the vulnerable party's reliance serves to heighten the other's state-imposed duty of care. On the other hand, if the vulnerable party appears to accept the risk of the exchange, and her counterpart forgoes protective measures because of this representation, the former frequently will be made to bear the responsibility for the resulting loss. In such a case, the injured party, by inducing the other's reliance, not only circumscribes her counterpart's freedom of action, she also helps to influence if not control her own unfortunate destiny.

Heightened State-Imposed Duties

Earlier, we saw that all actions can be described as either misfeasant—affirmatively creating a risk of harm—or nonfeasant—failing to alleviate a preexisting dangerous condition—and that the rules of responsibility for each differ dramatically. Where one engages in an affirmative act, the general rule is that the actor owes a duty to use reasonable care to avoid imposing foreseeable risks upon others.[102] One normally owes no duty, however, to act on behalf of another.[103] Thus, where an individual fails to eradicate a dangerous condition not of her own making, she usually is immune from liability to anyone who falls victim to it.

Both of these rules change, at least to some extent, when applied to imbalanced relational encounters. Take the duty-imposing rule of misfeasance. This duty typically is far different for those engaged in relationships than it is for those acting unilaterally. Indeed, where one party to a relationship possesses superior knowledge of the risks of an encounter, and a superior capacity to control or eliminate them, she ordinarily is allocated a heightened duty of care. This is especially true of those that provide public services, like common carriers or utilities, which must refrain from exposing their customers to insulting or abusive behavior[104] and must take extra precaution to protect them from harm.[105] Unlike other risk-creators, these parties do not produce and dispense danger in some chaotic fashion; rather, they do so more deliberately as part of expert enterprises. Through research and experience, these enterprises come to know the hazards of their activity much better than mere random actors. With this knowledge, these purveyors of goods and services invite others to enter the environment of risk which they create. Those who accept this invitation, however, normally lack the sophistication to assess the dangers which will confront them. Because of this, these patrons often depend upon their more knowledgeable counterparts to ensure their safety throughout the course of their relationship. Given this reliance, it is fair that these "dominant" parties bear greater responsibility for their affirmative actions.

For similar reasons, those enjoying a superior relational position may be held liable for failing to take certain actions on behalf of their customers. As you will recall, the duty to act only arises where there exists between the parties a "special relationship." Special relationships are created in two ways: either through an imbalance in the parties' respective abilities to control the risks of their encounter (as described above), or through an undertaking by one which places the other in a worse position.[106] For both scenarios, the control-reliance dependency inherent in the parties' relationship justifies imposing a more onerous duty of care upon the dominant partner. This explains why a department store is obligated to come to the aid of a patron caught in an escalator located on its premises when those merely shopping in the store are not.[107] Or why an employer may be required to provide medical assistance to an employee injured at its workplace even though her coworkers may not be under the same obligation.[108] In each case, the vulnerable party expects protection from her dominant counterpart and relies upon her to provide it. Thus, whether the dominant party acts or fails to act, her social responsibility will be far greater than others engaged in nonrelational endeavors.

Reliance Induced by Objective Consent

One should not get the impression that reliance is just a one way street to be traveled only by the meek and vulnerable. On the contrary, even in imbalanced relationships like those described above, both parties may rely on the objective expressions or implied representations of the other. While the weaker party's reliance often derives from the nature of the relation itself, usually the dominant party is induced to forego protective measures because of her counterpart's objective manifestation of consent to assume the risk of the encounter. Such a representation may be made formally, as by signing a contractual waiver or release, or informally, as by engaging in certain types of expressive behavior.[109] Where each party relies on the express or implied communications of the other, the dispenser of justice must determine which party is to shoulder the responsibility for the other's forbearance, or whether the burden should be borne between them. While a few of these cases are easy to resolve, in most a detailed comparative analysis is necessary to determine the respective interests of the parties and the extent to which each party's rights have been impaired by the conduct of her counterpart.

Immediate Reliance

The easiest cases are those in which the vulnerable party appears to consent to an imminent act, and the party who receives this message immediately proceeds to deliver it. We already have seen an example of this scenario in the case of *O'Brien v. Cunard S.S. Co.*[110] There, it will be recalled, a woman who stood in a vaccination line and witnessed numerous others before receive their inoculations, held up her arm to the surgeon administering the injections. After she too was vaccinated, she brought an action for battery against the steamship line employing the surgeon. Although in most cases patients rely on medical practitioners to protect their interest in bodily integrity, in this case the plaintiff's reliance interest was not tangible enough to sustain her claim for relief. Instead it was the surgeon's reliance which carried the day. Because the surgeon interpreting the plaintiff's behavior could reasonably believe that she consented to the injection, he was privileged to proceed with the vaccination.

In cases like this, where the offending conduct is committed immediately in response to the objective manifestations of the aggrieved party, the reliance of the actor is complete. Looking for signs of assent, the actor initiates the encounter only after being convinced that she possesses a special license to do so. Were this reliance interest not given priority, even the most common and innocuous exchange transactions would not be possible. A valet who drives off with a restaurant patron's vehicle might be accused of trespass to chattels or conversion. The same liability might extend to a bellhop who carries the bags of a hotel guest. Even handshakes and hugs might be legally dangerous. To prevent such absurd results, one must be held accountable for the objective appearance of her actions, at least insofar as others will rely upon them to take some immediate action of their own.

Reliance and Future Relations

The determination of justice is far more difficult where the vulnerable party's consent is given at the beginning of a long-term relationship which will expose her to risks well into the future. Here, the "consenting" party may have little idea of the dangers she will face as the relationship progresses. Moreover, the party relying on this expressed willingness may have plenty of time and a myriad opportunities to test the apparent consenter's resolve to assume the risk of injury. Under these circumstances, it is not enough to conduct the traditional duty analysis of tort law, for the objective consent of one party may substantially influence the responsibility of the other. Nor is a standard contract approach sufficient; indeed, even where one party appears to contract for the risk of harm, the heightened duty of protection owed by her dominant counterpart may vitiate that commitment.[111] In such cases, rather, it is necessary to undertake a more searching investigation of the parties' entire relationship and the mutual expectations engendered by it. Did the objective expression of consent influence the manner of the other's act, or induce the action entirely? If so, what autonomy interest was given up or exchanged by the incapacitated party?

One cannot answer these questions without giving serious consideration to the concept of reciprocity.[112] Where the exchanged values are unequal, reciprocity may demand that the apparent consent of the vulnerable party be avoided, and, in accordance with distributive justice, that the state's restriction of the dominant actor's conduct be enforced. Life, for example, may be interest so important for autonomy that it is inherently incommensurable (i.e., it may be an inalienable right). Otherwise, if the parties' reliance interests are roughly equivalent, or if the dominant actor's forbearance is more burdensome, the vulnerable party's objective consent may be effective in relieving her injurer of this responsibility.

Case Illustrations of Relational Analysis

A few illustrations will demonstrate how this comparative relational analysis should work. In *Dobratz v. Thomson*,[113] a water skier was fatally injured while performing a stunt routine during a waterskiing show sponsored by Webfooter Water Shows Inc., an nonprofit water ski club. Prior to joining the club, the decedent executed a lengthy release relieving the club and its members of liability from any injury sustained during a club "event." Employing traditional rules of contract interpretation, the Wisconsin Supreme Court held the release unenforceable as a matter of law because of its ambiguity.

The court found the release deficient in several respects. First, it observed that the release failed to specify that the activity of skiing was specifically within its scope. Moreover, the contract did not indicate the types of skiing stunts that would be required, or the level of dangerousness they posed. Nor did it define which of the many club "events" were covered. Finally, because the release purported to extend to injuries occurring upon "the premises," the court found that one could construe the waiver as limited to accidents occurring on dry land.

From an objective point of view, this interpretation of the written contract seems highly questionable. Need a recreational club, whose name is identified by a particular sport, define for prospective club members, who have chosen to participate in that activity, the nature of the sport itself? Is it really feasible for the risk-creator to explain the variety of ways the sport may be performed, and the variety of risks attending each permutation? Can the club possibly identify all possible venues in which risk may be created or the temporal vagaries of its realization? If such prevision were required, every ex ante assumption of risk would be rendered ineffective.

The court's analysis is far more defensible when the entire relationship of the parties is examined. Several aspects of the relationship were emphasized by the court, although only as background information or as a means of interpreting the release. For example, the court indicated that the decedent had no prior association with Webfooter before joining the club in January, February or April of 1985 (the record is unclear on this point). In fact, the decedent, who the court observed was a "beginner," had never before belonged to a water ski club. Although the club was aware of this fact, it is not clear that the club took any special precautions to explain its activities. Indeed, at the time the agreement was formed, the club had neither determined its show schedule nor finalized the routines to be performed. Following the execution of the release, the decedent participated in an unknown number of practice sessions. Webfooter's show tour, which included two performances per week, commenced in June of that year. The accident causing the decedent's death occurred just a month later.

From this description, we can tell a great deal about the duration, nature and extent of the parties' relationship. The actual relation between Webfooter and the decedent was relatively short—seven months at best, and perhaps no more than three. Indeed, the decedent was a newcomer not only to the sport, but to this general "category" of relationship. It follows that he would be less likely than an experienced skier to appreciate the dangers of stunt maneuvers prior to entering the contract. Because the itinerary of the club was not spelled out at the time the release was executed, or for some time thereafter, the decedent could not know whether he was qualified for the stunts which ultimately were included in the performances. It is not unlikely that, given his beginner status, he relied upon the club's expertise in evaluating his ability to participate in the shows. Having been accepted as a member, he might reasonably expect that he already was qualified to participate in the club's shows, that the club would train him to perform difficult stunts for which he was presently unqualified, or that they would not allow him to take part in stunts which exceeded his capability. Nothing occurred to dispel this expectation during the tenure of their brief and unhappy relationship. Thus, it could well be that the decedent's reliance on the club for protection superseded the club's expectation of immunity from liability for injuries sustained by novices like the decedent. Despite the pretensions of the *Dobratz* court, this conclusion can be derived only from a relational exegesis, and not from any objective reading of the contract.

Comparison of another case, decided by a court in the same jurisdiction just three years before, proves the point. In *Trainor v. Aztalan Cycle Club, Inc.*,[114] a motocross racer was injured when he failed to negotiate a sharply peaked mogul during a practice round of an event sponsored by the defendant-club. As a condition to participating in the race, the plaintiff had signed a release form nearly identical in all material respects to that found fatally ambiguous in *Dobratz*. Nevertheless, the Wisconsin Court of Appeals, in an opinion later discussed and approved by the Supreme Court in *Dobratz*, held the release valid and enforceable.

How, you might ask, could this be? If the court's task is to interpret objectively the language of such agreements, and if the content of the two contracts is substantially the same, than one would expect uniform results. That different results obtain in these two situations confirms that factors extrinsic to the contracts in question are being heavily weighted. As an examination of the *Trainor* opinion reveals, the most important of these factors is the relationship of the parties.

Unlike the skier in *Dobratz*, the plaintiff in *Trainor* was an experienced practitioner of his sport of choice. During his three-year career as a motocross racer, he had fallen from his bike nearly 100 times, sometimes sustaining injuries in the process. He was familiar with the defendant's racecourse, describing it as one of the most dangerous in the business. Indeed, prior to executing the release, the plaintiff, at the defendant's suggestion, personally inspected the course. Following his inspection, he complained to the defendant's officers that several of the "double jumps" were too steep. Nevertheless, they refused to alter the course. Plaintiff decided to participate in the race anyway. The day before the race, he executed the release, wherein he agreed that "he was 'rel[ying] upon his own inspection and his own skill, judgment, and ability and not upon such safety precautions as may be taken by [the sponsors].'"[115] The plaintiff had signed many such releases in the past, although he declared that he never had read any of them.

The relational differences in *Trainor* and *Dobratz* are manifest. Not only was Trainor a frequent member of the relevant relational category, a relation which extended not months but several years, he apparently had previous contacts with this specific sponsor. Thus, in contrast to the skier in *Dobratz*, Trainor was not an individual likely to need or expect special protection. Indeed, he communicated this fact to the sponsor when he personally inspected the course, reported his concerns, and yet proceeded to participate in the race. At that point, the sponsor might reasonably rely upon his conduct as an expression of his willingness to accept the known dangers of the course. This was confirmed by Trainor's written assurance in the release that, in entering the race, he assumed all risk of injury and was relying for safety only upon his own skill and judgment. Whereas this was a hollow expression in *Dobratz*, since it was unsupported by prior experience or specific conduct, in *Trainor* it was consistent with the expectations arising from the relationship itself.[116]

Dominant Party Reliance

One might question whether the cyclist in *Trainor* was really an unsophisticated or "vulnerable" party entitled to a heightened duty of protection. While he was no racecourse operator, he was familiar nonetheless with the dangers associated with the sport of motocross racing and with the hazards of the defendant's track in particular. *Trainor* might be read, then, not as a case of mutual reliance, but as an example of unilateral reliance only. Still, this does not mean that the former situation never arises. Indeed, there is no paucity of cases which demonstrate how the reliance of a "dominant" party may outweigh that experienced by one with considerably less knowledge of relational risks.

The recent Tennessee case of *Houghland v. Security Alarms & Services, Inc.*[117] is a perfect example. There, the Supreme Court of Tennessee had occasion to consider the validity of a waiver provision in a home security alarm agreement in which the plaintiff-subscribers agreed to release the security company from "all hazards which were covered by insurance."[118] The agreement also contained a liquidated damages clause which fixed its liability at a specified sum. One night, while the plaintiffs were out, their home was burglarized. The thieves walked away with jewelry and silver valued at $185,000, only $81,144 of which was covered by the plaintiff's personal insurance. The court upheld the waiver provision, stating that "[t]here is nothing in public policy to render inoperative or nugatory the contractual limitations contained in the...agreement."[119] Although the court did not explicitly determine whether the plaintiffs consented to the waiver, a relational analysis might have sustained the exculpatory clause on this ground as well.

The relationship here consisted of several formal and informal interactions between the Houghlands and the security company. The initial agreement, with the exculpatory clause, was signed by the parties in 1977. The service under the contract included home alarms and a "loop" system telephonically connecting the Houghlands' home to a central office maintained by the security company. When the loop system was activated, the central office was required to send a representative or police officer to the premises to determine the source of the alarm.

Two years later, the Houghlands contacted a representative of the security company to discuss the possibility of installing additional security equipment in their home. Specifically, they inquired about a transceiver system which would automatically call the central office even if the phone lines were disconnected. At about the same time, a company agent indicated by letter the company's policy of dispatching appropriate law enforcement personnel on all burglary alarms, although the company disclaimed any responsibility for their actions. The Houghlands decided to purchase the transceiver, and a rider to that effect was added to the original 1977 contract.

During the next nine months, the alarm at the Houghland residence was set off accidentally three times. Each time, the central office of the security system contacted the police who were dispatched to the Houghland residence. The last of these incidents was just five days before the burglary in question.

On that night, the central office received a signal which appeared to indicate a problem with the telephone line in the Houghland's neighborhood. Shortly thereafter, a second signal was received from the Houghlands' residence, this one showing that the "entire loop" had "gone open." Similar signals were received from other homes in the area. A representative of the security company was dispatched to investigate these signals. Upon visually inspecting the Houghland house from the outside, the representative observed no signs of entry. Because the Houghlands had refused to supply the company with keys to their home, as they might have done under their contract, the representative called the Houghland's son-in-law, who had been designated by the couple as the party to contact in an emergency. The son-in-law declined the representative's offer to enter the home and check the alarm, believing the matter could wait until the morning. The next morning, the Houghland's housekeeper discovered the break-in.

When one focuses on the unfolding relationship among the parties to this contract, it seems appropriate that the Houghlands bear the loss caused by the burglary of their home. Undeniably, the nature of the relationship itself was likely to induce a certain amount of reliance on the part of the Houghlands. Indeed, the sole purpose of the agreement was to provide the purchasers greater security and protection than they might receive from public authorities.

This presumed reliance, however, was both vitiated and counterbalanced. In this case, the Houghlands' expectations were colored by their actions. When the original agreement was signed, the service offered to accept greater liability on a graduated scale of increasing rates. The Houghlands declined. In addition, the Houghlands refused to release their house keys to the service. Both decisions evince a certain distrust, and a disavowal of further protection. Relying on these impressions, the service might reasonably believe that the Houghlands were willing to purchase cheaper protection with potentially greater risk. While these manifestations affected the initial decision to extend security service to the Houghlands, the subsequent relations of the parties influenced the expectation of how that service would be performed thereafter. Both the history of false alarms and, more importantly, the decision of the son-in-law to deny access to the home inhibited the service's ability to respond effectively to the alarm signal. Thus, the actions of the Houghlands may have induced a reliance by the service more real than any which they themselves had incurred in entering the agreement.

As this example illustrates, the objective analysis needed to accurately evaluate the mutual reliance of the parties is far more expansive and overtly relational than that required by neoclassical contract law. Where the parties lack equal knowledge or bargaining power, their formal contract should not conclusively determine their respective rights and responsibilities. Instead, the entire course of the parties' relationship should be examined. This analysis would include consideration of any informal communication or interaction that might have shaped the expectations of either participant. Ultimately, the mosaic assembled from this analysis may undermine the presumption of reliance arising from the categorical characteristics of the relation. Even if such a special relationship is absent, the relational analysis described above still provides a more vivid and deeply textured picture of the risk allocations effected by the parties.[120]

If it appears at the conclusion of this analysis that the plaintiff consented to accept the risk and the defendant relied on this expression, then the risk should be borne completely by the plaintiff. If, however, the defendant's proof is lacking in either of these respects, then usually she should assume full responsibility for the risk. Where it has been determined that the plaintiff's exposure to the risk was less than consensual, however, her recovery might be mitigated under a comparative fault analysis if her conduct is proven to be unreasonable.[121]

Parting Shots

What can be learned from this brief survey? While not exhaustive, and certainly not empirical, it demonstrates that courts often employ relational considerations in interpreting exculpatory agreements. And, although these considerations are rarely acknowledged openly for their significance, they can and many times do play a major role in the objective analysis of such agreements. This covert undercurrent completes a relational scheme animating both express and implied assumption of risk analyses. Under this scheme, relational principles dominate the preliminary inquiry into the allocation of risk—i.e., in the determination of duty—but thereafter are supposed to disappear from view. Often they do not. Although the formal analysis purportedly shifts to a search for consent, relational considerations like reliance surreptitiously reappear to influence this determination as well. The problem is that one can never tell when these relational notions will surface. Their invocation often is as unpredictable and fleeting as the whims of the mediums who summon them. Though this relational presence is useful and often compelling, its random dispersal throughout the law of torts creates a concatenation of disjointed rules which inevitably results in ambiguity and inconsistency in assumption of risk analysis. To correct this deficiency, courts must become more sensitive to the unique considerations—like relational imbalance, consent and reliance—which lie at the heart of any acceptable scheme of risk allocation. Until they do, fairness and justice will remain only illusory and unobtainable objectives for those that must stand in judgment before them.

.

Epilogue

We have now, I think, the necessary ingredients for developing a new, or at least clearer, understanding of the interrelationship between justice and tort law. Justice, we have seen, is a relational idea that explains our need to be treated fairly by others. A political and moral virtue, the concept of justice permeates all of our associations: from the simplest interpersonal encounter to the most fundamental social contract with our lawgiver. It should not be surprising, then, to find each of these aspects of justice—the private and the public—interwoven into every tort action. In the private sphere, the concept of corrective justice requires that those who treat us wrongly be held responsible to us for the consequences of their actions. This system of rectification derives from our moral sense of equality (in annulling undeserved interpersonal imbalances) and retribution, and explains the bilateral nature of our tort litigation system. On the public plane, tort justice requires that our disputes with others be decided fairly by a neutral arbiter—in our system, the judiciary. It demands, among other things, that the rules for resolving such disputes be reasonable. To meet this requirement, tort rules do not have to mirror deontological first principles; rather, they need only serve the ends of the prevailing political association. In our liberal democratic system, the primary objective of government has always been to secure the autonomy of every individual by protecting each from the harmful acts of others. Our tort rules further this objective by distributing varying normative responsibilities to individuals according to the riskiness of and need for their activities, and the vulnerability of those with whom they interact. Applied universally to all, the tort rules imposing these responsibilities placate our demand for distributive (or social) fairness from our lawgiver. This is true even though, when implemented in specific cases, the rules may not always render ideal results. As long as they are based on some fair distributive criteria, they will sufficiently quench our insatiable thirst for justice.

Having achieved this understanding, it would seem that our search for the truth has finally come to an end. Yet our quest is still not quite complete. We began this journey back in the Introduction speculating about whether the traditional tort system was a morally bankrupt institution. If nothing else, we now have at least a plausible answer to that question. Both the structure and content of tort law, I have argued, were originally founded on sound ethical principles which resonate with our most basic political sensibilities. Nevertheless, this conclusion, enlightening as it may be, was not the ultimate destination of our epistemic sojourn. Rather, we pondered whether the changes made to the tort system over the last century or so would ultimately enhance the law's delicate moral fabric, or would eventually ensure its destruction. If my account of justice and tort law is correct, we finally possess the critical faculties necessary to answer this crowning question, and with them, the power to predict the future of this volatile area of law.

Finding a Jurisprudential Niche

Before making such a prognostication, however, we first must take a closer look at the theory that I have fashioned as my divining rod. Although my vision of tort law's moral foundation is somewhat novel, I certainly am not the first, nor will I be the last, to offer a positive or normative theory of tort law. As we saw in the Introduction, many moralists before me have attempted to explain, criticize and/or justify our system of civil reparations. Indeed, it was the cacophonous clash of these previous efforts which inspired me to write this book. While I may have rejected some of their conclusions, nearly all of these early pioneers have influenced my own thinking on this enormously rich subject. In fact, the theory which I have presented in the preceding pages is largely a patchwork of ideas harvested from others and reconfigured in a slightly new way. You might call my creation a kind of philosophic Frankenstein. Like any mysterious creature, however, this chimeric figure is likely to be feared and misunderstood. To prevent this from happening, we must take a moment to get to know this stranger a little bit better. In short, we need to find out both what makes my theory unique and what distinguishes it from the theoretical hobgoblins that have stalked these woods before.

The Pluralist-Monist Schism

Without even examining its substantive pillars, one can readily see how the sheer scope of this new theory sets it apart from many of its predecessors. For example, Jules Coleman, one of the earliest and most prolific tort moralists, has consistently denied the possibility of discovering a universal ethic underlying all of tort law. Instead, Coleman has argued that tort law is a mixture of markets and morals.[1] Specifically, Coleman asserts that although much of negligence and intentional tort doctrine may be founded on the notion of corrective justice, the concepts of strict liability and necessity usually are not. These doctrines, he argues, often are premised on principles of economic efficiency.[2]

Similarly, George Fletcher, another leader in the moralist movement, also has disavowed any broad metatheory of tort law. Like Coleman, Fletcher sees tort law as possessing schizophrenic dual personalities: one animated by a moral spirit, the other preoccupied with economic efficiency. Yet Fletcher's account of this disorder is not identical to Coleman's. Far from it. Fletcher portrays the morality/efficiency dichotomy as a struggle between two distinct theoretical paradigms. According to Fletcher, the paradigm of reciprocity relies upon John Rawls' first principle of justice.[3] In cases within this paradigm, which typically invoke the theory of strict liability but also may include negligence claims, conduct causing injury to another is wrongful if the actor imposes greater risk upon others than she herself would be willing to endure. In other negligence cases, however, Fletcher sees the paradigm of reasonableness at work. Under this decidedly economic paradigm, Fletcher notes, conduct is unreasonable, notwithstanding its moral quality, only if the cost of avoiding an accident is less than the costs produced by the accident itself.[4]

My theory, by contrast, does not recognize the pathological identity crisis diagnosed by Fletcher or Coleman. Rather, it views tort law as emanating from a surprisingly healthy, and unified, moral psyche. In my view, all of tort law, including the theories of strict liability and negligence, can be explained as embodying the ideals of autonomy and equality, and as implementing the ethical principles of corrective and distributive justice. If the law imposes varying degrees of freedom and responsibility under different circumstances—prohibiting conduct in some cases, while merely requiring the payment of money in others—it is not because it lacks a pervasive moral foundation, but because its moral structure is supple, resilient and adaptive enough to cover any kind of transaction or relation.

Other Metatheories Distinguished

I am not completely alone in this belief. A small, but significant contingent of tort scholars have offered metatheories of their own. Richard Epstein's *A Theory of Strict Liability* is perhaps the best known attempt at providing a comprehensive account of tort law.[5] Rather than explain the way tort law actually is, however, Epstein has presented a vision of how the law ought to be. According to this vision, causation is the fundamental moral concept which justifies the imposition of liability against those who inflict harm upon their neighbors. Thus, Epstein endorses a scheme of strict liability with defenses in lieu of our current fault-based system of civil justice.

While Ernest Weinrib has offered an equally expansive theory of tort law, his normative approach relies upon an entirely different core concept. Weinrib asserts that the structure of the tort system is determined by corrective justice, which requires that disputes be resolved within the unique bilateral relation existing between the doer (defendant) and sufferer (plaintiff) of an injury.[6] Weinrib notes, however, that corrective justice provides no substantive formula for deciding which injurious acts are tortious, and thus deserving of rectification. This void, he argues, can and should be filled by Kant's golden rule: treat people not as a means to an end, but as ends in themselves.[7] For Weinrib, then, moral responsibility is not a matter of causation alone; rather, it arises from one's failure to act in accordance with a deontological directive.

In one sense, these metatheories are very much like my own. Each identifies autonomy as the base value which tort law attempts to foster and protect. Yet beyond this fundamental affinity, there are substantial differences, perhaps large chasms, separating our theories. As noted above, neither Epstein nor Weinrib tell us why tort law developed the way it has. Epstein doesn't even attempt to do so; Weinrib, though successful in explaining the law's formal structures, offers no reason for the law's apparent fickle notions of wrongdoing. My theory, by contrast, endeavors not only to provide a normative framework for tort law, but to demonstrate how such basic tort concepts as intent, negligence and strict liability have long coexisted within this delicate, freedom-enhancing matrix. In addition, both Epstein's and Weinrib's views of tort law are distinctly one-dimensional. Epstein, we know, is fixated on the notion of causation, finding it morally potent enough to support a whole scheme of civil liability. Weinrib, on the other hand, is transfixed by Kantian ethics. In his world, actors must follow a universal law of mutual respect or risk incurring a state-imposed financial sanction. Whether founded on causation or categorical imperative, each unary theory possesses limited justificatory power. What's worse, these narrow models cannot be assembled into some grander theoretical blueprint; in fact, they are inherently irreconcilable. While Epstein proposes to dispense with the notion of fault, Weinrib makes fault, in its truest moral sense, the epicenter of his tort universe. My theory avoids this pitfall. Rather than grounding tort law on any single concept (other than the general ideal of autonomy), the liberal paradigm I have offered seeks to show how the seemingly disparate ideas of causation and wrongdoing, and of negligence and strict liability, are seamlessly interrelated. Without causation there can be no rights or duties, and without these, the concept of wrongdoing is simply incomprehensible. Likewise, just as an act of negligence imposes unreasonable risks upon others, so too does an abnormally dangerous activity. In the end, each type of conduct demonstrates the actor's selfish and unfair usurpation of a disproportionate share of autonomy: the negligent actor by behaving in a way forbidden to others; the strict liability actor by conducting an abnormally risky activity in an inappropriate location, and then refusing to pay for this privilege. My theory sees these concepts not as antithetical, but as part of a complex mosaic that, when seen from afar, captures the illusive visage of justice.

On Combining the Forms of Justice

One of the most important, and most misunderstood, pieces of this mosaic is the intricate interconnection between corrective and distributive justice. Conventional thinking has long viewed these concepts as mutually exclusive. Indeed, Aristotle, in his *Nichomachean Ethics*, described each form of justice as completely unique and independent.[8] Distributive justice, he noted, is based on a geometric proportion and is invoked whenever some third party holds goods that two or more others desire. Corrective justice, by contrast, requires first a wrongful transaction, and second that the wrongful gains and losses of that encounter be arithmetically annulled. Extrapolating from this dichotomy, many contemporary scholars have declared that the two aspects of justice can never be commingled or combined.[9] Such a merger, they suggest, would adulterate the conceptual purity of each ethical form. While this interpretation is true in part, it also contains a serious analytical flaw. No doubt, altering a central characteristic of either paradigm—say, by requiring that goods always be distributed in arithmetically equal shares, or by correcting wrongful transactions by imposing liability in proportion to the wealth of the defendant—would cause each paradigm to disappear and transmute into something different. However, this does not mean that the two paradigms cannot be used in tandem to create a metasystem of justice that is not only fully complementary, but synergistic as well. This, in fact, is how I see classical tort law.

As I have argued throughout this book, distributive justice actually fills a void left open by the form of corrective justice. Distributive justice, you will recall, determines how resources are allocated by the state to its citizens. Corrective justice, on the other hand, determines how resources are allocated between two or more private parties following a wrongful transaction. It does not, however, provide any means for deciding which transactions are wrongful and which are not. This is where distributive justice comes in. Conduct is wrongful in a social and political sense only if the actor exercises more autonomy than she deserves. The state, through law, identifies the freedoms we are entitled to enjoy and distributes this liberty to us in a variety of ways. Tort law is one of these mechanisms. By providing rules and standards of behavior, the doctrines of tort law tell us when we have exercised more than our distributive share of freedom, and thus, when our conduct is wrongful. Only after this determination is made does the concept of corrective justice prescribe how to eradicate the parties' respective gains and losses of autonomy.

Silencing Tort Law's Critics

Recognizing this interrelationship between corrective and distributive justice is an important first step in defending tort law against its most vocal critics, namely, feminists and members of the Critical Legal Studies movement. For example, Leslie Bender, one of the most prominent feminist critics, sees tort law as part of a patriarchical social system designed by men to oppress women.[10] According to Bender, tort law embraces norms—such as objectivism, liberalism and separatism—that are intrinsically "male", and excludes inherently feminine values like subjectivism, relationalism and collectivism. This is bad, says Bender, because it ignores the feminine perspective of reality and denies women a true voice in shaping social policy.

Richard Abel, another tort detractor, also views the tort system as oppressive, but on an even larger scale. An avowed "Crit", Abel believes that tort law has been used by the rich and powerful to subjugate the poor and underprivileged.[11] According to Abel, capitalist tort law exploits and alienates victims, who are mostly poor, by basing their entitlement to compensation on the fault of their wrongdoers rather than on the financial need occasioned by their injuries. Even when a few victims are able to successfully surmount the onerous fault barrier, Abel laments, the tort system only permits them to recover damages worthy of a pauper, thereby devaluing their human dignity and reinforcing the material inequalities that hold them down.

While there is some merit to these criticisms, they ultimately miss the mark. The tort system, like any other social institution, is a reflection of the culture that creates it. As was noted in the Introduction, tort law was spawned during the feudal era of medieval England. As a result, it was designed primarily to protect the status of wealthy male landowners, not to promote equality among people of different social castes. This does not mean, however, that feudal law rejected the notion of distributive justice, or that it implemented a repressive distributive regime. It suggests only that early tort law was premised on allocative criteria—like bloodlines and property ownership—which, although objectionable by today's standards, were generally accepted and efficacious at the time.

In any event, once the institution of feudalism began to die out, and the basis for this archaic distributive scheme disappeared, tort law did not remain mired in the past, but adapted to the change. Beginning with the rise of parlimentarianism in England, and culminating in the American Revolution, the class status orientation of the Middle Ages was gradually replaced by the freedom movement of the Enlightenment. Along with this social transformation came an equally prodigious development in the distributive characteristics of tort law. Instead of basing liability rules on the parties' wealth or heritage, the "new" American tort law sought to distribute rights and duties in accordance with principles of liberty, equality, merit, need and risk. The rich and powerful were no longer accorded an exalted or privileged status. Under the flexible need criterion, the well educated and knowledgeable were held to a higher standard than those less naturally endowed. Further, the rich, who controlled the means of production and so possessed the power to create massive engines of destruction (like cars and railroads), now were accountable for the disproportionate risk they imposed upon others. Conversely, those who traditionally had suffered under feudal law—i.e., the weak and the vulnerable—began to enjoy the benefit of assistance and protection. Just as the need criterion had increased the responsibility of some, it served to reduce the burden on others. Children and the aged were required to act only in accordance with their unique mental and physical capabilities. Those confronted by emergencies, as well as those defending themselves or others, were afforded greater liberty to secure their interests from invasion. Product consumers, apartment dwellers, common carrier passengers, medical patients, employees and business invitees, who at one time had all been exploited by their more powerful relational counterparts, soon were wielding tremendous clout in the marketplace. Even women, who formerly were denied the right to sue, enjoyed newfound freedom, including, ultimately, the ability to recover for psychic injuries caused by abusive or outrageous conduct.[12] Far from promoting oppression, modern tort law, with its liberal distributive influence, had actually emerged as the great defender of the disadvantaged. In my view, it remains so today.

Assessing the Modern Developments

The crucial question now is whether tort law can continue to fulfill this role despite the onslaught of change that recently has been levelled against it. The answer, of course, depends upon the nature of the changes themselves: Do they improve or uplift the law, or do they only serve to despoil or subvert it? What makes this question so difficult to resolve is that the changes do not all share a uniform vision. In fact, they pull in opposite directions, and so threaten to tear apart the law's sinewy moral cartilage.

Directional Discord

The tension over tort law's future direction exists at several different levels of abstraction. Liberals desire to strip away old doctrine and replace it with new theories and concepts. Conservatives, on the other hand, want to forestall any further change, and to undo changes that have been made in the past. Many theorists, usually liberals, seek to transform the tort system into a public policy-making institution; others, typically conservatives, would like to preserve the tort system's traditional role as a private means of dispute resolution. Certain federalists believe the federal government should take a more active stand in regulating tortious behavior; states righters, by contrast, want to wrest control away from the national government and regain the power to regulate the general health, welfare and safety of their citizens. Finally, while many legislators would like to supplant tort law through legislative fiat, many judges are bent on extending the reach of tort law through common law precedent.

Substantive Changes

These opposed forces of change have clashed on both the procedural and substantive fronts of tort law. Given the scope of this book, however, I will focus only on the battles being waged over the law's four substantive components: duty, causation, damages and defenses. While some of these changes have already been discussed in earlier chapters, my purpose here is to more fully develop these analyses and to place them in a broader social context. Stepping back from the minutia, we shall see the development of two distinct but interrelated trends. On the one hand, liberal state courts have pushed the boundaries of tort law into previously unexplored territories; on the other hand, more conservative legislators (at both the state and federal levels) have attempted to prune back tort law in virtually all of its most fundamental particulars. Which approach is preferable? Actually neither, at least not entirely. When subject to careful scrutiny, it becomes apparent that although each approach offers some promise, both stand on somewhat shaky moral ground.

Long-Awaited Advances

Of course, not all of the recent innovations in the tort area are troublesome. In fact, some of these changes are unquestionably desirable, and have met with little opposition. For example, with respect to the element of duty, courts overwhelmingly have either abolished or eviscerated the privity barrier[13] and the entrant classification system for owners and occupiers of land.[14] Moreover, in all but a handful of states, the absolute defense of contributory negligence, which was used in the nineteenth century to insulate employers from liability, has been replaced by the more flexible concept of comparative fault.[15] In each case, the doctrine being discarded was a remnant of the antiquated status system which had shaped early (English) tort law. Each doctrine, in turn, has been superseded by concepts that reflect the values of liberty and equality so sacred to Americans and so intrinsic to American democracy. For instance, the privity and entrant status limitations have given way to a rich, multifactored analysis which does not automatically protect the interests of one party over the other, but considers and attempts to balance the interests of *all* parties to a lawsuit.[16] Likewise, in place of the one-sided rule of contributory negligence, which tossed out claims of even the most minimally careless plaintiffs, the doctrine of comparative fault now requires that the plaintiff's conduct be considered along with and compared to the behavior of her counterpart, and that the responsibility for their encounter be allocated proportionally between them.[17] Adding these concepts to the lexicon of tort law surely does not vitiate the law's moral pedigree, nor does it alter the law's private character. Quite the contrary. Such changes not only help to purge tort law of its historical baggage, they also serve to repair its distributive framework and, in the end, preserve its political and moral integrity as an instrument of private dispute resolution.

New Duties Securing Ethereal Interests

Other adjustments to the duty requirement, however, are more suspect and have been less warmly received. Beginning around the mid-twentieth century, state courts have actively and profoundly enlarged the scope of many entrenched tort duties. To illustrate, the duty to compensate for emotional distress, as a parasitic component of more tangible injuries, was expanded in two ways. First, where the plaintiff was directly exposed to injurious conduct, but did not actually sustain physical harm, she was permitted to recover for her resulting psychological discomfort.[18] In recent years, this right of recovery has been extended to claims of cancerphobia, which typically are prompted by the claimant's exposure to toxic substances.[19] Second, even where the plaintiff was not within the danger zone, but merely observed an injury sustained by a close relation, she was allowed compensation for any severe emotional scars left upon her by the event.[20]

Beyond the realm of emotional distress, duties protecting familial relations have been heightened in even more direct ways. Loss of consortium, a form of general damage formerly limited to husbands, has been extended to the entire immediate family, including wives,[21] parents[22] and children.[23] And while injuries to unborn children were awarded only reluctantly in the past, courts now are more receptive to causes of action founded on "wrongful birth"[24] and "wrongful life."[25] One can see a similar progression in the field of economic injuries. Although once recoverable only as an aftereffect of a physical harm, economic loss soon came into its own as an independent element of damage. Today, many courts are willing to award compensation for pure economic loss, without physical injury, so long as these financial costs are readily foreseeable.[26]

The mere recitation of these changes reveals a possible basis for objection. All share an obvious bias in favor of one party (the victim) over another (the alleged tortfeasor). Yet slanting the rules in this way is not necessarily unjust. Indeed, if such newfound duties rectified the law's clear moral deficiencies, they would be readily embraced regardless of their selective impact. The problem is that these changes do not simply correct a skewed moral tally sheet; in fact, they seem to create more difficulties than they cure. In rendering duty-enhancing decisions of this sort, courts seem almost oblivious to the broader ramifications of the responsibility mills they set in motion.

These unrecognized consequences are not only political in nature, but social and moral as well. On the political side, courts seem to forget that the creation of additional tort duties necessarily means increasing the involvement of government in our affairs, often inviting the state's intrusion into some of our most intimate relationships and experiences. Indeed, courts today are frequently asked to make a wide variety of extremely delicate and highly sensitive determinations that many of us would not request of a trusted friend or a respected religious advisor, let alone a state official or twelve strangers. From estimating the cost of our psychological trauma, to placing a price on the love and companionship shared by our family members and even to valuing our right to live a "normal" life without debilitating birth defects, tort law has made our private lives a decidedly public matter.

In the social sphere, too few courts recognize how opening the courthouse doors to claimants with the most trivial or specious injuries prevents the most seriously harmed victims from quickly recovering the compensation they so richly deserve and so desperately need. For example, in class actions, where such liberal duty rules are frequently utilized, claimants with inchoate or speculative injuries quickly flock to sign on. They realize that, with little effort or cost, they can receive generous awards for their largely unquantifiable claims. But as the hoards of plaintiffs swell, the litigation process slows to a crawl and the funds available for compensation shrink. In the meantime, seriously injured victims who need immediate financial relief from their mounting medical bills often opt out and settle for amounts that are grossly insufficient to repair their losses. Those who hang on seldom fair any better. In some cases, their share of the final judgment is pitifully small; in others, the defendant, having paid an increased number of less serious claims, is forced into bankruptcy, thus effectively eliminating the possibility of any recovery whatsoever.

This curious state of affairs points up a couple of cruel moral ironies. By providing greater protection against harm to those only marginally in need, these well-intentioned courts have sacrificed the security of the most needy of all. What's more, by expanding everyone's peripheral freedoms to mental tranquility and economic well-being, these new duties have stifled more basic freedoms of other actors, like drug and vaccine manufacturers, who engage in activities that could safeguard us from far more menacing harms. These sundry effects, whether viewed alone or in combination, seem perilous enough to warrant our concern.

Legislative Reaction

Motivated by such misgivings, some state legislatures set out to nip this trend in the bud. A particular target of attack were the theories of wrongful birth and wrongful life, which raised tricky questions of science and ethics. For reasons of policy and practicality, a few states passed laws forbidding or limiting either or both causes of action.[27] For the most part, however, the reformers have not sought to prevent the list of traditional injuries from expanding, but have determined to cut back on the recoverability of the traditional injuries themselves. Many state statutes now limit the amount of noneconomic (parasitic emotional distress) damages that may be recovered in certain civil actions.[28] Others place onerous restrictions on punitive damages, often imposing heavy evidentiary burdens on the plaintiff and/or capping her recovery.[29] And in our nation's capitol, Congress recently endorsed a product liability bill that contained similar provisions.[30]

While some of these measures seem to make sense, others appear to share the same bugaboos as the changes that inspired them. For instance, if punitive damages are deemed noncompensatory, and thus possess only deterrent value, then their award may be curtailed without fear of undermining the principle of corrective justice. Even if such recovery is meant to repair part of the moral damage inflicted by a malicious wrongdoer, a position endorsed by some jurisdictions, an award of punitive damages seems hopelessly maladapted for that purpose. Either one of these goals—i.e., deterrence or corrective justice—could be accomplished in ways far more efficacious than meting out a monetary penalty in a tort action. While criminal sanctions are available as a powerful deterrent to antisocial behavior, mediation and equitable remedies can be used to heal the dignitary wounds left by wrongful transactions.[31] As a clincher, by eliminating or reducing punitive relief, the state can help to ensure that defense compensation funds are not dissipated by the first few lucky plaintiffs to file suit, but are available to those with outstanding medical expenses and lost wages.

On the other hand, when general damages are arbitrarily limited to some fixed dollar amount, one can soon detect the smell of mischief in the air. Unlike punitive damages, general damages like pain and suffering, emotional distress and loss of life's pleasures are exclusively compensatory; thus, they clearly fall within the purview of corrective justice. Since corrective justice requires a case-by-case assessment of each defendant's unique conduct (gain) and each plaintiff's personal injury (loss), a rule which predetermines and objectifies the value of one factor necessarily corrupts the whole equation.

By way of illustration, suppose a car dealer sells a defective vehicle knowing that it will explode upon even a slight impact. A, who purchased the car, is severely burned when the vehicle crashes and bursts into flames. Assume further that A is likely to incur more than a million dollars of medical expenses over the course of her lifetime. A state statute, however, limits recovery of noneconomic damages to $250,000. Given the nature of the car dealer's conduct, and the severity of A's injuries, including her enormous economic loss and indescribable suffering, a multimillion dollar award of general damages seems to be in order. Yet the statute forecloses such relief. Accordingly, neither the dealer's wrongful gain, nor A's wrongful loss, will ever be fully extinguished. This is especially true in jurisdictions which also limit punitive damages, since the shortfall in compensatory damages can not be made up with an exemplary award. The resulting deficit to A, and others like her, is every bit as unjust as that experienced by the severely injured class action plaintiffs mentioned above, who must compete with others less deserving for a chance at receiving compensation.

Heightened Duties and the Drift Toward a Distributive Paradigm

Equally pressing moral and political quandaries have been created by the recent jurisprudential march toward strict, or at least stricter, liability. Almost everywhere you look these days, it seems that tort law is imposing stiffer and stiffer standards of behavior upon parties in positions of power and responsibility. Doctors are held to national standards[32] or standards set by their patients' expectations.[33] Under the doctrine of res ipsa loquitur, they may even be held liable without proof of negligence if they are unable to establish their innocence.[34] Product manufacturers, too, have been subject to especially exacting performance standards in the construction, design and marketing of their goods. Indeed, under the doctrine of strict products liability, a manufacturer may be held financially accountable for injuries caused by its products regardless of the amount of care it used in making them.[35] And manufacturers are not the only parties in the distributive chain who bear this burden. Practically any entity that comes in contact with a "bad" product shares this onerous responsibility. Component part makers,[36] wholesalers and distributors,[37] retailers,[38] used product sellers,[39] lessors,[40] bailors,[41] franchisors,[42] successor corporations,[43] electric companies,[44] trademark licensors,[45] real estate developers[46] and building contractors,[47] among others, all have been held strictly liable for playing some role in sending a defective product through the stream of commerce. Although employers have long been subject to vicarious liability for the negligence of their employees, today almost anyone who hires another to fix a hazardous condition or to perform a risky activity can be made to pay if something goes wrong.[48] But perhaps the most radical extension of this concept is in the area of parental responsibility. In an increasing number of jurisdictions, parents are being held strictly accountable for the destructive acts of their children.[49] The upshot of this whole trend seems to be, if the fate of others rests in your hands, you'd better be prepared to face the consequences when inevitable accidents occur.

Property Usages, Personal Services and Private Wrongs

The proliferation of such heightened behavioral standards, though foreboding, is in itself no reason to sound an alarm. Indeed, there is nothing inherently shocking about imposing greater legal obligations upon parties who engage in high-risk activities or who enjoy an epistemic advantage over their relational counterparts. As we have seen, the distributive criteria of risk and need, respectively, justify such disproportionately large allocations of responsibility. There also is nothing necessarily wrong with allowing members of a single community to set, interpret or apply the standard of strict liability. In fact, this tactic works quite well when the conduct in question has a peculiarly local character and effect. Unusual uses of property and the rendition of medical services fall neatly within this category.

Products Liability and Public Wrongs

Problems arise, however, when the activity regulated is of pandemic proportions, as is the case with the mass production and distribution of products. In this context, the imposition of strict liability is premised on the notion that such large enterprises are able to absorb the added liability and spread it around to their employees, shareholders and customers. The trouble here is that both the doctrine and policy of strict products liability suffer from terminal philosophical malignancies.

Corrective Justice Problems

As discussed in Chapter Sixteen, the theory of strict products liability, as currently conceived, is squarely antithetical to the concept of corrective justice. Except in manufacturing defect cases, the product seller's liability in each lawsuit is measured not only by the actual loss sustained by the plaintiff, as is required by corrective justice, but also by the number of other injuries caused by its product line, and even by the potential dangers posed by the product to the public at large. While this distended analysis insidiously destroys the law's corrective matrix from within, the policy of loss spreading attacks it directly from without. Under this policy, the wealth of the defendant, rather than the wrongfulness of her conduct, is the controlling factor in dispensing liability. Indeed, it makes no difference, for purposes of loss spreading, how much money the manufacturer spends on research and development, how sophisticated its quality control procedures are, or even how many people's lives are improved by its product. The only thing that matters is whether the manufacturer, rather than the injured consumer, is better equipped financially to diffuse the impact of the loss. Rather than promoting corrective justice, this policy threatens to replace that moral paradigm altogether with a purely distributive scheme.

Distributive Justice Problems

Even in this aspect, however, strict products liability proves to be a failure. While most distributive justice systems are created by legislatures, which speak for all citizens, the distributive policy of strict products liability is fashioned by the courts, and applies only on an ad hoc basis to the small percentage of people who happen to be involved in product-related accidents, and who are unable to resolve their own disputes. Compounding this problem, the individuals within the court system who establish the distributive rule are not experts, nor do their tastes and sensibilities reflect the norms of others who use the same internationally distributed product. Instead, they are amateur fact-finders who dispense regulatory judgments in accordance with their own, often peculiar, community standards of fairness.

Federal and State Reform

Federal and state reformers have recognized some of these problems, and have attempted to correct them. For example, as was noted in the Introduction, Congress has passed a wide variety of health and safety statutes that either expressly or impliedly preempt contrary state law. Airplanes, drugs, medical devices, poisons and clothing are just a few of the common products that are now either partially or exclusively regulated by the federal government.[50] In asserting its supremacy over the states, Congress has acknowledged that these products create public, rather than private, risks that must be evaluated by professional experts, not novices. At the same time, many state legislatures have enacted sweeping products liability reform statutes that either add proof requirements and/or defenses that resurrect the concept of fault, or retreat entirely from the doctrine of strict liability and return to the theory of negligence.[51]

These state measures, and their federal counterparts, appear to be a step in the right direction. The establishment of federal product standards provides a rational and fair way to allocate distributive responsibilities to those who market the same product all over the world. Likewise, basing the liability of manufacturers and other product sellers on the wrongfulness of their conduct ensures that tort law will retain its corrective purpose, and will not be vitiated or consumed by some inconsistent theory of justice. Perhaps most importantly, by promulgating broad, universal norms of behavior, these enactments and others like them finally repudiate the localized, piecemeal approaches of the past, and start us on a bold new path toward creating uniform strategies for handling this increasingly public problem.

Public Solutions to a National Crisis

Some may fear that consumers will suffer because of these changes. I am not convinced. With rigorous agency regulation, competitive markets and heightened standards of conduct, products of the future are likely to be just as safe, or quite possibly safer, than those sold today. Even if I am wrong, and consumer injuries rise, I don't believe the answer lies in the courts. Because product safety is now a national concern, we need to respond to the crisis with public solutions. This means creating general or specific compensation systems, like those developed under the National Childhood Vaccine Injury Act[52] and the Federal Mine Safety and Health Act of 1977,[53] which generally protect manufacturers from liability,[54] while still compensating injured victims for their losses. In the end, such a system is our best, and perhaps only, hope for stimulating the development of innovative and useful new products, protecting consumers from product-related injuries and avoiding the moral and political pitfalls that currently plague the law of products liability.

Changes to the Causation and Damage Requirements

Up to this point, the changes we have examined all have involved the element of duty, either in its conception or application. Yet the recent manipulations of tort law do not end there. Over the past several decades, state courts have slowly redefined such time-honored concepts as causation and damage. And these are no trivial changes. Indeed, the activity in these areas, though less pervasive, is more prolific, and certainly more profound, than any of the developments noted above.

Market and Risk Share Liability

It is virtually impossible to discuss the changes made to the causation requirement without also considering how our conception of damage has changed, for the line separating these two elements has become inscrutably blurred. For example, some jurisdictions have endorsed theories of market share[55] or risk share liability[56] which allow an injured claimant to recover damages against a product manufacturer without producing evidence that the named manufacturer made the offending item. In these cases, the plaintiff need only bring into court one or more of the manufacturers of that good; the burden then shifts to each defendant to disprove causation.[57] Those defendants who fail to meet this burden are held liable in proportion to their share of the relevant market for the product. At first blush, it appears that the courts have simply eliminated, or at least seriously devalued, the causation requirement. After all, if a manufacturer no longer possesses its sales or distribution records, and thus is incapable of presenting the necessary exculpatory evidence, it may be held liable despite the complete lack of its causality. There is another way of looking at this outcome, however. To the extent the manufacturer's liability tracks its national sales of the product, its responsibility is an accurate reflection of the amount of public risk it has created. Causation under this analysis is not at issue. The manufacturer *did* produce *these* products, and some members of the consuming public *were* actually placed at risk, even if they ultimately suffered no injury. What has been changed is the law's definition of harm. The endurance of risk, without more, has become an injury for which the law may provide compensation.

The Lost Chance Doctrine

Other new tort doctrines share this same duality. In some medical mal-practice cases, for instance, courts have imposed liability against doctors who, by their negligence, have decreased their patients' chances of surviving a par-ticular malady.[58] This responsibility holds true even though, at the time these patients were first diagnosed, they already had a less than fifty-percent chance of living to a normal life expectancy. As in market share cases, the patients here cannot prove factual cause under the traditional "but for" test since, even without the doctors' negligence, they were probably going to die. If the patient (through her estate) is permitted to recover, it must be because (1) the causation requirement has been significantly diluted or eliminated, or (2) she is being com-pensated not for her premature death, but for the lost statistical possibility that she might survive. Either way, the change effected is momentous.

Increased Risks and Medical Monitoring

A couple of remaining doctrinal innovations in this area require far less guesswork. In fact, these less cryptic changes were designed with one pur-pose in mind: to recognize risk exposure as new form of harm. The theo-ry of enhanced or increased risk declares this purpose directly. Under this doctrine, a plaintiff exposed to a toxic substance can recover damages if she can show that the contact increased her chances of developing a dis-ease (usually cancer) sometime in the future.[59] Another theory compen-sates for enhanced risk in a more indirect, but also more tangible way. Where the plaintiff's toxic exposure increases her risk of future harm, she can claim reimbursement for any medical expenses that are reasonably necessary to monitor her condition.[60] So long as the monitoring is a prob-able consequence of the toxic exposure, the plaintiff may recoup the costs of such things as check-ups and testing which ultimately may lead to early detection and treatment of the disease. From these theories, it is clear that risk enhancement is no longer just a trigger which activates the risk-creator's duty to repair more serious physical harms; it now is an injury *in itself* which, either in the abstract or as the basis for medical monitoring, may warrant independent compensation.

From Corrective to Distributive Justice

In Chapters Thirteen and Sixteen, we observed how revolutionary these developments truly are. In effect, they culminate the distributive drift only suggested by the other changes mentioned above. Indeed, if the doctrine of strict products liability and its supporting policy of loss spreading supply the dream of making the tort system an ad hoc, judicially administered public compensation scheme, the alterations to the causation and damage requirements are rapidly making that dream a reality.

Tort law used to be concerned with correcting the ill effects of transactions and relations. Although such tortious encounters varied widely, they all had one thing in common: causality. One or more parties through the power of human agency brought about a sequence of events that ultimately ended up in a clash of interests. This causality created the duty of the protagonist to her specific victim, it defined the victim's entitlement to protection from the protagonist, and perhaps most importantly, it empowered the victim to interfere with the protagonist's freedom in order to restore the status quo.

But the causation-destroying, risk-deploring theories mentioned above have changed all this. Take the doctrines of market share or risk share liability. In every case where such theories are asserted, most of the defendant-manufacturers have no relationship with or connection to the plaintiff. Although they may have made a product similar to the one consumed by the plaintiff, they did not produce the specific item that actually caused her injury. Thus, insofar as *this particular plaintiff* is concerned, they have committed no *private* act of wrongdoing. Nevertheless, courts in such cases are not much worried about correcting the uniquely personal moral rift existing between the plaintiff and her actual injurer. No, they are far more concerned with deterring everyone who marketed the product, and in compensating anyone who might have been harmed by it.

Of course, you don't need causation or even a tort case to accomplish either of these goals. All you need is a system of distributive justice which, on the one hand, imposes a tax on manufacturers in accordance with the riskiness of their products, and on the other, establishes a claims program that awards compensation to injured victims with little or no showing of fault or causal responsibility. As noted previously, such distributive plans are not immoral or politically dangerous if created by legislators or other public policy decision-makers and reduced to general law so they may apply uniformly to all those who fall within the group designated for regulation or protection. When implemented by judges and juries in random civil actions, however, these aspirations constitute a direct threat to the concept of corrective justice in general, and to the private justice objectives of tort law in particular.

Inhibiting the Trend:
The Demise of Joint Liability

One response to this distributive trend has been to limit the recovery of damages against defendants found collectively responsible for the individual injuries of others. In other words, instead of precluding group or industry-wide liability in the absence of causation, some state legislatures have restricted the amount of damages that the plaintiff may require each defendant to pay. Some statutes eliminate joint liability for all types of harm;[61] others, like the product liability bill recently proposed by Congress,[62] limit its application to economic damages only.[63]

By way of example, assume that a plaintiff sustains $100,000 of damage and names three defendants, A, B, and C, who may or may not have caused her injuries. After trial, the jury determines that defendant A increased the risk of harm to the plaintiff or the public by 10 %, that defendant B's contribution was 30 % and C's was 60 %. Under these circumstances, A could only be made to pay $10,000 of the plaintiff's judgment, B $30,000 and C the remaining $60,000.

This theory seems fair on paper, but in reality is patently misdirected and potentially unjust. On the defendants' side of the axis, the abolition of joint liability poses somewhat of a paradox. While it ensures that each defendant will not pay more of a judgment than is consistent with her assigned responsibility, it does nothing to correct the problem of holding noncausal defendants liable in the first place for losses produced by others. In fact, it is quite possible that, where one or more of the defendants becomes insolvent, the only real wrongdoer will escape liability entirely, and the remaining innocent parties will be left holding the bag. In such a case, doing away with joint liability will be even more burdensome to the plaintiff. If, in the above hypothetical, C, who was adjudged 60 % responsible, were to become judgment-proof, the plaintiff would be able to recover only 40 % of her damages, or $40,000. From a corrective justice standpoint, this may not be as unfair as first appears. Each defendant is accountable only to the extent of her own fault, thus extinguishing her wrongful gain. Yet we have seen that the plaintiff's loss also is supposed to figure prominently in this rectificatory process. Limiting the amount of each defendant's liability in proportion to her wrongdoing, therefore, may throw off the calculation of true responsibility, since it ignores all or part of the effect such conduct had upon the life of her victim. In any event, requiring the plaintiff to bear a large portion of accident costs which she had no part in producing seems unacceptable as a matter of social policy, and so points up the need for further reform in this area.[64]

Dismantling the Defense of Assumption of Risk

Tort law's final frontier of change has been in the realm of affirmative defenses. We saw at least one such innovation earlier on. The doctrine of comparative fault, we noted, has proven to be a morally satisfactory means of both annulling wrongful gains and losses, and of distributing responsibility among a group of individuals causally connected to a harmful transaction.

The other significant development in this area, however, has not been such a resounding success. As discussed in Chapter Nineteen, many courts and legislatures recently have reformulated the doctrine of assumption of risk. Some have dismembered it and sewn its parts into the body of doctrines like duty or comparative fault.[64] Others have eliminated it entirely, relegating all risk-allocation questions to the jury for comparative analysis.[65]

Each of these approaches, however, suffers from a sort of moral anemia. While they do not condone wicked or antisocial behavior, they are incapable of acknowledging the power of individual choice. For example, where a plaintiff knowingly and voluntarily encounters a dangerous condition carelessly created by another, these newer approaches do not bar her recovery, but allow her case to reach the jury. The jury, in turn, may divide the parties' respective responsibilities in any way they see fit. This seems puzzling since, if the plaintiff's choice is true, she appears to have no moral standing to shift the loss on to anyone else. Indeed, by electing to accept the danger, the plaintiff effectively negates the duty of the risk-creator, and reaps the benefit of enjoying an expanded spectrum of opportunity. She also deals the cards to her own fate, and does so fully aware of the hand she will have to play. If the concept of autonomy is to have any meaning in such a case, it would appear that the plaintiff should be held completely accountable for the consequences of her decision. Yet the more recent approaches to assumption of risk, which hopelessly splinter responsibility among all parties to a lawsuit, are too weak and indecisive to take this strong moral stand. Instead, they dilute the notion of liberty by declaring that, our desires notwithstanding, some Big Brother remains duty-bound to protect us from making the "wrong" moral or personal choices. Such an attitude could hardly be more repugnant to the interests of tort law or to the civil justice system in general. Indeed, besides offending our most fundamental political principles, this view threatens to vitiate the bases of our social relationships (by substituting duty for need, love or altruism), and, in the end, to destroy the sense of self-reliance which we use to formulate and implement our life plans. If we are to avoid such obvious stumbling blocks, we must reverse the changes that make them seem so frightening, and so imminent, and replace them with more appealing doctrines that will carry tort law into the twenty-first century.

Into the Great Beyond

But how do we know what our needs will be ten, twenty, or thirty years in the future, and how will we be able to tell if tort law is properly suited to meet those needs? Certainly, evaluating tomorrow's tort law will not be as easy as holding the law's many doctrines and policies up to a ready moral standard and determining whether they pass muster. This is because twenty-first century torts will be dramatically different from those we recognize today. Unprecedented changes in science, technology and society will force the law to adapt quickly to avoid becoming outdated. The advent of the computer age, in particular, will irretrievably alter the nature and scope of our relationships with others, and so will require us to rethink many of tort law's most sacred concepts.[66]

Duty is a good case in point. As we have seen, tort duties often are founded on special relationships in which one party possesses superior knowledge and bargaining power over the other. In the digital age, however, these relational imbalances may become considerably less prevalent, and far less severe. Indeed, as more people begin to cruise the information superhighway, the whole idea of a special relationship could become an anachronism. Consumers will be able to browse Web sites created by manufacturers and service providers and acquire almost unlimited information about the goods and services they offer. And when these net surfers become confused by a piece of esoteric material, they will be able to search cavernous library databases or enter a plethora of expert discussion groups to obtain clarification. With so much information available at the click of a mouse, duties designed to correct vast knowledge differentials may begin to shrink or recede. At the same time, however, the promise of instantaneous, universal communication seems to ensure that certain other duties will proliferate. Consider the hacker who plants a computer virus which infects and ultimately destroys files and hard drives all over the world. Or the cyber-terrorist who alters or steals information which is crucial to national defense, or to air traffic safety or to the safe operation of nuclear power plants across the country. Are the duties of these new age wrongdoers as expansive as the risks they create, or will we have to find some new way of limiting responsibility? There are no easy answers to this seminal, postmodern question.

Indeed, it is not even clear which interests will be protected in cyberspace. Since most people will work or transact via computer from the comfort of their homes, fewer people will find themselves in involuntary encounters while driving their cars, walking the streets or operating dangerous industrial equipment. Thus, we are likely to witness a significant decrease in the types of serious physical injuries which have preoccupied tort law throughout its history. Yet as these harms decline, invasions of another, more intangible sort are sure to skyrocket. Every aspect of our lives will be stored in tiny bits of electronic information which will be accessible to people all over the world. As a result, we will experience a rash of new injuries: our personal databases will be compromised or destroyed, our ideas will be copied or stolen, our most private secrets will be divulged and scrutinized, and our reputations will be sullied and smeared, all in ways never before imagined.

While these prospects seem incredibly daunting, they are not beyond tort law's capacity to prevent or correct them. To respond to these changes in a meaningful fashion, however, the law will have to adopt a new methodology for conceptualizing tortious wrongs. Instead of focusing almost exclusively upon the tortfeasor's conduct (characterizing it as either intentional, negligent or involving an abnormal danger), tort law must begin to examine the peculiar nature of the plaintiff's injury, the unique contours of the parties' relationship, and the precise manner in which the harm occurred. Only by searching for such new paradigms of interaction will the institution of tort law keep pace with this breakneck stampede into the unknown. As long as it does, we can rest assured that the wrongs of the information era will not escape our moral grasp, but will inevitably succumb to the timeless dominion of justice.

Notes

Notes to
Introduction

1. Following the Norman Invasion, the crown devoted most of its resources to securing the property of the realm. Indeed, the earliest writs created by the royal courts were designed to resolve property disputes. *See* THEODORE F.T. PLUCKNETT, A CONCISE HISTORY OF THE COMMON LAW 355–62 (5th ed. 1956). The king's courts also retained exclusive jurisdiction over felonies like murder, treason and larceny. *Id.* at 442–49. It was not until the thirteenth century, with the introduction of traveling judicial eyres, that an action of trespass was recognized. *Id.* at 366–67. This action, which redressed such misconduct as assault, imprisonment and taking away chattels, is believed to be the forerunner to the modern theory of torts. *Id.* at 366, 458–61, 465–67.

2. *Id.* at 366.

3. *Id.* at 465–67.

4. *See* FREDERIC W. MAITLAND, THE FORMS OF ACTION AT COMMON LAW 65 (1941); *see generally* George E. Woodbine, *The Origin of the Action of Trespass*, 33 YALE L.J. 799 (1923).

5. Woodbine, *supra* note 4.

6. There is some disagreement on this point. Professor Street argued that the concept of negligence was unknown to the law of trespass. *See* THOMAS A. STREET, FOUNDATIONS OF LEGAL LIABILITY 76 (1906). Oliver Wendell Holmes, on the other hand, contended that the theory of trespass never was premised on the concept of absolute liability. *See* OLIVER W. HOLMES, THE COMMON LAW 89 (1938). Other scholars have taken more of a middle ground, but seem to acknowledge the presence of fault in the early common law. *See* CECIL H.S. FIFOOT, HISTORY AND SOURCES OF THE COMMON LAW, TORT AND CONTRACT 191 (1949); PERCY WINFIELD, LAW OF TORTS 49 (2d ed. 1943).

7. FIFOOT, *supra* note 6, at 191; PLUCKNETT, *supra* note 1, at 460.

8. This terminology comes from the seventeenth century case of Weaver v. Ward, 80 Eng. Rep. 284 (K.B. 1616). There, a soldier engaged in a military skirmish accidentally discharged his weapon, striking the plaintiff. The court indicated that the soldier might be excused from liability if he could show that the incident was "utterly without his fault."

9. PLUCKNETT, *supra* note 1, at 468–72; *see* Charles O. Gregory, *Trespass to Negligence to Absolute Liability*, 37 VA. L. REV. 359, 363–65 (1951).

10. *See generally* BERNARD SCHWARTZ, THE LAW IN AMERICA 1–21, 55–59 (1974) (discussing the selective reception of the common law by American courts and the gradual change in tort and other areas of law).

11. The Massachusetts case of Brown v. Kendall, 60 Mass. (6 Cush.) 292 (1850) is often credited as being the first American decision to openly recognize the requirement of

fault in a trespass action. However, much the same conclusion seems to have been reached in the earlier New York case of Harvey v. Dunlop, 39 N.Y.C.L. Rep. 193 (Hill & Dennio Supp. 1843). There, the court had declared: "No case or principle can be found, or if found can be maintained, subjecting an individual to liability for an act done without fault on his part." *Id.*

12. Nevertheless, there remained at least one area of the law where causal responsibility was still the key to recovery. In cases involving ultrahazardous activities, like blasting, a defendant who caused injury to his neighbor could be held liable for the damage inflicted even if he conducted the activity with care and diligence. *See* Gregory, *supra* note 9, at 370–82. However, this form of strict liability was rejected by many courts during the mid-nineteenth century and did not win general approval among the states for several decades thereafter. *See* JOHN W. WADE ET AL., PROSSER, WADE AND SCHWARTZ'S CASES AND MATERIALS ON TORTS 67–75, nn. 7, 8 (9th ed. 1994).

13. *See generally* Samuel J.M. Donnelly, *The Fault Principle: A Sketch of Its Development in Tort Law During the Nineteenth Century*, 18 SYRACUSE L. REV. 728 (1967) (examining the development of the fault principle in American tort law); *see also* Gregory, *supra* note 9 (same).

14. Insofar as tort law allows private parties to release the anger and frustration that comes from injurious encounters, it also serves the ulterior function of social control.

15. This view recently has been disputed by Gary Schwartz in an article entitled *Tort Law and the Economy in Nineteenth-Century America: A Reinterpretation*. Gary T. Schwartz, *Tort Law and the Economy in Nineteenth-Century America: A Reinterpretation*, 90 YALE L.J. 1717 (1981). In that piece, Professor Schwartz examined reported tort cases from New Hampshire and California. He concluded that, although large industrial concerns in those states enjoyed theoretical protection from the adoption of fault-based liability rules and the development of duty and contributory negligence defenses, in practice courts often were reluctant to apply these concepts broadly. *Id.*

16. The cigarette manufacturing industry's duty to warn is preempted by the Federal Cigarette Labeling and Advertising Act of 1965, 15 U.S.C.A. § 1334 (West 1982 & Supp. 1993). *See* Cippollone v. Liggett Group, Inc., 505 U.S. 504 (1992).

17. The Federal Insecticide, Fungicide, and Rodenticide Act, 7 U.S.C. § 136v (1988 & Supp. IV 1992) has been held to preempt the duty of labeling pesticides. *See* King v. E.I. du Pont de Nemours & Co., 996 F.2d 1346 (1st Cir. 1993); Arkansas-Platte & Gulf Partnership v. Van Water & Rogers, Inc., 959 F.2d 158 (10th Cir. 1992); Papas v. Upjohn Co., 926 F.2d 1019 (11th Cir. 1991).

18. Most courts have held that The Medical Device Amendments (MDA) of 1976 to the Federal Food, Drug and Cosmetic Act of 1938, 21 U.S.C. § 360(k)(a) (1981 & Supp. 1992) preempt all claims and cases involving Class III medical devices that received pre-market approval from the FDA. *See, e.g.,* Martello v. Ciba Vision Corp., 42 F.3d 1167 (8th Cir. 1994), *cert. denied*, 115 S. Ct. 2614 (1995); LeMay v. Eli Lilly & Co., 881 F. Supp. 428 (E.D. Wis. 1995); Mitchell v. Collagen Corp., 870 F. Supp. 885 (N.D. Ind. 1995). A few courts have created exceptions for claims involving express warranty and fraud. *See, e.g.,* Michael v. Shiley, Inc., 46 F.3d 1316 (3d Cir. 1995); Caraballo v. Intermedics, Inc., 886 F. Supp. 974 (D.P.R. 1995); Ministry of Health v. Shiley, Inc., 858 F. Supp. 1426 (C.D. Cal. 1994). Until recently, courts were split on whether preemption should apply to medical devices which received FDA appproval because they were sub-

stantially equivalent to other products already on the market. *Compare* Reeves v. AcroMed Corp., 44 F.3d 300 (5th Cir.), *cert. denied*, 115 S. Ct. 2251 (1995) (finding preemption) *with* Lohr v. Medtronic, Inc., 56 F.3d 1335 (11th Cir. 1995) (finding no preemption). In June of 1996, however, the United States Supreme Court held that the MDA do not preempt state product liability claims which challenge devices marketed under the substantial equivalency exception. *See* Medtronic, Inc. v. Lohr, 116 S. Ct. 2240 (1996).

19. *See generally* Richard C. Ausness, *Federal Preemption of State Products Liability Doctrines*, 44 S.C.L. REV. 187 (1993) (providing a broad overview of preemptive federal legislation and proposing a model of statutory interpretation).

20. Some states have modified the statute of limitations. *See* IDAHO CODE § 6-1401 (1980) (no liability beyond the product's "useful safe life"); ILL. REV. STAT., ch. 110 para. 13-213 (1979) (adopting twelve-year repose period); KAN. STAT. ANN. § 60-3303 (1981) (similar to Idaho). Several states have adopted a "state-of-the-art" defense. *See* ARIZ. REV. STAT. ANN. § 12-683–686 (1978); IOWA CODE § 668.12 (1986); MICH. COMP. LAWS § 600.2946 (1978); MO. REV. STAT. § 537.764 (1987) (failure-to-warn claims only). Other states have partially or totally exempted nonmanufacturers from strict liability. *See* DEL. CODE ANN., tit. 18, § 7001 (1989) (permits a "sealed container defense" unless the manufacturer is insolvent or otherwise not subject to liability); GA. CODE ANN. § 51-1-11.1 (1987) (bars nonmanufacturer liability under a theory of strict products liability); MD. CTS. & JUD. PROC. CODE ANN. § 5-311 (1982) (permits sealed container defense); MINN. STAT. § 544.41 (1980); MO. REV. STAT. § 537.72 (West 1987). A few states have enacted comprehensive products liability statutes. *See, e.g.,* IND. CODE § 33-1-1.5-1–1.5-8 (Supp. 1981); OHIO REV. CODE ANN. § 2307.71–.80 (Anderson Supp. 1989). *See generally* JAMES A. HENDERSON, JR. & AARON D. TWERSKI, PRODUCTS LIABILITY: PROBLEMS AND PROCESS 859–62, 875–79 (2d ed. 1992) (identifying specific state acts and charting the changes they effect).

21. In reaction to an assumed crisis in medical malpractice insurance rates and availability, all fifty states in the mid-1970s passed some form of legislation regulating various aspects of the patient-health care provider (HCL) relationship. Although the number of different medical malpractice statutes is as great as the number of states, many state enactments share certain common features. Among the more frequently adopted provisions are: (1) new statutes of limitations applicable only to medical malpractice claims; (2) prohibitions on the specification of dollar amounts in the ad damnum clauses of complaints; (3) enforcement of the collateral source evidentiary rule; (4) limitations on attorneys' fees; (5) creation of medical review panels (MRP) to review prospective malpractice claims; (6) limitations on plaintiffs' total recoveries; (7) limitations on the dollar liability of the health care provider; (8) institution of state-run patients' compensation funds; and (9) limitations on plaintiffs' ability to receive lump sum recovery of damages. *See* JAMES A. HENDERSON, JR. & RICHARD N. PEARSON, THE TORTS PROCESS 891 (3d ed. 1988) (citing Florida Medical Assoc., MMPC 16 (Manne ed. 1985)); *see also* MICHAEL D. MCCAFFERTY & STEVEN M. MEYER, MEDICAL MALPRACTICE, BASIS OF LIABILITY 463 (1985) (surveying state medical malpractice statutes).

22. Several state statutes limit recovery of pain and suffering damages. *See* COLO. REV. STAT. § 13-21-102.5 (1987) (allows recovery of $250,000 unless damage established by clear and convincing evidence, in which case limit is increased to $500,000); IDAHO CODE § 6-1603 (1987) (limits recovery to $400,000 adjusted by inflation); KAN. STAT. ANN.

§ 60-19a01 (caps general damages at $250,000); MD. CTS. & JUD. PROC. CODE ANN. § 11-108 (Supp. 1987) (caps general damages at $350,000). A few states have established new standards and limitations for punitive damages. *See* ALA. CODE § 6-11-21 (1987) (caps punitive damages at $250,000 absent evidence of pattern or practice of intentional wrongful conduct); COLO. REV. STAT. § 13-21-102 (1987) (caps punitive damages at three times the actual damages awarded and requires that one-third of this amount be paid to state general fund); FLA. STAT. § 768.73 (1986) (limits recovery of punitive damages to three times compensatory damages and mandates that 60% be paid to Public Medical Assistance Trust Fund); GA. CODE ANN. § 51-12-5.1 (Michie Supp. 1990) (provides only one punitive damage award per act or omission in products liability action and 75% must be paid to state treasury); UTAH CODE ANN. § 78-18-1 (1989) (requires proof by clear and convincing evidence of intentional fraud or knowing and reckless indifference; 50% of punitive damages exceeding $20,000 are remitted to state treasury).

23. The trend has been to recognize more intangible forms of harm, including emotional distress unaccompanied by physical manifestations, *see* St. Elizabeth Hosp. v. Garrard, 730 S.W.2d 649 (Tex. 1987) (citing similar cases in n.3), *overruled on other grounds by* Boyles v. Kerr, 855 S.W.2d 593 (Tex. 1993), and hedonic damages, *see* Sherrod v. Berry, 629 F. Supp. 159 (N.D. Ill. 1985), *rev'd and remanded on other grounds*, 856 F.2d 802 (7th Cir. 1988).

24. *See* Potter v. Firestone Tire & Rubber Co., 863 P.2d 795 (Cal. 1993) (fear of cancer); *see also* Jackson v. Johns-Manville Sales Corp., 781 F.2d 394 (5th Cir.) (same), *cert. denied*, 106 S.Ct. 3339 (1986); In re Moorenovich, 634 F. Supp. 634 (D. Me. 1986) (same).

25. *See* Potter, 863 P.2d 795 (allowing reovery of medical monitoring expenses where the plaintiff's monitoring is a reasonably certain consequence of the toxic exposure and the recommended monitoring is reasonable); *accord* Ayers v. Township of Jackson, 525 A.2d 287 (N.J. 1987).

26. *See* Gideon v. Johns-Manville Sales Corp., 761 F.2d 1129 (5th Cir. 1985) (allowing recovery for increased risk of cancer caused by inhaling asbestos fibers); Sterling v. Velsicol Chem. Corp., 647 F. Supp. 303 (W.D. Tenn. 1986) (characterizing enhanced susceptibility to disease as a presently existing condition); Elam v. Alcolac Inc., 765 S.W.2d 42 (Mo. Ct. App. 1988) (treating increased risk of cancer as the present invasion of a legally protected interest); *Ayers*, 525 A.2d 287 (allowing recovery for increased risk of cancer, but requiring that the risk be quantified); *see generally* Melissa Moore Thompson, *Enhanced Risk of Disease Claims: Limiting Recovery to Compensation for Loss, Not Chance*, 72 N.C. L. REV. 453 (1994) (surveying cases).

27. *See* Falcon v. Mem. Hosp., 462 N.W.2d 44 (Mich. 1990) (lost chance of surviving amniotic fluid embolism); Wollen v. DePaul Health Ctr., 828 S.W.2d 681 (Mo. 1992) (lost chance of surviving gastric cancer); Herskovits v. Group Health Coop., 664 P.2d 474 (Wash. 1983) (lost chance of surviving lung cancer).

28. *See* Sindell v. Abbott Labs., 607 P.2d 924 (Cal. 1980) (named defendants must constitute a substantial share of the relevent market); Abel v. Eli Lilly & Co., 343 N.W.2d 164 (Mich. 1984) (state market approach; all sellers of subject product must be joined as defendants), *cert. denied*, 469 U.S. 833 (1984); Hymowitz v. Eli Lilly & Co., 539 N.E.2d 1069 (N.Y. 1989) (national market approach; no causation-based excuse permitted); Martin v. Abbott Labs., 689 P.2d 368 (Wash. 1984) ("risk share" approach adopted);

Collins v. Eli Lilly & Co., 342 N.W.2d 37 (Wis. 1984) (only one manufacturer of the subject product need be named as defendant; causation-based excuse permitted), *cert. denied*, 469 U.S. 826 (1984).

29. *See* Hall v. E.I. du Pont de Nemours & Co., 345 F. Supp. 353 (E.D.N.Y. 1972) (allowing recovery where there are a small number of possible defendants and all jointly controlled the risks of the subject product, as through a trade association).

30. *See* Summers v. Tice, 199 P.2d 1 (Cal. 1948) (where two defendants act tortiously, but only one actually causes harm to the plaintiff, each bears the burden of proving that she was not the cause); *see also* RESTATEMENT (SECOND) OF TORTS § 433B(3) (1965).

31. *See* McBride v. United States, 462 F.2d 72 (9th Cir. 1972); Hicks v. United States, 368 F.2d 626 (4th Cir. 1966); Daniels v. Hadley Mem. Hosp., 566 F.2d 749 (D.C. Cir. 1977); Whitfield v. Whittaker Mem. Hosp., 169 S.E.2d 563 (Va. 1969).

32. Some have suggested that the tort system be replaced by private insurance schemes or public compensation systems. *See, e.g.*, JEFFREY O'CONNELL, ENDING INSULT TO INJURY: NO-FAULT INSURANCE FOR PRODUCTS LIABILITY AND SERVICES (1975); Mark Franklin, *Replacing the Negligence Lottery: Compensation and Selective Reimbursement*, 53 VA. L. REV. 774 (1967); Stephen D. Sugarman, *Doing Away With Tort Law*, 73 CAL. L. REV. 535 (1985); *see generally* GUIDO CALABRESI, THE COST OF ACCIDENTS: A LEGAL AND ECONOMIC ANALYSIS 3–13 (1970) (discussing several different proposals).

33. Aristotle's explanation of corrective justice appears in Book V of the Nichomachean Ethics. *See* ARISTOTLE, THE NICHOMACHEAN ETHICS V (D. Ross trans., revised by J.L. Ackrill & J.O. Urmson 1990) (Oxford Univ. Press, World Classics ed.) The concept of corrective justice is discussed at length in Chapter Eight.

34. *See* Richard W. Wright, *Substantive Corrective Justice*, 77 IOWA L. REV. 625, 627–29 nn.6, 7, 10–14 (1992) (citing the plethora of recent articles on the subject).

35. *Id.*

36. *See* Ernest J. Weinrib, *Corrective Justice*, 77 IOWA L. REV. 403, 411–12 (1992).

37. *Id.* at 421–24.

38. *See* Jules L. Coleman, *The Mixed Conception of Corrective Justice*, 77 IOWA L. REV. 427, 427 (1992); *see generally* JULES L. COLEMAN, RISKS AND WRONGS (1992).

39. *See* Jules L. Coleman, *The Practice of Corrective Justice*, 37 ARIZ. L. REV. 15, 28–29 (1995) (noting that although the duty to repair in corrective justice is pre-political, it is conditioned on the legal and political practices existing in the relevant community); *see also* Coleman, *supra* note 38, at 329–45 (defining wrongful conduct as the violation of important interests and legally recognized rights, not as a display of moral disrespect).

40. *See* Stephen R. Perry, *The Moral Foundations of Tort Law*, 77 IOWA L. REV. 449 (1992).

41. *See* Stephen R. Perry, *Comment on Coleman: Corrective Justice*, 67 IND. L. REV. 381, 403–04 (1992). Perry also grounds corrective justice on the violation of rights. *Id.* at 507–08.

42. *See* Wright, *supra* note 34.

43. *But see* Peter Benson, *The Basis of Corrective Justice and Its Relation to Distributive Justice*, 77 IOWA L. REV. 515 (1992) (discussing also distributive justice and justice in exchange); Perry, *supra* note 40 (discussing distributive justice); Wright, *supra* note 34 (also discussing distributive justice).

44. *See* RICHARD A. POSNER, THE PROBLEMS OF JURISPRUDENCE 328 (1990); Larry A. Alexander, *Foreword: Coleman and Corrective Justice*, 15 HARV. J. L. & PUB. POL'Y 621,

627–28 (1992); Jules L. Coleman, *Tort Law and the Demands of Corrective Justice*, 67 IND. L. J. 349, 361–62 n.12 (1992).

45. There is another scenario in this paradigm which does not generally involve tort law. This is where the actor unilaterally performs a service for another which bestows upon her a tangible benefit. Because the recipient has been unjustly enriched, the actor is entitled to compensation for her service. This transaction is typically referred to as a quasi-contract or a contract implied in law and is covered by contract law or the equitable doctrine of unjust enrichment. *See* Judy Beckner Sloan, *Quantum Meruit: Residual Equity in Law*, 42 DEPAUL L. REV. 399–462, n.1 (1992).

Notes to Chapter 1
Private and Political Justice

1. *See* ARISTOTLE, THE NICHOMACHEAN ETHICS 108–09, V.1, 1129b13–1130a26 (D. Ross trans., revised by J.L. Ackrill & J.O. Urmson 1990) (Oxford Univ. Press, World Classics ed.).

2. *Id.* at 117, V.5, 1131b11–33.

3. *Id.* at 65–67, III.7, 1115a35–1116a29.

4. *Id.* at 74–76, III.11, 1118a26–1119a26.

5. Ernest J. Weinrib, *Corrective Justice*, 77 IOWA L. REV. 403, 405 (1992).

6. *See* JOHN RAWLS, A THEORY OF JUSTICE 58–59 (1971).

7. *Id.* at 85–88.

8. Of course, in limited circumstances, a private party may also obtain an injunction to prevent a prospective wrongdoer from engaging in some potentially harmful activity.

Notes to Chapter 2
Justice and Rights

1. H.J. McClosky has argued that a right *is* an entitlement to certain goods. H.J. McClosky, *Rights*, 15 PHIL. Q. 115–127 (1965). Under this view, the entitlement is absolute, and cannot be outweighed by conflicting rights. I do not use the term in this strict sense. As used here, rights may be abstract (such as the right to be free from harm) and conditional (in most cases requiring a balancing of competing interests).

2. H.L.A. Hart, *Are There Any Natural Rights?*, 64 PHIL. REV. 175, 178 (1955).

3. Unlike secondary rights, primary rights may derive from natural law. There may be some interests so basic to human flourishing—like life and liberty—that everyone is entitled to their enjoyment, even when they are denied by positive law. *See* JOHN M. FINNIS, NATURAL LAW AND NATURAL RIGHTS 225 (1980); *see generally* Hart, *supra* note 2 (identifying and discussing the natural right to liberty). It is unlikely, however, that the abstract principles of natural law could determine the relative powers of action enjoyed by parties whose primary rights come into conflict. For example, when a motorist is faced with an impending head-on collision (through no fault of her own), does she have the right to protect her own life by swerving onto the sidewalk and killing a pedestrian? Here, each party

enjoys the natural right to life. While the motorist may be entitled to a natural right to self-defense or self-preservation, may she exercise that right against some innocent third party? Natural law provides no answers to these sticky moral dilemmas. In such cases, it would seem, the motorist's secondary right of action, if any, must emanate from the fact-specific provisions of the positive law.

4. The concept of rights clusters is discussed in further detail in JOEL FEINBERG, RIGHTS, JUSTICE AND THE BOUNDS OF LIBERTY 130 (1980).

5. *Id.* (explaining how a hiker stranded on a snow-covered mountain would be justified in entering the cabin of another and burning the furniture in order to stay warm).

6. This view has been disputed by some rights theorists. Theodore Benditt, for example, has contended that rights *are* absolute. THEODORE M. BENDITT, RIGHTS 40 (1982). According to Benditt, "*if* a right exists at *t*, then it cannot be overridden, or non-accorded, or in any way made inoperative except as the right-holder wishes not to act, or insist, on it." *Id.* The notion that rights are absolute also has been endorsed by Joel Feinberg. *See* JOEL FEINBERG, SOCIAL PHILOSOPHY (1973). Feinberg views rights as a type of property which may not be dispossessed. Under this theory, one must distinguish between recognizing and according rights in cases of conflict. Whereas superseded prima facie rights are neither recognized nor accorded to the "losing" party, absolute rights are unconditionally recognized even if they are not accorded in certain situations. *Id.*

7. J.L. Mackie, who advocates this view, explains prima facie rights as follows:

> [T]he rights that in the end people have, their final rights, must result from compromises between their initially conflicting rights. These compromises will have to be worked out in practice, but will be morally defensible only insofar as they reflect the equality of the *prima facie* rights. This will not allow trivial interests of any to be sacrificed for the advantage of others, to be outweighed by an aggregate of less vital interests. Rather we might think in terms of a model in which each person is represented by a point-center of force, and the forces (representing *prima facie* rights) obey an inverse square law, so that a right decreases in weight with the remoteness of the matter on which it bears from the person whose right it is. There will be some matters so close to each person that, with respect to them, his rights will nearly always outweigh any aggregate of other rights, though admittedly it will sometimes happen that issues arise in which the equally vital interests of two or more people clash.

J.L. Mackie, *Can There Be a Right-Based Moral Theory?*, in PETER FRENCH ET AL., STUDIES IN ETHICAL THEORY 356 (1978); *see also* JOSEPH RAZ, THE MORALITY OF FREEDOM 184 (1986) ("A general right is…only a prima facie ground for the existence of a particular right in circumstances to which it applies.").

Notes to Chapter 3
Harm

1. *See* JOEL FEINBERG, RIGHTS, JUSTICE AND THE BOUNDS OF LIBERTY 45 (1980).
2. *Id.*

3. *Id.* at 62 (focusing on wants linked to a life plan).

4. *Id.* at 32–33, 46.

5. *Id.* at 33, 46.

6. *Id.* at 45. Feinberg believes this interference must be objective and not merely premised on the victim's subjective frustration in failing to have her want satisfied. *Id.* at 62–64.

7. However, if the confinement is of long duration it may produce the type of physical or psychological harm which is irreversible.

8. *See* DiCosta v. Aeronaves De Mexico, 973 F.2d 1490 (9th Cir. 1992) (recognizing a cause of action for those in the zone of danger, but confirming that spectators held no right of recovery).

9. *See* Harris v. Jones, 380 A.2d 611 (Md. 1977) (employee sensitive about his stuttering affliction not permitted to recover against supervisor who constantly ridiculed and mimicked him).

10. It is not unjust to deny recovery on the basis of such administrative concerns. In political associations, justice is dispensed by the state through its courts. But the state's capacity to secure justice is limited; it can only afford so many courtrooms, judges and administrative personnel. Thus, justice itself is a limited commodity which must be carefully distributed by the state in accordance with some fair criteria. *See infra* Chapter Seven (discussing the requirements of distributive justice); *see also* H.L.A. HART, THE CONCEPT OF LAW 161–63 (1961). The administrative concerns discussed in the text are premised on the criteria of need and merit. Thus, the greater the wrong to the victim, the more urgent her need for justice will be; and the greater the victim's need, the more meritorious her claim-right will be. On the other hand, where the victim's harm is trivial or speculative, the priority of her claim is much lower. Allowing such claims equal access to the courts disturbs this fair proportion and threatens to deplete the resources necessary to vindicate more substantial wrongs. This would be a far greater injustice than denying even a multitude of marginally worthy claims.

11. *See* Dougherty v. Stepp, 18 N.C. 371 (1835).

12. *Cf.* Coleman v. Employment Sec. Dept., 607 P.2d 1231 (Wash. Ct. App. 1980).

Notes to Chapter 4
Causal Responsibility

1. So long as they are foreseeable.

2. Even where the parties have contracted, the concept of causal responsibility provides a state-sanctioned reason for enforcing the agreement strictly against its signatories and not others foreign to it.

3. Although, as has been indicated previously, it is only by virtue of such duties that we enjoy the right to be free from the harmful intrusions of others.

4. In the right circumstances, even a private citizen can act to prevent the commission of a crime in her presence. Under the common law, a private citizen may arrest an actor for a felony if the crime actually occurred and she reasonably believes the actor committed the offense. Private citizens must directly witness a misdemeanor offense committed by

the actor in order to effect an arrest. A private citizen may use nondeadly force if she reasonably believes that an actor is committing or has committed a felony or misdemeanor and such force is necessary to prevent the commission or consummation of the offense. *See* RESTATEMENT (SECOND) OF TORTS §§ 118, 119 (1965).

5. They may not always restrict the autonomy of the risk-creator, and when they are so authorized, the form of their response will vary with the circumstances.

6. *See* Cordas v. Peerless Transp. Co., 27 N.Y.S.2d 198 (Sup. Ct. 1941).

7. As a general rule, one may not use force to recover personal property. *See* RESTATEMENT (SECOND) OF TORTS § 106 (1965). However, if the property owner acts promptly after the dispossession, she may employ reasonable, nondeadly force to take back her chattel. *See id.* § 103. Yet she must be careful. Should she use excessive force in her reclamation attempt, she may be held liable for any loss cuased by the abuse of her privilege. *See id.* § 107.

8. *Cordas*, 27 N.Y.S.2d at 202.

9. *Id.*

10. *Id.*

11. This hypothetical is loosely premised on an example used by Jules Coleman in his recent book, *Risks and Wrongs. See* JULES L. COLEMAN, RISKS AND WRONGS 274 (1992). In Coleman's example, however, the injured party does not misbehave, she simply slips on the snow-covered sidewalk. Under those circumstances, Coleman broadly concludes that causation principles would play no role in the determination of the property owner's liability. Rather, he argues that the property owner's liability is premised solely upon her normative responsibility in failing to shovel the snow. This seems correct. Indeed, it explains why in my illustration A would be required to bear her own loss. Under the facts as presented, my duty to shovel the snow does not extend to those like A who voluntarily slide across my sidewalk. I also believe, however, that my nonliability may be premised upon my lack of causal responsibility for the injuries sustained by A. To the extent that A's actions were intentional, she held the power to prevent her own misfortune. Had she elected to behave prudently or to take her mischief elsewhere, the accident on my sidewalk would not have occurred.

Notes to Chapter 5
Wrongdoing

1. *See* H.L.A. HART & TONY HONORÉ, CAUSATION IN THE LAW (2d ed. 1980); JUDITH JARVIS-THOMPSON, RIGHTS, RESTITUTION AND RISK 201–02 (1986); Steven R. Perry, *The Moral Foundations of Tort Law*, 77 IOWA L. REV. 449 (1992).

2. In 1991, 179,422 people were injured using ladders or stools; 152,770 people were injured in the bathtub or shower; and 1,693,175 people were injured on stairs, ramps, landings and floors. In 1991, 1,600,000 people were injured and 41,200 people died in motor vehicle accidents. *See* U.S. Department of Commerce, Economics and Statistics Administration Bureau of the Census; Statistical Abstract of the U.S., 131 & 611 (1993).

3. Wrongfulness is being used here in the narrow moral sense of unfairness. Where someone acts without the intent to cause harm, her conduct is not immoral in the general

sense of that term. However, it may be unjust in the particular sense of being unfair. One who acts unfairly breaches two duties. By transgressing a state-imposed rule requiring fair conduct, she violates a duty owed to society generally. If her action also exposes others to danger, she would owe an additional, specific duty to secure the interests of those endangered. If she breaches that duty, her conduct is a personal wrong only to the members of the protected class. It would not, however, be personally wrongful or unfair to others lacking such an entitlement. Thus, in the illustration mentioned in the text, if driving my car *is* in some sense a private wrong, it would be deemed inappropriate only for those unlucky motorists who happen to be in my path. It would not be personally wrongful to others who because of time or distance are completely immune from the potential destructive force of my car.

4. This is not to say that inaction can never amount to wrongdoing, only that under the facts of my hypothetical, harboring ill will toward the frustrated race car driver is not an act capable of condemnation. Later, we shall see that, when one is in a special relationship with another, such that she owes her counterpart a duty of protection, her failure to provide the required benefit can be every bit as wrongful as an affirmative act of misconduct.

5. In this sense, a duty is simply the constraining effect which an entitlement has upon the bearer. Sometimes it may require the bearer to provide her with an affirmative benefit; on other occasions it may dictate merely that the duty-bound party refrain from invading her vested interests. In either case, two things are clear: no entitlement can exist without a corresponding duty, and once such a duty is created, it establishes between the parties a special relational bond.

6. One of these elements is negative in nature and only implied by what we have observed above. It is the absence of the entitled party's consent to relieve the duty-bound actor of the responsibility she would otherwise owe. In a political system founded on the liberty of choice, such consent would effectively eliminate the other's duty of care and replace it with a right to appropriate the holder's interests. If consent is lacking, however, the three other elements discussed within must be established to show that an act is wrongful.

7. I will not distinguish between duties, which arise involuntarily, and obligations, which are created by agreement. *See* JOHN RAWLS, A THEORY OF JUSTICE 114 (1971). From here on, the terms will be used interchangeably.

8. Aristotle was a strong proponent of this view. He suggested, and few would contest, that the object of life is the pursuit of some conception of virtue. The ultimate good, according to Aristotle, is happiness. But happiness can be achieved in many different ways by aspiring to one of a number of other virtues. For the scholar, happiness is the pursuit of knowledge. For the artist it is aesthetics. For the cleric, piety. No matter what one's objective, all must formulate some life plan designed to achieve this end. That is, each individual must take the steps necessary to attain her own conception of virtue.

Two conditions are indispensable to this objective. One is the existence of choice between favorable and unfavorable options. Choosing good over evil is, after all, what we mean by virtue. The other condition for following a life plan is freedom of action. Most virtues cannot be obtained passively; rather, they require the performance of good acts which demonstrate an excellence of character. Both the ability to choose and the liberty to act are attributes of autonomy.

To exercise the freedoms of choice and action, one must possess a measure of independence. This has a couple of implications. It means, first off, that the individual is essentially self-sufficient. By self-sufficiency, I have in mind one who possesses the mental faculties required for making rational decisions and the physical capability of carrying them out. In addition, the individual must be free from outside compulsion. Compulsion may take the form of either manipulation or coercion by force or threat. Because individuals subject to such compulsion are deprived of choice and/or action, they enjoy very little autonomy.

Such is the predicament of those existing in a state of nature. Although everyone appears to enjoy unrestricted freedom, this is an illusion for all but the strongest and most cunning within the group. In reality, those less naturally endowed possess no freedom at all. They are always vulnerable to the coercive will of the rulers, who may appropriate their possessions, limit their actions or take their lives without fear of reprisal. For individuals trapped in this sorry state, there is no guarantee of survival, and little hope of human fulfillment.

Human flourishing can be secured, if at all, only in a political association. Here, the rule by force is replaced by a rule of law. Through law, the state protects each individual from the aggression of others. No longer subject to the demands of others, all citizens now possess the freedom to pursue a life plan.

9. See H.L.A. HART, THE CONCEPT OF LAW 167–68 (1961); see also RAWLS, supra note 7, at 114–17; JOSEPH RAZ, THE MORALITY OF FREEDOM 182 (1986); H.L.A. Hart, *Are There Any Natural Rights?*, 64 PHIL. REV. 175, 187–88 (1955) (discussing general rights).

10. See HART, supra note 9, at 167.

11. *Id.* at 185.

12. *Id.* at 183–84.

13. *Id.* at 184.

14. *Id.* at 185.

15. The discussion of mutual restrictions in this paragraph is based on *id.* at 185–87; see also RAZ, supra note 9, at 176–77.

16. *Id.* at 180; see also THEODORE M. BENDITT, RIGHTS 18–19 (1983) (aunt not mother).

17. Hart believes the mother would not have a right to enforce the promise. See HART, supra note 9, at 180. *But see* David Lyons, *Rights, Claimants & Beneficiaries*, 6 AM. PHIL. Q. 173, 180–84 (1969) (taking opposite view).

18. See RESTATEMENT (SECOND) OF CONTRACTS § 302 (1981) (dealing with intended beneficiaries).

19. *Id.* § 90 (premising the right on promissory estoppel).

20. As was the case in Erie R. Co. v. Stewart, 40 F.2d 855 (6th Cir. 1930) and Will v. S. Pac. Co., 116 P.2d 44 (Cal. 1941).

21. Except where the duty arises from a referendum-type initiative or a legislatively enacted statute. Even here, it would be hard to say that those in the minority actually gave their consent.

22. This assumes that there is a direct and continuous causal connection between the actor's conduct and the injury sustained by the victim. The critical question as to causation in intentional torts is whether the actor's conduct is a substantial factor in bringing about the type of harm which she intended from her original act. See Tate v. Canonica, 5 Cal. Rptr. 28, 35 (Ct. App. 1960) ("[N]o consideration is given to the fact that after the event it appears highly extraordinary that it should have brought about such harm or that the actor's conduct has created a situation harmless unless acted upon by other forces for which the actor is not responsible.... [T]he notion of independent intervening cause has no

place in the law of intentional torts, so long as there is a factual chain of causation."); *see also* U.S. Fidelity & Guar. Co. v. Am. Employer's Ins. Co., 205 Cal. Rptr. 460, 465 (Ct. App. 1984).

23. 162 N.E. 99 (N.Y. 1928)

24. As H.L.A. Hart has observed, this aspect of a right "form[s] a kind of moral property of individuals to which they are as individuals entitled." *See* HART, *supra* note 9.

Notes to Chapter 6
Two Senses of Justice

1. *See generally* ARISTOTLE, THE NICHOMACHEAN ETHICS 106–09, V.1 (D. Ross Trans., revised by J.L. Ackrill & J.O. Urmson 1990) (Oxford Univ. Press, World Classics ed.) (explaining justice in the broad sense).

2. *Id.* at 109–117, V.2–4 (discussing justice in the particular sense, and comparing it to the broad sense of justice).

3. *Id.* at 108–09, V.1, 1129b13–1130a26.

4. *Id.* at 110, V.2, 1130a26–b18.

5. *See* Steven J. Heyman, *Aristotle on Political Justice*, 77 IOWA L. REV. 851 (1992).

6. *See* ARISTOTLE, POLITICS I.2, 1252b27–1253a19 (Carnes Lord trans. 1984).

7. *See* ARISTOTLE, *supra* note 1, at 108, V.1, 1129b13–1130a6.

8. *Id.*

9. *Id.* at 107, V.1, 1129a23–b13.

10. *Id.* at 48, III.1, 1110a1–10.

11. *Id.* at 125–26, V.8, 1135a5–b15.

12. *Id.* at 127, V.8, 1135b15–1136a2.

13. *Id.*

14. Some types of behavior which many would consider immoral are not proscribed by law. A good example is the rule of nonliability for failures to provide assistance to others in distress. *See* RESTATEMENT (SECOND) OF TORTS § 314 (1965); *see also* Yania v. Bigan, 155 A.2d 343 (Pa. 1959) (wherein the court held that a bystander had no duty to rescue); Bishop v. City of Chicago, 257 N.E.2d 152 (Ill. App. Ct. 1970) (wherein the court held that a bystander owed no duty to rescue another, no matter how easily and safely it might be accomplished). Other forms of conduct which *are* legally forbidden do not seem to offend our moral sensibilities. Such might be the case where one drives five miles per hour above the speed limit on a deserted, rural road, or goes through a stop light in the dead of night when no other cars are within sight.

15. The assumption here is that all those deserving the protection of such a right are similarly deprived.

16. For example, in racial discrimination cases prior to the enactment of civil rights laws.

17. *See* MODEL PENAL CODE § 2.02 (1962) (describing types of mens rea, including criminal intent).

18. *See* RESTATEMENT (SECOND) OF TORTS § 8A (1965) (tortious intent is an actor's desire to produce the consequences of his act, or his belief that such consequences are substantially certain to result from it).

19. *See infra* Chapter Ten.

20. *See* ARISTOTLE, *supra* note 1, at 109–10, V.2, 1130a6–b18.

21. Except for another human being. Aristotle specifically mentions "honour or money or safety." *Id.* at 110, V.2, 1130a26–b18.

Notes to Chapter 7
Distributive Justice

1. *See* ARISTOTLE, THE NICHOMACHEAN ETHICS V.3, 112, 1131a6–27 (D. Ross trans., revised by J.L. Ackrill & J.O. Urmson 1990) (Oxford Univ. Press, World Classics ed.).

2. *Id.* at 113–14, V.3, 1131a27–1132a2.

3. *See* Ernest J. Weinrib, *Corrective Justice*, 77 IOWA L. REV. 403, 408 (1992).

4. *See* ARISTOTLE, *supra* note 1, at 112, V.3, 1131a6–27.

5. *Id.* at 113, V.3, 1131a27–b14.

6. Why is "need" considered a fair distributive criterion? Any political association involves a kind of compact between the state and the individuals who comprise it. The state provides the means necessary to survival; in return, the members of the association must obey the laws which make survival possible. As a result of this arrangement, each individual would seem to have an affirmative entitlement to the basic necessities of life. *See* NEIL MACCORMICK, LEGAL RIGHT AND SOCIAL DEMOCRACY: 15, 42–43 (1982); *see also* JOHN M. FINNIS, NATURAL LAW AND NATURAL RIGHTS 170–71 (1980); JOHN RAWLS, A THEORY OF JUSTICE 14–15, 75–83 (1971) (discussing the "difference principle" that economic inequalities are just only if they benefit the least advantaged members of society). Such primary goods are indispensable to our mental and physical well-being, which in turn represent the most basic attributes of our autonomy. While most individuals will be able to provide these necessities for themselves, there will always be some who cannot. In such cases, it would be fair to distribute a greater share of these primary goods to the needy, who will enjoy no autonomy without them, than to others more fortunate. Indeed, it is only because those less well off have agreed to follow the rule of law that those more fortunate have been able to attain that station. For if the state breaks the compact (by failing to provide necessities to the needy), and releases the underclass from the obligation to obey the law, there is little doubt that the well-to-do will be the first target of aggression. *See* FINNIS, *supra*, at 172–73.

7. I say it is limited because no one in a political association may enjoy absolute freedom. Instead, every individual must refrain from intentionally causing harm to others.

8. For example, the First Amendment right to free speech not only affords me the liberty of expressing myself, it also imposes upon others the duty to refrain from stopping me. Conversely, my duty not to trespass upon the property of my neighbor does not just limit my autonomy, it establishes my neighbor's right to prevent me from doing so.

9. Distributive justice ensures that both public and private laws promulgated by the state fairly allocate autonomy rights among all citizens. Every law either bestows some positive liberty or, more commonly, secures some negative liberty. Public law usually involves positive liberties. For example, the Constitution preserves our basic freedoms of speech, press, assembly and free exercise of religion. And, as we have seen, certain mater-

ial entitlements, such as welfare, are created and distributed through statutory law. Conversely, private law, including the law of torts, usually establishes our negative liberty interest in being left alone by others. Even though such laws often are used to resolve private disputes, they are still a matter of distributive justice. This is evident when one considers the nature of private law. Private law empowers private citizens to take some preventative or corrective action against those that threaten or harm them. These powers are triggered by certain rules of conduct. If an individual fails to conform to the behavioral requirement of the private law, the state's distributive restriction on the offending conduct is enforced by requiring the offender to make reparation to the party harmed. As with any type of distribution, the responsibility allocated to the actor by the state must be fair. If the law imposes behavioral requirements arbitrarily, allowing some individuals more autonomy than others similarly situated, then it fails the test of proportional equality, and is unjust.

10. Intellectual property law is concerned with protecting creative ideas. Such protection is provided by a variety of legal mechanisms, including utility patents, trade secrets, copyrights, trademarks, design patents, plant patents, plant variety protection, semiconductor mask work production, false advertising remedies, misappropriation, and publicity rights. The elements of an intellectual property right are: (1) the subject matter it covers; (2) the substantive requirements for obtaining it; (3) the method of obtaining it; (4) its content; and (5) its duration. *See* DONALD S. CHISUM & MICHAEL A. JACOBS, UNDERSTANDING INTELLECTUAL PROPERTY LAW §§ 1A, 1B (1992); *see also* EARL W. KINTER & JACK LAHR, AN INTELLECTUAL PROPERTY PRIMER 2–3 (2d ed. 1982).

11. Adverse possession functions as a method of transferring interests in land without the consent of the prior owner, and even in spite of the dissent of such owner. It rests upon social judgments that there should be a restricted duration for the assertion of "aging claims" and that the lapse of a reasonable time should assure security to a person claiming to be the owner. *See* RICHARD R. POWELL & PATRICK J. ROHAN, POWELL ON REAL PROPERTY 7:1012[2][a] (1975). The theory upon which adverse possession rests is that the adverse possessor may acquire title at such time as an action in ejectment by the record owner would be barred by the statute of limitations. *Id.*

The law of adverse possession differs among jurisdictions, partly because of differently worded statutory provisions, and partly because of different judicial attitudes about what constitutes "possession," and about the circumstances which will justify calling possession "adverse." Nonetheless, state courts are in general agreement that to be successful, an adverse possession claimant must prove that her possession of another's land was: (1) hostile and under a claim of right; (2) exclusive; (3) open and notorious; (4) actual; and (5) continuous for the requisite period. In addition, the owner must have notice of the adverse claim of the possessor. *Id.* Such possession must be shown by clear and convincing evidence. *Id.*

The kind of possession necessary to establish title to property by adverse possession need not always be personal possession by the adverse claimant, but may sometimes be established by conduct of another person so authorized by the claimant. The character of the disputed property is crucial in determining what degree of control and what character of possession is required to establish adverse possession. Thus, wild and undeveloped land that is not readily susceptible to habitation, cultivation, or improvement does not require the same quality of possession as residential or arable land, since the usual acts of ownership are impossible or unreasonable. *Id.*

12. Assuming the parties to a contract have roughly equal bargaining power, one dissatisfied with her bargain usually may not rescind the agreement without falling into breach. *See* Weaver v. Am. Oil Co., 276 N.E.2d 144 (Ind. 1971).

13. *See* The Medicaid Act, 42 U.S.C. §§ 1396–1396n (1982) (establishing a comprehensive scheme whereby the federal government assists states in providing medical assistance to aged, blind, or disabled individuals whose income and resources are insufficient to meet the costs of necessary medical services).

14. *See* U.C.C § 2-302 (1978) (stating that a court may refuse to enforce a contract or particular clause that it finds to be unconscionable); *see also* RESTATEMENT (SECOND) OF CONTRACTS § 178 (1981) (stating that a term or agreement is unenforceable where public policy outweighs the interest in enforcement).

15. *See* Int'l Harvester Co. v. Sartain, 222 S.W.2d 854 (Tenn. Ct. App. 1948) (suppliers of electricity are burdened with the requirement that they exercise the highest degree of care which skill and foresight can obtain); *see also* Lewis v. Buckskin Joe's, Inc., 396 P.2d 933 (Colo. 1964) (amusement park operator and driver of stagecoach ride had duty of exercising highest degree of care toward paying stagecoach passengers); Harvey v. Zell, 73 S.E.2d 605, 608 (Ga. 1952) (gas company must use highest degree of care to prevent injury from gas escaping from the company's lines); Oliver v. Union Transfer Co., 71 S.W.2d 478 (Tenn. Ct. App. 1934) (common carriers have a heightened duty of care towards their passengers).

16. How can one tell whether an incapacitated party has truly chosen to expose herself to a risk of harm, or if the risk has been imposed upon her against her will? There are several considerations which would be relevant to this delicate evaluation. These include the probability of harm from the act (one that a person with average capacities would accept?); the seriousness of the harm (based on the value of the interest invaded); the probability that the victim's goal would result from the risky activity; the value of the goal in furthering the victim's life plan; and the necessity of the risk in the activity (are there alternatives which would accomplish the goal with less risk?). *See* JOEL FEINBERG, RIGHTS, JUSTICE AND THE BOUNDS OF LIBERTY 115 (1980). If, on balance, it appears that no reasonable person in the victim's position would have encountered the danger, the state might distribute to the injury-producing actor a greater responsibility to refrain from the risky activity, even though the victim herself appeared to prefer it. In other words, in effecting such a distribution, internal and external incapacities serve as valid subcriteria for treating the actor differently from all others.

17. *See* RESTATEMENT (SECOND) OF CONTRACTS § 14 (1981) (stating that a person under eighteen years of age can incur only voidable contractual duties); *accord* Pettit v. Liston, 191 P. 660 (Or. 1920); *see also* RESTATEMENT (SECOND) OF CONTRACTS § 15 (1981) (stating that a person who is cognitively or behaviorally impaired can incur only voidable contractual duties); *accord* Ortelere v. Teacher's Retirement Bd., 250 N.E.2d 460 (N.Y. 1969) (same).

18. *See* Roth v. Union Depot Co., 43 P. 641, 647 (Wash. 1896) ("[I]t would be a monstrous doctrine to hold that a child of inexperience—and experience can come only with years—should be held to the same degree of care in avoiding danger as a person of mature years and accumulated experience.").

19. Older children, however, might be held liable for engaging in adult or inherently dangerous activities. *See* Goodfellow v. Coggburn, 560 P.2d 873 (Idaho 1977) (driving tractor); Williams v. Esaw, 522 P.2d 950 (Kan. 1974) (riding motorcycle); Dellwo v. Pearson, 107 N.W.2d 859 (Minn. 1961) (operating motorboat); *see also* RESTATEMENT (SEC-

OND) OF TORTS § 283A (1965) (stating that a child's conduct must conform to that of a reasonable person of like age, intelligence and experience).

20. There is a strong argument that the responsibility owed to a party suffering a relational incapacity does not derive from a general distributive duty, but arises from a special duty assumed by the party in the dominant position.

21. *See* Ploof v. Putnam, 71 A. 188 (Vt. 1908).

22. *Id.* at 175.

23. These consideration were derived from FEINBERG, *supra* note 16, at 32, 114–15. Once these considerations are weighed, and the distributive regulation is established, implementation of the rule will have a bilateral effect. Not only will the rule inform the behavior of those who participate in the regulated activity, it also will shape the expectations of those individuals affected by their actions. Such expectations, in turn, will influence how these others will act in response to the risk. For example, if acquiring a license were the only distributive restriction on the act of driving a car, all but the most brazen would stay off the streets. In such a scenario, there is a reverse reciprocal relationship between the autonomy rights of drivers and pedestrians. As the freedom to drive without traffic constraints increases, the freedom to walk the streets safely declines. Thus, so long as the driver does not exceed her distributed right to drive (or violate her responsibility to obtain a license), pedestrians injured by the driver nevertheless have not been wronged, since they were not guaranteed the freedom from such a danger. This highlights an obvious but important point. Built into any social scheme is a certain degree of acceptable or unpreventable risk that all must bear as a cost of enjoying the benefits of political association.

24. Whether the risk is great or small, if the interest invaded is not critical to the victim's exercise of autonomy, the state would not be justified in restricting the injury-producing activity. Here, there is no right in need of protection.

25. Such restrictions, or regulations, are usually promulgated by government agencies. These agencies, for example, can dictate how employers are to maintain their physical plants, *see* Occupational Safety and Health Act of 1970, 29 U.S.C.A. § 651 *et seq.* (West 1985 & Supp. 1993), and how (and when) drug companies are to market their products, *see* Federal Food, Drug, and Cosmetic Act of 1938, 21 U.S.C.A. § 301 *et seq.* (West 1972 & Supp. 1993). If the regulation is not followed, the entire activity can be curtailed even if no one is injured.

26. For example, Johns-Manville was forced to file for bankruptcy because of the extensive liability it incurred from selling asbestos. *See* In re Johns-Manville Corp., 36 Bankr. 743 (S.D.N.Y. 1984); *see generally* Note, *The Manville Bankruptcy: Treating Mass Tort Claims in Chapter 11 Proceedings*, 96 HARV. L. REV. 1121 (1983).

Notes to Chapter 8
Corrective Justice

1. Margaret Jane Radin has argued that the purpose of corrective justice may not be to rectify all wrongful losses, but merely to redress them in some way. Such redress may not require that the victim receive compensation for the damages sustained in an injurious transaction. Rather, it may only dictate that the wrongdoer make some gesture of suppli-

cation to the victim. This gesture could be the payment of money or anything else of value to the wrongdoer. The significance of this gesture is twofold. It extinguishes the victim's moral outrage over the act and/or its consequences. And, perhaps even more importantly, it demonstrates society's concern for the moral worth of the victim. *See* Margaret Jane Radin, *Compensation and Commensurability*, 43 DUKE L.J. 56, 73–74 (1993).

2. Aristotle does not explain what makes an interaction wrongful. Thus, commentators have attempted to fill this void with theories of their own. As noted in the introduction to this book, Ernest Weinrib has argued that an encounter is wrongful when the conduct of the initiator evinces a disrespect for the *moral or abstract* right of the victim. *See* Ernest J. Weinrib, *Corrective Justice*, 77 IOWA L. REV. 403, 421–24 (1992). Jules Coleman and Stephen Perry both argue that wrongfulness involves the violation of a *legal* right. *See* JULES L. COLEMAN, RISKS AND WRONGS 329–45 (1992) (also arguing that wrongdoing may consist of an unjustifiable invasion of an interest which is not protected by a right); Stephen R. Perry, *The Moral Foundations of Tort Law*, 77 IOWA L. REV. 449, 507–08 (1992).

Because of the breadth of these theories, it is not possible to review them in detail here. In any event, each has received extensive consideration elsewhere. Weinrib's theory recently has been criticized by Richard Wright. *See* Richard W. Wright, *Substantive Corrective Justice*, 77 IOWA L. REV. 625, 631–64 (1992). An entire symposium has been dedicated to analyzing Coleman's work. *See Symposium on Risks and Wrongs*, 15 HARV. J.L. & PUB. POL'Y 621 (1992) (reviewing Coleman's book, *Risks and Wrongs*). Perry's view was discussed in Claire O. Finkelstein, *Tort Law as a Comparative Institution: Reply to Perry*, 15 HARV. J.L. & PUB. POL'Y 940 (1992). Insofar as my view of tort justice also is rights-based, it bears a greater resemblance to the theories of Coleman and Perry, though beyond this affinity the differences are considerable. The theories of Weinrib and Coleman are considered further in the Epilogue.

3. Jules Coleman has suggested that corrective justice does not require that the actor benefit from her act, only that the injured party sustain a wrongful loss. See Jules L. Coleman, *Corrective Justice and Wrongful Gain*, 11 J. Legal Stud. 421, 425-26 (1982). There is some support for this in the *Ethics*. At one point Aristotle comments:

> [I]t makes no difference whether a good man has defrauded a bad man or a bad man a good one, nor whether it is a good or a bad man that has committed adultery; the law looks only to the distinctive character of the injury, and treats the parties as equal, if one is in the wrong and the other is being wronged, and if one inflicted injury and the other has received it.

ARISTOTLE, THE NICHOMACHEAN ETHICS 114–15, V.4, 1131b14–1132a25 (D. Ross Trans., revised by J.L. Ackrill & J.O. Urmson 1990) (Oxford Univ. Press, World Classics ed.) (emphasis added).

However, in this passage, Aristotle is not so much delineating the requirements of corrective justice as he is distinguishing that form of justice from the demands of distributive justice. Distributive justice determines how public resources are allocated among individuals in the first instance. This distribution establishes the status quo which exists between parties prior to voluntary or involuntary interactions. Corrective justice, Aristotle notes, has no concern with the fairness of this original distribution. It simply does not matter, for purposes of corrective justice, that some individuals are more morally or materially deserving of the resource than others. Once this distribution is disrupted, such that one party suffers some cognizable loss, corrective justice demands rectification regardless of the character or status of the parties. This appears all that Aristotle intends to profess when he states that the law "looks only to the distinctive character of the injury."

Support for this interpretation is found elsewhere in the *Ethics*. Indeed, as I have already noted, Aristotle's formula for determining rectification is premised on finding the mean between loss *and gain*, between deficiency and excess. Arguably it would be impossible to make such a determination with only one-half of the necessary factors. Still, it might be argued that in some cases no tangible benefit accrues to the actor, and thus the "gain" factor necessarily is absent. But Aristotle clearly rejects this notion. He notes that corrective justice would apply even where one party's only purpose in acting was to inflict a wound upon another. *Id.* at 115, V.4, 1132a2–25. Here, the actor receives an abstract or personal benefit from her aggressive conduct. As Aristotle clarifies, "the term gain is applied generally to such cases—even if it be not a term appropriate to certain cases, e.g. to the person who inflicts a wound—and 'loss' to the sufferer; at all events when the suffering has been estimated, the one is called loss and the other gain." *Id.*

4. *Id.* at 110, V.2, 1130a26–b18.

5. Besides money, one may seek to gain "honours" or safety. *Id.*

6. *Id.* at 115, V.4, 1132a2–25.

7. *See* THE ORATIONS OF DEMOSTHENES 333 (C.R. Kennedy trans. 1856).

8. *Id.* at 330.

9. *Id.* at 330–31.

10. *See* H.L.A. HART, THE CONCEPT OF LAW 160–61 (1961).

11. *See* ARISTOTLE, *supra* note 3, at 115–16, V.4, 1132a2–b9.

12. There are some who believe that corrective justice is a procedural mechanism only. *See, e.g.*, Steven D. Smith, *The Critics and the 'Crisis:' A Reassessment of Current Conceptions of Tort Law*, 72 CORNELL L. REV. 765 (1987); Catherine Pierce Wells, *Tort Law as Corrective Justice: A Pragmatic Justification for Jury Adjudication*, 88 MICH. L. REV. 2348 (1990).

13. *See* ARISTOTLE, *supra* note 3, at 115, V.4, 1132a2–25.

14. *Id.* ("[T]he nature of the judge is to be a sort of animate justice.").

15. This triadic procedural structure was not a novel idea even in Aristotle's day, as most private disputes already were handled in this way. In ancient Athens, the parties presented their cases to a magistrate, who made an initial determination whether there were sufficient grounds for the action to proceed. *See* A.R.W. HARRISON, THE LAW OF ATHENS 85–92 (1971). If so, the magistrate enpanelled a jury to hear the dispute. *Id.* at 154–68.

16. *See* ARISTOTLE, *supra* note 3, at 114–116, V.4, 1131b14–1132a2, 1132a25–b9.

17. *Id.* at 116, V.4, 1132a25–b9.

18. *Id.* at 115, V.4, 1132a2–25.

19. Although even here the analysis may not be so simple. If the object was taken intentionally, then the wrongdoer not only has inflicted a material harm upon the victim, she also has committed the abstract harm of repudiating the victim's primary right against theft. In this case, part of the wrongdoer's gain is in breaking a rule that others must obey. Simply returning the stolen property does not seem to annul this more abstract, political gain.

20. In explaining corrective justice, Aristotle states that "[i]f an official has inflicted a wound, he should not be wounded in return, and if someone has wounded an official, he ought not to be wounded only but punished in addition." *See* ARISTOTLE, *supra* note 3, at

117, V.5, 1132b11–33. His reasoning here seems to be that the arithmetic proportion of corrective justice does not mean simply measuring the injustice by the loss inflicted (and imposing the same on the wrongdoer), but requires a consideration of both the culpability of the wrongdoer's conduct and the gravity of the victim's injury.

21. In hindsight, however, we can see how my careless indifference might cause others injury. Besides creating sharp obstacles for pedestrians, it was not unfathomable that dropping the nail might create an insidious hazard for motor vehicles traveling over the roadway.

Notes to Chapter 9
Justice in Exchange

1. *See* ARISTOTLE, THE NICHOMACHEAN ETHICS 117, V.5, 1131b11–33 (D. Ross trans., revised by J.L. Ackrill & J.O. Urmsom 1990) (Oxford Univ. Press, World Classics ed.).

2. *Id.*

3. *Id.* at 119, V.5, 1133a17–b3.

4. *Id.* at 118–19, V.5, 1132b33–1133a17.

5. *Id.* at 119, V.5, 1133a17–b3.

6. *Id.* at 121, V.5, 1133b20–1134a11.

7. *Id.* at 119, V.5, 1133a17–b3.

8. *Id.* at 119–21, V.5, 1133a17–1134a11.

9. *See* James Gordley, *Equality in Exchange*, 69 CAL. L. REV. 1587 (1981) (suggesting that equality of exchange underlies much of modern contract law).

10. *See* ARISTOTLE, *supra* note 1, at 111, V.2, 1130b18–1131a6.

11. *Id.* at 109–10, V.2, 1130a6–b18.

12. Slaves and serfs were notable exceptions. *See* VICTOR EHRENBERG, THE GREEK STATE 32–36 (1960).

13. *See infra* Chapter Nineteen.

Notes to Chapter 10
Retributive Justice

1. Jules Coleman endorses this view. He argues that even if an injurer has a duty to rectify a loss caused by her conduct, it is not unjust for some other party to discharge that duty. *See* Jules L. Coleman, *The Mixed Conception of Corrective Justice*, 77 IOWA L. REV. 427, 443–44 (1992).

2. *See* Jean Hampton, *Correcting Harms Versus Righting Wrongs: The Goal of Retribution*, 39 UCLA L. REV. 1659, 1663 (1992). Sometimes, however, these consequences can be important in determining the type and degree of retribution warranted by the act. As general rule, the more serious the injury inflicted, the greater the retributive response will be. We saw this earlier in the case of the ancient Greeks, who ostracized those who caused the death of another, even if only by misadventure. *See* THE ORATIONS OF DEMOSTHENES 333 (C.R. Kennedy trans. 1856).

3. *See* Herbert Morris, *Persons and Punishment* in PUNISHMENT AND REHABILITA-

TION 40 (J. Murphy, 1st ed. 1985).

    4. *Id.* at 42–44.

    5. *See* Hampton, *supra* note 2.

    6. *Id.* at 1686.

    7. *Id.* at 1685–87.

    8. *See* Margaret J. Radin, *Compensation and Commensurability*, 43 DUKE L.J. 56 (1993).

    9. *See* ORATIONS, *supra* note 2.

    10. By now, the parallels between private retributive justice and corrective justice should be evident. Both are concerned with rectifying wrongful acts. Corrective justice admits overtly the bilateral nature of the adjustment between the parties. It requires that the gains of grasping behavior be given up, and that the proportional deficit of the victim be repaired. Although retributive justice focuses primarily on the act, rather than its consequences, part of the recompense for that act is the nullification of the wrongdoer's message of superiority over the victim. This too entails restoring a balance between the parties. *See* Hampton, *supra* note 2, at 1698.

    Besides this structural similarity, the two concepts share a substantive affinity. Recall that corrective justice is not just concerned with neutralizing gains and losses which are corporeal. It also redresses abstract harms. This includes attacks upon the ideal of autonomy evidenced by intentional conduct. Since autonomy is indispensable to survival, any direct repudiation of this concept is not merely personal or political, but moral. Retributive justice seeks to punish such behavior for very much the same reason. Acts which are deliberately harmful denigrate their victims by denying them the basic human right of autonomy. It is this lack of respect which inspires the deepest primordial feelings of anger and contempt which define our retributive instinct. *See* RICHARD POSNER, THE PROBLEMS OF JURISPRUDENCE 316, 322–23 (1990).

    11. *See* Emily Sherwin, *Why is Corrective Justice Just?*, 15 HARV. J.L. & PUB. POL'Y 839, 844 (1992).

    12. *See* H.L.A. HART, THE CONCEPT OF LAW 159–60 (1961).

    13. *Id.*

Notes to Chapter 11
The Anatomy of a Tort

    1. For primary rights this structure is complete; secondary rights, however, require the additional ingredient of factual causation. *See infra* Chapters Twelve and Thirteen.

    2. A tort may consist of conduct which is fault-based or fault-free. It may result in injury to person, property, psyche, expectation or relation. And it may arise spontaneously and involuntarily, or during the course of a well-planned, long-term relationship.

    3. In some cases, the conduct in question does not *actually* have to be wrongful; it is sufficient that it *appears* wrongful to others. Thus, tort law permits one in danger to take defensive action against her attacker so long as it reasonably appears that there is a need for such a response. *See* RESTATEMENT (SECOND) OF TORTS § 63 (1965) (recognizing a privilege of self-defense); *see also* WILLIAM L. PROSSER ET AL., CASES AND

MATERIALS ON TORTS 107 (8th ed. 1988) (noting that self preservation is the first law of nature).

4. Without wrongful conduct, any interaction with another is permissible or at least benign. On the other hand, wrongful conduct which causes no harm to another may be punishable as a crime against the state, but it does not give rise to any private right of action.

5. *See, e.g.*, Lambert v. Bessey, 83 Eng. Rep. 220, 221 (1681) ("In all civil acts, the law doth not so much regard the intent of the actor, as the loss and damage of the party suffering."); Mitchell v. Alestree, I. Vent. 295 (1676) (horse trainers liable for injuries to bystanders regardless of the degree of care exercised).

6. Brown v. Kendall, 60 Mass. (6 Cush.) 292 (Mass. 1850).

7. *See, e.g.*, Ball v. Nye, 97 Am. Dec. 56 (1868) (defendant liable for damage caused by the percolation of filthy water from his mine); Hay v. Cohoes, 2 N.Y. 159 (1849) (defendant conducting blasting on his own property held liable for damage to plaintiff's property even though no negligence shown).

8. *See* RICHARD A. EPSTEIN, A THEORY OF STRICT LIABILITY (1980).

9. Ordinarily, one cannot owe a duty to one's self. Duty is a bilateral notion that requires two beings: one who must give and another who is entitled to receive. If one conceives of the self as constantly changing and evolving, however, then the same person may have different identities at different stages of her life. Each version of the self may be as unique as the personalities of two independent individuals. Consider Jerry Rubin, who changed from a 1960's peace activist into a Wall Street investment mogul. Or Byron "Whizzer" White who went from being an acclaimed football player to becoming a Justice of the United States Supreme Court. Under this view, a prior self may owe a duty to its future incarnations to refrain from conduct which might jeopardize their happiness or existence.

10. This responsibility is imposed by the doctrines of assumption of risk, contributory negligence or comparative fault, and mitigation of damages. The recipient also has a responsibility not to harm the actor, unless she is justified in doing so.

11. *See* RESTATEMENT (SECOND) OF TORTS § 333 (1965) (stating that a landowner owes no duty to a trespasser to make his land safe, to warn of dangers on it, or to protect him in any other way); *see also* Sohn v. Katz, 169 A. 838 (N.J. 1934) (extending landowner immunity to household members); *see generally* Francis Hermann Bohlen, *The Duty of a Landowner Toward Those Entering His Premises of Their Own Right*, 69 U. PA. L. REV. 142, 237 (1921).

12. *See* RESTATEMENT (SECOND) OF TORTS § 343 (1965) (stating that a property owner must exercise reasonable care for the safety of his invitee; duty includes fixing or warning of known dangers and inspecting for hidden dangers); *see also* Home Ins. Co. v. Spears, 590 S.W.2d 71 (Ark. 1979) (holding a landowner liable to an invitee who was injured on the owner's bridge); Campbell v. Weathers, 111 P.2d 72 (Kan. 1941) (holding a store owner liable to a customer retrieving a box from a storeroom).

13. The same relationship between responsibility and autonomy would seem to exist even where the recipient does not voluntarily expose herself to danger. Thus, one who crosses the street without looking carefully for oncoming traffic may not act willfully, yet she assumes some of the responsibility for any resulting injury she may sustain. In this situation, her right to be left alone by motorists using the street would be diminished by the extent of her own negligence.

14. An exception would be where the recipient possesses greater knowledge, skill or training than the average individual. Here, the recipient may have a heightened responsibility to prevent her own harm.

15. *See* Glittenberg v. Doughboy Recreational Indus., 491 N.W.2d 208 (Mich. 1992)(holding that manufacturers of above-ground swimming pools do not have a duty to warn of the obvious danger of diving head first into the shallow water of such pools).

16. *See* Broussard v. Continental Oil Co., 433 So. 2d 354 (La. Ct. App.) (under similar facts, holding that the hand drill manufacturer was not required to place on the drill a specific warning of the risk of explosion), *cert denied*, 440 So.2d 726 (La. 1983).

17. *See infra* Chapter Fifteen.

18. *See* JOHN RAWLS, A THEORY OF JUSTICE 350 (1971).

19. *See* ARISTOTLE, THE NICHMACHEAN ETHICS 107–08, V.1, 1129a23–1130a6 (D. Ross trans., revised by J.L. Ackrill & J.O. Urmson 1990) (Oxford Univ. Press, World Classics ed.).

20. As Judge Cardozo remarked in *Palsgraf*, "The plaintiff sues in her own right for a wrong personal to her, and not as the vicarious beneficiary of a breach of a duty to another." Palsgraf v. Long Island R.R. Co., 162 N.E. 99, 100 (N.Y. 1928).

21. Winterbottom v. Wright, 152 Eng. Rep. 402 (1842).

22. *Id.* at 405.

23. In the product liability context in which it arose, it is now all but a dead letter. *See* MacPherson v. Buick Motor Co., 111 N.E. 1050 (N.Y. 1916).

24. *See, e.g.,* Western Seed Prod. Corp. v. Campbell, 442 P.2d 215 (Or. 1968), *cert. denied*, 393 U.S. 1093 (1969).

25. *See, e.g.,* Mentzer v. New England Tel. & Tel. Co., 177 N.E. 549 (Mass. 1931) (telephone company); Reimann v. Monmouth Consol. Water Co., 87 A.2d 325 (N.J. 1952) (water company); Strauss v. Belle Realty Co., 482 N.E.2d 34 (N.Y. 1985) (electric utility); H.R. Moch Co. v. Rensselaer Water Co., 159 N.E. 896 (N.Y. 1928) (waterworks company).

26. *See, e.g.,* Chatman v. Millis, 517 S.W.2d 504 (Ark. 1975) (psychiatrist not liable for diagnosing patient's father as being a homosexual); Freese v. Lemmon, 210 N.W.2d 576 (Iowa 1973) (physician who treated patient for a seizure not liable for injuries sustained by patient during subsequent motoring accident).

27. Usually the concept of foreseeability fills the bill. *See infra* notes 28 & 29.

28. *See, e.g.,* DeCastro v. Boylan, 367 So. 2d 83 (La. Ct. App. 1979) (policeman hit by thief driving stolen car held not protected by statute requiring cars to be locked and keys removed); Traylor v. Coburn, 597 S.W.2d 319 (Tenn. Ct. App. 1980) (child injured while crossing road in front of school bus not within class protected by statute requiring school bus to remain stationary).

29. The act of dumping toxic waste in a water source, for example, may affect tens of thousands of individuals over a wide geographical expanse for decades.

30. *See* Lynch v. Fisher, 34 So. 2d 513 (La. Ct. App. 1948); Ramsey v. Carolina-Tenn. Power Co., 143 S.E. 861 (N.C. 1928).

31. *Palsgraf*, 162 N.E. 99; *see also* Diamond State Tel. Co. v. Atl. Refining Co., 205 F.2d 402 (3d Cir. 1953); Tucker v. Collar, 285 P.2d 178 (Ariz. 1955); Isaacs v. Huntington Mem. Hosp., 695 P.2d 653 (Cal. 1985).

32. *See* St. Elizabeth Hosp. v. Garrard, 730 S.W.2d 649, 652 n.3 (Tex. 1987) (citing

cases), *overruled on other grounds by* Boyles v. Kerr, 855 S.W.2d 593 (Tex. 1993).

33. Defamation actions protect this interest. *See* RESTATEMENT (SECOND) OF TORTS chap. 24 (1977) ("Invasions of Interest in Reputation").

34. These are covered in actions for tortious interference with contractual relations. *Id.* §§ 766–766C.

35. Reliance damages may be redressed in misrepresentation actions. *Id.* § 549. Violation of a reliance interest may also support a negligence action premised on a wrongful undertaking. *Id.* § 323(b).

36. *See* Coleman v. Employment Sec. Dept., 607 P.2d 1231 (Wash. 1980).

37. *See* Dun & Bradstreet, Inc. v. Greenmoss Builders, Inc., 472 U.S. 749 (1985) (presumed damages recoverable where subject speech does not involve matter of public concern); *see also* RESTATEMENT (SECOND) OF TORTS § 569 (1977).

38. *See* Ernest J. Weinrib, *Toward a Moral Theory of Negligence Law*, 2 LAW & PHIL. 37 (1983).

39. In the sphere of public law, states have enacted codes to protect public health, welfare, safety *and morals*. Most of these laws, however, have been either repealed or ignored. Sunday blue laws, obscenity laws, and laws against prostitution, abortion and sodomy all represent largely failed efforts to promote a certain conception of virtue. On the federal level, the short history of the eighteenth amendment (prohibiting the sale of alcoholic beverages), U.S. CONST. AMEND XVIII, *repealed by* U.S. CONST. AMEND. XXI, stands as a testament to the inadequacy of law as a mechanism for self-directed moral suasion.

40. The examples in tort law are legion. Early trespass theory permitted recovery by an injured claimant regardless of the culpability of the offender. If the harm was the result of a direct and affirmative act, liability was imposed even if the actor could not have prevented the outcome. *See Lambert*, 83 Eng. Rep. at 221 (wherein the court focused upon the loss and damage of the injured party); *Mitchell*, I. Vent. 295 (horse trainer held liable for injuries to bystanders regardless of care exercised). Even today, the same fate awaits an adult who lacks the mental capacity to avoid certain harm to others. This disregard of moral fault also seems evident in the "fault-free" theory of strict liability for abnormally dangerous activities. *See infra* Chapter Sixteen.

41. *See* Yania v. Bigan, 155 A.2d 343 (Pa. 1959) (defendant held to have no duty to rescue even though he encouraged the decedent to jump into an open trench filled with water); *see also* W. PAGE KEETON ET AL., PROSSER AND KEETON ON TORTS 375 (5th ed. 1984) ("The law has persistently refused to impose on a stranger the moral obligation of common humanity to go to the aid of another human being who is in danger, even if the other is in danger of losing his life.").

42. *See* RESTATEMENT (SECOND) OF TORTS § 46 & cmt. d (1965) (requiring severe emotional distress precipitated by "conduct so outrageous in character, and so extreme in degree, as to go beyond all possible bounds of decency, and to be regarded as atrocious, and utterly intolerable in a civilized community.").

Notes to Chapter 12
The Question of Factual Cause

1. Richard Epstein has argued that causation still is or should be the *only* prerequisite to tort liability. *See* RICHARD A. EPSTEIN, A THEORY OF STRICT LIABILITY (1980). *But see* Richard W. Wright, *Substantive Corrective Justice*, 77 IOWA L. REV. 625, 629 n.13 (1992) (collecting criticisms of Epstein's theory). Though few have followed this view, it suggests the lofty status traditionally enjoyed by this concept in this area of the law.

2. The Latin phrase "sine qua non," which literally means "without which not," is commonly expressed as the "but for" test: but for this one event, another would not have occurred. BLACK'S LAW DICTIONARY 221 (6th ed. 1990); *see* D.M.A. Strachen, *Scope & Application of the "But For" Causal Test*, 33 MOD. L. REV. 386 (1970).

3. "NESS" is an acronym for "Necessary Element in a Sufficient Set" of causes or conditions. *See* H.L.A. HART & TONY HONORÉ, CAUSATION IN THE LAW 108–129 (2d ed. 1985); *see also* Richard W. Wright, *Causation in Tort Law*, 73 CAL. L. REV. 1735, 1775–88 (1985).

4. *See* RESTATEMENT (SECOND) OF TORTS § 431 (1965).

5. *See* ARNO C. BECHT & FRANK W. MILLER, THE TEST OF FACTUAL CAUSATION IN NEGLIGENCE AND STRICT LIABILITY CASES 9–10 (1961).

6. Ybarra v. Spangard, 154 P.2d 687 (Cal. 1944) (where an unconscious plaintiff received unusual injuries during medical treatment, members of a surgical team who provided the treatment had the burden of showing that their actions were not a cause of the plaintiff's injuries).

7. This theory is applied primarily in medical malpractice cases where the plaintiff is mistreated or misdiagnosed. It allows recovery for the lost opportunity of receiving reasonable treatment, even where it appears more likely than not that the patient would have succumbed to her illness if properly cared for. *See* Herskovits v. Group Health Coop. 664 P.2d 474 (Wash. 1983).

8. *See* Nutt v. A.C.&S., Inc. 466 A.2d 18 (Del. Super. Ct. 1983) (wherein the court held that claims for fear of future asbestos-related harm were compensable with a demonstrable physical change in bodily condition); Michals v. William T. Watkins Mem. United Methodist Church, 873 S.W.2d 216 (Ky. Ct. App. 1994) (wherein the court held that a claim for increased risk may be maintained if supported by physical injury).

9. *See* Potter v. Firestone Tire & Rubber Co., 863 P.2d 795 (Cal. 1993) (allowing recovery of medical monitoring costs where the plaintiff more likely than not will develop an illness in the future); Burns v. Jaquays Mining Corp., 752 P.2d 28 (Ariz. Ct. App. 1987) (holding that claimants were entitled to recover the costs of medical surveillance to forestall the development of cancer).

10. Where two or more parties act negligently, but it is unknown which of the tortfeasors caused the plaintiff's injuries, the theory of alternative liability shifts the burden of disproving causation to each defendant; those who fail to satisfy this burden may be held liable, even though her causal agency has not been proven. *See* Summers v. Tice, 199 P.2d 1 (Cal. 1948).

11. *See* Hall v. E. I. du Pont de Nemours & Co., 345 F. Supp. 353 (E.D.N.Y. 1972); Burnside v. Abbott Labs., 505 A.2d 973, 984 (Pa. Super. Ct. 1985) ("Enterprise liability

exists where (1) the injury-causing product was manufactured by one of a small number of defendants in an industry; (2) the defendants had joint knowledge of the risks inherent in the product and possessed a joint capacity to reduce those risks; and (3) each of them failed to take steps to reduce the risk but, rather, delegated this responsibility to a trade association.").

12. Under market share liability, a plaintiff injured by a defective product may recover damages against manufacturers of that good, even though the plaintiff is incapable of proving which manufacturer actually sold the item which caused her loss; the liability of each manufacturer, however, is limited to a percentage of the plaintiff's damage reflective of its market share of sales of that product during the relevant time period. *See* Sindell v. Abbott Labs., 607 P.2d 924 (Cal. 1980).

13. In brief, I shall argue that the essence of factual causation is factual responsibility for a result. It simply identifies those actors whose exercise of autonomy has violated a distributive duty by inhibiting the autonomy of others. By establishing a unique link between wrongdoers and victims, in turn, it also helps to satisfy the concerns of distributive, corrective and retributive justice alike. Nevertheless, because these justice requirements are dynamic and relative to different relations and acts, the need for causal responsibility is not absolute, but will vary from case to case.

14. The other forces referred to here could include nonfeasance; i.e., it is possible for an act of misfeasance to combine with someone's nonfeasance to produce an injurious result.

15. Hart and Honoré propose a solution to such a conundrum. They suggest that omissions of this sort may be deemed causes if they are abnormal; that is, if the failure to act marks a deviation from the normal course of events. *See* HART & HONORÉ, *supra* note 3, at 33–44. This approach, however, does not provide much assistance in our search for causes in the crosswalk hypothetical. If the accident occurs in a benevolent society where altruism is the norm, then all bystanders who fail to act are causes of the pedestrian's injuries. And what if one of the onlookers is the pedestrian's parent or a school crossing guard? Under Hart and Honoré's approach, these individuals might not be causal agents if most parents and crossing guards would not have acted. Surely this is not an acceptable conclusion. In such a scenario, the custom of carelessness among guardians would be determinative of our definition of causation. Yet society might want such guardians to protect their charges even if they are not in the habit of doing so. Without causation, however, there can be no tort liability for such guardians; and without the incentive of liability, the dereliction of these individuals is unlikely to change.

16. *See* Tarasoff v. Regents of Univ. of Cal., 551 P.2d 334, 343 (Cal. 1976).

17. In such a situation, a disastrous accident would be avoided unless some unforeseeable causal agent circumvents the sitter's efforts to keep the tyke safe. This might occur, for example, if a miscreant suddenly pushed the child into the street.

18. Anderson v. Minneapolis, St. P. & S. S. M. Ry. Co., 179 N.W. 45 (Minn. 1920).

19. *See* RESTATEMENT (SECOND) OF TORTS § 431(a) (1965).

20. *Id.* § 433 (explaining "substantial factor" considerations).

21. *Id.* § 433(b).

22. *Id.* § 433(a).

23. *Id.* § 433(c).

24. One other consideration not mentioned in section 433 of the Restatement, but frequently appearing in tort cases, is whether someone else actually desired (subjectively intended) to produce the result. *See* Watson v. Ky. & Ind. Bridge & R. Co., 126 S.W. 146

(Ky. 1910). Where this is so, the deliberate actor attempts to influence or control the outcome. Accordingly, her act of volition is likely to be a primary factor in producing the result.

25. This would not be difficult in a world where all injury-producing behavior was affirmative, isolated, and sequential, so that no two causes ever concurred. But obviously this is a fantasy. In our world, every event has innumerable causes. Some of these causes are natural, others are the product of human agency. Of course, tort law, as part of our system of social justice, is only concerned with rectifying injuries which result from the actions of individuals. Thus, there must be some device which allows us to separate natural from human causes; and within the latter, to distinguish between those human actions which have a salient effect upon the interests of others and those that do not.

26. Taken from David A. Fischer, *Causation in Fact in Omission Cases*, 1992 UTAH L. REV. 1335, 1349 (based on the case of Saunders Sys. Birmingham Co. v. Adams, 117 So. 72 (Ala. 1928)).

27. Obviously, if the harm sustained by the plaintiff derives from a natural condition, she will be left to bear the loss on her own. That is, of course, unless some human being was required to control it.

28. If D unknowingly lacked the reflexes necessary to apply the brakes more quickly, or was presented by an emergency which shortened her reaction time, she would not be negligent, and there would be no need to consider the issue of factual responsibility.

29. Indeed, by determining which agent's (or agents') exercise of autonomy controlled a tortious injury, it identifies the party (or parties) who are uniquely vulnerable to the secondary rights of the victim.

Notes to Chapter 13
Factual Cause and Justice

1. Several recent theories ignore the harm requirement and permit recovery for exposure to risk. *See* Jackson v. Johns-Manville Sales Corp., 781 F.2d 394 (5th Cir. 1986) (allowing claims for fear of cancer and for the reasonable probability of developing cancer in the future), *cert. denied*, 106 S.Ct. 3339 (1986); In re Moorenovich, 634 F. Supp. 634 (D. Me. 1986) (recognizing a claim for fear of developing cancer in the future); Sherrod v. Berry, 629 F. Supp. 159 (N.D. Ill. 1985) (awarding hedonic damages), *rev'd and remanded on other grounds*, 856 F.2d 802 (7th Cir. 1988); Herskovits v. Group Health Coop., 664 P.2d 474 (Wash. 1983) (permitting claim for lost chance of survival).

2. Laws prohibiting prostitution may appear to be founded on a concern for the virtue of both the entrepreneur and her customers. However, to the extent that such covert transactions facilitate the spread of social diseases, prostitution laws actually may have a legitimate social welfare purpose.

3. Natural law theorists and positivists agree on this point. Under natural law theory, an unjust law is no law at all and thus is entitled to no respect. *See* THOMAS AQUINAS, TREATISE ON LAW 78 (Gateway ed. 1964). According to positivist theory, obedience to the command of law cannot be ensured through sanction only. There must be some measure of voluntary submission to the law. This submission occurs only when the law is just. *See* H.L.A. HART, THE CONCEPT OF LAW 196–97 (1961).

4. The injured party could then be compensated out of a state fund designated for that purpose.

5. *See* Richard A. Posner, The Problems of Jurisprudence 316, 322-23 (1990). Today, a tort plaintiff may recover nominal damages against a wrongdoer who willfully invades her rights, even if no actual damage is done. This permits the victim to denigrate the asserted superiority of the wrongdoer and reestablish the equality between them. *See* Jean Hampton, *Correcting Harms Versus Righting Wrongs: The Goal of Retribution*, 39 UCLA L. Rev. 1659, 1698 (1992). This is a personal remedy against the party responsible for the harm. No remedy divorced from the wrongdoer could serve the same end. In negligence cases involving extreme culpability, the victim similarly is permitted to punish the wrongdoer through an award of punitive damages.

6. *See* Emily Sherwin, *Why is Corrective Justice Just?*, 15 Harv. J.L. & Pub. Pol'y 839, 844 (1992).

7. Even where there is some justification for imposing liability against the factually responsible actor, there may be good reason for finding some other party to compensate the injured party. There are three types of noncausal parties who, although not directly subject to the victim's claim-right, may be asked to defray the costs of her injuries. The first type includes individuals who have acted wrongfully in the same or similar way as the tortfeasor; the second consists of entities which have consented to assume the loss; the third includes persons employed by, or who own stock in, a primarily responsible party, and others who purchase that party's goods or services. The first group typically is comprised of insurance subscribers who pay higher premiums because of previous incidents. Such individuals indirectly subsidize the losses sustained by other insureds in similar accidents. The second group generally is comprised of insurance companies which write private policies or participate in public compensation systems. The third group includes just about anyone who has ever bought a product or worked for a corporation.

Imposing liability against noncausal parties, like those in this last group, may seem to create justice concerns on its own. After all, if such actors have not inflicted harm upon anyone, they usually may not be subject to an ex post duty of compensation. To impose such an obligation, under these circumstances, would itself constitute a wrongful interference with the actors' autonomy interests.

However, this would not be so, as for the first group mentioned above, where the actors' conduct violated some other distributive duty. For example, risky activity may be prohibited or regulated ex ante, not just restricted ex post. Thus, those who engage in such activities, and who are also subject to more onerous prohibitory or regulatory duties, have no autonomy interest to act in the forbidden manner. Requiring them to remunerate victims of similar actions would not seem unfair, since the autonomy restriction it represents would be far less than that imposed by the ex ante rules. On this ground, justice might require that they contribute to the reparation of private losses which resulted from the same category of activity, but which were not in fact "caused" by their conduct.

The liability borne by insurance companies is founded on a distinctly different rationale. Their duty to absorb the costs of accidents is not premised on prior wrongful conduct, but on consent. In return for a stated premium, these enterprises have assumed special duties to provide compensation to those injured in transactions with others. So long as the justice concern of reciprocity is satisfied, such commitments may provide sufficient justification for diverting losses from causal wrongdoers.

8. For example, compare the negligent driver's benefit in not being alert to the pedestrian's loss of a limb.

9. As in cases involving "eggshell" plaintiffs. *See* McCahill v. N.Y. Transp. Co., 94 N.E. 616 (N.Y. 1911).

10. *See* HART, *supra* note 3, at 161–63.

11. Medical malpractice is the other area where the public interest may justify weakening the causation requirement. The doctrines of res ipsa loquitur and lost chance allow injured patients to recover against health care providers without proving their causal responsibility. *See* Ybarra v. Spangard, 154 P.2d 687 (Cal. 1944) (adopting version of res ipsa loquitur which shifts the burden of disproving causal negligence to defendants) and *supra* note 1. Physical and mental health are primary goods. They are not a matter of personal desire, but are essential for the life plans of all individuals. The provision of these goods, therefore, has a definite public character. Indeed, a state which fails to protect these basic welfare interests offers no advantage for its citizens, and may be susceptible to disobedience. Here, the public interest in competent medical care, and in doctors who will not hide the truth, may supersede the private interests of retributive and corrective justice furthered by the concept of causal responsibility.

12. In most cases, such products will be regulated by ex ante duties of safety. Imposing ex post liability against the manufacturers of such products, even where causation is speculative, is a less restrictive autonomy sanction than enforcing the ex ante regulation.

Notes to Chapter 14
Intentional Torts

1. "Fault-free" in the sense used here, means that the risk posed by the activity is an inevitable and unavoidable by-product of its performance. As will be discussed in Chapter Sixteen, however, such a description may in fact be misleading. To the extent that high risk endeavors expose others to unacceptable levels of danger, those who perform them may be at fault for creating such excess hazards without compensating the individuals who must bear their consequences.

2. These defenses usually are founded on the protection of the individual's welfare interests. In defending these interests, the actor may not do more than is necessary to return to the status quo. In an Aristotelian sense, she may not act graspingly, but must only seek the intermediate between the loss expected and any gain she could acquire in countering the attack.

3. Unless there is a claim of justification, in which case this issue would have to be resolved as well.

4. *See generally* William Prosser, *Transferred Intent*, 45 TEX. L. REV. 650 (1967) (discussing the doctrine of transferred intent).

5. *See* Hughes v. Emerald Mines Corp., 450 A.2d 1 (Pa. 1982).

6. *See* Vosburg v. Putney, 50 N.W. 403 (Wis. 1891).

7. As in assault actions.

8. As in actions for trespass to land.

9. *See* RESTATEMENT (SECOND) OF TORTS §§ 13, 18 (1965).

10. *See id.* § 21.

11. *See* Mohr v. Williams, 104 N.W.2d 12 (Minn. 1905) (a doctor who operated on the wrong ear of the patient was held liable for battery even though he successfully reparied a serious condition in that ear).

12. *See* Perry v. Jefferies, 39 S.E. 515 (S.C. 1901) (defendant, in a mistaken belief that he owned certain property, entered the land and cut and removed timber belonging to the plaintiff).

13. *See* Drabek v. Sabley, 142 N.W.2d 798 (Wis. 1966) (defendant unreasonably attacked a boy who threw a snowball at him).

14. *See* RESTATEMENT (SECOND) OF TORTS § 35 (1965).

15. *See id.* §§ 35(1)(c), 42. The Restatement gives the following illustration of how a false imprisonment may lead to physical harm:

> 3. A locks B, a child six days old, in the vault of a bank. B is not conscious of the confinement, but the vault cannot be opened for two days, and during that time B suffers from hunger and thirst, and his health is affected. A is subject to liability to B for false imprisonment.

Id. § 42 cmt. b, Illus. 3.

16. *See* Davis & Allcott Co. v. Boozer, 110 So. 28 (Ala. 1926).

17. *See* Hardy v. LaBelle's Distrib. Co., 661 P.2d 35 (Mont. 1983) (a temporary employee accussed of stealing a watch voluntarily came to the manager's office and took a lie detector test in order to clear her name).

18. *See* RESTATEMENT OF TORTS § 46 (1947 & Supp. 1948).

19. *See* Clark v. Assoc. Retail Credit Men, 105 F.2d 62 (D.C. Cir. 1939); Duty v. Gen. Fin. Co., 273 S.W.2d 64 (Tex. 1954).

20. *See* RESTATEMENT (SECOND) OF TORTS § 46(1) & cmt. d (1965).

21. *See id.* § 46(1) & cmt. i.

22. *See* Young v. Stensrude, 664 S.W.2d 263 (Mo. Ct. App. 1984) (defendant showed the plaintiff and others a pornographic movie at a business meeting after describing the film as educational).

23. *See* RESTATEMENT (SECOND) OF TORTS § 158 (1965).

24. *See id.* § 158 ("One is subject to liability to another for trespass, irrespective of whether he thereby causes harm to any legally protected interest of the other...."); *see also* Glade v. Dietert, 295 S.W.2d 642, 645 (Tex. 1956).

25. *See* Katko v. Briney, 183 N.W.2d 657 (Iowa 1971) (use of spring gun to defend abandoned farm house against thief was unreasonable).

26. *See* RESTATEMENT (SECOND) OF TORTS § 218 cmts. e & g (1965).

27. *See id.* § 221 & cmt. b. The tortfeasor need not know that another has a possessory interest in the chattel, nor intend to invade the other's possessory interest in it. It is sufficient that the tortfeasor deals with the chattel in a way that is destructive of the other's possession or ownership of the property. *Id.*

28. *See id.* § 218 cmt. g.

29. *See id.* § 222A(2)(a)(b)(c).

30. *See id.* § 222A(2)(d)(e)(f).

Notes to Chapter 15
Negligence

1. However, some courts now allow recovery to plaintiffs who merely have developed an increased risk of being injured in the future, *see* Gideon v. Johns-Manville Sales Corp., 761 F.2d 1129 (5th Cir. 1985); Elam v. Alcolac Inc., 765 S.W.2d 42 (Mo. Ct. App. 1988), or who have been deprived of a chance of surviving some malady, *see* Falcon v. Mem. Hosp., 462 N.W.2d 44 (Mich. 1990); Wollen v. DePaul Health Ctr., 828 S.W.2d 681 (Mo. 1992); Herskovits v. Group Health Coop., 664 P.2d 474 (Wash. 1983).

2. Ordinarily, such acts are not restricted ex ante (though, of course, some forms of negligent conduct may be regulated), but are allowed to proceed unobstructed. Once they produce injury in another, however, they may be subject to the less restrictive sanction of tort law compensation.

3. *See* RESTATEMENT (SECOND) OF TORTS § 289 (1965).

4. Except where the recipient possesses superior skill, knowledge or experience which heightens her responsibility to look out for herself, regardless of the actor's duty.

5. *See* Tarasoff v. Regents of Univ. of Cal., 551 P.2d 334, 343 (Cal. 1976).

6. *See* Harris v. Pa. R.R. Co., 50 F.2d 866 (4th Cir. 1931) (ship operator owed duty to crew member who fell overboard); Carey v. Davis, 180 N.W. 889 (Iowa 1921) (employer owed unconscious, overheated farm laborer a duty to shelter him properly); Rival v. Atchison, T. & S. F. R. Co., 306 P.2d 648 (N.M. 1957) (employer owed duty to furnish prompt medical treatment to employee).

7. *See* Cross v. Wells Fargo Alarm Serv., 412 N.E.2d 472 (Ill. 1980); *Carey*, 180 N.W. at 892; *see also* RESTATEMENT (SECOND) OF TORTS § 323 & cmt. c (1965).

8. *See* Randy E. Barnett, *The Sound of Silence: Default Rules and Contractual Consent*, 78 VA. L. REV. 821, 900–02 (1992).

9. *See* United States v. Lawter, 219 F.2d 559 (5th Cir. 1955) (defendant undertook to rescue woman using helicopter but performed rescue negligently).

10. *See* Abresch v. Northwestern Bell Tel., 75 N.W.2d 206 (Minn. 1956) (telephone company undertook to call fire department for plaintiff); Dudley v. Victor Lynn Lines, Inc., 138 A.2d 53 (N.J. Super. Ct. App. Div. 1958) (employer's promise to call doctor for decedent caused decedent's wife to forego obtaining other assistance), *rev'd on other grounds*, 161 A.2d 479 (N.J. 1960); DeLong v. Erie County, 455 N.Y.S.2d 887 (Sup. Ct. App. Div. 1982) (911 dispatcher failed to secure police response to decedent's call for assistance).

11. *See* Brown v. MacPherson's, Inc., 545 P.2d 13 (Wash. 1975) (defendant led avalanche expert to believe the plaintiffs would be warned of danger).

12. General duties, we have seen, are justified because political association, and thus the pursuit of virtue, is not feasible without them. They require that we act honestly towards one another and that we cause our neighbors no harm. Yet they do not proscribe all harmful activity. Indeed, life could not proceed in such a vacuum. So in applying this general duty, the state must determine which harmful activities to restrain and which to permit. It need not distribute these burdens equally among all individuals, provided it has good reason for imposing greater responsibilities on some rather than others. Where there is no just criterion for making this distinction, the excessive duty is unfair even though it

aims at the laudable objective of preventing harm. If, however, the uneven distributions of responsibility are made in accordance with a fair proportion, they are just and must be obeyed.

13. *See* Haldane v. Alaska Airlines, Inc., 126 F. Supp. 224 (D. Alaska 1954) (wherein the court held that the airline's agent had a duty to warn decedent, who drowned by exiting wrong door, of dangers of exiting through that door without a flotation device); Tunkl v. Regents of Univ. of Cal., 383 P.2d 441 (Cal. 1963) (wherein the court held invalid as against public policy an exculpatory agreement between a patient and a non-profit hospital); Houston Lighting & Power Co. v. Reynolds, 712 S.W.2d 761 (Tex. Ct. App. 1986) (wherein the court held that the defendant-power company had a duty to warn the plaintiff about the danger of handling aluminum tent poles near a 35,000 volt power line).

14. *See* Hoyt v. Rosenberg, 182 P.2d 234 (Cal. Ct. App. 1947) (wherein the court held that the defendant-minor, who injured another child while playing "kick the can", was to be judged by the standard of care reasonably expected from boys of like age and development under similar conditions); RESTATEMENT (SECOND) OF TORTS § 283A (1965) (the standard of care for a child is that of a reasonably able child of like age, intelligence and experience under like circumstances); *see also* McGregor v. Marini, 256 So. 2d 542 (Fla. Dist. Ct. App. 1972); Gaspard v. Grain Dealers Mut. Ins. Co., 131 So. 2d 831 (La. Ct. App. 1961).

15. *See supra* note 14.

16. *See* RESTATEMENT (SECOND) OF TORTS § 298 cmt. m (1965).

17. *See* Young v. Park, 417 A.2d 889 (R.I. 1980) (physician is bound to exercise the same degree of diligence and skill as exercised by physicians in good standing engaged in the same type of practice in similar localities); Chamness v. Odum, 399 N.E.2d 238 (Ill. Ct. App. 1979) (chiropractor); Heath v. Swift Wings, Inc., 252 S.E.2d 526 (N.C. Ct. App. 1979) (pilot).

18. *See* Pub. Serv. Co. v. Elliott, 123 F.2d 2 (1st Cir. 1941) (if plaintiff knew more than the ordinary uninstructed layman about the properties of electricity his conduct would be judged in light of that superior knowledge); *see also* RESTATEMENT (SECOND) OF TORTS § 289 cmt. a (1965).

19. While this is primarily a basis for imposing strict liability (which I will discuss in Chapter Sixteen), it also appears in negligence cases. *See* Allen v. Ellis, 380 P.2d 408 (Kan. 1963) (child held to adult standard of care while driving an automobile); Dellwo v. Pearson, 107 N.W.2d 859 (Minn. 1961) (child operating a motorboat held to heightened adult standard); *see also* Giarratano v. Weitz Co., 147 N.W.2d 824 (Iowa 1967); Bosak v. Hutchinson, 375 N.W.2d 333 (Mich. 1985); RESTATEMENT (SECOND) OF TORTS §§ 416, 427 (1965).

20. *See* Tunkl, 383 P.2d 441 (medical services).

21. *See* Cordas v. Peerless Transp. Co., 27 N.Y.S.2d 198 (Sup. Ct. 1941) (cab driver held at gunpoint abandoned vehicle while still in motion; held not negligent).

22. Many of these responsibilities, in fact, are not merely incorporated into the ex post rules of tort law, but are embodied in ex ante rules of conduct. For example, a parent who fails to properly care for a child may be temporarily dispossessed of the child or may lose her parental rights completely. *See, e.g.,* In re Raymond G., 281 Cal. Rptr. 625 (Ct. App. 1991) (child was properly removed from parents when parents negligently failed to provide adequate food to child).

23. *See* Bybee Bros. v. Imes, 155 S.W.2d 492 (Ky. 1941); Conery v. Tackmaier, 149 N.W.2d 575 (Wis. 1967).

24. Where both parties to an interaction possess superior knowledge or skill, the responsibility of the actor would be no greater than the reasonable person. In essence, the superior characteristics of the plaintiff and defendant would cancel each other out.

25. Tort law has recognized many of these special relationships, including those involving doctors and patients, common carriers and passengers, innkeepers and guests, business invitors and invitees, employers and employees, parents and children, students and schools, landlords and tenants, captains and shipmates and product manufacturers and consumers. *See* W. PAGE KEETON ET AL., PROSSER AND KEETON ON TORTS 376–77 (5th ed. 1984).

26. This responsibility may be implied in fact from the relationship itself (and so would be founded on the parties' consent) or may arise by operation of a state-imposed distributive duty because of the reliant party's presumed lack of choice in encountering the harm posed by the other's conduct (thus making her resulting injury a wrongful invasion of autonomy).

27. For example, product manufacturers often induce the trust and reliance of their customers by advertising the durability, dependability or safety of their goods.

28. *See Giarratano*, 147 N.W.2d 824; *Bosak*, 375 N.W.2d 333; *see also* RESTATEMENT (SECOND) OF TORTS §§ 416, 427 (1965).

29. *Allen*, 380 P.2d 408 (sixteen-year-old held to an adult standard of care because he was driving an automobile); *Dellwo*, 107 N.W.2d 859 (twelve-year-old operating a motorboat); *see also* RESTATEMENT (SECOND) OF TORTS § 283A cmt. c (1965).

30. Judge Learned Hand indicated as much in his famous "formula" for negligence: an actor is negligent if the burden of avoiding the loss was less than the product of the probability of the loss and its expected magnitude (B<PL). *See* United States v. Carroll Towing Co., 159 F.2d 169 (2d Cir. 1947).

31. *See Tunkl*, 383 P.2d 441 (holding void as against public policy an exculpatory agreement entered into between a patient and a nonprofit hospital).

32. *See Haldane*, 126 F. Supp. 224 (holding that the defendant-airline's agent should have warned the plaintiff-passenger of the dangers of exiting through the side door of a seaplane); *Houston Lighting & Power Co.*, 712 S.W.2d 761 (the defendant-utility had a duty to warn the plaintiff of the danger of handling aluminum tent poles near a 35,000 volt power line).

33. *See* RESTATEMENT (SECOND) OF TORTS § 402A cmt. b (1965). Today, this special responsibility has been extended to manufacturers of other products. Indeed, in many jurisdictions, it is per se unconscionable for the manufacturer of *any consumer product* to contractually limit recovery of damages for personal injuries. *See* U.C.C. § 2-719(3) (1978).

34. *See* Becker v. IRM Corp., 698 P.2d 116 (Cal. 1985) (holding landlord strictly liable for injuries resulting from latent defects on the leased premises), *overruled by* Peterson v. Superior Ct., 899 P.2d 905 (Cal. 1995); Hilder v. St. Peter, 478 A.2d 202 (Vt. 1984) (holding that in the rental of any residential dwelling unit, the landlord supplies an implied warranty that the premises will be maintained in a safe, clean and habitable condition).

35. These considerations were drawn from JOEL FEINBERG, RIGHTS, JUSTICE AND THE BOUNDS OF LIBERTY 114–15 (1980).

Notes to Chapter 16
Strict Liability

1. Besides the theories of abnormally dangerous activities and products liability discussed below, strict liability is also found in the areas of nuisance and respondeat superior.

2. Rylands v. Fletcher, 159 Eng. Rep. 737 (Ex. 1865); L.R., 1 Ex. 265 (E.C. 1866); L.R., 3 H.L. 330 (H.L. 1868).

3. *Id.*

4. *Id.*

5. *See* RESTATEMENT OF TORTS § 520 (1938).

6. *Id.*

7. *See* RESTATEMENT (SECOND) OF TORTS § 519 (1977).

8. *See* Harper v. Regency Dev. Co., 399 So. 2d 248 (Ala. 1981); Correa v. Curbey, 605 P.2d 458 (Ariz. 1979); Williams v. Amoco Prod. Co., 734 P.2d 1113 (Kan. 1987); Valentine v. Pioneer Chlor Alkali Co., 864 P.2d 295 (Nev. 1993); Thigpen v. Skousen & Hise, 327 P.2d 802, 804 (N.M. 1958); New Meadows Holding Co. v. Wash. Water Power Co., 687 P.2d 212 (Wash. 1984); Bennett v. Larsen Co., 348 N.W.2d 540 (Wis. 1984).

9. *See* RESTATEMENT (SECOND) OF TORTS § 520(a)–(f) (1977).

10. *See* Langan v. Valicopters, Inc., 567 P.2d 218 (Wash. 1977).

11. *See* RESTATEMENT (SECOND) OF TORTS § 520 cmt. l (1977).

12. *See* Corprew v. Geigy Chem. Corp., 157 S.E.2d 98 (N.C. 1967) (abrogating the privity limitation); Coakley v. Prentiss-Wabers Stove Co., 195 N.W. 388 (Wis. 1923) (delineating exceptions to the privity doctrine).

13. *See, e.g.,* Swengal v. F. & E. Wholesale Grocery Co., 77 P.2d 930 (Kan. 1938) (holding that where personal injury is caused by unwholesome or contaminated food or drink, liability may be imposed absent privity); Peters v. Johnson, Jackson & Co., 41 S.E. 190 (W. Va. 1902) (wherein the court allowed plaintiff, who used a drug but had not purchased it, to recover damages against the druggist).

14. MacPherson v. Buick Motor Co., 111 N.E. 1050 (N.Y. 1916).

15. The fate of the privity doctrine was sealed just a few years later with the adoption of section 402A of the Restatement (Second) of Torts. Under that section, the absence of privity could no longer be used as a defense to a product liability claim. Specifically, comment l to section 402A provides:

> In order for the rule stated in this Section to apply, it is not necessary that the ultimate user or consumer have acquired the product directly from the seller, although the rule applies equally if he does. He may have acquired it through one or more intermediate dealers. It is not even necessary that the consumer have purchased the product at all. He may be a member of the family of the final purchaser, or his employee, or a guest at his table, or a mere donee from the purchaser. The liability stated is one in tort, and does not require any contractual relation, or privity of contract, between plaintiff and the defendant.
>
> "Consumers" include not only those who in fact consume the product, but also those who prepare it for consumption. Thus, the housewife who contracts tularemia while cooking rabbits for her husband is includ-

ed within the rule stated in this Section, as is also the husband who is opening a bottle of beer for his wife to drink. Consumption includes all ultimate uses for which the product is intended. Thus, the customer in a beauty shop to whose hair a permanent wave solution is applied by the shop is a consumer. "User" includes those who are passively enjoying the benefit of the product, as in the case of passengers in automobiles or airplanes, as well as those who are utilizing it for the purpose of doing work upon it, as in the case of an employee of the ultimate buyer who is making repairs upon the automobile which he has purchased.

RESTATEMENT (SECOND) OF TORTS § 402A cmt. l (1965).

16. For a general discussion of these two phases in the development of product liability law, see James A. Henderson, Jr. & Aaron D. Twerski, *Closing the American Products Liability Frontier: The Rejection of Liability Without Defect,* 66 N.Y.U. L. REV. 1263 (1991). In that article, Professors Henderson and Twerski describe two subsequent phases in the evolution of product liability law. In the period between 1960 and 1980, liability rules generally expanded, especially in the area of generic product risks. Although further marginal extensions were made to product liability doctrine during the 1980s, a clamor for reform began to arise by the end of that decade.

17. Escola v. Coca Cola Bottling Co., 150 P.2d 436 (Cal. 1944).

18. There, the plaintiff-waitress was injured when a soft drink bottle exploded in her hand. The offending bottle had been manufactured by Owens-Corning and was subsequently sold to Coca Cola Bottling Company. After filling and capping the bottle, Coca Cola had sold and delivered it to the plaintiff-waitress's employer. The plaintiff sued Coca Cola under the negligence theory of res ipsa loquitur, contending that the bottler either failed to detect a flaw in the glass container or overly pressurized its contents. Despite evidence of the bottler's substantial quality control efforts, the majority concluded that there was sufficient evidence for a jury to infer that the problem with the bottle originated with Coca Cola, and nowhere else within the distributive chain. In his now famous concurring opinion, Traynor pointed out that the expansive version of res ipsa loquitur endorsed by the majority really did not prove the bottler's negligence at all, but was more like a theory of strict liability. After cataloguing the numerous strict liability concepts which already had infiltrated this area of the law—from adulterated food statutes to the theory of implied warranty of merchantability—Traynor recommended that the burdensome requirements of negligence law be discarded in favor of a new theory of strict liability in tort.

19. *Id.* at 433.

20. Henningsen v. Bloomfield Motors, Inc., 161 A.2d 69 (N.J. 1960).

21. Greenman v. Yuba Power Prods., Inc., 377 P.2d 897 (Cal. 1963).

22. *See* RESTATEMENT (SECOND) OF TORTS § 402A (1965). Section 402A provides as follows:

> "Special Liability of Seller of Product for Physical Harm to User or Consumer," § 402A (1): One who sells any product in a defective condition unreasonably dangerous to the user or consumer or to his property is subject to liability for physical harm thereby caused to the ultimate user or consumer, or to his property, if: a) the seller is engaged in the business of selling such a product, and b) it is expected to and does reach the user or consumer

without substantial change in the condition in which it is sold. (2) The rule stated in Subsection (1) applies although a) the seller has exercised all possible care in the preparation and sale of his product, and b) the user or consumer has not bought the product from or entered into a contractual relation with the seller.

Id.

23. *Id.* § 402A(2)(a).

24. *See, e.g.,* Caterpillar Tractor Co. v. Beck, 593 P.2d 871, 883 (Alaska 1979); Kerns v. Engelke, 390 N.E.2d 859, 862 (Ill. 1979); O'Brien v. Muskin Corp., 463 A.2d 298, 303 (N.J. 1983).

25. *See* RESTATEMENT (SECOND) OF TORTS § 402A(1) (1965).

26. The consumer expectation test is contained in comments g and i to section 402A of the Restatement (Second) of Torts. These comments provide, in relevant part, as follows:

> Cmt. g, "Defective Condition": The rule stated in this Section applies only where the product is, at the time it leaves the seller's hands, in a condition not contemplated by the ultimate consumer, which will be unreasonably dangerous to him....
>
> Cmt. i, "Unreasonably Dangerous".... The article sold must be dangerous to an extent beyond that which would be contemplated by the ordinary consumer who purchases it, with the ordinary knowledge common to the community as to its characteristics....

Id. § 402A cmts. g & i.

27. It is now generally agreed that section 402A was developed as a result of the evolution of both negligence and warranty laws to protect people who were injured by dangerous products. *See* Oscar S. Gray, *Reflections on the Historical Context of Section 402A*, 10 TOURO L. REV. 75 (1993). The warranty pedigree of section 402A is most evident in the consumer expectation test used for determining product defectiveness. Like the contract-based theory of warranty, the new theory of strict liability in tort seemed most concerned with whether the consumer received what she had bargained for in the purchase transaction with the manufacturer. *See* Gray v. Manitowoc Co., 771 F.2d 866, 869 (5th Cir. 1985) ("[C]onsumer expectation test of section 402A is rooted in the warranty remedies of contract law, and requires that harm and liability flow from a product characteristic that frustrates consumer expectations." (citing Page Keeton, *Products Liability and the Meaning of Defect*, 5 ST. MARY'S L.J. 30, 37 (1973)); Kotler v. Am. Tobacco Co., 685 F. Supp. 15, 19 (D. Mass. 1988) (the expectations of a reasonable consumer determine whether or not goods are merchantable); Barker v. Lull Eng'g Co., 573 P.2d 443, 454 (Cal. 1978) (the consumer expectation test "reflects the warranty heritage upon which the California product liability doctrine in part rests."). Strict liability in tort was preferable to warranty law, or so the founders of section 402A thought, because warranties were (and to some extent still are) subject to numerous contract-based defenses, like privity disclaimers and notice, which impeded consumers from recovering for injuries caused by defective products. *See* William L. Prosser, *The Fall of the Citadel*, 50 MINN. L. REV. 790 (1966); George L. Priest, *Strict Products Liability: The Original Intent*, 10 CARDOZO L. REV. 2301 (1989).

28. *See* Mazetti v. Armour & Co., 135 P. 663 (Wash. 1913); *see also* RESTATEMENT (SECOND) OF TORTS § 402A cmt. b (1965) ("Since the early days of the common law

those engaged in the business of selling food intended for human consumption have been held to a high degree of responsibility for their products.... In the earlier part of this century this ancient attitude was reflected in a series of decisions in which the courts of a number of states sought to find some method of holding the seller of food liable to the ultimate consumer even though there was no showing of negligence on the part of the seller.").

29. Recently, the Supreme Court of California abandoned the consumer expectation test in complex design cases where the product defect is beyond the common everyday experience of the jury. *See* Soule v. Gen. Motors Corp., 882 P.2d 298 (Cal. 1994).

30. *See, e.g.,* Schell v. A.M.F., Inc., 567 F.2d 1259 (3d Cir. 1977); Raney v. Honeywell, Inc., 540 F.2d 932 (8th Cir. 1976); Byrns v. Riddell, Inc., 550 P.2d 1065 (Ariz. 1976).

31. *See* John W. Wade, *Strict Tort Liability of Manufacturers,* 19 S.W. L.J. 5, 17 (1965).

32. *See* United States v. Carroll Towing Co., 159 F.2d 169 (2d Cir. 1947).

33. Kelley v. R.G. Indus., Inc., 497 A.2d 1143 (Md. 1985).

34. *See* Halphen v. Johns-Manville Sales Corp., 484 So. 2d 110 (La. 1986) (defining asbestos as per se defective); Beshada v. Johns-Manville Prods. Corp., 447 A.2d 539 (N.J. 1982) (rejecting a state-of-the-art defense in failure to warn claims arising out of exposure to asbestos).

35. The name is Henderson and Twerski's. *See* JAMES A. HENDERSON, JR. & AARON D. TWERSKI, PRODUCTS LIABILITY: PROBLEMS AND PROCESS 531–58 (2d ed. 1992).

36. *See* Enright v. Eli Lilly & Co., 570 N.E.2d 198, 203 (N.Y. 1991) ("[A] widely distributed product, if defective, presents a risk to a broad range of potential victims. For that reason, although the need for deterrence is not unique to the products liability context, it [deterrence] may have added weight there.").

37. *See* Shackil v. Lederle Labs., 561 A.2d 511 (N.J. 1989); Smith v. Eli Lilly & Co., 527 N.E.2d 333 (Ill. Ct. App. 1988).

38. Actually, an abnormally dangerous activity may appear even more blameworthy than one performed carelessly. Ordinarily, those conducting abnormally dangerous activities are aware of the risks associated with their enterprises. They proceed with the activity in order to make a profit, even though it will cause harm to a certain faction of the population. Negligent acts usually lack this type of calculation. Thus, they may evince less of the disrespect for human life demonstrated by some strict liability activities.

39. Such conduct also is considered "unreasonable" under the theory of nuisance. According to section 826 of the RESTATEMENT (SECOND) OF TORTS, an intentional invasion of another's real property interests is unreasonable if either "(a) the gravity of the harm outweighs the utility of the actor's conduct, or (b) the harm caused by the conduct is serious and the financial burden of compensating for this and similar harm to others would not make the continuation of the conduct not feasible." RESTATEMENT (SECOND) OF TORTS § 826 (1965). Although section 826 involves an intentional tort, the rationale of that provision (to regulate unusually dangerous activities and to make otherwise valuable enterprises absorb their externalized costs) seems equally applicable to less deliberative conduct. In any event, in most cases of strict liability, those who carry on such enterprises will know to a substantial certainty that some people in the community will be harmed by their conduct, thus satisfying the legal definition of intent.

Notes to Chapter 17
Calculated Transactions

1. Other privileges include defense of property, recovery of property, authority and justification.

2. *See generally* RESTATEMENT (SECOND) OF TORTS § 63–75 (1965) (comprehensively summarizing the rules of self defense); *see also* Silas v. Bowen, 277 F. Supp. 314 (D.S.C. 1967) (defendant was justified in shooting plaintiff's foot with a shotgun after plaintiff grabbed the defendant by the shoulder); Germolus v. Sausser 85 N.W. 946 (Minn. 1901) (noting that the privilege of self-defense terminates when harm is no longer imminent); Drabek v. Sabley, 142 N.W.2d 798 (Wis. 1966) (defendant found liable for beating boy who had thrown a snowball at him); Keep v. Quallman, 32 N.W. 233 (Wis. 1887) (noting that self-defense applies only if one has reasonable grounds to fear an immediate attack); McDonald v. Terrebonne Parish Sch. Bd., 253 So. 2d 558 (La. Ct. App.)(self-defense privilege is limited to use of reasonable force based on relative age, size and strength of the parties), *cert. denied*, 255 So. 2d 353 (La. 1971).

3. *See* Ploof v. Putnam, 71 A. 188 (Vt. 1908) (dock owner liable for casting off plaintiff's boat during stormy weather); *see also* RESTATEMENT (SECOND) OF TORTS §§ 197, 263 (1965) (explaining private necessity); Francis Hermann Bohlen, *Incomplete Privilege to Inflict Intentional Invasions of Interests of Property and Personality*, 39 HARV. L. REV. 307 (1926).

4. Vincent v. Lake Erie Transp. Co., 124 N.W. 221 (Minn. 1910).

5. *See* Perry v. Jefferies, 39 S.E. 515 (S.C. 1901) (defendant held liable for taking timber from plaintiff's land notwithstanding reasonable belief that he owned it); Dexter v. Cole, 6 Wis. 319 (1888) (mistake of fact will not protect an actor who misappropriates the property of another); *see also* Clarke B. Whittier, *Mistake in the Law of Torts*, 15 HARV. L. REV. 335 (1902).

6. Ranson v. Kitner, 31 Ill. App. 241 (1888).

7. *See* Talmage v. Smith, 59 N.W. 656 (Mich. 1894) (defendant held liable for intentionally throwing stick which missed target but struck and injured plaintiff); Carnes v. Thompson, 48 S.W.2d 903 (Mo. 1932) (defendant held liable for intentional striking of unintended plaintiff); Lopez v. Surchia, 246 P.2d 111 (Cal. Ct. App. 1952) (defendant held liable for intentional shooting of unintended plaintiff); *see also* William L. Prosser, *Transferred Intent*, 45 TEX. L. REV. 650 (1967) (discussing the doctrine of transferred intent).

8. This appears to be a slight majority approach. *See* Gortarez v. Smitty's Super Valu, Inc., 680 P.2d 807 (Ariz. 1984) (noting that an intervenor steps into the shoes of the person he's defending and is privileged to act only if that person actually would be privileged to defend himself); Sandman v. Hagan, 154 N.W.2d 113 (Iowa 1967) (same); Young v. Warren, 383 S.E.2d 381 (N.C. Ct. App. 1989) (same).

9. This is the approach advocated by the Restatement. *See* RESTATEMENT (SECOND) OF TORTS § 76 (1965); *see also* Brouster v. Fox, 93 S.W. 318 (Mo. Ct. App. 1906) (defendant is privileged to use reasonable force to defend another, as long as his mistake is reasonable); Beavers v. Calloway, 61 N.Y.S.2d 804 (Sup. Ct.), *aff'd*, 66 N.Y.S.2d 613 (App. Div. 1946) (same); JOHN SALMOND, LAW OF TORTS 44 (8th ed. 1934).

10. *See* Wagner v. Int'l Ry. Co., 133 N.E. 437 (N.Y. 1921) (noting that an endangering

act is wrongful both to the victim and to his rescuer).

11. The equitable doctrine of quantum meruit also enhances the autonomy of altruistic intervenors. If an actor, who is not an officious intermeddler, renders to a distressed party assistance with a reasonably definite, quantifiable value, the party receiving such a benefit is required to compensate the altruist for her efforts. *See* Klintz v. Read, 626 P.2d 52, 55 (Wash. Ct. App. 1981); *see also* RESTATEMENT OF RESTITUTION § 1 (1937) (a "person who has been unjustly enriched at the expense of another is required to make restitution."); *see generally* John W. Wade, *Restitution for Benefits Conferred Without Request*, 19 VAND. L. REV. 1183 (1966).

12. *See Lopez*, 246 P.2d 111 (defendant unreasonably shot boy who was fighting with his son); *see also* George P. Fletcher, *The Right and the Reasonable*, 98 HARV. L. REV. 949 (1985).

13. *See* RESTATEMENT (SECOND) OF TORTS § 323 & cmt. c (1965); *see also* United States v. Lawter, 219 F.2d 559 (5th Cir. 1955) (defendant held liable for negligently undertaking to rescue plaintiff with a helicopter); Carey v. Davis, 180 N.W. 889 (Iowa 1921) (defendant held liable for undertaking to aid vulnerable plaintiff and leaving him in worse condition).

14. *See* Abresch v. Northwestern Bell Tel., 75 N.W.2d 206 (Minn. 1956) (defendant held liable for undertaking to call fire department but failing to do so); Dudley v. Victor Lynn Lines, Inc., 138 A.2d 53 (N.J. 1958) (defendant held liable for inducing decedent's wife to forego obtaining other assistance by promising her that he would call a doctor), *rev'd on other grounds*, 161 A.2d 479 (N.J. 1960); Brown v. MacPherson's, Inc., 545 P.2d 13 (Wash. 1975) (defendant held liable for inducing avalanche expert to believe plaintiffs would be warned of danger); DeLong v. Erie County, 455 N.Y.S.2d 887 (Sup. Ct. App. Div. 1982) (911 dispatcher failed to secure police response to decedent's call for assistance).

15. Implied assumption of risk actually arises in two different interactive paradigms. In calculated transactions, the risk-taker voluntarily (and impliedly through her conduct) encounters a dangerous condition created by another, but without the other's instigation or knowledge. Here, the risk-taker is denied recovery for her injuries because of the benefit she derives from the exercise of her choice and because of her causal responsibility in initiating the encounter. In relations, the risk-taker voluntarily accepts dangers that arise during a planned association with someone else. In cases within this paradigm, the risk-taker's rights are limited because of the effect her choice has upon the autonomy of her counterpart. This latter variety of implied assumption of risk will be discussed in greater detail in Chapter Nineteen.

16. *See* Knight v. Jewett, 834 P.2d 696 (Cal. 1992) (separating implied assumption of risk into two categories: primary—in which no duty is owed by the defendant—and secondary—in which the defendant breaches a duty owed to the plaintiff, yet the plaintiff proceeds to encounter the "unreasonable" danger created by that conduct); Blackburn v. Dorta, 348 So. 2d 287 (Fla. 1977) (same); Meistrich v. Casino Arena Attractions, Inc., 155 A.2d 90 (N.J. 1959) (same).

17. The Tennessee Supreme Court recently catalogued the many different ways in which courts have vitiated or eliminated the preclusive bar of assumption of risk:

> Of the forty-five states, other than Tennessee, that apply principles of compara-

tive fault, only five states—Georgia, Nebraska, Mississippi, Rhode Island and South Dakota—retain assumption of risk as a complete bar to recovery. Ten states abolished the doctrine entirely as a separate affirmative defense before, or without any reference to, the adoption of the state's particular comparative-negligence law. Ten other states by statute have abolished or subsumed the defense of assumption of risk into their comparative fault schemes. The remaining nineteen states which have judicially considered the appropriate role of assumption of risk in light of a statutory or judicial adoption of comparative negligence or fault principles have also altered or abolished the common law doctrine.

See Perez v. McConkey, 872 S.W.2d 897, 903 (Tenn. 1994) (itself holding that implied assumption of risk no longer applies as a complete bar to recovery in a negligence action) (citations omitted).

18. In many jurisdictions, implied assumption of risk cannot be used as a defense to the violation of a protective statute. *See* Blanton v. Kellioka Coal Co., 232 S.W. 614 (Ky. 1921) (child labor act); Bolitho v. Safeway Stores, Inc., 95 P.2d 443 (Mont. 1939) (pure food act); Koenig v. Patrick Constr. Corp., 83 N.E.2d 133 (N.Y. 1948) (factory safety act).

Notes to Chapter 18
Random Transactions

1. This is not to say that, statistically speaking, injuries are more likely the result of some other person's conduct than of the injured party's own actions, although, given our basic survival instinct, such a conclusion does not seem far-fetched. Rather, I am merely suggesting that of those transactions that actually wind up in litigation, very few will involve injuries which are solely induced by the plaintiff herself. Indeed, given the costs of litigation, and the dismal chances for success, only a bold or foolish lawyer would agree to take such a case.

2. 162 N.E. 99 (N.Y. 1928).

3. It might be argued, however, that the railroad, as an owner or occupier of land, owed a duty to prevent the creation of dangerous artificial conditions on its premises, or at least to remove them when and if they developed. Alternatively, as a common carrier, the railroad might have possessed a heightened duty to protect its passengers from harm. Under either analysis, the railroad could have been obligated to screen passengers for explosives or secure large objects, such as the standing scale, to the wooden boards of the platform.

4. This explains why the pugilist who intentionally throws a punch at another, but fails to strike her, may be held liable for assault, while the negligent pedestrian who bumps into a passerby is not responsible for the contact.

5. This is not always the case. If, for example, the first actor's conduct is wrongful because she creates a hidden danger, it may not be possible for the second actor to discover the condition before encountering it. This might be the case where an invitor fails to properly light a stairway and, as a result, her invitee falls down the steps.

6. *See* W. PAGE KEETON ET AL., PROSSER AND KEETON ON TORTS 471 (5th ed. 1984).

Notes to Chapter 19
Relations

1. There is considerable disagreement among academics about what makes contracts enforceable. Charles Fried has argued that promises provide the moral glue which bind together contracting parties. *See* CHARLES FRIED, CONTRACT AS PROMISE: A THEORY OF CONTRACTUAL OBLIGATION (1981). Grant Gilmore, on the other hand, has noted the importance of reliance in enforcing promissory obligations. *See* GRANT GILMORE, THE DEATH OF CONTRACT (1974). For Ian MacNeil, the relationship of the parties, rather than the words they exchange, determines the nature and scope of their commitment to each other. Ian R. MacNeil, *Contracts: Adjustment of Long-Term Economic Relations Under Classical, Neoclassical, and Relational Contract Law*, 72 Nw. U.L. REV. 854 (1978). Recently, however, Randy Barnett has argued that consent more than any other concept provides the moral grounding for contractual agreements. Randy E. Barnett, *A Consent Theory of Contract*, 86 COLUM. L. REV. 269 (1986).

2. Product warranties may be either express or implied. Implied warranties arise by operation of law without any specific statement by the manufacturer or seller. *See* U.C.C. §2-314 (1978). However, express warranties are created only where the seller makes an affirmative representation about the product to the user or consumer. *See* U.C.C. §2-313 (1978). Under section 2-316, the seller, using the appropriate language, may disclaim either type of warranty. *See* U.C.C. §2-316 (1978). For example, all implied warranties are excluded by expressions like "as is." *Id.* Furthermore, section 2-719 of the U.C.C. permits the seller to limit the remedies which may be asserted under a product warranty. *See* U.C.C. §2-719 (1978) (an agreement may provide for remedies in addition to or in substitution for those provided by the U.C.C. and may limit or alter the measure of damages recoverable under the U.C.C., as by limiting the buyer's remedies to return of goods and repayment of the price or to repair and replacement of non-conforming goods and parts).

3. *See* Randy E. Barnett, *The Sound of Silence: Default Rules and Contractual Consent*, 78 VA. L. REV. 821, 880 (1992) (where there is an unexpressed (and possibly non-conscious, but nonetheless genuine) tacit assumption shared by both parties, it almost invariably reflects the commonsense expectations of the relevant community).

4. Assumption of risk rests upon the victim's consent and requires actual knowledge of danger. However, contributory negligence may rest upon constructive knowledge. Under the concept of constructive knowledge, the victim is held responsible for dangers she did not actually perceive if a reasonable person could or should have discovered such risks. *See* Grey v. Fibreboard Paper Prods. Co., 418 P.2d 153 (Cal. 1966).

5. *See* Ford v. Gouin, 834 P.2d 724 (Cal. 1992) (water skier denied recovery against ski boat operator for injuries incurred when he struck tree); Brown v. Green, 884 P.2d 55 (Cal. 1985) (terms of lease established that lessee assumed responsibility for removing abestos-laden material from property); *see also* JOHN G. FLEMING, THE LAW OF TORTS 242–69 (7th ed. 1987) (providing analysis of assumption of risk).

6. Daniel Kahneman, Paul Slovic and Amos Tversky provide the most detailed description and analysis of these heuristics in their book, *Judgment Under Uncertainty: Heuristics and Biases. See* JUDGMENT UNDER UNCERTAINTY: HEURISTICS AND BIASES (D. Kahneman, P. Slovic & A. Tversky, eds. 1982).

7. For more on the "availability" heuristic, see Amos Tversky & Daniel Kahneman, *Availability: A Heuristic for Judging Frequency and Probability*; Michael Ross & Fiore Sicoly, *Egocentric Biases in Availability and Attribution*; and Shelly E. Taylor, *The Availability Bias in Social Perception and Interaction*, which all appear in JUDGMENT, *supra* note 6, at 163–200.

8. *See* Shelly E. Taylor, *The Availability Bias in Social Perception and Interaction*, in JUDGMENT, *supra* note 6, at 191–92.

9. *Id.* at 192–94.

10. *Id.*

11. The "representativeness" heuristic has been a frequent source of commentary and analysis among decision-making and problem-solving theorists. *See generally* JUDGMENT, *supra* note 6, at 23-98 (containing a number of articles which discuss this heuristic).

12. *See* Amos Tversky & Daniel Kahneman, *Judgment Under Uncertainty: Heuristics and Biases* in JUDGMENT, *supra* note 6, at 4-11.

13. *Id.* at 14–18.

14. The overconfidence phenomenon is addressed more fully in JUDGMENT, *supra* note 6, at 287–351.

15. Utilizing these heuristics, Howard Latin, in his paper entitled *Problem-Solving Behavior and Theories of Tort Liability*, has proposed an expansive model for reforming the liability rules of tort law. *See* Howard A. Latin, *Problem-Solving Behavior and Theories of Tort Liability*, 73 CAL. L. REV. 677 (1985). Latin's theory starts from the philosophical perspective that the fundamental objective of tort law is accident avoidance. To accomplish this objective, he argues, it is necessary to consider the problem-solving capacities of parties who will or are likely to interact. He notes that there are some actors who may be suited to assess the consequences of their behavior but never do. He explains: "In many settings, people lack sufficient information and expertise to assess risks properly; they are inattentive to known risks; they do not understand the applicable liability doctrines; and compelling nonlegal incentives shape their behavior." *Id.* at 692. For these individuals, Latin laments, the imposition of tort liability will seldom promote the social engineering goal of accident avoidance.

Thus, Latin proposes that tort liability be "assigned whenever possible to categories of actors who do, *in reality*, think about accident prevention, loss spreading, and the effects of legal rules, and whose behavior may therefore be significantly influenced by potential liability." *Id.* at 681. "The central social question," he explains, "is not whether average people could conceivably make cost-minimizing decisions," but "whether they really do so in specific accident contexts...." *Id.* at 696.

From this premise, Latin attempts to go the next step in defining and identifying both those individuals who are likely to conduct cost-benefit analyses of their activities and those who likely will not. The former group, whom he labels "high-attention" problem solvers, are characterized by their ability to understand material risks and applicable liability doctrines, their attention to risks and legal rules while engaged in risky conduct, and their penchant for assessing the costs and benefits of alternative choices when subject to liability for a designated type of accident loss. *Id.* at 697. Individuals or entities which lack any one of these attributes are unlikely to be effective cost minimizers and so are included within the latter category of "low-attention" problem solvers. *Id.*

"High-attention" problem solvers are distinguished by their sophisticated decision-making processes. Ordinarily, these processes include specialists who concentrate on limited problem issues. In addition, they are able to acquire feedback from previous decisions and adapt policy choices from this experience. Finally, they are subject to supervision by others whose job it is to control the pecuniary costs of the activity. *Id.* at 694–95. Because it is nearly impossible for these features to coexist without an institutional structure, almost all "high-attention" problem solvers are found in organizational, commercial or professional settings.

Latin uses this profile to develop a liability system matrix. Under this matrix, each of the parties in a tortious interaction is first identified as either a "high-attention" or "low-attention" problem solver. After the appropriate characterizations have been made, the interactive axis itself must be defined as unilateral or bilateral. A unilateral problem solving axis exists where only one of the parties is a "high-attention" problem solver; where the parties are either both "high-attention" or both "low-attention" problem solvers, a bilateral axis exists. *Id.* at 701.

Liability rules are then assigned to the relationship. Negligence or contractual analysis is used in bilateral contexts involving two "high-attention" problem solvers. Strict liability applies to "high-attention" defendants in unilateral contexts. Where the plaintiff is the unilateral "high-attention" problem solver, she must bear her own loss. And, when both parties share a "low-attention" profile, their dispute should be settled within a compulsory insurance system. *Id.* at 697 (see chart in Figure 1).

Latin notes that bilateral "high-attention" relationships are rather rare in tort cases because both parties must satisfy all the criteria of efficient decision-making. However, he provides several examples of unilateral problem-solving contexts. These include common carriers and passengers, operators of abnormally dangerous activities and those harmed by such activities, sports arenas and spectators, intentional tortfeasors and their victims, and product manufacturers, including auto makers, and their customers. *Id.* at 710–26.

Despite appearances, Latin rejects a relational moniker for his liability matrix. Rather, he characterizes his model as "situational." Distinguishing Calabresi and Hirschoff's better cost avoider approach, *see* Guido Calabresi & Jon Hirschoff, *Toward a Test for Strict Liability in Torts*, 81 YALE L. REV. 1055 (1972), which requires a comparison of the parties' respective problem solving capabilities, Latin states that his theory depends instead on a separate "qualitative" judgment of each party's abilities. He reasons that "it would generally be easier for legal institutions to decide qualitatively whether typical parties are informed problem solvers in a given accident setting than to evaluate their relative decision-making and preventative capabilities." Latin, *supra* note 15, at 703.

Despite this disclaimer, a comparison of Latin's model to current tort theories reveals its obvious "relational" traits. Under contemporary tort theory, the attributes or conduct of the plaintiff play no role in the assignment of liability rules imposed against the defendant. In Latin's model, however, the applicable rule can only be determined by evaluating the plaintiff's problem solving abilities. Although the abilities of the parties are considered separately, this assessment has no meaning apart from the specific context of their relationship. And, because each party's problem-solving prowess can differ radically from one risk to the next, the relationship of the parties, relative to the risk, is fluid, not static, and so will require an independent investigation in each case for each risk.

Whatever its formal description, Latin's paradigm, at a minimum, invokes the basic relational framework of analysis slowly influencing the direction of modern tort theory. Though eschewing consideration of the specific interactions of the parties, and its effect on their behavior, Latin's qualitative risk-assessment model confirms the importance of the relative status and attributes of the parties in broadly defining the context of their relationship. Moreover, like the theory of Calabresi and Hirschoff, Latin's theory also emphasizes the significance of that relation beyond its constituent members by considering the social distributive effects of the parties' private risk allocation decisions. This itself is noteworthy, since it introduces into the analysis normative content foreign to corrective justice. Perhaps of most relevance for our present inquiry, this theory further sharpens our understanding of risk-assessment by specific categories of actors, and so promises to be instructive for any analysis of risk-allocation questions.

16. *See* Trainor v. Aztalan Cycle Club, Inc., 432 N.W.2d 626 (Wis. Ct. App. 1988).

17. Studies show that consumers who are familiar with certain products often will fail to recognize or will disregard warnings or instructions placed upon those goods. For example, in one recent study a number of above-ground swimming pool owners were asked to examine a pool as if they were about to purchase it. Half were shown a pool with a warning against diving; the other half were shown a pool with no warning at all. For each group, the presence or absence of the warning was seldom remembered by the participants. Even where the warning was seen, it had no effect upon the participants' perception of the danger presented by the pool. And for those who were already inclined to dive into pools, the warning had no effect upon their behavior. *See* Gerald Goldhaber & Mark deTurck, *Effects of Consumers' Familiarity With a Product on Attention To and Compliance With Warnings*, 11 J. PROD. LIAB. 29 (1988); *see also* Alan L. Dorris & Jerry Purswell, *Warnings and Human Behavior: Implications for the Design of Product Warnings*, 1 J. PROD. LIAB. 254 (1977) (in study involving 100 high school and college students, all participants failed to notice a warning placed on a hammer).

18. This tendency was documented by Dorothy Nelkin and Michael Brown in their book, *Workers at Risk. See* DOROTHY NELKIN & MICHAEL S. BROWN, WORKERS AT RISK (1984). Nelkin and Brown surveyed industrial workers about their perception of and attitudes towards the risks they encountered on the job. Many of the respondents echoed the sentiment expressed by Daniel, a chemical operator in a chemical plant. He opined:

> When I first started working I was scared to death when I saw cyanide, hydrochloric acid, and all that high powered stuff. But now I'm used to it. I know what's around, what I'm working with. The jitters go away. It don't scare me.... We joke about the risks. We got a lot of rodents that run around, like mice and stuff, and they're always chewing on something. Someone will say, "hey, watch out for that little rat. He's got cyanide in him and he'll explode."

Id. at 85.

19. *See* Michael S. Brown, *Patient Perceptions of Drug Risks and Benefits*, 1 RISK 203 (1990); Ilan B. Vertinsky & Donald A. Wehrung, *Risk Perception and Drug Safety Evaluation*, 2 RISK 281 (1991).

20. Although bicycle accidents account for a large number of all accidental injuries sustained in the United States, many people view bicycling as a relatively safe activity. In one recent study, people were asked to evaluate and rank the risks in ninety activities, industries or products. Bicycles appeared seventy-fifth on the list, behind such things as nuclear power (6th—statistically one of our safest energy sources), food preservatives (35th), aspirin (50th), food coloring (62nd) and skyscrapers (69th). *See* Paul Slovic, Gary C.

Fischoff & Robert J. Lichtenstein, *Facts and Fears: Understanding Perceived Risk*, in SOCIETAL RISK ASSESSMENT: HOW SAFE IS SAFE ENOUGH? 203–04 (R. Schwing & W. Albers, eds. 1980) (see chart in Table 8).

21. *See* ELEANOR SINGER & PHYLLIS M. ENDRENY, REPORTING ON RISK (1993).

22. *See* David Shaw, *Media Speak to a Public Ripe to Find Health Danger*, LOS ANGELES TIMES, Sept. 13, 1994, at A1; David Shaw, *Headlines and High Anxiety*, LOS ANGELES TIMES, Sept. 11, 1994, at A1; *see also* Paul Slovic, Baruch Fischhoff, and Sarah Lichtenstein, *Facts Versus Fears: Understanding Perceived Risk*, in JUDGMENT, *supra* note 6, at 467–68.

23. *See* David Shaw, *Alar Panic Shows Power of Media to Trigger Fear*, LOS ANGELES TIMES, Sept. 12, 1994, at A19.

24. *Id.*

25. *See* Slovic et al., *supra* note 20, at 195 ("newness" listed as one of eight criteria used to assess risk); *see also* PETER HUBER, LIABILITY 156–59 (1988) (noting how the newness of a product or technology makes it more susceptible to liability and less attractive to insure); *see generally* Peter Huber, *Safety and the Second Best: The Hazards of Public Risk Management in the Courts*, 85 COLUM. L. REV. 277 (1985).

26. *See* Paul Slovic, Baruch Fischhoff & Sarah Lichtenstein, *Facts Versus Fears: Understanding Perceived Risk*, in JUDGMENT, *supra* note 6, at 485–86.

27. *See* Slovic et al., *supra* note 20, at 192–94, 211 (concluding that "[t]he perceived potential for catastrophic loss of life emerges as one of the most important risk characteristics....").

28. *See* Clayton P. Gillette & James E. Krier, *Risk, Courts, and Agencies*, 138 U. PA. L. REV. 1027, 1076–77 (1990). Professors Gillette and Krier explain the important effect of "control" on the perception of risk as follows:

> Voluntary exposure pre-supposes knowledge. Knowledge coupled with freedom of action facilitates individual choice and efforts to control events bearing on the choice. To be forced to face a risk, on the other hand, or to be ignorant of it, or to sense that no one is really in command of it, leaves one's well-being in the hands of others, or of no one. Either alternative is obviously inferior, under most circumstances, to being in charge.

Id.

29. *Id.*

30. *See* Ortelere v. Teachers' Retirement Bd., 250 N.E.2d 460 (N.Y. 1969) (mentally ill); *see also* RESTATEMENT (SECOND) OF CONTRACTS §§ 14, 15 (1981) (dealing with infants, and individuals with mental illness or defect).

31. *See* Laura Henning, *On Their Own*, LOS ANGELES TIMES, Oct. 30, 1994, at K1 (describing HOME and HOPE programs in which parents purchase housing with federal and local grants and lease it to their mentally disabled children who learn to become independent by living in and maintaining the residences).

32. *See* Tunkl v. Regents of Univ. of Calif., 383 P.2d 441 (Cal. 1963) (exculpatory provision between patient and nonprofit hospital held void as against public policy); Meiman v. Rehabilitation Ctr., Inc., 444 S.W.2d 78 (Ky. 1969) (exculpatory agreement between patient, who sought treatment after leg amputation, and rehabilitation facility void as against public policy); Cardona v. Eden Realty Co., 288 A.2d 34 (N.J. Super. Ct. App.

Div. 1972) (clause which releases tenement landlord of liability for future acts is invalid); *see also* RESTATEMENT (SECOND) OF TORTS § 402A cmt. b (1965); U.C.C. § 2-719 (3) (1978).

33. Unlike intrinsic incapacities, the disabilities which flow from such relations are not peculiar to the parties themselves, but arise from their relative status within a particular interactive context. Thus, they are not permanent but changeable from case to case.

34. Examples might include innkeepers and guests, common carriers and passengers, business invitors and invitees, etc. The market for the services offered in such relations typically is more competitive than for necessities, thus affording more choice to their potential consumers. Still, given the expertise of these proprietors, and the control they exercise over the administration of their services, they are routinely subject to a general duty to protect their patrons.

35. Although many such relations involve necessities, this is not always the case. Where the relationship is not vital to the weaker party's basic welfare, her transactional capacity is less impaired, and the chances for obtaining her true consent are far better. Thus, the presumption of relational incapacity may be overridden by a weaker showing of reliance by the proprietor. In such a case, the justice concern of reciprocity will be a factor in determining whether, or to what extent, the proprietor's general duty may be limited by the consent of the other. Where the proprietor acted only because the patron consented, the patron's permission of the action may create a less onerous special duty which replaces the state-imposed restriction of it. Yet even here, if the patron's harm is substantial enough (affecting a primary good such as bodily integrity), it may outweigh whatever intangible autonomy restriction the proprietor may have suffered. In such a case, the presumption of incapacity will prevail, and the proprietor will be held to the state standard of responsibility.

There *are* occasions where such a presumption could be overcome. If the weaker party encounters a danger either created or not suppressed by her counterpart, and with deliberation elects to expose herself to it, her choice seems to bear all the hallmarks of volition. Such might be the case, for example, where an industrial employee, in a reckless game of chicken, intentionally thrusts her hand into the pinch point of a punch press. Alternatively, a worker who receives greater compensation for accepting the risks of her occupation might be said to have chosen this accommodation voluntarily.

36. *See* Suter v. San Angelo Foundary & Mach. Co., 406 A.2d. 140 (N.J. 1979); Cremeans v. Willmar Henderson Mfg. Co., 566 N.E.2d 1203 (Ohio 1991). The remarks of Ben, a chemical plant repairman, reflect this bleak reality:

> Most guys won't tell their foreman, "I'm not going to do that," because they just got hired and they'll lose their jobs. If you have a family, a house, a car, and bills to pay, you forget about your personal feelings about certain things. We really don't have a choice. I can't refuse to work knowing that tomorrow I can't get another job. I can't look for a year and a half for a job. I'd lose everything. I don't think it's right for them to say, "Well, if you don't like it, leave."

NELKIN & BROWN, *supra* note 18, at 92.

37. *See* Jordan v. Goddard, 442 N.E.2d 1162 (Mass. App. Ct. 1982).

38. *See* United Novelty Co. v. Daniels, 42 So. 2d 395 (Miss. 1949).

39. *See* Moran v. Faberge, Inc., 332 A.2d 11 (Md. 1975).

40. While the Restatement of Contracts renders all waivers of liability for intentionally

inflicted harm void as against public policy, *see* RESTATEMENT (SECOND) OF CONTRACTS § 195 (1981), the Restatement of Torts takes a less extreme position, *see* RESTATEMENT (SECOND) OF TORTS §§ 892A, 496B (1965). Under the latter authority, one may assume the risk of an intentional act if the choice is both knowing and voluntary. Why didn't the drafters of the Restatement of Torts make such clauses unenforceable as did their colleagues in the contract realm? Temporal context seems to be the most likely explanation. Sections 892A and 496B were adopted in 1965, shortly after the Uniform Commercial Code was drafted, and long before its widespread acceptance. Both contract and tort law have been greatly "liberalized" since that time. The Restatement of Contracts § 195(1), which was adopted in 1981, reflects this more liberal view.

41. *See* U.C.C. § 2-719(3) (1978) ("Consequential damages may be limited or excluded unless the limitation or exclusion is unconscionable. Limitation of consequential damages for injury to the person in the case of consumer goods is prima facie unconscionable but limitation of damages where the loss is commercial is not.").

42. *See* Winterstein v. Wilcom, 293 A.2d 821 (Md. Ct. Spec. App. 1972).

43. *Compare* Murphy v. Steeplechase Amusement Co., 166 N.E. 173 (N.Y. 1929) (wherein the plaintiff fell during an amusement park ride which contained a moving belt designed to upset the riders).

44. *See* Rowland v. Christian, 443 P.2d 561 (Cal. 1968).

45. *See* Boyl v. Cal. Chem. Co., 221 F. Supp. 669 (D. Or. 1963).

46. *See* Hudson v. Craft, 204 P.2d 1 (Cal. 1949); *see also* RESTATEMENT (SECOND) OF TORTS § 892C (1977) (voiding consent and allowing recovery where the defendant's conduct violates a criminal statute designed to protect a class of persons of which the plaintiff is a member).

47. This, in effect, is the approach advocted by section 112(B) of the Model Uniform Product Liability Act which eliminates assumption of risk as a bar to recovery and permits the jury to consider whether and to what extent the plaintiff's recovery, if any, should be mitigated by her conduct. *See* MODEL UNIFORM PRODUCT LIABILITY ACT § 112(B) (1979).

48. When individuals mutually assent to assume or assign the risks of their relationship, a private agreement is formed. More often than not, such agreements allocate responsibility for certain consequences of the encounter to one party or the other. Of course, there may be exceptions where the parties agree to share the burdens of their association. For example, the parties may decide in advance that if personal injury results from their relation, they will split the cost of repairing the damage. In most cases, however, risks are not shared in this way. Instead, all of the anticipated risks are catalogued and divvied up between the parties. Each risk then becomes the sole responsibility of the party to whom it is assigned. To illustrate, in some product warranties the manufacturer agrees to repair or replace a defective good while the consumer consents to bear the cost of all consequential damage that it may produce. Here, the entire risk of product damage is allocated to the manufacturer, and the risk of other loss—including damage to other property and personal injury—is assumed completely by the consumer. As indicated earlier, however, such a clause might contravene section 2-719(3) of the Uniform Commercial Code which states that a remedy modification excluding consequential damage in a consumer transaction is presumed unconscionable. *See supra* note 41.

49. This is not particularly surprising since in many of these disputes, the tortfeasor,

who controls the risks inherent in the relation, already possesses a heightened tort duty to protect her more vulnerable counterpart.

50. *See* RENA A. GORLIN, CODES OF PROFESSIONAL RESPONSIBILITY 376 (3d ed. 1994) (citing Ethical Principles of Psychologists and Code of Conduct § 6.07).

51. *See* Falcon v. Mem. Hosp., 462 N.W.2d 44 (Mich. 1990).

52. *See* McKethean v. Wash. Metro. Area Transit Auth., 588 A.2d 708, 712 (D.C. 1991) (common carrier owes a duty of reasonable care to its passengers); Hernandez v. Rapid Bus Co., 641 N.E.2d 886 (Ill. App. Ct. 1994) (bus company's voluntary undertaking to see that passengers made it safely from school bus to school building gave rise to duty to protect student from foreseeable criminal attack by fellow school bus passenger); *see also* RESTATEMENT (SECOND) OF TORTS §§ 314A(1) (a) cmts. d & e (1965) (stating that where a special relationship exists, such as between a common carrier and its passengers, the carrier undeniably has a duty to protect its passengers from foreseeable harm arising from criminal conduct of others).

53. Implied warranties of habitability were developed by courts to combat housing shortages, standardized leases and discrimination which place today's tenants, as consumers of housing, in a poor position to bargain effectively for express warranties and covenants requiring landlords to lease and maintain safe and sanitary housing. *See* Radaker v. Scott, 855 P.2d 1037, 1042 (Nev. 1993); Wade v. Jobe, 818 P.2d 1006, 1010 (Utah 1991); Hilder v. St. Peter, 478 A.2d 202, 208 (Vt. 1984); Adams v. Gaylock, 378 S.E.2d 297, 299–300 (W. Va. 1989); Moxley v. Laramie Builders, Inc., 600 P.2d 733, 755 (Wyo. 1979); Nastri v. Wood Bros. Homes, Inc., 690 P.2d 158, 161 (Ariz. Ct. App. 1984); *see also* Becker v. IRM Corp., 698 P.2d 116 (Cal. 1985) (wherein the court held a landlord strictly liable for injuries resulting from latent defects within the leased premises), *overruled by* Peterson v. Superior Ct., 899 P.2d 905 (Cal. 1995).

54. *See* Henningsen v. Bloomfield Motors, Inc., 161 A.2d 69 (N.J. 1960); *see also* U.C.C. § 2-314 (1978).

55. *See* Morgan v. Yuba County, 41 Cal. Rptr. 508 (Dist. Ct. App. 1964).

56. *See* Florence v. Goldberg, 375 N.E.2d 763 (N.Y. 1978).

57. *See* Coffee v. McDonnell-Douglas Corp., 503 P.2d 1366 (Cal. 1972).

58. *See* Blackburn v. Dorta, 348 So. 2d 287 (Fla. 1977).

59. There are certain exchanges which appear patently unequal. The right given up by the consenter may be a primary good like bodily integrity or an indispensable material resource, or the power and abilities of the parties may be grossly disproportionate. In these cases, consent to the transfer seems suspect. If, in fact, consent has been coerced or cajoled, then the resulting exchange may be harmful to the apparent consenter. Under such circumstances, what is the state to do? Accept expressions of consent at face value and allow the exchange to stand? Or should it scrutinize such expressions for true volition?

The answers to these questions depend upon one's view of the role of the state. Libertarians might argue that the state should never interfere in the private relations of its citizens. Social democrats, on the other hand, might contend that the state has a duty to protect citizens from all actual harms, even those shrouded by a veil of consent. Modern tort law embraces the latter view. It precludes the private modification of distributive protections under circumstances evincing a lack of consent.

60. In some circumstances, the state may decline to enforce its protective duties on behalf of actors who are injured in encounters where their consent to assume a risk is

objective only. This is especially likely where one party's actions have a profound effect on the behavior of those with whom she interacts. To illustrate, in a case of mutual combat, assume A promises to let B strike her in the face, so long as B extends A the same courtesy. Here, it is the giving of permission by A which will account for B's subsequent decision to throw a punch. Even if A was just joking, and so did not subjectively consent to the blow, her apparent consent may have had such a compelling influence on the parties' interaction that she will be held to bear the consequences of her prank. In this situation B's reliance on A's promise trumps whatever protection A normally would have received from the state's distributive prohibition against battery. Alternatively, the state may refuse to enforce its rules of responsibility if doing so would violate public policy. Such might be the case in the above hypothetical where A and B have engaged in a relation which possesses no social utility, and poses great potential for breaching the peace. Regardless of whether A subjectively agreed to the contact, the state may wish to discourage her behavior by denying her any preemptive or corrective remedy.

61. 28 N.E. 266 (Mass. 1891).

62. *Compare* Knight v. Jewett, 834 P.2d 696 (Cal. 1992) (in which the Supreme Court of California rejected the claim of a woman who sustained injuries in a "touch" football game on the ground that the player who inflicted the injury-producing contact owed her no duty of care).

63. As evidence of this reluctance, consider the case of Hardy v. Southland Corp., 645 A.2d 839 (Pa. Super. Ct. 1994). There, the plaintiff slipped and fell in a convenience store after stepping upon the defendant's rain-slicked, linoleum floor. Although the plaintiff admitted that she had glanced at the floor and had noticed that it was wet, the court found that she did not assume the risk of falling. In reaching this conclusion, the court observed that

> the testimony does not establish that appellant [the plaintiff] ever interrupted her normal walking gait, noticed the condition of the floor, pondered it for a moment and then proceeded anyway realizing that it may be slippery.... The "preliminary conduct" of walking into the store is not such that should be regarded as accompanied with assuming the risk of a fall on a slippery floor. Appellant did not become aware of the "known danger" until just before she took the step which caused her injury. Indeed, in order to avoid the danger it might have been necessary for her to stop herself in mid-stride. In our opinion these are not circumstances to which the doctrine should apply as an affirmative defense. Rather, these circumstances invite comparison of negligence under applicable law.

Id. at 841.

64. *See* Dobratz v. Thomson, 468 N.W.2d 654 (Wis. 1991); *Trainor*, 432 N.W.2d 626.

65. *See* RESTATEMENT (SECOND) OF CONTRACTS § 195 (1981); RESTATEMENT (SECOND) OF TORTS §§ 496B & 892A (1965).

66. RESTATEMENT (SECOND) OF CONTRACTS § 195 (1981).

67. *Id.*

68. 383 P.2d 441 (Cal. 1963).

69. *Id.* at 446.

70. *See* Okla. Nat. Gas Co. v. Appel, 266 P.2d 442 (Okla. 1954).

71. *See* Turek v. Pa. R. Co., 64 A.2d 779 (Pa. 1949).

72. *See* Gardner v. Jonathan Club, 317 P.2d 961 (Cal. 1950).

73. *See* George v. Bekins Van & Storage Co., 205 P.2d 1037 (Cal. 1949).

74. *See* Makower v. Kinney Sys., 318 N.Y.S.2d 515 (Sup. Ct. 1970).

75. *See* Sys. Auto Parks & Garages, Inc. v. Am. Econ. Ins. Co., 411 N.E.2d 163 (Ind. Ct. App. 1980).

76. *See* Denver Union Term. Ry. Co. v. Cullinan, 210 P. 602 (Colo. 1922).

77. *See* Sporsem v. First Nat'l Bank, 233 P. 641 (Wash. 1925).

78. *See* Thomas v. Hous. Auth., 426 P.2d 836 (Wash. 1967).

79. *See* Discount Fabric House v. Wis. Tel. Co., 345 N.W.2d 417 (Wis. 1984).

80. *See* Scott v. Pac. W. Mountain Resort, 834 P.2d 6, 11 (Wash. 1992); Meyer v. Naperville Manner, Inc., 634 N.E.2d 411 (Ill. Ct. App. 1994).

81. *See* Wagenblast v. Odessa Sch. Dist., 758 P.2d 968 (Wash. 1988).

82. *Tunkl*, 383 P.2d 441; *see also* W. PAGE KEETON ET AL., PROSSER AND KEETON ON TORTS § 68, at 482–84 (5th ed. 1984).

83. *See Dobratz*, 468 N.W.2d 654.

84. *See* Boyce v. West, 862 P.2d 592 (Wash. Ct. App. 1993); Murphy v. N. Am. River Runners, Inc., 412 S.E.2d 504 (W. Va. 1991); Arnold v. Shawano County Agric. Soc'y, 330 N.W.2d 773 (Wis. 1983); *see also* ARTHUR L. CORBIN, CORBIN ON CONTRACTS § 1472, at 596 (1962 & Supp. 1991); SAMUEL WILLISTON, A TREATISE ON THE LAW OF CONTRACTS § 1759A, at 144 (3d ed. 1972 & Supp. 1991); RESTATEMENT (SECOND) OF TORTS § 486B, cmt. b (1965).

85. *Tunkl*, 383 P.2d at 446.

86. Some courts take a different view of primary implied assumption of risk. They hold that, where the doctrine applies, the defendant either owed no duty to the plaintiff in the first place, or that if such a duty was owed, it was not breached. *See Blackburn*, 348 So. 2d 247.

87. *See Knight*, 834 P.2d 696.

88. The importance of risk reciprocation was first noted by professor George Fletcher in his pioneering work, *Fairness and Utility in Tort Theory*. *See* George P. Fletcher, *Fairness and Utility in Tort Theory*, 85 HARV. L. REV. 537 (1972). In that piece, Professor Fletcher offered two paradigms of tort law. One, labelled the paradigm of reasonableness, explains tort theory in utilitarian terms. This is the traditional approach which has achieved predominance in negligence cases. The other theory, which he called the paradigm of reciprocity, takes a deontological perspective. Under the reciprocity theory, liability is determined by comparing the risks created by each of the parties and imposed upon the other. If the risks thus imposed by the plaintiff upon the defendant reciprocate or exceed those created by the defendant, she may not recover for her loss. In essence, the imposition of reciprocal risk amounts to a waiver of that party's security from risk in return for the privilege of engaging in her own high risk activity.

This idea of reciprocity seems to emanate quite naturally from a scheme of corrective justice. Under this system, it will be recalled, a party who disrupts the preexisting state of equality among individuals is accountable for restoring the equilibrium if her conduct is wrongful. In defining wrongfulness, Fletcher invokes a version of the Rawlsian first principle of justice: all in society have the right to the maximum security from risk compatible with a like security for everyone else. One who imposes more risk than she incurs violates this principle. *Id.* at 550.

Although this approach has received some legitimate criticism, *see* Jules L. Coleman,

Moral Theories of Torts: Their Scope and Limits, Part I, 1 LAW & PHIL. 371 (1982), it remains important for the originality of its perspective. By invoking a comparative analysis, the reciprocity paradigm forces at least an initial consideration of the parties' relations. It emphasizes that fairness in the allocation of risk is not an isolated but relative concept. Having broken this new ground, Fletcher's theory has paved the way for more expansive excursions into relational tort theory. *See, e.g.,* Howard A. Latin, *Problem-Solving Behavior and Theories of Tort Liability*, 73 CAL. L. REV. 677 (1985) (proposing a liability matrix determined by the relative capacities of interacting parties to perceive and control the risks of their association). Fletcher's theory is considered further in the Epilogue.

90. Mississippi, in 1910, was the first state to adopt a general comparative negligence act. By the mid-1960s, contributory negligence was replaced by comparative fault in six other states, including Georgia, Nebraska, Wisconsin, South Dakaota, Arkansas and Maine. *See* Alvis v. Ribar, 421 N.E.2d 886, 891–92 (Ill. 1981).

91. Many early courts held that one who voluntarily exposed herself to known dangers was guilty of contributory negligence. *See* Wallace v. Great Atl. & Pac. Tea Co., 85 F. Supp. 296 (N.D. W. Va. 1949); Wright v. City of St. Cloud, 55 N.W. 819 (Minn. 1893); Tharp v. Pa. R. Co., 2 A.2d 695 (Pa. 1938); Smith v. City of Cuyahoga Falls, 53 N.E.2d 670 (Ohio Ct. App. 1943).

92. *See, e.g.,* ARK. STAT. ANN. § 27-1763 (1979); CONN. GEN. STAT. ANN. § 57-572h(c) (West Supp. 1985); Brown v. Kreuser, 560 P.2d 105 (Colo. 1977); Wilson v. Gordon, 354 A.2d 398 (Me. 1976); Bolduc v. Crain, 181 A.2d 641 (N.H. 1962); Wentz v. Deseth, 221 N.W.2d 101 (N.D. 1974); *see also* UNIFORM MODEL PRODUCT LIABILITY ACT § 112(B) (1) (1979) ("When the product seller proves, by a preponderance of the evidence, that the claimant knew about the product's defective condition and voluntarily used the product or voluntarily assumed the risk of harm from the product, the claimant's damages shall be subject to reduction to the extent that the claimant did not act as an ordinary reasonably prudent person under the circumstances.").

93. Except in a jurisdiction with a modified comparative fault system. In such a system, the plaintiff is barred from recovery if her fault is either equal to or greater than that of the defendant. *See* V. SCHWARTZ, COMPARATIVE NEGLIGENCE § 2.1 (2d ed. 1986).

94. *See, e.g., Blackburn*, 348 So. 2d 287; Salinas v. Vierstra, 695 P.2d 369 (Idaho 1985); Meistrich v. Casino Arena Attractions, Inc., 155 A.2d 90 (N.J. 1959).

95. Although the result is a finding of "no duty," it appears that California reaches this conclusion using the terminology of "primary implied assumption of risk," and not the language of duty. *See Knight*, 834 P.2d 696.

96. *Id.* at 703.

97. *Id.* at 704.

98. *Id.* at 707.

99. Justice Kennard, who authored a dissenting opinion in *Knight*, seems to have recognized this point. She states that the essential distinction to be drawn in assumption of risk cases is not between primary risks and secondary risks, but between risk choices that are deliberate, and thus consensual, and those that are merely careless. *Id.* at 715. Consent to a risk, she notes, "will negative liability... and thus provides a complete defense to an action for negligence." *Id.*

100. *Se, e.g.,* IND. CODE ANN. § 34-4-33-2(a) (Burns Supp. 1985); Keegan v. Anchor Inns, Inc., 606 F.2d 35, 41 n.8 (3d Cir. 1979) (interpreting Virgin Islands' compartive fault

statute); Braswell v. Economy Supply Co., 281 So. 2d 669 (Miss. 1973); Gustafson v. Benda, 661 S.W.2d 11 (Mo. 1983).

101. *See Knight*, 834 P.2d at 720 (Kennard, J., dissenting) ("In those cases that have merged into comparative fault, partial recovery is permitted, not because the plaintiff has acted unreasonably, but because the unreasonableness of the plaintiff's apparent choice provides compelling evidence that the plaintiff was merely careless and could not have truly appreciated and voluntarily consented to the risk....").

102. *See* Palmer v. A.H. Robins Co., 684 P.2d 187, 209 (Colo. 1984); Dooley v. Everett, 805 S.W.2d 380, 384 (Tenn. Ct. App. 1990); *see also* W. PROSSER, THE LAW OF TORTS 324 (4th ed. 1971).

103. *See* Buchanan v. Rose, 159 S.W.2d 109, 110 (Tex. 1942) (stating that a mere bystander who did not create the dangerous condition confronting the plaintiff is not required to become a good Samaritan and prevent the plaintiff's injury); *see also* Williams v. State, 664 P.2d 137 (Cal. 1983); Hurley v. Eddingfield, 59 N.W. 1058 (Ind. 1901); Buch v. Amory Mfg. Co., 44 A. 809, 810 (N.H. 1898).

104. *See* Krupnick v. Hartford Accident & Indem. Co., 34 Cal. Rptr. 2d 39 (Ct. App. 1994); Wallace v. Shoreham Hotel Corp., 49 A.2d 81 (D.C. 1946); *see also* Calvert Magruder, *Mental and Emotional Disturbances in the Law of Torts*, 49 HARV. L. REV. 1033, 1051 (1936); RESTATEMENT (SECOND) OF TORTS § 48 (1965) (recognizing liability of common carrier for insults by servants).

105. *See* Katamay v. Chicago Transit Auth., 289 N.E.2d 623, 635 (Ill. 1972); Schindler v. So. Coach Lines, Inc., 217 S.W.2d 775, 778 (Tenn. 1949); Fillpot v. Midway Airlines, Inc., 633 N.E.2d 237 (Ill. App. Ct. 1994).

106. *See* Farwell v. Keaton, 240 N.W.2d 217 (Mich. 1976) (boy who placed unconscious friend in the back seat of his car, drove to various locations throughout the night and then left the car parked in the friend's driveway without notifying his parents, was held liable for the friend's death); RESTATEMENT (SECOND) OF TORTS § 324(b) (1965) (where one who is under no duty to act, takes charge of another who is helpless to adequately aid or protect himself, he is subject to liability to the other for any bodily harm caused by the actor discontinuing his aid, if by so doing he leaves the other in a worse position than when the actor took charge of him).

107. *See* L.S. Ayres & Co. v. Hicks, 41 N.E.2d 195 (Ind. 1914).

108. *See* Tippecanoe Loan & Trust Co. v. Cleveland R. Co., 106 N.E. 739 (Ind. Ct. App. 1915).

109. It is important to note, however, that in either case the expressive party need not actually agree to bear the risk of harm; rather, she need merely give that appearance.

110. 28 N.E. 266 (Mass. 1891).

111. The concept of reliance has endured a rather checkered past under both contract and tort theories of recovery. It has been a kind of family black sheep. Never quite fitting into either theory, it was often overshadowed by the traditional favorite siblings of the law, autonomy and culpability. Like any obstreperous youth, however, reliance has proven to be too volatile to ignore. Gradually, and only recently, it has come to enjoy acceptance and even a measure of respectability in both tort and contract law.

In contract, the enforceability of promises historically depended upon the existence of some indicia that the commitment was seriously made. Early on, certain procedural formalities satisfied this requirement. These included seals of promisors and written documents. *See* E. ALLAN FARNSWORTH, CONTRACTS § 2.16 (2d ed. 1990). Eventually, consideration became recognized as the primary type of validation device. This entailed a showing that each party bargained for a legal detriment to be incurred by the other. *See* Hamer v. Sidway, 27 N.E. 256 (N.Y. 1891) (uncle bargained for nephew's abstinance from smoking, drinking and swearing before age twenty-one in exchange for $5000).

The doctrine of consideration, however, proved incapable of doing justice in certain cases. The earliest of these involved intrafamily promises and promises made to charitable institutions. Though made gratuitously, these overtures often induced the promisee to incur some sort of legal detriment. Under classical contract theory, such promises were unenforceable because they lacked the element of a bargain. *See* JOHN E. MURRAY, JR., MURRAY ON CONTRACTS §§ 61, 62 (3d ed. 1990). Eventually, this result came to be viewed as unfair. Because of the parties' relationship, the detrimental reliance suffered by the promisee appeared particularly authentic and damaging. Accordingly, in modern contract theory, such reliance is deemed sufficient to validate these promises and render them enforceable. *See* RESTATEMENT (SECOND) OF CONTRACTS § 90 (1981).

The same rationale was extended to unilateral contracts partially performed. To consummate such an agreement, the promisee must entirely complete the act requested by the promisor. In other words, the offer of the promisor could not be accepted by a return promise; it could only be accepted by the completion of performance. *See* Petterson v. Pattberg, 161 N.E. 428 (N.Y. 1928). Thus, even after the promisee commenced performance, incurring significant expense in the process, the promisor could revoke the offer of payment. *Id.* Although the promisee could seek restitution for benefits conferred upon the promisor, she could not enforce the agreement or recover for preparation expenses not resulting in a direct benefit to the promisor. *Id.*

Appreciating the significance of reliance in this context, the drafters of the Restatement of Contracts (Second) adopted a rule which remedied the inequity in this outcome. Under section 45 of the Restatement, the promisee's reliance, by beginning performance, rendered the promise of the promisor irrevocable, creating in the promisee an option to consummate the contract by completing performance or to discontinue without further legal responsibility. RESTATEMENT (SECOND) OF CONTRACTS § 45 (1981). Under this rule, reliance replaced consideration as the criterion for evaluating the seriousness and thus enforceability of the promise.

The long tentacles of this concept soon spread to other types of cases unsatisfactorily resolved under the doctrine of consideration. The construction contractor who relied on the bid of a subcontractor (in submitting its own bid for the general contract) formerly was without a remedy if the subcontractor changed or revoked its offer after the general contract was awarded but before the contractor had an opportunity to accept the bid. *See* James Baird Co. v. Gimbel Bros., Inc., 64 F.2d 344 (2d Cir. 1933). Under section 87(2) of the Restatement (Second) of Contracts, however, the contractor's reliance now makes the subcontractor's bid irrevocable. *See* RESTATEMENT (SECOND) OF CONTRACTS § 87(2) (1981). Similarly, an oral promise which violates the applicable mandate of the statute of frauds nevertheless may be enforceable if the promisee justifiably relies on that promise to her detriment. *See* RESTATEMENT (SECOND) OF CONTRACTS § 139 (1981).

In all of these cases, both parties had exchanged promises in an attempt to effectuate a classic contract. Substituting for consideration, the reliance principle was used as the glue binding the parties to a mutual commitment. This principle, however, proved far too unctuous to be contained within the confines of an agreement. Under section 90 of the Restatement of Contracts (First and then Second) justifiable reliance could be used to enforce any promise, whether or not it was given in exchange for or in anticipation of a return promise or benefit. RESTATEMENT (SECOND) OF CONTRACTS § 90 (1981). Even where parties simply negotiated, and thus had not yet extended definite promises of performance, conduct inducing reliance has been found to create promissory-like obligations. *See* Hoffman v. Red Owl Stores, 133 N.W.2d 267 (Wis. 1965).

This ascendancy of reliance prompted Professor Gilmore, in his famous book of the same name, to proclaim *The Death of Contract*. GILMORE, *supra* note 1. In his view, the reliance principle eroded the theoretical underpinnings of contract doctrine. No longer was contract enforcement dependent on bargained for exchanges. Nor was the will of the parties, as an expression of their autonomy, important for the imposition of legal responsibility. Instead, reliance had shifted the focus to the conduct of the promisor and the injury sustained by the promisee, two hallmark criteria for assessing tort obligations. Yet, despite Gilmore's observation, reliance traditionally has not played a major role in the development of tort theory.

The source of this slight can be traced back to the early forms of action in England. Much of what we now call tort law evolved from the writ of trespass. To obtain such a writ, the claimant was required to show that his injury was occasioned by an act of misfeasance. This meant that the defendant must have created and imposed the risk of harm against the claimant through some affirmative undertaking. *See* THEODORE F.T. PLUCKNETT, A CONCISE HISTORY OF THE COMMON LAW 465–67 (5th ed. 1956). Here, the culpability of the conduct and its connection to the harm were clear enough to warrant a state imposed sanction. Indeed, during its infancy, a successful action for trespass could entail payment of both a civil (bot) and criminal fine (wite). *See* Wex S. Malone, *Ruminations on the Role of Fault in the History of the Common Law*, 31 LA. L. REV. 1, 1-3 (1970). Mere inaction or nonfeasance did not become actionable until the later writ of trespass on the case was adopted, and even then the claimant's burden of proof was much tougher. *See* Charles O. Gregory, *Trespass to Negligence to Absolute Liability*, 37 VA. L. REV. 359, 363–65 (1951).

Promissory commitments do not fit comfortably within the early common law distinctions drawn between misfeasance and nonfeasance. As a verbal or written overture of future conduct, it is a type of inchoate undertaking. It is more than mere nonfeasance in that at least *some* connection or relationship has been created between the parties. Nevertheless, it is less than misfeasance, since it may never result in any affirmative conduct, nor in the creation of a hazardous condition. Because of the uncertain characteristics of promissory obligations, the reliance principle has been slow to gain recognition or acceptance in the tort area.

Older decisions were loath to find a tort duty arising from a promise, even where it had induced the promisee's detrimental reliance. In the well-known case of *Thorne v. Deas*, 4 Johns. 84 (N.Y. 1809), the business partner of a sea merchant promised that he would obtain insurance for cargo to be shipped from New York to North Carolina. He failed to do so, and when the ship was lost at sea, the sea merchant sued in tort for the value of cargo. The New York court rejected the claim. Although the sea merchant had refrained from insuring the cargo on the strength of the promise, the court held that there was no duty because the partner had not undertaken affirmative steps to acquire the insurance. The unexecuted promise amounted to mere nonfeasance, and thus was not actionable in tort.

Since *Thorne*, courts have become increasingly comfortable imposing tort liability for negligent undertakings which result in detrimental reliance, even where the reliance consists of only economic loss. *See* Vereins-Und Westbank v. Carter, 691 F. Supp. 704 (S.D.N.Y. 1988) (attorney liable to third party for contents of opinion letter); Citizens State Bank v. Timm, Schmidt & Co., 335 N.W.2d 361 (Wis. 1983) (accounting firm may be liable to third party for negligently prepared financial statements); M. Miller Co. v. Cent. Contra Costa Sanitary Dist., 18 Cal. Rptr. 13 (Dist. Ct. App. 1961) (engineering company held liable to third party for negligently prepared soil report). Promissory reliance also has won some resounding victories for tort claimants sustaining severe physical injuries. For example, an employer which promised to obtain medical assistance for an sick employee was found liable for his death because the employer failed to call for a doctor. *See* Dudley v. Victor Lynn Lines, Inc., 138 A.2d 53 (N.J. Super. Ct. App. Div. 1958), *rev'd on other grounds*, 161 A.2d 479 (N.J. 1960). And the husband of a woman who was promised by a county sheriff's department that she would be warned of the impending release of a dangerous prisoner was allowed to sue the county for failing to issue such a warning. *See Morgan*, 41 Cal. Rptr. 508. In neither of these cases was there an undertaking beyond the promise. Nevertheless, because of the severity of the injuries sustained (death in both cases), and the existence of tort-like "special relationships" between the promisors and promisees, the violation of the reliance principle justified recovery in tort.

112. The justice of reciprocity is not concerned only with what interests relational parties gave up. It also looks to see what they have gained. Where the transaction is for necessities, the bargained-for gain is obvious. But where the transaction is discretionary, one must evaluate the subjective benefit which the parties hoped to acquire from their association. After all, the whole purpose of political association is to ensure for each individual the freedom necessary to pursue whatever it is she subjectively believes to be virtuous or necessary to achieving her own conception of virtue. For bungee jumpers, race car drivers and sky divers this may mean engaging in high-risk activities which test the bounds of the human condition. In the minds of these individuals, the great subjective good derived from such activities may counterbalance or outweigh their attendant risks. Because private law generally, and tort law in particular, is ill-equipped and unauthorized to judge the moral propriety of such preferences, it usually permits such individuals the freedom to engage in any activity, risky or otherwise, which they believe will further their life plans. So long as a modicum of reciprocity is apparent, and consent is true, the responsibilities for participating in such joint endeavors should be, and often are, left to the determination of the parties themselves.

113. 468 N.W.2d 654 (Wis. 1991).

114. 432 N.W.2d 626 (Wis. Ct. App. 1988).

115. *Id.* at 628.

116. It might also be said that the cyclist was factually responsible for his resulting injury because he influenced and controlled the actions of the track owner, and by so doing, decided his own fate.

117. 755 S.W.2d 769 (Tenn. 1988).

118. *Id.* at 771.

119. *Id.* at 773.

120. As the foregoing illustrations demonstrate, the reliance principle stands uniquely suited to facilitate the analysis of assumption of risk questions. It supplies the structural

framework for bridging the philosophical gap between the doctrine's dual schizophrenic personalities of tort and contract. Better still, it provides the analytic methodology to accomplish this very complicated task.

Whereas tort concerns the social responsibility of injury-producing behavior, contract seeks to protect the autonomy of those who may desire to encounter it. The reliance principle coalesces these interests with a relational perspective. In determining whether one has justifiably relied, it is necessary to examine both the representations made and the conduct of those who act upon it. In the assumption of risk context, it requires that we assess both the risk-seeker's manifested intention to encounter the risk, and the risk-creator's "reliance" in offering the risk in its present form.

With this connection established, the policy objectives of the respective theories may be introduced into the analysis with conceptual consistency. Contract tells us to look carefully for consent in the promise to accept the risk, and to be wary of overreaching. Similarly, tort allows us to scrutinize the relative status of the parties to determine if one party must provide and the other receive special protection from her counterpart. Tort also invites consideration of other policy factors, including the extent of culpability, deterrence and loss shifting.

Despite these apparent advantages, the relational approach inherent in the reliance principle has never been formally recognized as a means of analyzing assumption of risk questions. As we have seen, most theories offered in this regard, both ancient and modern, tend to provide only unilateral solutions to this bilateral dilemma. It is because of these myopic approaches that the law in this area has been, and continues to be, so arbitrary and confusing.

121. It is fairly uncommon for a willing victim to be the only factually responsible party to an injurious encounter. In many cases, the dominant and servient parties may share factual responsibility for a harmful outcome. Here, an all-or-nothing determination of responsibility may not do. Assuming that the dominant party bears a distributive responsibility which has not been altered by private agreement, and that she is at least in part factually responsible for the resulting injury of the other, it may be appropriate to subject the parties' actions to comparative analysis. In such a situation, several factors would inform the determination of liability, including the magnitude of the risk created by the dominant party's conduct, the other's awareness of the risk and ability to avoid it, the personal and social value of the actions of each, the nature of the parties' relationship and the circumstances surrounding their interaction. See MODEL UNIFORM PRODUCT LIABILITY ACT § 111(B)(3) (1979) & drafter's analysis of that section. Thus, in the motocross illustration, where the activity of racing was only recreational, the rider was fully aware of all risks, and the dangers though significant were limited primarily to participants, the rider might be made to bear the lion's share of responsibility for any losses incurred, if he were not completely barred from recovery.

Notes to Epilogue

1. *See generally* JULES L. COLEMAN, MARKETS, MORALS, AND THE LAW (1988).
2. *See* JULES L. COLEMAN, RISKS AND WRONGS 371–406 (1992).
3. *See* George P. Fletcher, *Fairness and Utility in Tort Theory*, 85 HARV. L. REV. 537,

550–51 (1972). As applied to the reciprocity thesis, this principle would provide: "we all have the right to the maximum amount of security compatible with a like security for everyone else." *Id.* at 550.

4. *Id.* at 559–60.

5. RICHARD A. EPSTEIN, A THEORY OF STRICT LIABILITY (1980).

6. *See* Ernest J. Weinrib, *The Special Morality of Tort Law*, 34 McGILL L.J. 404, 408–09 (1989).

7. *See* Ernest J. Weinrib, *Toward a Moral Theory of Negligence Law*, 2 LAW & PHIL. 37 (1983).

8. *See* ARISTOTLE, THE NICHOMACHEAN ETHICS, 114–15, V.4, 1131b14–1132a25 (D. Ross Trans., revised by J.L. Ackrill & J.O. Urmson 1990) (Oxford Univ. Press, World Classics ed.).

9. *See, e.g.,* Peter Benson, *The Basis of Corrective Justice and Its Relation to Distributive Justice*, 77 IOWA L. REV. 515, 535–47 (1992); Ernest J. Weinrib, *Corrective Justice*, 77 IOWA L. REV. 403, 416–18 (1992); Richard W. Wright, *Substantive Corrective Justice*, 77 IOWA L. REV. 625, 702–08 (1992) (though suggesting that, in claims of nuisance and eminent domain, the two forms of justice may coexist in the same body of law). *But see* Stephen R. Perry, *The Moral Foundations of Tort Law*, 77 IOWA L. REV. 449, 512–13 (1992) (proposing a theory of localized distributive justice for correlating moral rights and obligations of reparation). This conclusion, while tantalizingly simple, is certainly not compelled by the wisdom of Aristotle. In fact, in Aristotle's day there simply was no conflict between corrective and distributive justice schemes. The Greeks knew no distinction between its citizens and the state; its citizens *were* the state. All full citizens both enacted laws and served on juries. Ultimately, the juries usurped legislative power by declaring the illegality or inappropriateness of the law and deciding cases in accordance with the dictates of their consciences. *See* VICTOR EHRENBERG, THE GREEK STATE 71–74, 77–80 (1960). Thus, decisions in these cases did not so much represent a state-imposed distribution of liberty to the parties, as do our modern tort cases, but simply served as an ad hoc attempt by fellow citizens to resolve disputes between their neighbors.

10. *See* Leslie Bender, *A Lawyer's Primer on Feminist Theory and Tort*, 38 J. LEGAL EDUC. 3 (1988); Leslie Bender, *An Overview of Feminist Torts Scholarship*, 78 CORNELL L. REV. 575 (1993); Leslie Bender, *Changing the Values in Tort Law*, 25 TULSA L.J. 759 (1990); Leslie Bender, *Feminist (Re)Torts: Thoughts on the Liability Crisis, Mass Torts, Power, and Responsibilities*, 1990 DUKE L.J. 848; Leslie Bender, *Is Tort Law Male?: Foreseeability Analysis and Property Managers' Liability for Third Party Rapes of Residents*, 69 CHI.-KENT L. REV. 313 (1993); Leslie Bender, *Teaching Torts as if Gender Matters: Intentional Torts*, 2 VA. J. SOC. POL'Y & L. 115 (1994).

11. *See* Richard L. Abel, *A Critique of Torts*, 37 UCLA L. REV. 785 (1990).

12. The theory of intentional infliction of emotional distress was first recognized in the case of Wilkinson v. Downton, 2 Q.B. 57 (1897), where the female plaintiff suffered severe emotional distress after being told by a mean-spirited (male) practical joker that her husband had been seriously injured in an accident.

13. In MacPherson v. Buick Motor Co., 111 N.E. 1050 (N.Y. 1916), the New York Court of Appeals abolished the privity limitation in product liability cases. Every other state jurisdiction has followed suit. M. STUART MADDEN, PRODUCTS LIABILITY § 1.2, at 12 (2d ed. 1988). Nevertheless, the privity rule still possesses some vitality in cases involving public or quasi-public defendants, *see* H.R. Moch Co. v. Rensselaer Water Co., 159

N.E. 896 (N.Y. 1928) (water company), or professionals, *see* Clagett v. Dacy, 420 A.2d 1285 (Md. Ct. Spec. App. 1980) (attorney).

14. Some courts have eliminated the classification system entirely. *See* Webb v. Sitka, 561 P.2d 731 (Alaska 1977); Rowland v. Christian, 443 P.2d 561 (Cal. 1968); Pickard v. City of Honolulu, 452 P.2d 445 (Haw. 1969). Others only recognize a distinction between persons who are invited onto the property and those who are not. *See* Wood v. Camp, 284 So. 2d 691 (Fla. 1973).

15. Only Alabama, Maryland, North Carolina and Virginia continue to recognize contributory negligence as a complete bar to recovery. *See* JOHN W. WADE ET AL., PROSSER, WADE AND SCHWARTZ'S CASES AND MATERIALS ON TORTS 578 n.2 (9th ed. 1994).

16. *See, e.g., Rowland*, 443 P.2d 561 (in a premises liability case, examining the following factors: the closeness of the connection between the injury and the defendant's conduct, the moral blame attached to the defendant's conduct, the policy of preventing future harm, the prevalence and availability of insurance, the foreseeability of harm to the victim, the burden to the defendant and the consequences to the community of imposing a duty, and the certainty of the plaintiff's injury).

17. There is perhaps one concern with the concept of comparative fault, at least in the way it presently is applied by most courts. Typically, where a system of comparative fault is in use, the jury is told to allocate responsibility by focusing on the characteristics of each party's conduct. This instruction is fine as far as it goes, but it doesn't quite go far enough. Corrective justice requires not only that we examine the behavior of the parties, but also that we consider the nature and extent of the plaintiff's loss, and assess the parties' causal contribution to the injurious transaction. For example, suppose defendant A, who had drunk himself into an alcoholic stupor, passed out while driving his car. A's car comes to rest in the passing lane of a freeway. Defendant B, who is traveling in the passing lane, sees A's car in plenty of time to move into the next lane. After checking her side mirror and seeing no other vehicles, B begins to make the lane change without applying her turn signal. B's car cuts in front of a vehicle operated by the plaintiff, who was driving in B's blind spot. The plaintiff, a nervous driver, jerks her steering wheel to the right, causing her vehicle to leave the roadway and crash into a culvert. The plaintiff sustains serious injuries in the collision. In a case such as this, using the parties' conduct as the sole basis for apportioning responsibility leads to potentially absurd results. While A's conduct (driving drunk and passing out behind the wheel) is socially reprehensible, it had the least impact upon the accident. Indeed, under the facts of the hypothetical, the obstacle created by A is just one of a thousand other reasons why a motorist such as B may need to change lanes while driving on a freeway. B, on the other hand, committed a rather trivial motoring faux pas (not signalling a lane change), but her conduct had a far more direct and powerful influence upon the chain of events leading to the mishap. Finally, the plaintiff herself was guilty of little more than overreacting in an emergency to save her own skin, yet with a touch of her brakes or a smoother turn to the right, the entire accident might have been avoided. Here, the justice of the encounter cannot be found in the parties' actions alone, but is a product of all the circumstances that caused their lives to intersect. Comparative fault, with its emphasis on conduct, seems to miss this point.

18. *See* Strazza v. McKittrick, 156 A.2d 149 (Conn. 1959) (truck crashed into the plaintiff's house while she was at home); Falzone v. Busch, 214 A.2d 12 (N.J. 1965) (plaintiff nearly struck by automobile).

19. *See* Jackson v. Johns-Manville Sales Corp., 781 F.2d 394 (5th Cir. 1986) (exposure to asbestos), *cert. denied*, 478 U.S. 1022 (1986); Payton v. Abbott Labs., 437 N.E.2d 171 (Mass. 1982) (DES).

20. *See* Dillon v. Legg, 441 P.2d 912 (Cal. 1968) (basing duty on the foreseeability of the victim's emotional injury, and using three criteria to determine the scope of foreseeability: (1) plaintiff's nearness to the location of the accident, (2) the directness of the emotional impact upon the plaintiff due to her sensory and contemporaneous observance of the accident, and (3) the closeness of the plaintiff's relationship with the victim).

21. *See* Hitaffer v. Argonee Co., 183 F.2d 811 (D.C. Cir. 1950).

22. *See* Howard Frank, M.D. P.C. v. Superior Ct., 722 P.2d 955 (Ariz. 1986) (allowing recovery for loss of companionship of minor and adult children alike).

23. *See* Berger v. Weber, 303 N.W.2d 424 (Mich. 1981).

24. A wrongful birth cause of action typically arises when a physician fails to adequately test a fetus for birth defects or diseases and the infant is born deformed or seriously ill. The parents then sue the physician to recover for the extraordinary expenses of raising a special child. *See* Smith v. Cote, 513 A.2d 341 (N.H. 1986) (allowing recovery for extraordinary maternal care costs, even beyond the age of majority, and for pecuniary losses resulting from the emotional distress in obtaining medical care and counselling). *Cf.* Hartke v. McKelway, 526 F. Supp. 97 (D.D.C. 1981) (permitting recovery of damages for emotional distress where, because of the defendant-doctor's negligence in performing a sterilization procedure, plaintiff gave birth to a normal child).

25. Wrongful life actions are brought on behalf of children born with serious illnesses or birth defects caused by their physicians' negligent diagnoses or treatments. *See* Turpin v. Sortini, 643 P.2d 954 (Cal. 1982) (allowing recovery of the extraordinary expenses arising from the condition, but denying recovery of general damages for pain and suffering); Procanik by Procanik v. Cillo, 478 A.2d 755 (N.J. 1984) (same).

26. *See* J'Aire Corp. v. Gregory, 598 P.2d 60 (Cal. 1979) (a restaurant which leased space from an airport was permitted to recover for revenue lost because of the failure of a contractor, which had been hired by the airport to renovate the restaurant, to finish the job in a reasonable and timely fashion); People's Express Airlines, Inc. v. Consol. Rail Corp., 495 A.2d 107 (N.J. 1985) (airline was permitted to recover for economic loss caused by a tank car accident which prompted the evacuation of an airport).

27. *See* Philip G. Peters, Jr., *Rethinking Wrongful Life: Bridging the Boundary Between Tort and Family Law*, 67 TUL. L. REV. 397, 415 (1992) (listing state statutes that preclude such causes of action).

28. *See* JOHN W. WADE ET AL., PROSSER, WADE AND SCHWARTZ'S CASES AND MATERIALS ON TORTS 519 (9th ed. 1994) (noting that about half of the state legislatures have enacted laws limiting the amount of damages recoverable).

29. Many states place strict caps on the amount of punitive damages which may be recovered in certain types of cases. *See, e.g.,* ALA. CODE §§ 6-11-20(4), 6-11-21 (Supp. 1988) ($250,000 cap); GA. CODE ANN. § 51 12-5.1 (Supp. 1988) ($250,000 cap in all but product liability cases); KAN. STAT. ANN. § 60-3701 (1987) (providing complex capping formula). Several jurisdictions deny such relief entirely unless the plaintiff can establish the defendant's misconduct by clear and convincing evidence. *See, e.g.,* IOWA CODE ANN. § 668A.1 (1987); KY. REV. STAT. ANN. § 411.184 (Michie Supp. 1988); OHIO REV. CODE ANN. § 2307.80 (Page's Supp. 1988).

30. *See* The Product Liability Fairness Act of 1995, S. 565, 104th Cong., 1st Sess. (1995) (proposing to cap punitive damages at the lesser of $250,000 or twice the amount of compensatory damages). President Clinton vetoed the bill, however, in May of 1996.

31. *See* Alan Calnan, *Ending the Punitive Damage Debate*, 45 DePaul L. Rev. 101 (1995) (recommending victim-offender mediation, public apology and/or personal service as more satisfactory corrective measures).

32. *See* Jordan v. Bogner, 844 P.2d 664 (Colo. 1993); Morrison v. MacNamara, 407 A.2d 555 (D.C. 1979); Shilkret v. Annapolis Emergency Hosp. Ass'n, 349 A.2d 245 (Md. 1975); Hall v. Hilbun, 466 So. 2d 856 (Miss. 1985).

33. *See* Canterbury v. Spence, 464 F.2d 772 (D.C. Cir. 1972) (in cases involving informed consent), *cert. denied*, 409 U.S. 1064 (1972); Scott v. Bradford, 606 P.2d 554 (Okla. 1979) (same).

34. *See* Ybarra v. Spangard, 154 P.2d 687 (Cal. 1944) (where the plaintiff who was scheduled for an appendectomy woke up with neck pain, the burden shifted to the operating room personnel to negate their negligence).

35. *See* Restatement (Second) of Torts § 402A(2)(a) (1965).

36. *See* Michalko v. Cooke Color and Chem. Corp., 451 A.2d 179 (N.J. 1982).

37. *See* Dunham v. Vaughan & Bushnell Mfg. Co., 247 N.E.2d 401 (Ill. 1969).

38. *See* Vandermark v. Ford Motor Co., 391 P.2d (Cal. 1964).

39. *See* Realmuto v. Straub Motors, Inc., 322 A.2d 440 (N.J. 1974).

40. *See* Price v. Shell Oil Co., 466 P.2d 722 (Cal. 1970).

41. *See* Washwell, Inc. v. Morejohn, 294 So. 2d 30 (Fla. Dist. Ct. App. 1974), *cert. denied*, 310 So. 2d 734 (Fla. Dist. Ct. 1975).

42. *See* Kosters v. Seven-Up Co., 595 F.2d 347 (6th Cir. 1979).

43. *See* Ray v. Alad Corp., 560 P.2d 3 (Cal. 1977).

44. *See* Stein v. So. Cal. Edison, 8 Cal. Rptr. 2d 907 (Ct. App. 1992).

45. *See* Torres v. Goodyear Tire & Rubber Co., 786 P.2d 939 (Ariz. 1990).

46. *See* Schipper v. Levitt & Sons, Inc., 207 A.2d 314 (N.J. 1965).

47. *See* State Stove Mfg. Co. v. Hodges, 189 So. 2d 113 (Miss. 1966), *cert. denied*, 386 U.S. 912 (1967).

48. *See* Maloney v. Rath, 445 P.2d 513 (Cal. 1968) (holding an automobile owner liable for injuries caused by the failure of her car's brakes, which had been overhauled by a repairman just three months before); *see also* Pacific Fire Ins. Co. v. Kenny Boiler & Mfg. Co., 277 N.W. 226 (Minn. 1937) (noting that the general rule of nonliability for acts of independent contractors is merely a preamble to the long list of its exceptions).

49. *See* Corely v. Lewless, 182 S.E.2d 766 (La. 1971) (applying the Code Napoleon). Some states accomplish this by statute. *See* Alice B. Freer, *Parental Liability for Torts of Children*, 53 Ky. L.J. 254 (1965) (listing statutes).

50. *See* Federal Aviation Act of 1958, 49 U.S.C.A. § 1301 *et seq.* (airplanes); Federal Food, Drug and Cosmetic Act of 1938, 21 U.S.C.A. § 301 *et seq.* (drugs and medical devices); Poison Prevention Packaging Act, 15 U.S.C.A. § 1471 *et seq.* (poisons); Flammable Fabrics Act, 15 U.S.C.A. § 1191 *et seq.* (clothing).

51. *See, e.g.,* Ind. Code Ann. § 33-1-1.5-4 (1983) (defendant is permitted to raise the following defenses: consumer's awareness of the defect or danger, unforeseeable misuse, unforeseeable modification, conformity to the state of the art); Mich. Comp. Laws § 600.2946 (1985) (permitting evidence of compliance with industry standards and gov-

ernment regulations, and excluding evidence of post-accident changes in the state of the art); OHIO REV. CODE ANN. § 2307.78 (Anderson Supp. 1988) (with certain exceptions, precluding assertion of strict liability claim against suppliers; proof of negligence required).

52. 42 U.S.C. 300aa-1 *et seq.* (1986) (creating an optional compensation system for victims of childhood vaccines; claimants may recover economic damages and a maximum of $250,000 general damages for harms contained on an injury table or for those harms otherwise proven to be causally connected to the vaccine).

53. 30 U.S.C. §§ 801–962 (1995) (providing benefits to partially or totally disabled miners who have developed pneumoconiosis "at least in part" because of their employment in a coal mine).

54. Since manufacturing defects are not intrinsic to an entire product line, but arise only sporadically because of some error in the construction process, products containing such defects may not pose the kind of public risks which would warrant exempting the manufacturer from liability.

55. *See* Sindell v. Abbott Labs., 607 P.2d 924 (Cal. 1980) (named defendants must constitute a substantial share of the relevant market); Abel v. Eli Lilly & Co., 343 N.W.2d 164 (Mich. 1984) (state market approach; all sellers of subject product must be joined as defendants), *cert. denied*, 469 U.S. 833 (1984); Martin v. Abbott Labs., 689 P.2d 368 (Wash. 1984) (plaintiff need only sue one manufacturer; manufacturer(s) may exculpate by disproving causation; unexculpated manufacturers held liable on pro rata basis unless able to produce evidence of market share); Collins v. Eli Lilly & Co., 342 N.W.2d 37 (Wis. 1984) (only one manufacturer of the subject product need be named as defendant; causation-based excuse permitted), *cert. denied*, 469 U.S. 826 (1984).

56. *See* Hymowitz v. Eli Lilly & Co., 539 N.E.2d 1069 (N.Y. 1989) (no causation-based excuse permitted; each manufacturer held liable in proportion to amount of public risk it created (i.e., in accordance with its national market share)).

57. The New York approach in *Hymowitz* is a notable exception. There, the named defendants were not permitted to disprove causation, but were held liable for an amount of the plaintiff's damages commensurate with their share of the national market for the offending product. *See id.*

58. *See* Falcon v. Mem. Hosp., 462 N.W.2d 44 (Mich. 1990) (lost chance of surviving amniotic fluid embolism); Wollen v. DePaul Health Ctr., 828 S.W.2d 681 (Mo. 1992) (lost chance of surviving gastric cancer); Herskovits v. Group Health Coop., 664 P.2d 474 (Wash. 1983) (lost chance of surviving lung cancer).

59. *See* Gideon v. Johns-Manville Sales Corp., 761 F.2d 1129 (5th Cir. 1985) (allowing recovery for increased risk of cancer caused by inhaling asbestos fibers); Sterling v. Velsicol Chem. Corp., 647 F. Supp. 303 (W.D. Tenn. 1986) (characterizing enhanced susceptibility to disease as a presently existing condition); Ayers v. Township of Jackson, 525 A.2d 287 (N.J. 1987) (allowing recovery for increased risk of cancer, but requiring that the risk be quantified); Elam v. Alcolac, Inc., 765 S.W.2d 42 (Mo. Ct. App. 1988) (treating increased risk of cancer as the present invasion of a legally protected interest); *see generally* Melissa Moore Thompson, *Enhanced Risk of Disease Claims: Limiting Recovery to Compensation for Loss, Not Chance*, 72 N.C. L. REV. 453 (1994) (surveying cases).

60. *See* Potter v. Firestone Tire & Rubber Co., 863 P.2d 795 (Cal. 1993) (allowing recovery of medical monitoring expenses where the plaintiff's monitoring is a reasonably certain consequence of the toxic exposure and the recommended monitoring is reason-

able); *Ayers*, 525 A.2d 287 (same).

61. *See, e.g.,* TEX. CIV. PRAC. & REM. CODE § 33.013 (1987) (recognizing a few exceptions where joint liability will apply).

62. *See* The Product Liability Fairness Act of 1995, S. 565, 104th Cong., 1st Sess. (1995) (basing liability for noneconomic damages on the defendant's percentage of comparative fault).

63. *See, e.g.,* CAL. CIV. CODE § 1431.2 (1986); NEB. REV. STAT. § 25-21, 185.10 (1995); N.Y. CIV. PRAC. L. & R. 1601 (McKinney Supp. 1996); OHIO REV. CODE ANN. § 2315.19(D)(1)(a)(b)(c) (Anderson 1995); *see generally* VICTOR E. SCHWARTZ, COMPARATIVE NEGLIGENCE § 15-4 (3d ed. 1994) (listing statutes).

64. I propose the following solutions. Assume a jury finds that defendant A is 60% at fault for causing the plaintiff's (P's) injuries, that defendant B is 30% responsible for the loss, and that P herself is 10% to blame for the accident. Assume further that P sustained $100,000 of economic loss and $300,000 of noneconomic (pain and suffering) damage. One approach is to make the defendants severally liable for both the economic and noneconomic portions of the judgment. Under this approach, each defendant would have to pay an amount of the judgment commensurate with her percentage of comparative fault. Thus, A would be liable for $240,000 of P's loss (60% of the $400,000 judgment), and B would be responsible for $120,000 of the total judgment (30% of $400,000). In the event any defendant becomes insolvent, however, the liability share of the insolvent defendant would be split between the remaining parties (defendant(s) and plaintiff) in accordance with a ratio determined by comparing their respective percentages of fault. So if A became insolvent, the $240,000 shortfall in P's recovery would be reallocated between B and P using a 3 to 1 ratio (comparing B's 30% comparative fault to P's 10% comparative fault). Thus, B would be required to pay an additional $180,000 of P's loss, and P would have to absorb an extra $60,000 of the judgment. In all, B would be liable for $300,000 ($120,000 representing B's 30% comparative fault + $180,000 representing B's proportional liability for A's share). P, on the other hand, must shoulder a total of $100,000 of her own loss ($40,000 representing P's 10% comparative fault + $60,000 representing P's proportional liability for A's share).

Another approach would hold A and B severally liable for P's noneconomic (pain and suffering) loss, but jointly liable for P's economic damage. Thus, if either A or B becomes insolvent, the remaining defendant would be required to pay the full economic judgment (reduced, of course, by P's percentage of fault). However, with regard to the noneconomic loss, the insolvent defendant's share of the damage would be split among the remaining parties (defendant(s) and plaintiff) in accordance with the above-described formula. Thus, in the above hypothetical, if A were to become insolvent, B would be required to pay the full $90,000 of economic loss which P is entitled to recover ($100,000 of total economic loss - $10,000 representing P's 10% of comparative fault), even though B was determined to be only 30% at fault. In essence, P is guaranteed payment for her medical costs and lost income. Of the remaining $300,000 of noneconomic loss, B would be expected under a comparative fault system to pay 30% or $90,000. P would be required to absorb 10% of this loss, or $30,000. Because of A's insolvency, P would face a $180,000 shortfall in her noneconomic loss recovery (A's 60% share of the total $300,000 of noneconomic loss). Under this second proposal, however, the remaining parties, B and P, would split A's share between them in accordance with their relative allocations of fault. Once again, the fault ratio between B and P is 3 (30%) to 1

(10%). Thus, B would be required to pay three dollars of the outstanding $180,000 judgment balance for every one dollar that P pays (or must absorb). This means that B will pay an additional $135,000 for the noneconomic damage, and P must eat the remaining $45,000 loss. In the end, B's total liability comes to $315,000 ($90,000 joint liability for economic loss + $90,000 comparative fault share of noneconomic loss + $135,000 proportional responsibility for shortfall). P, on the other hand, is required to shoulder $85,000 of her entire $400,000 loss ($10,000 comparative fault share of economic loss + $30,000 comparative fault share of noneconomic loss + $45,000 proportional responsibility for shortfall).

Neither of these proposals is perfect. The first approach does not ensure that all of P's economic losses will be satisfied by the remaining, solvent defendant(s). For example, if P's economic loss had amounted to $200,000 (and her noneconomic loss remained at $300,000), B, the solvent defendant who was adjudged 30% at fault, would be required to pay only $150,000 in damages. Here, $50,000 of P's medical expenses or lost wages would go unreimbursed (even when P's economic loss—$200,000—is reduced by her percentage of fault—10% or $20,000—$30,000 of P's special damages remain uncompensated). Although the second approach corrects this shortcoming, it also requires that the remaining defendant pay a disproportionately higher amount of the shortfall than the plaintiff. Under the facts given above, B's $315,000 liability tab is well over two and a half times greater than her 30% comparative responsibility (which was determined to be $120,000), while P's final liability of $85,000 is barely twice the amount of her comparative fault (which was determined to be $40,000).

Despite these drawbacks, however, each approach seems preferable to either a traditional joint liability scheme or a pure form of several liability. Under a pure several liability system, B would be obligated to pay only $120,000 (30%) of the judgment. Of course, under such an approach, P would have to bear $280,000 of loss (well over half of the total) for an accident she barely had a hand in causing. Indeed, according to P's 10% comparative fault assessment, she should only have to swallow $40,000 of the damages. Conversely, if a traditional joint liability rule were in place, B would have to pay P's entire $360,000 judgment ($400,000 total - $40,000 of P's comparative fault). Each of these schemes is egregiously unfair to one party. My proposed solutions, on the other hand, require both parties to share the burden of any shortfall by premising their additional responsibilities on a distributive ratio that comports with our sense of justice.

65. *See, e.g.,* Knight v. Jewett, 834 P.2d 696 (Cal. 1992); Blackburn v. Dorta, 348 So. 2d 287 (Fla. 1977); Salinas v. Vierstra, 695 P.2d 369 (Idaho 1985); Meistrich v. Casino Arena Attractions, Inc., 155 A.2d 90 (N.J. 1959).

66. *See, e.g.,* ARK. STAT. ANN. § 27-1763 (1979); CONN. GEN. STAT. ANN. § 57 572h(c) (West Supp. 1985); Brown v. Kreuser, 560 P.2d 105 (Colo. 1977); Wilson v. Gordon, 354 A.2d 398 (Me. 1976); Bolduc v. Crain, 181 A.2d 641 (N.H. 1962); Wentz v. Deseth, 221 N.W.2d 101 (N.D. 1974); *see also* UNIFORM MODEL PRODUCT LIABILITY ACT § 112(B)(1) (1979) ("When the product seller proves, by a preponderance of the evidence, that the claimant knew about the product's defective condition and voluntarily used the product or voluntarily assumed the risk of harm from the product, the claimant's damages shall be subject to reduction to the extent that the claimant did not act as an ordinary reasonably prudent person under the circumstances.").

67. *See* WILLIAM KNOKE, BOLD NEW WORLD (1996) (discussing the social changes that are likely to occur during the information age of the twenty-first century).

Index